About CROP

CROP, the Comparative Research Prog
from the academic community to the problems of poverty. The programme
was initiated in 1992, and the CROP Secretariat was officially opened in
June 1993 by the Director General of UNESCO, Dr Federico Mayor.

In recent years, poverty alleviation, poverty reduction and the
eradication of poverty have moved up the international agenda, with
poverty eradication now defined as the greatest global challenge facing
the world today. In cooperation with its sponsors, the International Social
Science Council (ISSC) and the University of Bergen (UiB), CROP works
in collaboration with knowledge networks, institutions and scholars to
establish independent, alternative and critical poverty research in order to
help shape policies for long-term poverty prevention and eradication.

The CROP network comprises scholars engaged in poverty-related
research across a variety of academic disciplines. Researchers from more
than a hundred different countries are represented in the network, which is
coordinated by the CROP Secretariat at the University of Bergen, Norway.

The CROP series on International Studies in Poverty Research presents
expert research and essential analyses of different aspects of poverty
worldwide. By promoting a fuller understanding of the nature, extent,
depth, distribution, trends, causes and effects of poverty, this series will
contribute to knowledge concerning the reduction and eradication of
poverty at global, regional, national and local levels.

For more information contact:

CROP Secretariat
PO Box 7800, 5020 Bergen, NORWAY
Phone: +47 55 58 97 44
Email: crop@uib.no
Visiting address: Jekteviksbakken 31
www.crop.org

Series editors

Juliana Martínez Franzoni, associate professor of political science, University
of Costa Rica

Thomas Pogge, Leitner professor of philosophy and international affairs,
Yale University

CROP INTERNATIONAL STUDIES IN POVERTY RESEARCH
Published by Zed Books in association with CROP

David Gordon and Paul Spicker (eds), *The International Glossary on Poverty*, 1999

Francis Wilson, Nazneen Kanji and Einar Braathen (eds), *Poverty Reduction: What Role for the State in Today's Globalized Economy?* 2001

Willem van Genugten and Camilo Perez-Bustillo (eds), *The Poverty of Rights: Human Rights and the Eradication of Poverty*, 2001

Else Øyen et al. (eds), *Best Practices in Poverty Reduction: An Analytical Framework*, 2002

Lucy Williams, Asbjørn Kjønstad and Peter Robson (eds), *Law and Poverty: The Legal System and Poverty Reduction*, 2003

Elisa P. Reis and Mick Moore (eds), *Elite Perceptions of Poverty and Inequality*, 2005

Robyn Eversole, John-Andrew McNeish and Alberto D. Cimadamore (eds), *Indigenous Peoples and Poverty: An International Perspective*, 2005

Lucy Williams (ed.), *International Poverty Law: An Emerging Discourse*, 2006

Maria Petmesidou and Christos Papatheodorou (eds), *Poverty and Social Deprivation in the Mediterranean*, 2006

Paul Spicker, Sonia Alvarez Leguizamón and David Gordon (eds), *Poverty: An International Glossary*, 2nd edn, 2007

Santosh Mehrotra and Enrique Delamonica, *Eliminating Human Poverty: Macroeconomic and Social Policies for Equitable Growth*, 2007

David Hemson, Kassim Kulindwa, Haakon Lein and Adolfo Mascarenhas (eds), *Poverty and Water: Explorations of the Reciprocal Relationship*, 2008

Ronaldo Munck, Narathius Asingwire, Honor Fagan and Consolata Kabonesa (eds), *Water and Development: Good Governance after Neoliberalism*, 2015

Abraar Karan and Geeta Sodhi (eds), *Protecting the Health of the Poor: Social Movements in the South*, 2015

Alberto D. Cimadamore, Gabriele Koehler and Thomas Pogge (eds), *Poverty and the Millennium Development Goals: A Critical Look Forward*, 2016

Alberto D. Cimadamore, Gro Therese Lie, Maurice B Mittelmark and Fungisai P. Gwanzura Ottemöller (eds), *Development and Sustainability Science: The Challenge of Social Change*, 2016

Einar Braathen, Julian May and Gemma Wright (eds), *Poverty and Inequality in Middle Income Countries: Policy Achievements, Political Obstacles*, 2016

PEASANT POVERTY AND PERSISTENCE IN THE TWENTY-FIRST CENTURY

THEORIES, DEBATES, REALITIES AND POLICIES

edited by Julio Boltvinik and Susan Archer Mann

Foreword by Meghnad Desai

ZED

Zed Books
London

Peasant Poverty and Persistence in the Twenty-first Century: Theories, Debates, Realities and Policies was first published in 2016 by Zed Books Ltd, The Foundry, 17 Oval Way, London SE11 5RR, UK.

www.zedbooks.net

Typeset in Plantin and Kievit by Swales & Willis Ltd, Exeter, Devon
Cover designed by www.kikamiller.com

A catalogue record for this book is available from the British Library.

ISBN 978-1-78360-844-7 hb
ISBN 978-1-78360-843-0 pb
ISBN 978-1-78360-845-4 pdf
ISBN 978-1-78360-846-1 epub
ISBN 978-1-78360-847-8 mobi

Printed and bound by CPI Group (UK) Ltd, Croydon, CR0 4YY

El Colegio de México hosted and Universidad Autónoma Metropolitana-Xochimilco sponsored the international seminar from which this book derived.

Julio Boltvinik dedicates this book to:

My beloved Araceli: wife, colleague and accomplice
My dear daughters Jana and Ema; my dear sons Uri and León
My cherished granddaughters Ariela, Victoria and Lucía

And to the memory of my co-editor, colleague and friend, Susan Archer Mann, who died shortly after having completed all the hard and outstanding work she did for many years to make this book possible.

Susan Archer Mann dedicates this book:

In loving memory of her dear friend and mentor Frederick H. Buttel for his contributions to revitalising and fostering a critical rural sociology.

CONTENTS

TABLES AND FIGURES

Tables

Figures

ACKNOWLEDGEMENTS

For the organisation of the international seminar
The International Seminar on Peasant Poverty and Persistence, which took place at El Colegio de México (Mexico City) on 13–15 March 2012, and from which this book derived, would not have been possible without the help of many persons. At the risk of omitting someone, I want to express my deep gratitude to some of them. To Asunción Lera St. Clair, Director of CROP when the idea of this seminar originated at a meeting of CROP's Scientific Committee in 2009, for her extraordinary and enthusiastic support. When her period as Director of CROP finished, the international seminar was an ongoing project. To Alberto Cimadamore, Director of CROP, who supported the project, signed an agreement with El Colegio de México and allocated funds to make it a reality. To my friend Armando Bartra, who spent many hours and a great deal of energy helping me organise the agenda and build a list of distinguished participants to invite to the seminar. Additionally, he convinced the authorities of Universidad Autónoma Metropolitana-Xochimilco (UAM-X) to co-organise the seminar and allocate funds to it. To Roberto Blancarte, then Director of CES (Centro de Estudios Sociológicos of El Colegio de México), who enthusiastically supported the role of El Colegio as host of the international seminar. To Arturo Alvarado, who became Director of CES a few weeks before the seminar and has been very supportive since then. To Salvador Vega y León, then Rector of UAM-X, who was not only supportive but also very enthusiastic about the project. To Yolanda Massieu Trigo, who was in charge of the postgraduate course on rural development at UAM-X and was also very enthusiastic and participated in the seminar. To Hans Egil Offerdal, who, while working for CROP Latin America and resident in Mexico, was the person who solved all the problems, prepared letters and budgets, arranged air tickets, wrote various drafts of the call for papers and cleared everything that had to be cleared with CROP headquarters. He was, and is, a friend.

Julio Boltvinik

For writing and producing the book

We express our gratitude to all the authors of chapters in the book for contributing their knowledge, the fruits of their research and their effort to this collective project. We are especially grateful for their open-minded attitude when we had to interact on points where we saw communication or conceptual difficulties. Disagreements remained, but in most cases they were clarified. Henry Bernstein generously gave us wise advice when we were preparing the book proposal. Jakob Horstmann, managing editor at CROP, has been very kind to us during all the long stages that we had to go through. David Barkin and Gordon Welty offered their spontaneous help in revising chapters written by non-native English-speaking authors. David Barkin also helped with the contents of some specific points in Leff's paper and in the introduction. The anonymous reviewer of the book proposal made some very useful suggestions. We also want to thank all the people at Zed Books, who have been patient and tolerant all the way through. Lastly, we express our warm gratitude to Judith Forshaw, who did excellent work copy-editing this long and complex book.

Julio Boltvinik and Susan Archer Mann

Susan Archer Mann thanks the University of New Orleans' Office of Research for a Creative Endeavor Award that enabled her to work on this book.

FIRST PART: INTRODUCING THE BOOK

FOREWORD

Meghnad Desai

1. Persistence of peasantry: a problem for theory or history?

The urgent and critical problem of the world is global poverty. Even by the flawed standards of the World Bank (see the Introduction by Boltvinik and Mann), there are about 1 billion people living in poverty in rural areas. The stipulated poverty levels are derisory for meeting basic requirements. The Asian Development Bank recently revised its poverty standard to include a margin of resources needed to adapt to vulnerability to climate risks. The World Bank's purchasing power parities (PPP) dollar level went up from $1.25 to $1.51. This led it to revise Asian poverty numbers from 20 per cent to 50 per cent of the total population. The much-publicised reduction in poverty in Asia has thus been eliminated by looking more carefully at the life experiences of the poor.

The purpose of these global exercises is more to arrive at a number than to understand the problem. Even so, a large part of the rural poor is engaged in some sort of agricultural activity. They are typically smallholders with their own cultivation, tenant farmers, share croppers (*métayer*) or landless labourers. In Asia, they are called farmers; elsewhere they are labelled peasants. The poverty of the peasantry is one theme discussed here. In his contribution, Bernstein discusses the data on agriculture and rural poverty in great detail, and casts his net broader than the category of 'peasantry' (own-account farmers) to include other categories of the rural poor. He also draws our attention to changes in rural poverty, and in poverty in general, rather than just the persistence of the peasantry. However, for sake of the present discussion, the questions posed are: why are there still peasants around the world? And why are they poor?

The fact that peasantry persists in the twenty-first century, three centuries and more after the advent of industrial capitalism, and whether that persistence explains the poverty of peasants are problems that are addressed in this excellent collection of essays. All the authors write within the general framework of Marxian political economy, although there are many cogent differences in their approaches. Many operate within the broad confines of Marx's writings, exploring *Capital* as well as *Grundrisse* and other texts. Others, such as Leff, Vergopoulos and Arizmendi, take a critical approach that challenges and extends the paradigm. The collection is thus a demonstration of the powers and limits of the Marxian method of analysing real-world problems as well as a study of the peasantry.

The problems are laid out by Julio Boltvinik and Susan Mann in their introduction and in Boltvinik's background paper (Chapter 1). They are then discussed by various authors. A common thread in the collection is that the persistence of the peasantry is an anomaly that needs to be – and can be – explained by Marxian political economy. The argument is that, if we take seriously the stadial theory of history as briefly but succinctly expounded in Marx's preface to *A Contribution to the Critique of Political Economy* (CCPE), summarising the longer argument that appeared later in *The German Ideology*, jointly written with Friedrich Engels, the transition from feudalism to capitalism should eventually eliminate all the pre-capitalist forms of production, leaving only fully developed capitalist production in the sphere of exchange.

There are several problems here. Not only is the passage in CCPE painfully short, but it is inadequate as a theory of history. It is Eurocentric: non-European social evolution is put into one grab bag category called the 'Asiatic Mode of Production'. Putting that aside, the daisy chain of primitive communism, ancient or slave mode, feudalism, capitalism and then socialism maps out the process of progress over time. The only transition that has been analysed at all seriously using Marxian theory is that from feudalism to capitalism, but even here there is no agreement among scholars about how it happened or whether it was uniform across different regions or even within Europe, or if it was ever complete. (The bibliography is large here.) Suffice it to say that the idea of a complete transition from one mode to the next is a drastic simplification and not descriptively accurate. What we typically have is the coexistence of forms from earlier modes with later ones. Such mixed categories were labelled 'social formations'. Most, if not all, capitalist economies have a persistence of pre-capitalist forms of organisation within them. It was thought once that such 'impure' social formations with their persistence of pre-capitalist forms were a sign of underdeveloped capitalism, which would wither away with a more rapid development of capitalism. This was, however, too simple a defence of the theory. Marx had what economists call the Ricardian disease – taking any observable tendency to its logical conclusion and considering that the prediction of a real outcome. Ricardo had subsistence wages for ever, and rents consuming profits to drive the economy into a stationary state with a zero profit rate. Marx envisioned the total triumph of capitalism across the globe due to the sheer logical necessity of his theory. Reality, however, eludes the predictions of theory.

The survival of pre-capitalist forms of production is not unusual. In many areas of the economy and in many regions, pre-capitalist forms have survived. Small businesses with owner workers, handicrafts in both simple necessities and luxury items – goldsmiths, jewellers, fine textile producers, and so on – can be found in the developed as well as the less developed world. In agriculture especially, the triumph of industrial forms in the manner of factory farms (much loved by Leninists in the Soviet Union) has been limited. The Mann–Dickinson thesis referred to in some of the essays here discusses this very aspect, although there are disagreements – especially as expressed by Julio Boltvinik – about the cogency of their argument. Bernstein offers a longer historical perspective on the development of agriculture as a global industry in his chapter (Chapter 5) and describes the shrinkage of peasantry across continents over time. Only in sub-Saharan Africa does own-account farming account for more than half of total rural activity, but even there the percentages are in the mid-fifties.

Even very large and efficient farms remain family farms in Europe and USA. As neoclassical economists would say, there are limits to the economies of scale and size in agriculture. Large, medium and small family farms are the predominant forms of organisation in agricultural production. Machines have displaced labour but they have not eliminated it. Vineyards have crucial limits to economies of size and the degree to which labour can be replaced. Fruit picking is seasonal and urgent. In Western Europe, where small peasant farms are an exception rather than a rule (in UK the category of peasantry is unknown), the surplus labour is recruited from a variety of sources – urban, temporary migrants and locals, for instance. Fully automated or mechanised farming remains in the future, if it ever becomes cost effective.

But other pre-capitalist forms survive. The survival of aboriginal tribes across the world is not an anomaly but an indication that even pre-feudal forms of organisation – hunting and gathering – can coexist with modern capitalism. As is cogently pointed out in the essay by Welty, Mann, Dickinson and Blumenfeld (Chapter 3), the reproduction of labour power takes place within the household, which is a pre- and non-capitalist form of production organisation. Indeed, the household has survived as the site for the production and upkeep of human labour across all modes of production that we know of. It survives because nothing more cost saving has been found to replace it over the centuries.

The fact that the reproduction of labour power – the most crucial input into the production of surplus value in the Marxian theory – takes place under non-capitalist conditions has much more serious implications for the theory than has been noticed even by feminist writers who have criticised the labour theory of value. The argument is as follows. Marx, like all classical economists, assumed that the exchange value of a commodity is determined by the labour content in its production. Implicitly this is so if the production is under capitalist conditions. But if labour power is produced under non-capitalist conditions, why should its value be determined by the standards of capitalist costing? The point is not just that the household does not charge surplus value in determining the reproduction cost of labour power, but that it might not use cost calculus in any form. If so, the exchange value of labour power is determined not by cost but by demand. The implications for value theory are serious.

Another way of putting this is to say, as Vergopoulos argues in his chapter (Chapter 9), that capitalism needs at least one sector in which the commodity producers are underpaid in order to sustain profitability in the system. My own view is more critical than that. It is an immanent critique. This is that when you examine Marx's very powerful proposition within the limits of even his own method, it does not hold water. This could and will be challenged. But then one of the purposes of this volume is to examine the theory itself as well as the reality it purports to explain.

Thus, whatever the optimistic projections of Marxian stadial theory, the transition from previous modes of production to capitalism is not and can never be complete. The persistence of pre-capitalist or even pre-feudal forms is to be expected. The issue that is raised by Boltvinik, Bartra, Arizmendi and Bernstein, among others, is whether the survival of the peasantry is a structural necessity for capitalism. Let me come to that.

Peasantry is a term most associated with Europe and, on the evidence presented here, the Western hemisphere. In England, there has been no reference to peasants since the Peasants' Revolt in the thirteenth century. Since the Black Death of the mid-fourteenth century, England has had farmers, not peasants. *Paysannerie* is a French expression and persists past the French Revolution. It typically refers to a family farm with a small amount of land owned or rented. In India, 80 per cent of farms are under 2 acres in size and classified as subsistence farms. Many farmers also work as seasonal farm labourers. Their livelihoods are precarious.

The persistence of peasantry, despite the poverty attendant on being a peasant, can be due to many things since it is not unique but is part of the general problem of the necessarily incomplete transition from feudalism and/or other pre-capitalist modes to capitalism. The authors in this collection would reject this view. They seek an explanation for the persistence of peasantry not in empirical factors such as inequality in landholding, rules such as partible inheritance, underdevelopment of the non-agricultural parts of the economy and hence a lack of alternative forms of employment, and only residually in choice. Lot of subsistence farms produce for their own consumption and are poor but outside the market framework (except when they hire themselves out as farm workers). The authors seek an explanation in the systematic exploitation of the peasantry due to its coexistence with capitalist agriculture. This is the crux of the themes explored here and so it needs careful attention. However, in his contribution, Leff challenges this Marxistic or economistic functional explanation to draw our attention to a cultural, ecological and anthropological perspective.

The contentious issue is whether the persistence of the peasantry is a functional part of capitalist agriculture. This question can be asked in two ways. Could capitalist agriculture survive without peasantry? Secondly, is the peasantry exploited if and when it enters into exchange relations with capitalist markets? Can we deploy the tools of Marxian value theory to analyse the question of the poverty of the peasantry? This takes us to a central theme of this collection. Let me proceed carefully and in some detail on the conceptual tools at hand and the way in which they are developed and deployed by the authors.

2. Abstract and concrete labour

Ricardo had shown – and has even logically proved – that rent from land was an unearned income for the landlords. Rent rose as inferior lands came into cultivation. The price of corn was determined by the cost of the marginal land. All supra-marginal lands earned a differential rent, and rent was zero on marginal land. In *Capital*, Volume III, Part VI (CW 37: 608–800), Marx discusses the many aspects of rent – differential rent, ground rent and peasantry. One of his ideas is to doubt that anyone would lease their land for zero rent. He was thinking of the English context.

Marx wanted to prove the similar proposition that profits of capital were unearned. His brilliant insight was to use the dual value form – use value and exchange value – which, according to classical political economy, every commodity had. Classical theorists were agreed that the exchange value of a commodity was determined by the labour time required in its production (or the labour time that the commodity, when sold, could command). They made no connection between the use value and exchange value of a commodity. Marx seized upon the uniqueness of human labour, which served as a measure of exchange value for all commodities but was itself – as labour power – sold as a commodity. He translated this into the proposition that profits were the money form of surplus value, which was the gap between the use value of labour time expended and the exchange value of labour power. The use value was extracted during the production process and was measured by the length of time extracted as well as by the intensity of the production process. The exchange value of labour power, like that of all commodities, was measured by the labour time involved in the production and reproduction of labour power.

This was the radical part of Marx's critique of political economy. It is and remains a powerful proposition and is central to many of the contributions in this collection, although there are differences between authors – Boltvinik and Bartra, for example. This is a central matter so I shall concentrate on this in my remarks.

First, it has to be said that, while this was a central proposition, it was not sufficient to show that all profits came from the surplus value produced by living labour. There is a long and extensive debate on the price–value transformation problem that pertains to Volume III, Part II of *Capital* (CW 37: 141–209), which was edited and published by Engels from Marx's manuscripts. (Marx had finished the manuscripts for all three volumes in the early 1860s before he prepared Volume I for publication in 1867. In the remaining sixteen years of his life, he did not revisit or revise the rest of the manuscript. The reason for this is much debated but need not concern us here.) Marx's treatment was a muddle. The world at large was not convinced with his demonstration and Eugen von Böhm-Bawerk published a trenchant critique of Marx's failure to prove his proposition.

Ladislaus von Bortkiewicz offered one solution of the problem in 1907 (all details in Desai 1979).

The issue is as follows: if profits are produced by living labour, why would capitalists employ non-human – constant – capital? This is especially so since the organic composition of capital – the ratio of constant capital to variable capital (or, in some versions, constant capital to total capital, i.e. constant plus variable capital), $g = C / V$ or $C / (C + V)$ – differs between individual employers. The rate of surplus value – the ratio of surplus value – to variable capital ($r = S / V$) multiplied by one minus the organic composition yields the value rate of profit: $\pi = r (1 - g) = S / (C + V)$. Marx assumed that r was equal across capitals. Since g was different, π was unequal across capitals. But all classical political economists agreed that the money rate of profits was equal across all capitals. What gives?

The solution involves a transfer of surplus value from capitals with low g to those with high g. Thus, while labour power creates surplus value, during the pricing process the larger capitals attract more surplus value to themselves. But why this should be the case is not clear. The numerical example in Volume III just gives a particular solution. Parallel to the accounts in value terms are the accounts in terms of production prices, which attach money prices to all inputs and then add a uniform rate of profit to arrive at market prices. The transfer of surplus value across different capitals happened during the pricing process. Marx did not explain why this was so and his worked-out example looked as if it were unfinished. That may have been a reason why he never finished Volume III of *Capital*. The central issue is this: if firms with a higher organic composition attract surplus value from those with a lower organic composition, how can you distinguish that from the argument that they make a larger surplus value because capital produces surplus value just as labour does? As neoclassical economists would assert, labour equipped with machinery is more productive than labour with simple tools.

Marx's failure to prove his basic proposition did not diminish his bigger historical message. At the level of the economy, his vision of a crisis-ridden system in dynamic disequilibrium going through booms and busts remained a powerful guide to mapping the course of capitalist economies. But there remain (in my view at least) problems with using the value theoretic apparatus for analysing concrete issues. First of all, the basic proposition is about abstract undifferentiated labour, i.e. unskilled manual labour power. While the wage in this case is determined by the cost of the production of subsistence, once you move away from abstract labour to concrete labour, Marx's discussion has problems. Thus, the ratio of the wages of skilled workers to those of unskilled workers cannot be analysed in this framework, although there has been some debate on this. One could say that the use value of skilled labour is an exact multiple of the use value of abstract labour in proportion to its wage ratio. But that is to say that the market determines wage differentials, not value calculus. The ratio cannot either be explained in terms of the exchange value of skilled labour being exactly in the same ratio to the exchange value of abstract labour as their wages are without again making the argument circular. Neoclassical political economy abandoned the Labour Theory of Value and linked use value and exchange value for each and every commodity. It also gave up labour time as the common measure of value.

3. Peasant labour

So much by way of introductory remarks. Peasant labour would seem to be the closest to abstract undifferentiated labour. It works with very little capital. Its exchange value is problematical since it is not sold on the market while the peasant works on his land. What the peasant sells is the final output, which includes the use value of labour time as well as the contribution of land, equipment and the hard-to-evaluate contribution of nature: for example, climate and weather conditions such as timely rainfall. Land is a constant input while nature is variable. (Leff points out in his contribution that this could be a much more vital point than the value calculus allows.) But we can, in the style of neoclassical economics, assume that the exchange value is the same as if the labour power were sold on the market. Bear in mind that the argument is somewhat circular here. If the basic level of consumption of the peasant household is limited by what little it has, the 'exchange value' is determined by the starvation consumption level. Marx had theorised about labour power as a commodity bought and sold on the market, and hence its exchange value was to be determined like that of all other commodities using the labour time required for its production. If labour power is not exchanged (as, say, within the household), its value is indeterminate in classical and Marxian theory. Indeed, the value category does not apply.

The issue of exploitation – whether by 'self', à la Chayanov, or by the predatory capitalist nearby – depends on the use value of labour time spent. The difference between the use value and the exchange value, which are both expressed in labour time, is the amount of surplus value. If, as Marx assumed, the use value is just the length of time spent, then the issue is simple. The raw difference in time spent at the farm during the production period minus the amount of time required to produce the consumption bundle (the time may be that of the women of the household) is surplus value. In a Chayanovian calculus, there is no exchange and hence the issue of surplus value does not arise. The peasant household works on the farm and in the house to produce the stuff that is consumed.

The result may be a poor level of consumption. But even that requires self-exploitation. If the harvest is good, the consumption level of the family will be better but still at a poverty level. If the harvest fails, the household will starve. There is zero surplus value. Value categories do not impinge.

If the context changes to a Marxian rather than a Chayanovian one, how does the calculus change?

The thesis by Julio Boltvinik is that it is the discontinuous nature of the labour input requirement during the agricultural production process that is the principal factor in understanding both the poverty and the persistence of the peasantry. There is idle time between sowing and harvesting and also idle time after harvesting (for example in the winter). This idle time has to be provided for in terms of subsistence consumption to reproduce labour power. But idle time is unpaid time. Thus, the use value of labour time is low relative to what it would be if production time and working time coincided. The consequence of this is that the presence of the peasantry, which bears the cost of idle time without charging for it, makes agricultural prices lower than they would be otherwise and this makes the peasantry structurally beneficial to capitalism.

Let us take this a step at a time. The peasant is his own cultivator of a small piece of land with some simple tools. In this, he is not the classic proletariat who has been divested of the means of production and has to sell his labour power (*Capital*, Volume I, Chapter 6, 'The buying and selling of labour power'; CW 35: Part I). Arizmendi makes this point by mentioning the different way in which the subsumption of the peasantry takes place. The peasant does not sell his labour power but the produce of his effort using land and some capital equipment. The total value of the output would then equal the labour time plus the wear and tear of capital, as per the standard calculus, plus the value of the contribution of the land input. To this we have to add, unlike in a manufacturing process, the effect of nature on output, which is variable from year to year. Thus, the value of output exceeds the value of labour input but maybe not by much. Does it include surplus value? Since it is the peasant's own cultivation, one should rule out surplus value or class it as self-exploitation in order to preserve the conventions of value accounting.

Whichever way we account for it, Boltvinik contends that it is the unpaid time which is the cause of peasant poverty and the reason for its persistence, which is profitable to capitalism. Bartra takes the view that the crucial factor is that the owner-cultivator does not charge differential rent, and this allows the peasant to absorb the shock of the low price he obtains for his produce. For Bartra, the exploitation of the peasant takes place in the product market as the price the peasant obtains as a small seller will be determined by larger players in the market. Notice that we have moved from value calculus in Boltvinik to price domain in Bartra. But they are both seeking explanation for what they agree is the poverty of the peasant.

Where does the exchange value of labour power come in here? For all the authors, labour power that is sold as a commodity – the cost of production and reproduction measured in labour time – determines the exchange value, just as it does for all commodities. The fact that labour power is perhaps the only commodity produced under non-capitalist conditions has to be noted, but this is not peculiar to the peasantry. However, peasant labour is not sold as a commodity. Its exchange value is therefore indeterminate. The radical implication of Boltvinik's argument could be that the subsistence level of the peasant (individual as well as household) is determined by the market value of his produce. This market value is low in terms of labour time, thanks to discontinuity in the production process, and/or in terms of the exploitative nature of the product market where the peasant has to sell his produce. For Bartra, the peasant is the marginal producer cultivating land with zero rent and hence able to survive low prices.

These are competing as well as complementary theories. Peasants have low productivity per acre or per worker but still survive. They are an adjunct to capitalist agriculture in two senses. Since peasants do not sell their labour power (except when they are casual farm workers), they are not part of the labour market. But since they sell their output, their exploitation takes a different form from that of the worker in an industrial production process who is alienated from the product of his work. Thus, without being fully part of capitalism, they suffer as a result of it.

The peasant has land that adds value to the final output. This is not properly accounted for. Leff regards the 'entropic degradation of land induced by the economic process' and its ecological effects as a more important dimension of peasant poverty than the seasonal work pattern. The contribution of nature is even more 'free' for the value accounting logic than the idle hours of the worker. Leff discusses three orders of productivity – ecological, technological and cultural – and wants to put the problem of the peasantry in an ecological context, which itself is a consequence of global capitalism. Elma Montaña illustrates this by examining three river basins and the condition of the peasantry in Argentina, Bolivia and Chile. The interaction of the natural conditions of soil, water supply and weather all go to determine the sustainability of peasant agriculture.

It may be that the peasantry demands a generalisation of the value theory. This, in my view, is not so much the way in which Boltvinik tackles the issue (more about that below). The issue is that, when labour is idle between production operations, nature is at work. It determines how much the hard work of sowing is rewarded in terms of the harvest. If value can be imparted only by labour time (after translating the contribution of constant capital in terms of equivalent labour time), then nature is valueless. But that is empirically absurd in agriculture. The value calculus may work for manufacturing and other industries, but not for agriculture. So, in agriculture, the value of the output must acknowledge the contribution of nature in a non-trivial way.

Let us take the issue of differential rent. How would one account for it within the Marxian calculus? The standard formula is $C + V + S$, all measured in labour time. How do we account for rent? It is a sort of surplus value since it is like profit. However, it is not a product of labour but rather of differential fertility. Let me try out a suggestion. Let differential fertility be denoted as f. For marginal land, f is zero. For all supra-marginal land, it is positive and can be ordered in an increasing sequence. So, for any land yielding rent, the value equation can be rewritten as $(C + V + S)(1 + f)$. Simply put, $f(C + V + S)$ is the value form of money rent. (This is rather simplistic and would need to be developed much more. As I mentioned above, in *Capital*, Volume III, Part VI, Marx discusses rent extensively.)

Julio Boltvinik takes a different approach to the generalisation of value theory. He wants to add to the standard value equation in Marx's

Simple Reproduction Scheme (SRS) a further condition that total output of wage goods (Department II output) has to be sufficient to reproduce the entire population. This is a normative condition that capitalism ought to allow reproduction at some minimum level of consumption (V in his notation). But there is no reason why it should. Capitalism is a mode of production and reproduction of capital, not a charity. Labour power is an essential input but not the responsibility of the system. The fact that, from the Poor Laws to the welfare state, something has been done about the poor does not detract from this proposition. Indeed, the reform of the Poor Laws in nineteenth-century England was the mark of the bourgeois revolution minimising such pre-capitalist commitment. Marx did not make this a condition. The reserve army marched on empty stomachs.

Boltvinik's notion can be taken together with the ideas of farmers' support and wage subsidies that are part of policy in many developed capitalist countries. This 'dividend' is collected via tax and redistributed. Let us begin with Boltvinik's equation, which is located in Marx's SRS:

$$(S_1 + S_2) + (V_1 + V_2) = v365N$$

Here, v is the average per capita consumption of the population. The equation defines the per capita per day consumption afforded by the system, but leaves the question of who gets what aside. Let us assume that the number of capitalists who consume $S_1 + S_2$ is n, which is a small fraction of N. If there is no taxation, then what the workers get is:

$$(V_1 + V_2) = v'365 (N-n)$$

Here, v' is the average per capita per day consumption of all workers and their households. Capitalists consume c per capita per day:

$$\{S_1 + S_2\} = c365n$$

The subsidy regime has to be financed by a tax on the capitalists. Thus:

$$[(V_1 + V_2) + t (S_1 + S_2)] = v365 (N-n)$$

Here, t is the tax on the capitalist's consumption, which is transferred to support the minimum living standard v. This is a simple way to frame welfare payments within a Marxian national income account (which is what Marx's SRS is a pioneer attempt at doing).

One should remember that Marx and Engels were staunchly against all schemes of egalitarian reform under capitalism (see Hollander 2008, especially Part 5, Chapter 13 'Economic organisation and the equality issue', pp. 385–409).

Conclusion

There is much more that can be said, but let the volume speak for itself. Here is a rich collection of innovative, critical essays spanning political economy in the broadest sense, including history, politics, and the ecology of global capitalism. I congratulate the authors and the editors on a successful venture.

References

Desai, M. (1979) *Marxian Economics.* Totowa NJ: Littlefield, Adams & Co.

Hollander, S. (2008) *The Economics of Karl Marx: Analysis and applications.* Cambridge: Cambridge University Press.

Marx, K. and F. Engels (1998) *Collected Works.* Various volumes. London: Lawrence and Wishart. Referred to in the text as 'CW'.

INTRODUCTION

Julio Boltvinik and Susan Archer Mann

1. The origins and contents of this book

This book is based on papers presented at the International Seminar on Peasant Poverty and Persistence in the Contemporary World, which took place at El Colegio de México, Mexico City on 13–15 March 2012. The seminar was originally conceived in 2009 at a Scientific Committee meeting of the Comparative Research Programme on Poverty (CROP), which is a programme of the International Social Science Council (ISSC) hosted by the University of Bergen, Norway. In that meeting, committee member Julio Boltvinik highlighted the fact that, among the world's poor, the great majority are peasants and that the specific topic of peasant poverty had not served as a central topic in any of the international seminars organised by CROP since its creation in 1992. His suggestion to organise a seminar on this topic was approved and Professor Boltvinik offered to write a background paper on peasant poverty and persistence to establish the themes to be addressed at it. This background paper is included as Chapter 1 in this book. The Universidad Autónoma Metropolitana-Xochimilco (UAM-X) co-sponsored this event together with CROP and El Colegio de México, and scholars from both the global North and the global South participated in this exciting transnational conference.

The strategy adopted for selecting seminar participants was twofold. On the one hand, distinguished scholars in the field of agrarian studies were personally invited to participate. On the other, CROP launched a call for papers through its broad network of contacts. The background paper was distributed to all the invitees and potential participants, who were asked to submit an abstract of their proposed paper and who were invited to react to the contents of the background paper and to address two main questions: what are the roots of peasant poverty? And why has the peasantry as a distinct form of production been able to persist into the twenty-first century in the face of global capitalist development? An academic programme committee was appointed to select the papers to be included in the seminar.

This book is organised in three parts, and the second part is divided into four sessions that mirror the actual sessions of the seminar in Mexico City. The first part includes the foreword and the introduction to the book; the second part includes the background paper and ten papers presented at the seminar (Chapters 1 to 11); and the third part, which closes the book, is a post-seminar paper prepared by Professor Boltvinik. This latter paper includes replies, clarification and precisions to the comments on and critiques of his original background paper, a deepening of some important topics, a succinct discussion of certain issues that are not included in this volume but are highly relevant to the subject of the book, and a typology of replies to the central questions of the seminar. Thus, the structure of the twelve chapters of the book comprises one pre-seminar paper, ten seminar papers, and one post-seminar paper. This structure provides the book with its distinguishing feature: its emphasis on dialogue and debate, on criticism and reply. Overall, the motto of CROP – 'mobilizing critical research for the prevention and eradication of poverty' – captures the purpose of this book.

2. On the definition of poverty and the low reliability of rural poverty data

The word *poverty* originated in everyday life. According to the Spanish dictionary *Diccionario de la Real Academia Española* (DRAE), the noun *poverty* means 'need, narrowness, lack of what is *necessary* to sustain life', while the adjective *poor* means 'in need, poverty-stricken and lacking the necessities to live'. According to the *Concise Oxford Dictionary*, the noun expresses the state of being poor and also the lack of the *necessities* for life, and the adjective refers to a person who 'lacks money or adequate means to live comfortably'. In an Arabic dictionary of 1311 AD, poverty is defined as the 'inability of the individual to satisfy his own *basic needs* and the needs of his dependants' (Spicker et al. 2007: 10). As seen, poverty and needs are inextricably linked in everyday life.

Amartya Sen (1981: 26, emphasis added) distinguishes two procedures for identifying who is poor: the direct method checks 'the set of people whose actual consumption baskets happen to leave some *basic need unsatisfied*. The 'income method's first step is to calculate the minimum income at which all the specified minimum needs are satisfied. The next step is to identify those whose actual incomes fall below that poverty line' (ibid.). For Sen, these two procedures:

> are not, in fact, two alternative ways of measuring the same thing, but represent two alternative *conceptions* of poverty. The direct method identifies those whose actual consumption fails to meet the accepted convention of minimum *needs*, while the income method is after spotting those who do not have the ability to meet these *needs*. (Sen 1981: 28, emphasis in original)

Both conceptions are present and combined in the dictionary definitions given. Poverty is either unsatisfied needs or the inability to satisfy them (as in the Arabic definition). Poverty and needs are also inextricably linked in social sciences.

In the poverty literature, one finds, among others, the additional following concepts:

• *Primary and secondary poverty*: 'The families living in poverty may be divided into two sections: 1) Primary Poverty. Families whose total earnings are insufficient to obtain the necessaries for the maintenance of merely physical efficiency. 2) Secondary Poverty. Families whose total earnings would be sufficient for the maintenance of merely physical efficiency were it not that some portion of it is absorbed by other expenditure, either useful or wasteful' (Rowntree 2000 [1901]: 86–7).

• *Relative poverty*: 'Individuals, families and groups in the population can be said to be in poverty when they *lack the resources* to obtain the types of diet, participate in the activities and have the living conditions and amenities which are customary, or are at least widely encouraged or approved in the societies to which they belong' (Townsend 1979: 31, emphasis added).

In its *Rural Poverty Report 2011* (IFAD 2010), the International Fund for Agricultural Development (IFAD) *estimated that about 1 billion rural people are poor*. IFAD reached this figure by following the World Bank's poverty measurement methodology, using a poverty line of $2 a day per person and an extreme poverty line of $1.25; in both cases, these amounts are expressed in the national currencies of each country, so that they can be compared with the income of the population, through so-called purchasing power parities (PPP). However, IFAD's figure, alarming and appalling as it is, clearly underestimates rural poverty. Thomas Pogge referred to World Bank figures resulting from the application of the same criteria in his lecture at the round table 'Poor thought: challenging the dominant narratives of poverty research', which took place at the University of Bergen on 12 May 2010 (Pogge 2010). He explained how these statistics shamelessly underestimated global poverty and presented a false trajectory of global poverty reduction that served the interests of neoliberal capitalism:

1. The evolution one depicts of world poverty in the long term, between 1981 and 2005, depends highly on the poverty line (PL) used. If one uses the 'official' WB [World Bank] PL of $1.25 (of purchasing power parities: PPP) per person per day, poverty in the 25 years decreases 27 per cent; but if one uses a $2 PL, poverty increases 1 per cent, and using a US$2.5 PL, it increases by 13 per cent. As seen, the lower the PL is, the more optimistic and more favourable is the outcome for neoliberal capitalism. In all three cases the total population in poverty would, respectively, be in 2005: 1.38 billion (b) with $1.25 PL; 2.56b with $2 PL; and 3.08b with $2.50 PL.

2. *WB's official PLs have been falling in real terms*, while the institution has intended to give the opposite impression: that its PLs have been rising. The truth is that in terms of 2009 purchasing power, the original PL of $1, which was used between 1990 and 1997, was $1.99; that of $1.08, used between 2000 and 2008 was $1.60; and that of $1.25, which is now being used, is equivalent to $1.37.

Hence, to observers unschooled in the dense details and intricate machinations of poverty statistics, the World Bank appears to be raising the poverty line but actually lowers it in terms of real purchasing power. By lowering the real poverty line, the World Bank suggests that poverty is falling. This adds falsehood to the open and shameless cynicism that is implied in offering to nearly half of the world's population a subsistence level that barely meets animal survival, which is what people would be able to attain with an income at the level of such squalid poverty lines.

IFAD data in the 2011 report refer only to developing countries and cover the period from 1988 to 2008. Note that 1988 is situated towards the end of the severe debt crisis of the 1980s which affected mainly Latin America and Africa. Therefore, the baseline year chosen is one of very high poverty rates, fostering the view that poverty is decreasing. IFAD calculations depart from World Bank estimates at the national level and are disaggregated by the institution using the proportion represented by rural poverty in total national poverty as derived from national estimates (each of which has its own poverty measurement methodology and definitions of 'rural' and 'urban').

As the report points out in the notes to Annex 1, which presents the figures for rural poverty and rural extreme poverty by region for developing countries, there 'are also two important assumptions behind the calculations':

> The first is that the incidence of rural poverty rates according to national surveys remains the same at the US $1.25/day poverty line. Ravallion, Chen and Sangraula (2007) showed that while this approximation is quite accurate for US $2/day poverty lines, it may be weaker for US $1.25/day. Because urban poverty lines are often higher than rural poverty lines, such an assumption may *underestimate* the incidence of rural poverty at the US $1.25/ day poverty line. The second assumption is that definitions of urban and rural populations are consistent across countries, and that the ratios of urban poverty lines to rural poverty lines are constant within regions. This is not the case, but intraregional variations are relatively limited. (IFAD 2010: 235, emphasis in original)

It is not only that the World Bank's calculations distort the evolution of world poverty and that IFAD's disaggregation of these figures add more doubts, but that the thresholds of $1.25 and $2 per person per day lack any support in any conception of human needs. This is shown in the example of Mexico, where a poverty line of $1.25 PPP results in a single-digit poverty incidence (5.3 per cent in rural areas and 1.3 per cent in urban settlements), while the two official poverty measures used by the Federal Government (Coneval) show it to be around 50 per cent of the population, and two other options estimate an incidence of around 80 per cent. The first of these is *Evalúa DF*, which uses the Integrated Poverty Measurement Method as its official procedure. The second is a reinterpretation of Coneval's results that replaces the intersection criterion (used by Coneval) with the union criterion (traditionally used in Latin America). Both options are applied to two sets of the poor population: one defined as those with an income below the poverty line, and the second as the population with unsatisfied basic needs. The four alternative indices to the World Bank's $1.25 per person per day result in very high multiples of the incidence of poverty using World Bank thresholds: the national incidence is 8.7, 9.7, 15.2 and 15.6 times higher respectively. The contrast is even more acute in urban areas, where the results are 61, 59, 35 and 31 times the World Bank estimates. It is quite obvious that these enormous distances between the World Bank's poverty line and Mexican official estimates make World Bank and IFAD figures, as well as goal 1 of the Millennium Development Goals, absolutely irrelevant for Mexico. (One can generalise this conclusion for many developing countries.) The next paragraph describes what you can buy in Mexico with $1.25 PPP and therefore what this World Bank ultra-poverty line means.

In May 2005, a PPP dollar was equivalent to 7.13 pesos, while the nominal exchange rate was 10.96 pesos per dollar. Therefore, the poverty line defined by the World Bank ($1.25) was equivalent to 8.91 pesos per person per day (81 per cent of the nominal value of a dollar at that time). It is hard to imagine how a person could, in 2005, meet her or his most basic needs with an income of less than 9 pesos a day. Suffice it to say that even the very frugal *food poverty line* defined by the Federal Government (which, until 2009, was the lowest of the three official poverty lines used) recognises that to acquire the *raw food basket* to meet average nutritional requirements, a person needs an income of $19.50 or $26.36 pesos (in rural and urban areas respectively). This means that people who have an income equal to the World Bank's ultra-extreme poverty line would be able to acquire only 46 per cent or 34 per cent of the minimum requirements for not being extremely (or food) poor, according to federal criteria in rural and urban areas respectively. This shows that such poverty lines are meaningless in terms of human needs.

Given the three groups of limitations present in World Bank/IFAD poverty estimates already mentioned – the ones identified by Pogge with respect to the World Bank's figures; those indicated for IFAD's disaggregation process between urban and rural levels; and the one outlined above for the poverty and extreme poverty thresholds – it is unnecessary to elaborate on the results obtained by IFAD as they cannot give an adequate picture of rural poverty levels and their evolution through time.

Although the measurement of poverty is not a central object of this book, one of the papers deals with alternative figures for one specific country (see Chapter 6).

3. Situating this volume in the history of peasant studies

The theoretical debates over peasant poverty and persistence that fill this volume have a long history. They are part of a century-old debate over the reasons for peasant persistence and the defining features of the uneven development of capitalism in agriculture. We cannot do justice in this brief introduction to the detailed history of agrarian studies over the past century. However, we can at least highlight the integral relationship between theory, history and political praxis, by pointing out how major political, economic and social events spurred transformations in agrarian social thought, as well as how the papers in this book contribute to this critical knowledge production.

Referred to as the 'agrarian question' in the late nineteenth and early twentieth centuries, debates over peasant persistence primarily took place between Marxist theorists and populist theorists (known as the Narodniks) over the nature of capitalist development in Russia. While nineteenth- and early twentieth-century theorists from various countries and representing diverse political perspectives had predicted the demise of non-wage forms of production in their grand theories of modernisation and industrialisation (Durkheim 1960 [1893]; Weber 1978 [1922]),[1] the stubborn persistence of peasant farms into the twentieth century presented a serious anomaly. Few countries had such immediate political pressures to address this issue as did early twentieth-century Russia. Indeed, it is no surprise that the most fertile political debates over peasant persistence grew on Russian soil, given the importance of the peasant–proletarian alliance for the Bolshevik Revolution of 1917, as well as for the New Economic Policy of the 1920s – a policy created to deal with the rural instability that threatened the young Soviet Republic.

Marx and Engels had predicted as early as 1848 in *The Communist Manifesto* that the cheap prices of capitalist commodities would 'compel all nations, on pain of extinction to adopt the bourgeois mode of production' (Marx 1970 [1848]: 39). However, this prediction came up short as capitalism failed to 'create a world after its own image' (ibid.) – particularly in the Russian countryside, where non-capitalist forms of production, such as peasant farms, engaged the bulk of the population in pre-revolutionary Russia. To address this uneven development, numerous Marxist theorists entered these agrarian debates – the most famous works being Karl Kautsky's *The Agrarian Question* (1988 [1899]) and V. I. Lenin's *The Development of Capitalism in Russia* (1967 [1899]).

These Marxist writings have been historically interpreted as foreshadowing the impending doom of the petty producer. While Marxist analyses have become more sophisticated and complex, sometimes even challenging these earlier interpretations (as in Chapter 12), the view that capitalism holds dominion over the fate of non-capitalist forms of production remains a point of reference to be discussed or accepted in some of the papers in this volume (see Chapters 1, 3, 4, 5 and 10).

In contrast, the Narodniks idealised peasant production and romanticised rural life (especially the peasant commune or *mir*) as part of a more general belief in the unique historical destiny of Russia to find a path of development different from that of the West. The premier theorist of that era to articulate this perspective was the Soviet agrarian economist Alexander V. Chayanov. His most famous works, published in English under the title *The Theory of Peasant Economy* (1966 [1925]),[2] elaborated his theory of peasant self-exploitation, a theory that is still invoked in explaining peasant persistence today, as various papers in this volume attest (see Chapter 9). The Narodniks' favoured path to development, which was based on petty commodity production and came to be known as an alternative 'third path' (being neither capitalist nor socialist), also remains alive in this volume, although it appears in the more *au courant* discourse of a path to sustainable development (see Chapter 7), as we shall discuss at more length below.

After World War II, these early twentieth-century debates were resurrected once again in the face of the global instability created when anti-colonialist and/or socialist revolutions caused the sun to set on many former European empires. Between 1945 and 1981, more than 100 new countries joined the United Nations, tripling the ranks from 51 to 156 nations (McMichael 1996: 25). However, colonial independence did not necessarily transform the uneven and unequal nature of global stratification. Many former colonies did not modernise or industrialise significantly; rather, large portions of their populations remained plagued by absolute poverty – lacking the basic necessities of human life, such as food, clean water and adequate shelter. Moreover, while national liberation movements had promised greater freedom and democracy in their anti-colonialist revolutionary zeal, these countries often ended up with small, indigenous elites enjoying great wealth and power amid the poverty of the masses, or what Frantz Fanon called 'the wretched of the earth' (Fanon 1967 [1961]).

Within the broader field of social change and development, the reasons for this extremely uneven and unequal global development became the central questions debated by theorists after World War II. The major conceptual schemes of these post-war theories reflected the Iron Curtain divide between capitalism and socialism that was established by the success of socialist revolutions in such largely agrarian countries as the USSR, China and Cuba. Modernisation theory was associated with bourgeois theory and its pro-free enterprise stance, whereas dependency theory and world systems theory were developed by Marxist and neo-Marxist theorists. No doubt, the heightened role of the US in these global conflicts – the Vietnam War, for instance, along with similar struggles in Chile, El Salvador and Nicaragua – galvanised mass movements both domestically and internationally that called for more critical approaches to understanding modernisation and development. This volume reflects the impact of these Cold War era debates, given that many papers contain references to the underlying theses of dependency and/or world systems theories.

Within the subfield of agrarian studies, anti-colonialist and socialist revolutions led a new generation of scholars to examine more critically the 'peasant wars of the 20th century' (Wolf 1969), as well as the distorted development that continued to characterise many former colonies and Third World countries. Indicative of this revitalised interest in peasant poverty and persistence, the early 1970s witnessed a proliferation of research, scholarly books and new specialised journals, such as *The Journal of Peasant Studies*, which recently celebrated its fortieth anniversary. Because this new research incorporated more critical and conflict-oriented theoretical perspectives than its rather stodgy predecessor – traditional rural sociology rooted in government-funded applied research and structural functional theory – it was heralded as 'the new sociology of agriculture' (Buttel et al. 1989).

Yet, here again, two distinct interpretations of rural development were advanced, and they continued to mirror the earlier Marxist/ Narodnik debate. Marxist and neo-Marxist scholars continued to view capitalism as the hegemonic mode of production shaping modern rural class structures, but paid more attention to historically specific and natural factors that delayed or averted this practice. Despite the greater complexity of these theories, their vantage point remained anchored in the logic of capitalist accumulation. In contrast, more micro-oriented approaches, which were often rooted in the neoclassical economic views of A. V. Chayanov or Max Weber, focused attention on the way in which the internal logic of non-wage forms of production (which differed from capitalist logic) presumably enabled them to resist capitalist penetration and remain permanent oases in a hostile capitalist world. These discussions also have become more sophisticated in recent years, as various papers in this volume suggest. For example, a number of papers discuss how features of agriculture that some authors (see, for example, Mann and Dickinson 1978; Contreras 1977) have seen as obstacles to capitalist development – such as the seasonality of production – have been functional in peasant persistence and poverty (see Chapters 1 and 6). Some authors highlight the important role of peasant cultural 'imaginaries' and their attachment to their historical and terrestrial roots (Chapter 7). Others highlight how peasants' engagement in diversified farming (Chapter 2) or forms of peasant multi-activity – such as seasonal wage labour at home or abroad in both agricultural and non-agricultural production – provide alternative sources of income for peasant households (Chapters 1 and 6). Still others point to the importance of peasants organising their communities along the principles of 'good living' or '*sumak kawsay*', in order to ensure both social and ecological reproduction (Chapter 11). Agrarian theories of late modernity also were influenced by the rise of the New Left. Whereas the Old Left had highlighted the battle between labour and capital as the primary axis of oppression in modern societies and had championed the working class as the major agent of revolutionary change, the New Left included the new social movements of late modernity, such as the civil rights movement, the women's movement, the anti-Vietnam War and other anti-imperialist movements, and the environmental movement. These new social movements addressed conflicts and cleavages generated by various forms of domination – by race, gender and global location, as well as the domination of nature. Historian Van Gosse refers to the New Left as a 'movement of movements' that encompassed all of the struggles for fundamental change from the 1950s to the 1970s (Gosse 2005: 5).

Spurred by the burgeoning environmental movement, in the 1970s various agrarian theorists wove into their analyses a growing awareness that the environmental destruction inflicted by and on human societies was beginning to encompass the entire earth. Not only had World War II revealed the devastating effects of nuclear arms, but non-renewable fuels such as coal, oil and gas, upon which modern, industrial societies are so dependent, were being exhausted. Control over these valuable fuel supplies became hotly contested – especially when the OPEC oil crisis in the early 1970s brought home to the First World how less developed societies were capable, through the organisation of cartels, of controlling the prices of some strategic resources. Although the replacement of natural raw materials by synthetics had begun in the early decades of the twentieth century and was largely under First World control, the abundance of non-biodegradable waste created by these synthetic fibres was becoming ever more apparent. In turn, the spillover effects of the toxic wastes generated by urbanisation, industrialisation and militarisation plagued the air, land and water of communities, not only locally but globally. It was frighteningly apparent that industrial societies had done more damage to the natural environment in 200 years than all previous civilisations combined (Balbus 1982: 362–3). Perhaps it took such world-scale damage to make people critically aware of the dangers of continuing on this path of environmental destruction. A

number of papers in this volume reflect this environmental awareness, and focus on the contributions of industrial-style farming to
ecological degradation and its effects on agriculture (see Chapters 2,
4, 7, 8 and 11) – an awareness that was largely absent in earlier versions of these agrarian debates.

The despoliation of the planet was further fostered by the
deregulation of economic life that accompanied the rise of
neoliberalism in the 1980s. When the state relinquishes the will and
capacity to regulate capital, this loss has irrational and self-defeating
consequences. The neoliberal political agenda excludes all possible
futures that would be incompatible with commodification. Indeed,
some observers have grimly noted: 'The logical end of neoliberalism
is the commodification of everything' (Leys and Harriss-White
2012). Already, the commodification of nature has gone far; this
process started before neoliberalism, but received a tremendous
impulse under it. Not only have farmland and fresh water supplies
been commodified, but also parts of the oceans (through the creation
and sale of exclusive fishing and drilling rights) and even air itself
(carbon trading is, in theory, a market for fresher air). One of
the papers in this volume focuses on the impact of this process in
terms of how the commodification of water supplies affects peasant
producers (Chapter 8), while other authors discuss the global 'land
grabs' currently taking place (Chapters 4, 5 and 10). The paper
by Luis Arizmendi (Chapter 4) couples what he calls the 'epochal'
environmental and food crises today to discuss the 'worldisation of
poverty' and how food circuits have 'become ... the most lucrative
business on the planet' for transnational capital.

In turn, even the functions of the state have been privatised
and commodified under the reign of neoliberalism: not just the
provisioning of public goods and services, such as utilities, but
activities hitherto seen as quintessentially public, such as schools,
prisons and policing. This attack on the public sphere is visible in
neoliberalism's austere structural adjustment programmes, which
have created further grotesque social inequalities on a world scale.
The impacts of these structural adjustment policies on the health and
welfare of peasant producers are addressed in this volume – especially
by authors who focus on indebted countries of the global South,
where these structural adjustment programmes were first imposed
(Chapters 3 and 9).

Perhaps the major contribution to agrarian studies by feminists of the second wave of the women's movement was their documentation of how gender matters in global development. Feminist scholars across the political spectrum empirically documented how modernisation and development had different impacts on women as opposed to men (Mann 2012; Chapters 9 and 10). Feminist scholars have argued that both Marx and Chayanov failed to adequately address the reproduction of labour power under capitalism and petty commodity production respectively; this argument is of particular relevance to the papers in this volume that mirror the early Marxist/ Narodnik debates. Chayanov's theory of 'self-exploitation' in the peasant economy essentially obscured the way in which the peasant household is the locus of domestic patriarchy (Mallon 1987; Hammel and Gullickson 2004; Welty 2012). Peasant households were never the equitable institutions Chayanov supposed; rather, women and children were vulnerable to abuse and exploitation by the male head of the household, often supported and reinforced by traditional customs and religion. Although Marx and Engels devoted more attention to the oppression of women (Marx 1986 [1882]; Engels 1972 [1884]), Marx's political economy of capitalism focused on the sphere of production and did not venture far into the ways in which labour power – either of the proletariat or of other classes – was reproduced on a day-to-day and intergenerational basis (Vogel 1983 [1973]; Hartmann 1981). Even today, agrarian studies are largely gender blind. As one observer wryly noted: 'It is remarkable how intellectual life for centuries was conducted on the tacit assumption that human beings had no genitals' (Eagleton 2003: 3–4).

Two papers in this volume directly address gender issues. Welty, Mann, Dickinson and Blumenfeld (Chapter 3) specifically address the social reproduction of labour power, while Damián and Pacheco (Chapter 6) document not only the negative effects of the North American Free Trade Agreement (NAFTA) on peasant producers but also how women, children and the elderly are left in the countryside as young and/or able-bodied men migrate to urban areas or abroad. Hopefully, this type of research will trigger more critical gender work in agrarian studies, particularly given how recent data estimate that women comprise just over 40 per cent of the agricultural labour force in the developing world, a figure that has risen slightly since 1980 and ranges from 20 per cent in the Americas to almost 50 per cent in East and Southeast Asia, as well as in Africa (FAO 2011). In turn, because the structural adjustment programmes imposed by neoliberal regimes are quick to cut state subsidies for health, education and welfare, women are more likely than men to be affected by longer working hours spent in care-giving labour. As David Harvey has observed, women 'bear the brunt' of neoliberal policies (Harvey 2007 [2005]: 170).

Together, the death of nature and the death of even the most meagre social safety nets led a number of theorists to contest altogether the assumption that modernisation and development (whether in its capitalist or socialist guise) resulted in progress. Concepts such as 'degrowth', 'maldevelopment' and 'necropolitics' became more evident in social thought,[3] as did critiques of the Enlightenment's meta-narrative of progress that had undergirded two centuries of modern Western thought. The critiques of progress by 'populist' theorists often highlight the benefits of pre-market subsistence production and its organic links to nature. Here, focus is placed on how the replacement of subsistence agriculture with modern cash crops results in a scarcity of the water, food, fodder and fuel that had sustained earlier peasant communities. Today, this third path is often couched in a discourse of ecological balance, and principles such as 'simple living' resonate strongly with such theorists.[4] Advocates of this path typically support grass-roots social movements and small, decentralised, democratic social organisations centred in local and community politics. Reliance on barter and social bonds of community replace market and financial institutions, while natural resources such as water and land are neither privatised nor commodified but treated as community responsibilities. The papers in this volume that highlight the indigenous '*milpa*' path to sustainable development (Chapter 2) or the benefits of organising social life along the principles of 'good living' (Chapter 11) exemplify this approach. Notably, these papers also highlight ethnicity and the important alternative bodies of knowledge and collective responsibility or accountability that characterise indigenous cultures.

Other authors focused their critique of progress on a more discursive level, attacking the master narratives of development (both bourgeois and Marxist) created by Eurocentric or Western thought. These critical perspectives – many of which fall under the rubric of 'postcolonial thought' today – argue that the very idea of 'modernity' is one of the 'central tropes' through which the West constructed itself as the centre and rest of the world as its periphery (Mary Louise Spratt quoted in Spurlin 2006: 3). In the field of peasant studies, this approach is best illustrated by the rise of subaltern studies, first in India and later in Latin America (Rodríguez 2001). Initially, subaltern studies was part of a broader trend in social history to provide histories 'from below' in order to rectify an elitist bias – especially colonialist and bourgeois-nationalist elitism. However, by the mid-1980s a rift opened up between scholars committed to subaltern class analysis and their forms of resistance and those who found that discursively deconstructing cultural power was more compelling in the face of the failures of modernity, positivism and the Enlightenment (Ludden 2002). While some scholars, such as Mohanty, coupled her earlier focus on decolonising Western thought with a later focus on capitalism and subaltern forms of resistance and consciousness (Mohanty 2006), others focused heavily on the discursive power of colonialism. In the latter case, subaltern studies largely became a postcolonial critique of modern, Enlightenment-based epistemologies written 'under Western eyes' (Mohanty 1984: 333), and debates centred on whether and how the subaltern could speak (Spivak 1988). This linguistic turn rendered into problems of subjectivity and epistemology the concrete and material problems of everyday life in the New World Order of transnational capitalism (Dirlik 1997).[5]

While none of the papers in this volume follow this discursive path, they still contend with the same failures of modernity and the rise of a New World Order that eludes earlier Cold War conceptual schemes. By the end of the 1980s, the 'three worlds' framework for understanding uneven capitalist development appeared obsolete. Not only had the Second World witnessed a significant demise with the implosion of the Soviet Union and the penetration of capitalism into the former communist bloc – both in Eastern Europe and in the Far East – but also industrial capitalism in the West was being decentred as offshoring, outsourcing and subcontracting abroad resulted in deindustrialisation. This meant that, for the first time in the history of capitalism, the capitalist mode of production was divorced from its historically specific origins in Europe and appeared as an authentically global abstraction (Dirlik 1997). Indeed, transnational capital is no longer just Euro-American, and neither is modernity. Rather, the situation is far more fluid and hybrid. Moreover, the increasing role of finance capital is unprecedented. Although theorists of imperialism had predicted the growing influence of finance capital in the early twentieth century (Hilferding 2007 [1910]; Lenin 1996 [1917]), the 'financialisation' of the globe, as one paper in this volume calls it (Chapter 9), has increased the complexity of contemporary capitalism, making it more difficult to understand, to control and to resist.

No doubt the situation looks bleak for the vast reservoir of disposable people bereft of social protections and for whom there is little to expect from neoliberalism except poverty, hunger, disease and despair. However, key topics of discussion at the international seminar on peasant poverty and persistence were forms of peasant resistance that respond directly to this neoliberal phase of transnational capitalism. In particular, there was a focus on La Vía Campesina – an organisation considered by many to be the most important transnational social movement in the world (Borras 2004; McMichael 2008; Patel 2006; 2013). This movement had its roots initially in Latin America but now has 148 member organisations in sixty-nine countries that cross five continents, and it claims to represent over 500 million rural families worldwide (Martínez-Torres and Rosset 2010). La Vía Campesina has levelled scathing attacks on World Bank land policies and has been involved in protests against the World Trade Organization (WTO) and the Free Trade Area of the Americas (FTAA). Its member organisations have even helped topple national governments in Ecuador in 2000 and in Bolivia in 2003. Although La Vía Campesina defines capitalism as the ultimate source of crises facing the global countryside and identifies transnational corporations as the worst enemy of peasants and small farmers, it also seriously addresses environmental and gender issues. It promotes ecological sustainability, demands parity between men and women within its organisation, and counterpoises the peasant 'moral economy' (Scott 1977) with the dominant 'market economy' model. It thereby brings all of these important social, economic and political concerns directly into the global debate over the future of agriculture (Martínez-Torres and Rosset 2010).

In summary, the seismic transformations in social life over the last half century require equally seismic transformations in social thought and political praxis if we are to understand and respond adequately to the crises of global rural poverty created by the twin processes of neoliberalism and transnational, flexible capitalism. While the papers in this volume address a century-old 'agrarian question', they do so in original, creative ways that better meet the conceptual needs of the social, political and economic problems thrown up by this New World Order.

4. Conceptualising the peasantry or the 'awkward class'

Just as the theoretical debates over peasant poverty and persistence discussed above exhibited much contested terrain, so does the very issue of defining the peasantry. The contributors to this volume share no single definition, but rather advocate a range of definitions that reflect a number of complicated and contentious issues.[6] The absence of a shared definition is not a failing of this text but reflects the historical reality that peasants as a social group have never fitted easily into the analytical categories used by social scientists, irrespective of their theoretical perspectives. For this reason, Teodor Shanin – one of the leading scholars of peasant societies in the twentieth century – referred to the peasantry as 'the awkward class' (Shanin 1972).[7]

In the pre-modern era, peasants often constituted an estate-like or caste-like subordinated group characterised not only by economic exploitation but also by limited social rights – both *de jure* and *de facto*, such as restrictions on geographical and social mobility and obligations to provide services and deference to the dominant groups. By the twentieth century, the spread of capitalism and market economies, with their attendant social upheavals and political movements, meant that many of these unfree or serf-like forms of labour and obligatory service had ended in much, but not all, of the globe (Edelman 2013).

As noted in the section above, scholarly interest in the peasantry initially arose in the late nineteenth and early twentieth centuries in response to the industrialisation and capitalist transformation of Central and Eastern Europe, with the most heated debates over how to conceptualise the peasantry taking place largely between the Marxists and populists of that era. The Chayanovian model viewed the peasantry as a unitary category with its own unique economic modus operandi whose focus on subsistence production and willingness to engage in self-exploitation to maintain its ties to the land distinguished it from more market-oriented and market-governed producers. By contrast, the Marxist-Leninist model highlighted how the peasantry would differentiate into distinct classes as capitalism and commodity production penetrated the countryside: rich peasants, who owned landed property and hired wage labour; middle peasants, who were small landowners operating on the basis of family labour alone; and poor peasants, who lacked sufficient land and therefore were forced to sell their labour to make ends meet. This differentiation would eventually signal the demise of the peasantry since it was assumed that small-scale petty commodity production could not compete over time in societies dominated by capitalism. In this volume, this approach is elaborated most fully by Henry Bernstein's contribution (Chapter 5; see also Bernstein 2010).

The famous peasant wars of the mid- to late twentieth century, coupled with the way in which Vietnamese peasants stood up to the most industrialised nation in the world, reawakened interest in the peasantry in the 1960s and 1970s. As peasants became armies and major actors on the global stage, their continued persistence and their political importance were evident. The flourishing of peasant studies in this era rejuvenated and extended the earlier debates that had focused largely on political economy. Often, attempts were made to distinguish 'peasants' from 'farmers' on the basis of their social relations of production and/or their relations to the market. This approach was exemplified in works such as Wolf (1969), Shanin (1971; 1972; 1973) and Mintz (1973), where the following questions became prominent. Did peasants own their own means of production, such as their land or farm equipment? Did they use family labour, hire labour, or hire themselves out as wage labourers? Were there seasonal differences in these occupational practices or did they maintain the same occupation throughout the year? Were their farm inputs and outputs commoditised or produced for use? Did they produce primarily for subsistence or to invest and expand their scale of operations? Were peasants more willing than other workers or producers to receive substandard wages or farm incomes because of their deep ties to the land? How were peasants exploited by other groups through rent, taxes, cheap labour and/or unequal market exchanges? When, if at all, do peasants cease being peasants if they still maintain rural units of production, even if those units are not economically viable? Do peasants have particular social and moral obligations to their communities that supersede market considerations and that entail obligatory ceremonial or ritual redistributions of wealth? The importance given to these different variables often distinguished the adversaries in any debate. For a fine example of an empirical study that examined many of these questions, see Deere and de Janvry (1979).

More recent conceptualisations reject a 'peasant' versus 'farmer' dichotomy and locate peasant farming on a continuum with entrepreneurial farming, although money and market relations still govern specific locations on this continuum (Van der Ploeg 2008). Here, key features of the peasantry include minimising monetary costs through cooperative relations that provide alternatives to the market, and non-monetary means of obtaining farm inputs and labour, as well as a greater prevalence of crop diversification to reduce economic and environmental risks (Edelman 2013).

Boltvinik (Chapter 12) quotes Alavi and Shanin (1988: xxxv, emphasis added), who refer to how V. P. Danilov et al. (in an article in Russian published in 1977) distinguish peasant family units and farmer family units:

> In Danilov's view the distinction based on the respective relations of production which delimits family labour from wage-labour under capitalism, must be supplemented by a further distinction based on *qualitative differences in the forces of production deployed*. Peasant production is family agriculture where natural forces of production, land and labour predominate. Farmers, on the other hand, represent family farms in which the man-made forces of production, mostly industrial in origin, come to play a decisive role. The particularity of family farming as a form of organisation of production does not disappear thereby, but the characteristics of its two different types can be distinguished more clearly.

An expanded analysis of Danilov's views can be found in Figes (1987).

Some authors in this text use the terms 'peasant' and smallholding 'farmers' interchangeably. At times, this interchangeable conceptual scheme is empirically driven – governed by the way in which existing data are organised. At other times, it is a political act. For example,

La Vía Campesina, mentioned in numerous contributions to this book, uses an umbrella concept that loosely defines peasants as 'people of the land'. This broad definition is not surprising, given that social movements seek to attract large numbers of supporters. La Vía Campesina includes small- and medium-sized Canadian farmers alongside poor peasants in the global South. It excludes large farms, not because of their size or social relations of production, but because of their support for unfettered trade liberalisation, industrial or chemical-intensive agriculture and genetically engineered crops. It also includes people involved in various occupations who live in rural areas, such as those engaged in handicraft production related to agriculture (Edelman 2013).

Indeed, it is often highlighted today how the rural poor engage in occupational multiplicity – or what authors Damián and Pacheco in this book call 'pluri-activity' – where they move between various occupations, such as from farming to wage labour, urban service work, and/or mercantile trade. While some scholars use the concept of 'peasant' to refer to these rural poor, others argue that the term is obsolete because of this occupational multiplicity – especially given how globalisation has intensified migration and the existence of transnational households (Kearney 1996). Still others warn against mistaking temporary migration and/or occupational multiplicity as reliable indicators of depeasantisation, since these activities can also lead to accumulation that enables rural viability (Bebbington 1999).

In sum, as Teodor Shanin (1973) argued almost half a century ago, conceptualisations of the peasantry must acknowledge the complexity of their social reality and recognise peasant heterogeneity across the globe and across historical time. Although there is no single, shared definition of peasants today, most scholars would agree that, while they have diminished as a proportion of the global population over time, their size in absolute numbers has increased, as has their impoverishment. Thus, a better understanding of the various reasons for peasant poverty and persistence is still of utmost importance in the new millennium.

5. Contributions of the authors

This section describes the contents of Part II of the book, starting with the **background paper** and the three additional papers included in **Session I: Theoretical perspectives on peasant poverty and**

persistence, which provide a wide variety of theoretical perspectives on these issues.

In the **background paper, 'Poverty and persistence of the peasantry', Julio Boltvinik** argues that peasant poverty is determined by the seasonality of agriculture as expressed in unequal labour demands throughout the year, concentrated in periods of sowing and harvesting, and by the fact that, in capitalist systems, prices only incorporate (as costs) the wages of days that have effectively been worked. Since peasant producers are price takers in the same markets as capitalist firms, the prices of their products can only reward them for the days that have been effectively worked. In other words, *the social cost of seasonality is absorbed by peasants, who therefore have to live in permanent poverty as* errant proletarians in search of additional income.

Boltvinik discovered (in the course of his polemic with Armando Bartra) that his theory of peasant poverty also explained peasant persistence – that capitalism cannot exist in a pure form in agriculture. *Without the peasants' supply of cheap seasonal labour, capitalist agriculture would be impossible* because there would be (virtually) no one prepared to work *only* during the sowing and harvesting periods. Hence, *this persistence is not only functional but indispensable to the existence of capitalist agricultural firms.* However, peasants will be obliged to sell their labour seasonally (and cheaply) only *if they are poor:* rich farmers in the USA can (and do) spend off-season periods in idleness. In other words, *agricultural capitalism can only exist in symbiosis with poor peasants, prepared (and compelled) to sell their labour seasonally.* Thus, a theory that explains peasant survival should also explain their poverty.

The background paper examines the nature of agricultural production by contrasting it with industry, emphasising seasonality. It also includes a brief characterisation of the peasant family unit. Various sections of the paper are devoted to discussions of diverse theoretical positions on the persistence of the peasantry.

The background paper describes a public polemic between Boltvinik and Armando Bartra, who, in his theory of the persistence of the peasantry (see below for more detail), argues that peasants persist because they act as a buffer mechanism for differential rent, which damages non-agricultural capital, diminishing it substantially. Playing this role explains peasants' persistence. Bartra admits that peasants absorb the full cost of seasonality. He argues that peasants are subject to *polymorphous exploitation* when they absorb this cost, when they sell their labour power and when they migrate. Bartra ends his polemic with Boltvinik by arguing that the main difference between them lies not in their diagnoses but in their proposals for dealing with peasant poverty. Whereas Boltvinik proposes that Third World countries should subsidise peasants, Bartra argues that, while subsidies have a positive role to play, the real solution lies in agricultural diversification. For Boltvinik, Bartra has an original theory of peasant persistence that largely complements his own.

The background paper then closely examines and critically assesses the Mann–Dickinson thesis, which shares features with the work of Ariel Contreras (1977). Boltvinik points out that both papers, being based only on *Capital*'s Volume II, disregard the equalisation of rates of profit (the process by which values are transformed into prices of production), as analysed by Marx in Volume III of *Capital*. As a result, they identify false obstacles to capitalist development in agriculture.

Boltvinik maintains that when the reality of discontinuous work in agriculture is introduced into Marx's theory of value, the value of labour power in agriculture will not be sufficient for the reproduction of the labour force: for example, the people who sowed will have died by harvest time. He notes that a third equation is needed in Marx's Simple Reproduction Scheme, which would specify the conditions needed for the reproduction of the working force. In order to maintain equilibrium in the scheme, the working time incorporated into the commodity needs to account for not just the live work undertaken by the worker during the days he works, but also the value of his labour power during the days when he does not work. He calls the resulting scheme a *general theory of value* to distinguish it from Marx's original theory, which is more accurately seen as a *theory of value for continuous labour processes*. Boltvinik's thesis here gave rise to a debate with Luis Arizmendi, as seen in the latter's paper for this volume.

The paper concludes by arguing that Third World countries should do what most developed countries do: subsidise their peasants or farmers and thereby recognise the *right of peasants to a minimum standard of living*. Boltvinik argues that, in the EU and the US, the cost of seasonal farm labour is absorbed by society as a whole through subsidies to agricultural production. Boltvinik enumerates three factors that explain why most peasant households in Mexico and the rest of the Third World live in abject poverty: first, their productivity is below that of their competitors in developed countries; second, their labour power is undervalued; and third, they absorb the cost of seasonality.

Chapter 2, by **Armando Bartra**, '**Rethinking rustic issues: contributions to a theory of contemporary peasantry**', begins by pointing out the irony in that the Great Crisis has led such a conspicuous agent of modernisation as the World Bank to call for the promotion of peasant production. For Bartra, the 'recipes for industrial agriculture [are] unsustainable', so he proposes to recover 'certain models of production ... developed by the great agricultural cultures that might be inspirational for the replacement paradigms' now required urgently. To elaborate his proposal, he goes into some detail to explain one of these holistic models: the *milpa* – the mixed maize field. He also associates the multicropping that is characteristic of the *milpa* with the multicultural values adopted by Mesoamerican pre-Hispanic civilisations.

One of Bartra's major contributions is that he has developed an original theory of the persistence of the peasantry centred on land rent. He argues that, as demand grows, additional production has to be derived from less fertile (marginal) land that produces agricultural products at higher costs. He states that 'differential rent is unavoidable when the same goods with different costs are regularly sold at the same price' (Bartra 2006). This would be the case if marginal lands were cultivated by capitalist enterprises. But if these lands are exploited by peasants, as they usually are, 'peasants can be forced to work below average profits and, on occasions, at the simple point of equilibrium'. Thus, peasants are essential as a buffer mechanism for land rent, and this helps explain their persistence. Bartra also points to unequal market exchanges as another basis of peasant exploitation. He argues that, rather than seeking government subsidies to compensate for the idle time associated with the seasonality of rural production, promoting diversified farming – as exemplified by the environmentally sustainable, indigenous, *milpa* fields – would be a more viable way to reduce peasant poverty.

In **Chapter 3**, '**From field to fork: labour power, its reproduction, and the persistence of peasant poverty**', **Gordon Welty**, **Susan Mann**, **James Dickinson** and **Emily Blumenfeld** argue that the historically specific and commodity-specific analysis underlying the Mann–Dickinson thesis is preferable to the 'ontology of industry and agriculture' proposed in Boltvinik's background paper. They also discuss how Boltvinik's analyses of both wage-based production and petty commodity production ignore the role of gender and patriarchy. They highlight not only how peasant women play important roles in subsistence production and the informal sector, but also how the political economy of domestic labour and the social reproduction of labour power are critical to an analysis of peasant persistence.

The authors highlight the *less visible and hidden universe of unpaid labour within the home that goes into the production and reproduction of labour power*. By doing so, they point to the gender inequality entailed in this process, as well as to the fact that unpaid domestic labour enables lower wages to be paid to workers in capitalist enterprises. They argue that many agrarian theorists have been gender blind to the patriarchal inequalities within peasant households, including A. V. Chayanov and his famous theory of peasant economy.

They counterpoise the background paper's thesis that capitalist agriculture cannot exist without a pauperised peasantry with the idea that capitalism relies on, creates and perpetuates many peculiar non-capitalist forms of production to operate both in industry and in agriculture. To them, it is not so much that the world's poor, especially the rural poor, are poor because of the way capitalism exploits the peasant's ability to undertake much of its reproduction, but because masses of humanity are now surplus and disposable. They discuss outsourcing, illegal migration, temporary work, the informal sector and permanent casuals – in short, the mass of surplus humanity located off the grid of capitalist accumulation proper. Their paper ends by arguing against the likelihood that subsidising peasant production is a viable solution to peasant poverty, as the background paper proposes. In their view, the current era of neoliberalism and flexible capitalism is one of the least ripe times in history to be calling for government subsidies to end peasant poverty.

In **Chapter 4, 'Baroque modernity and peasant poverty in the twenty-first century'**, **Luis Arizmendi** agrees with Armando Bartra that, given the global food crisis, the controversy around the complex relationship between capitalism and the peasantry in the twenty-first century has become central. According to Arizmendi, the myth of progress mistakenly associates peasant poverty with the persistence of pre-modern, pre-capitalist forms, thus evading capitalist domination as the basis for peasant poverty. Indeed, capitalism's 'rule' is that the wages received by rural workers 'will never be adequate for satisfying their needs'. This fact forces peasant households to invent mixed strategies for their social reproduction, combining petty commodity production with wage work.

'Baroque modernity' refers to this peculiar combination of modern and pre-modern forms aimed at resistance in times of adversity. For Arizmendi, the best approach to deciphering its historical complexity has been developed in Latin America, where the relationship between the peasant economy and the capitalist economy has been investigated not as a relation of exteriority, nor as the contact between two forms of production that are articulated from outside, but rather as a relation of domination in which the capitalist economy absorbs and penetrates the peasant economy, placing the latter at its service.

To understand this complex relationship, Arizmendi further develops the concept of subsumption. In this, he departs from Marx's concepts of formal subsumption (where the worker is a wage worker dispossessed of his or her means of production) and real subsumption (where capital introduces new technology and controls it); instead, he couples the insights of Bolívar Echeverría (who showed that these forms of subsumption are not necessarily successive) with the work of Armando Bartra, arguing that capital can dominate labour from the sphere of commodity circulation – the market through unequal exchange. This constitutes a type of *indirect formal subsumption* which makes possible the exploitation of labour (the extraction of surplus value) without the commodification of labour power. Based on these ideas, Arizmendi creates new labels. For peasants, 'seasonal time wages' represent the *specific formal subsumption of the labour force*, while unequal exchange represents the *non-specific formal subsumption of labour by capital*. Both externalise annual reproduction costs, leaving them in the hands of peasant producers.

In analysing the evolution of food regimes throughout the world, Arizmendi distinguishes a stage of self-sufficiency (up to the 1970s); a stage of artificial food dependency, where the main providers are US food corporations; and a new stage sparked by the collapse of international food reproduction. In this latter stage, to avoid assuming the annual reproduction costs of labour power, capital 'places on the shoulders of the *campesindios* not the ecological rebalancing of the planet but rather the externalities produced by both global warming and experimentation with genetic engineering'.

In the persistence in Latin America of ecological and communitarian forms of contact with nature, Arizmendi finds a set of proposals for coping with the current food and environmental crisis. In order to overcome the world food crisis, for him it is crucial to promote the design of strategic policies based on principles of human security that prioritise the reproduction of life, rather than capitalist accumulation.

Opening this part's **Session II: Historical and empirical approaches** to the issues of peasant poverty and persistence is **Chapter 5, Henry Bernstein**'s **'Agriculture/industry, rural/urban, peasants/workers: some reflections on poverty, persistence and change'**. Bernstein responds to Boltvinik's 'stimulating' background paper, pointing to both shared and contested terrain. He applauds Boltvinik's focus on the reproduction of rural households for broadening what too often are capital-centric arguments about 'obstacles to capitalist agriculture', where peasant persistence is treated simply as residual. Bernstein synthesises in a table the distinctive features of agriculture vis-á-vis industry as described in the background paper. However, Bernstein finds problematic the highly abstract nature of the background paper, in which abstractions are not grounded in *theory as history*, nor is the theory tested empirically. He proposes an alternative and complementary approach that is both historically and empirically informed.

Bernstein adopts a broad definition of agriculture which includes farming as well as economic interests, institutions and activities that affect the activities and reproduction of farmers. He argues that '*one cannot conceive of the emergence and functioning of agriculture in modern capitalism without the centrality and reconfigurations of new sets of dynamics linking agriculture and industry, and the rural and urban* (and indeed the local, national and global)'.

Bernstein also highlights the high levels of commodification that exist in many rural areas of the globe and that undermine any notion that existing production units are pre-modern or pre-capitalist. He contends that, by the time of independence in Asia and Africa, *subsistence among peasants had been commodified*. This means that their *reproduction could not take place outside commodity relations and the discipline they impose*, and this results in a tendency towards the decomposition of once pure classes of agrarian labour, since they have to diversify their forms and spaces of employment (and self-employment) to meet their simple reproduction needs. Bernstein questions whether poor peasants should be considered 'peasant' farmers at all or more accurately viewed as wage workers. While they 'might not be dispossessed of *all* means of reproducing themselves', most do not *possess* sufficient means for their reproduction; this 'marks the limits of their viability as petty commodity producers'. Based on data from the World Bank's *World Development Report 2008*, Bernstein argues that 'own-account farming is the primary economic activity for more than half of the adult rural population *only* in sub-Saharan Africa'. He suggests that capitalism has successfully penetrated the countryside, resulting in the depeasantisation of agricultural labour.

Bernstein rejects farm subsidies as a solution to rural poverty, arguing instead that the key question is the broader struggle over employment and real wage levels. He adds: 'And if I had to emphasise only one aspect of the remarkable trajectories of capitalist farming over the last 150 years ... it would be its remarkable development of the productive forces, of the productivity of labour, in farming.' For Bernstein, without these achievements, feeding the large urban populations of the globe today would be impossible. This is an interesting point for debate, as some authors in this volume (Vergopoulos, for instance) hold the opposite view.

Chapter 6, 'Employment and rural poverty in Mexico', by **Araceli Damián** and **Edith Pacheco** discusses the findings of empirical research on peasant poverty and persistence in Mexico. After providing an overview of the history of the Mexican countryside since the Revolution of 1910, the authors contend that today only some regions of the country have modern agriculture, while most peasants continue to use rudimentary technology. Although rural to urban migration explains why the rural population dropped from 66.5 per cent in 1930 to 23.2 per cent in 2010, part of this migration was circular and seasonal, with peasants combining work in the city and in the countryside. In turn, Mexican peasants have long provided cheap seasonal labour to US agriculture and to other US economic activities, and these migrants send important money remittances back home. The authors conclude that circular migration to the USA contributes to the persistence of the peasantry in Mexico.

Damián and Pacheco provide a detailed analysis of two surveys: the special section on agriculture of the National Employment Survey (known as ENE from its name in Spanish), or the agricultural module, undertaken from 1991 to 2003; and the National Household Income and Expenditure Survey (known as ENIGH from its name in Spanish), which is carried out every two years. From the first survey they estimate that slightly more than one-third of all households reporting agricultural income own land and can be classified as peasant units. Applying the Integrated Poverty Measurement Method to the second survey, they present rural poverty incidence data and classify the poor in three strata: indigence, extreme poverty and moderate poverty. These figures show that *most rural inhabitants are poor (around 95 per cent since 1984)*. Nevertheless, the internal structure of rural poverty has changed: the percentage of indigents (the poorest stratum) has declined from 74 per cent in 1984 and 74.7 per cent in 2000 to 58 per cent in 2010, while there have been increases in the other two strata.

The remainder of their paper analyses the results of the agricultural module, which identified workers using a period of reference of the previous six months (instead of the last week, as is usually the case in employment surveys all over the world). Given the seasonal nature of agricultural work, it is not surprising that the module identified *1 million more workers in agriculture* than were previously identified using a one-week reference period. As Damián and Pacheco point out: 'This result constitutes the first evidence of the high level of intersectoral occupational mobility of agricultural workers in Mexico in a context in which the seasonality of production plays a central role.'

The authors emphasise that their findings must be placed in the context of a decreasing contribution of agriculture to gross domestic product (GDP) and a decreasing proportion of the working age population engaged in agriculture. Nevertheless, 60 per cent of the working population in rural areas was still engaged in agricultural production in 2003, based on data from the agricultural module. The authors also found that *'very few rural households were able to live exclusively off the land, since only 8.3 per cent had all household workers engaged in agricultural activities'*. They also found that *fewer than one in six agriculturally engaged persons belonged to households able to live exclusively off the land*; that the broad participation in agricultural activity in rural contexts (only 24.6 per cent of the labour force lives in households that are totally non-agricultural) *points to the persistence of the peasantry*; and that widespread peasant multi-activity 'is largely due to the seasonal nature of agricultural work'.

At the end of their paper, Damián and Pacheco highlight the huge gaps between agricultural and non-agricultural wages and between the proportion of people with access to social security in rural and non-rural areas. They also point to how the poorest peasant households show high rates of labour participation even in the very young age group (ages 12 to 17) and among those aged 65 years and over. The authors conclude that 'there is evidence that the peasantry absorbs the economic and social cost of capitalist labour seasonality and instability of work, constituting an industrial reserve army'.

Session III is titled **Environment, food crisis and peasants**. Its first paper – **Chapter 7, 'From the persistence of the peasantry in capitalism to the environmentalism of indigenous peoples and the sustainability of life'**, by **Enrique Leff** – argues that explanations of peasant poverty and persistence have to adopt a more historical, anthropological, social and ecological perspective that relies less on economic reasoning. For Leff, a shift from traditional Marxist to eco-Marxist explanations is required to better address the issues of political ecology and environmental sustainability and to show how peasant poverty is also the product of a *historical process of entropic degradation of their environment and their livelihoods*.

Leff argues for an alternative theory of value, claiming that the main problem of the Marxist theory of value is not that it fails to include the discontinuity of work in seasonal production processes, as argued in the background paper, but *that nature is not valued and that nature does not determine value or surplus value*. For him, *the problem is crystal clear: nature contributes to production*. Yet, in Marxist theory, *only labour time, determined by technological progress, contributes to value*; 'nature has been externalised by the economy'. Herein lies a major theoretical difference between Leff's views and those of many other authors in this volume who rely on Marx's theory of value.

Eco-Marxism is praised by Leff for highlighting the hidden *second contradiction of capital*, or how capitalism destroys the ecological conditions for its own social reproduction. While the peasantry has survived through complex socio-cultural and political mechanisms of resistance, Leff asks how long can we expect nature to survive when its resiliency mechanisms have been eroded. For him, this problem can be solved only through a 'shift in economic paradigms ... the deconstruction of economic rationality and the construction of an environmental rationality'.

Moreover, the questions posed are not only about the conservation of biodiversity or the persistence of peasantry, but also about the survival of the living planet and human life. If capitalist-induced entropic degradation is what is driving the ecological destruction of life support systems and cultural resiliency, then the future persistence of the peasantry will depend on envisioning and constructing a sustainable mode of production, one based in the *negentropic potentials of life*. This implies a labour process oriented towards enhancing and magnifying the principle of life: the process of photosynthesis. Thus Leff proposes a sustainable negentropic paradigm of production that is 'articulated in a spatial and temporal frame of non-modern cultural imaginaries and ecological practices'. For him, the privileged spaces in which to deploy this strategy of *negentropic* production are the 'rural areas of the world' inhabited by indigenous peasant peoples.

Leff ends his paper by highlighting the importance of 'the social imaginaries of the sustainability of traditional peoples', the persistence of their attachments to their historical and territorial roots, such as those being expressed today through the principle of well-being – *sumak kawsay* – and their ability to trust that another world is possible.

Chapter 8, 'South American peasants and poor farmers facing global environmental change: a development dilemma', by **Elma Montaña** reports the findings of a research project on the vulnerability of rural communities in watershed basins of Argentina, Bolivia and Chile. In this comparative study of dry land areas of these three countries, she maps out different adaptive strategies undertaken by capitalists, large landowners and poor peasants in response to dwindling water supplies, as well as the strikingly different government policies of each of these countries: Chile's neoliberal agenda, Argentina's welfare state and Bolivia's policies to revitalise indigenous communities. She also notes how expected changes in climate and hydrology are likely to affect the availability of drinking and irrigation water, threatening productive systems and the subsistence of rural dwellers. Montaña carefully illuminates the social divisions created by *water access*. In explaining how the expected decrease in the rivers' flows will exacerbate the disadvantages of small producers, thereby polarising the hydraulic societies still more, she quotes a popular saying that captures the political economy of these hydraulic societies: 'Water flows uphill towards money.' This social inequality is driven to its extreme in Chile, where water is transformed into a commodity by the prevailing neoliberal, pro-market, public policy.

Indeed, the manner in which droughts are faced in each case is related to water governance. In Mendoza, Argentina, the supply of irrigation water is proportional to the land area and water is inherent to the land, so it cannot be used on other farms. In Chile, water can be used anywhere by those who buy shares; this is a very competitive system in which 'water is concentrated in the hands of the most powerful producers'. In Bolivia, conflict is mitigated by the relative homogeneity of producers and their cultures. In turn, trade unions and irrigators' associations make up for the lack of financial resources with solidarity and mutual aid mechanisms, creating more favourable settings in which conflicts can be resolved by taking into consideration an interest in the commons. Yet, in all three basins, migration as a result of poverty is a common element.

Linking water with the notion of poverty evokes the issue of scarcity. However, as Montaña points out, physical scarcity is produced when water availability is limited by nature; *economic and political scarcity* occurs 'when people are barred from accessing an available source of water because they are in a situation of political subordination'.

Although Montaña explores the strengths and weaknesses of various adaptive strategies, she shares with other authors the view that the most viable strategy for peasant persistence requires an emphasis on diversified farming and environmental sustainability.

In **Chapter 9, 'Financialisation of the food sector and peasants' persistence'**, **Kostas Vergopoulos** examines the relationships between the following elements: the present financial and economic crises; financialisation in general and the financialisation of the agro-industrial food circuit in particular; the generalised increase in food prices; peasant poverty and persistence; and recent policies to enhance both food security and family-based agrarian production. He discusses how those responsible for the recent financial crisis are desperately trying to mitigate the consequences of the burst housing bubble by replacing it with new speculative bubbles of commodities and food. Vergopoulos argues that the major world economic event in recent years has been the 'food tsunami': a quick acceleration of food prices combined with decreasing production and the breakdown of productivity in the world food economy. According to the US Department of Agriculture, there has been a sharp decline in agrarian productivity by acre of cultivated land, as well as a decrease in US cereal stocks. On the other hand, the 'worldwide struggle for water and against the threat of pervasive desertification represents an overwhelming limiting factor for many ... food projects'. Vergopoulos goes beyond the conventional causes of increases in food prices and argues that the structural penetration of capitalism into agricultural production is an additional cause. He further states that inflation in food prices has an impact on the *overall global valorisation of capital.*

Although Vergopoulos views the entrance of traders and international banks into the domain of foodstuffs as tantamount to an invasion by 'true carnivores', he still sees speculation in food commodities as only the tip of the iceberg. He identifies the root of the problem as 'structural mutations created by the extension of capitalism into the agri-food sphere'.

In addition, Vergopoulos examines why food security policies and the return to family-based forms of food production are being encouraged. For a number of years, both the World Bank and the Food and Agriculture Organization of the United Nations, (FAO) have emphatically encouraged and financed the worldwide implementation of 'food security' programmes based on the consolidation of family farming. Quoting Chayanov, Vergopoulos argues that the family mode of production permits a maximisation of the agrarian product while minimising prices and production costs. Hence, the poorer peasants are, the more competitive they become. As such, peasant poverty and persistence, far from being a relic of the past, is simply an inexpensive safety net for capitalist food crises.

He adds that, under the capitalist mode of production, the supply of the 'special' commodity of labour power must be ensured through a non-capitalist (read: family labour production) process – in order to keep its price substantially, structurally and permanently low. He concludes:

Peasants' poverty, instead of being a handicap, represents the competitive advantage of this type of production and a way out of the current impasse. By the same token, we can understand not only why peasants remain poor, but also why they certainly will not disappear and why the capitalist mode of production in the agri-food sector is now tending to restore the land to its traditional residents and workers ...
The relation between the two worlds – capitalist and peasant – might well turn out to be as deeply opposite and antagonistic, but also as deeply functional, as it has been in the past.

Opening **Session IV: Policy, self-reliance and peasant poverty** is **Chapter** 10, **Farshad Araghi**'s '**The rise and fall of the agrarian welfare state: peasants, globalisation, and the privatisation of development**'. Araghi analyses what he calls 'agrarian welfare systems', or food regimes that managed labour and food supplies in different historical epochs. He discusses the role of overseas colonialism in 'constructing export-dependent monocultures that subsidised the reproductive needs of European labour and capital'. Similarly, the success of settler colonial states also lowered food costs, which, in turn, 'lowered the value of labour power and enhanced the rate of surplus value' for capital. This 'global food regime' came to a 'political end' as a consequence of 'socialist movements at home' and 'peasant and anti-colonialist movements in the colonies' towards the end of the nineteenth century and in the early twentieth century.

For Araghi, a new stage of 'long national developmentalism' began with the Russian Revolution. It was the success of the Soviets in linking national and colonial questions with the peasant question and in supporting the demands of an insurgent peasantry that put the 'Third World and its development on the agenda of the United States'. The compromise forced upon the US by these conditions was a 'market-led national developmentalism' that was designed to 'placate postcolonial peasant movements by accommodating their land hunger within a market-led framework', and to 'demobilise ...

and ... unlink them from urban nationalist and/or socialist movements'. Here, US-sponsored land reform, dominated by a 'family farm' ideology, was seen as a 'way of creating a stable and highly conservative social base'.

Yet, as Araghi points out: 'Ironically, a global agrarian programme that ... had sought to create a class of peasant proprietors as a stable social base for the postcolonial states, *ipso facto* created the conditions for a process of depeasantisation on a world scale.' He identifies two dynamic forces that created these conditions: 1) the expansion of monetised and commodity relations, exposing emerging small farms to market forces that favoured large-scale producers; and 2) the emerging world market, which substantively undermined home market formation and nation-based divisions of labour. The disposal of increasing US grain surpluses as food aid or concessional sales further depressed world prices of grain and encouraged Third World food imports and food import dependency. In Araghi's view, *'peasantisation and depeasantisation are neither unilinear nor mutually exclusive national processes'.* Moreover, *peasant dispossession from class differentiation in this period occurred at a sluggish rate and, in the end, was subordinated to peasant dispossession via urban displacement.* This *relative depeasantisation* process took place in the period between the 1950s and the 1970s.

In contrast, *absolute depeasantisation* defines the character of global dispossession in the late twentieth century and beyond under postcolonial neoliberal globalism. The 1970s witnessed a profound capitalist crisis and, as a response, capital's *counterrevolution*, which implied capital withdrawal from reformist social compacts. The *retreat from development* was a component of a systemic counteroffensive that sought to reverse the protection of society from the market. From 1973 onwards, the 'privatisation of the agrarian welfare state to the advantage of northern transnational agribusinesses and capitalist farms' generated 'absolute depeasantisation and displacement'. Debt-enforced structural adjustments in many agrarian sectors of the globe led to: 1) the deregulation of land markets and the reversal of land reform policies; 2) drastic cuts in farm subsidies, price supports and irrigation support; 3) the expanded commodification of seeds and seed reproduction; 4) a marked and growing dependence on chemical and hydrocarbon farm inputs; and 5) the promotion of agro exports at the expense of food crops. In this period, 'the "invisible hand" of the debt regime ... functioned as the "visible foot" of the global enclosures of our times'.

Asymmetric power relations, argues Araghi, forced millions of petty producers in the South to compete with heavily subsidised transnational corporations in the North. The inability to compete led in turn to massive peasant dispossession by displacement. Araghi describes how the global enclosures of postcolonial neoliberal globalism have led to the creation of masses of semi-dispossessed peasantries who have lost their non-market access to their means of subsistence, but still hold formal ownership to some of their means of production. As a result, agrarian direct producers are thrown into 'the vortex of globalisation as masses of surplus labour in motion'. Key to this project was the WTO's Agreement on Agriculture, which is an agreement between the United States and Europe to resolve their overproduction crisis by expanding the space of commercial dumping in the South.

In his concluding paragraphs, Araghi adds that an *unprecedented global land grab is underway as speculative investors, who now regard 'food as gold', are acquiring millions of hectares.* The human cost of such actions will be dispossessed and displaced peasants, who, in India, according to one source, will be 'equal to twice the combined population of UK, France, and Germany'.

Chapter 11, **'Overcoming rural poverty from the bottom up'**, by **David Barkin** and **Blanca Lemus** is a heterodox paper that focuses on the market itself as the principal obstacle to peasants escaping the poverty imposed on them by their participation in the capitalist circuit of accumulation. The authors argue that millions of rural denizens have adopted different strategies for confronting their structural weaknesses using communal principles of collective action and traditional organisation. Indeed, many rural organisations have chosen to collectively administer and control their social and natural resources. To achieve their goals, peasant communities also must ensure a diversified productive structure that allows members to satisfy their basic needs, as well as to produce goods used for exchange.

Although there are many examples of these alternative forms of organising rural production, social scientists have largely ignored them. In contrast, this paper draws from the proposals of diverse indigenous and peasant groups whose own organisation of the rural production process forms part of their diagnosis for overcoming peasant poverty. Their collective commitments to an alternative framework for production and social integration offer a realistic but challenging strategy for local progress. Barkin and Lemus enumerate the following principles that have been widely agreed upon in broad-based consultations among these peasant communities: autonomy, solidarity, self-sufficiency, productive diversification, and sustainable management of regional resources. An emphasis on local or regional economies, the use of traditional and agro-ecological approaches in production and the integrated management of ecosystems constitute the foundations for the groups' ability to guarantee a minimum standard of living for all their members. These communities also require a commitment to participate in production, thus eliminating unemployment.

A major thrust of this paper is its critique of the notion of progress where well-being is measured in terms of economic growth or other objective indicators. Barkin and Lemus highlight three major features of this critique. First, they suggest alternative measures of well-being, such as an index of 'gross domestic happiness'. They argue that 'throughout the world we are suffering a deterioration in our quality of life, resulting from the weakening or destruction of social and solidarity networks ... and the accelerated destruction of the ecosystems on which we depend'. Questioning the meaning of progress requires a multidisciplinary vision and a re-evaluation of some of the fundamental elements that we normally associate with traditional society.

Second, the authors emphasise *degrowth* and *good living (sumak kawsay)* in contrast to the development paradigm that, in their view, entails the transformation and destruction of both the natural environment and social relations. *Sumak kawsay* implies *recognising the 'rights of nature'* and a complex citizenry that accepts social as well as environmental commitments. The basic value in a 'good living' regime is *solidarity*. The success of such a regime requires that the essential function of the market is transformed so that it can serve society rather than determine social relations, as it does at present.

Third, the authors embrace communality. This concept includes: direct or participatory democracy; the organisation of community work; community possession and control of land; a common cosmology; and a respect for community leadership. Communality is a contract one accepts on the understanding that it involves commitment to the well-being of the group as a whole, even if a particular situation works against an individual's interests. It implies a concept of democracy that is simultaneously an ethical agreement. Their overall view is captured well near the end of their paper where Barkin and Lemus state:

it might be that much of the poverty to which most of the literature is addressed has its origins in the individualism and alienation of the masses whose behaviour is embedded in the Western model of modernity, a model of concentrated accumulation based on a system of deliberate dispossession of the majority by a small elite ... To escape from this dynamic, the collective subject that is emerging in the process offers a meaningful path to overcoming the persistence of poverty in our times.

Chapter 12 by **Julio Boltvinik, 'Dialogues and debates on peasant poverty and persistence: around the background paper and beyond'**, responds to the various papers in this volume in diverse ways and expands some of the initial discussions in the background paper. First, in Table 12.1, Boltvinik lists the commentaries and criticisms included in five of the chapters of the book. He organises his reactions (and his deepened analysis) in four groups: 1) general clarifications (divided into three groups: genesis and theoretical bases of his theory; what he does not say; and what he does say in the background paper); 2) precisions on seasonality; 3) backups for his theory (where he examines the positions by Lenin, Danielson, Kautsky and Luis Cabrera, finding expected and unexpected support for his theory); and 4) replies to the authors in this book. Replies are organised in two groups. Short replies to non-central commentaries are presented in Table 12.2, while longer replies to Welty et al., Bernstein, and lastly Arizmendi and Leff together are presented in section 2.

Outstanding points in sections 1 and 2 are Boltvinik's discovery of a precedent to his theory in Danielson's theory of the 'freeing of winter time' as the fundamental cause of peasant poverty; his unveiling of a little known facet of Lenin's work that rejects, ambiguously, the theory of the vanishing peasantry; the complementarity between

Boltvinik's theory and Kautsky's theory on the demographic role of the peasantry; the importance of discussing the alleged neglect of nature in Marx's labour theory of value, the Lauderdale Paradox, or the contradiction between use value and exchange value; and, lastly, the profound insight, generated in Boltvinik's debate with Arizmendi, on discontinuities and the labour theory of value – that is, that any theory of capitalism has to include its necessary coexistence and articulation with the peasantry (or family farm).

Section 3 summarises the distinctive features of agriculture, drawing on Bernstein's Table 5.1 to create Table 12.3. The list of features included in this table is longer than those in earlier analyses by both authors. One of the features added, inspired by Bartra's chapter, contrasts the natural character of agriculture's main means of production (land, water and climate) with human-produced machinery in industry. Boltvinik also adds a column that describes how each feature impinges on the technical and economic logic of the production process in agriculture.

Section 4 is a heterogeneous list of topics not covered in the book but that are important to understand the plight (and possible futures) of peasants. Originally, this chapter was meant to cover the contents of this list in depth, but this was precluded by space limitations.

The chapter, and the book, ends with section 5, which builds two typologies of replies included in this volume, one for each of the two central theoretical questions – on poverty and on the persistence of the peasantry. The section discusses both the replies sustained by the contributors to this book and those by other authors. The end result of this exercise is synthesised in Tables 12.4 and 12.5.

Notes

1 These earlier grand theories of modernisation are discussed in Araghi (1995).

2 *The Theory of Peasant Economy* includes two of Chayanov's works that were published in Russian as *Peasant Farm Organisation* and *The Theory of Non-Capitalist Economic Forms.*

3 For more on 'degrowth', see Barkin and Lemus (Chapter 11 in this volume); for 'maldevelopment', see Shiva (1989); and for 'necropolitics', see Mbembe (2001).

4 As noted above, an example can be found in this volume where Barkin and Lemus discuss how the concept of 'sumak kawsay' or 'good living' is defined in the preface to the new Ecuadorian Constitution as a new form of citizens' coexistence, in harmony and diversity with nature, in order to achieve a good life.

5 For a challenge to these approaches, see Vivek Chibber (2013), who makes a strong case that the

non-Western world can be conceptualised using the same analytical lens that we use to understand developments in the West. He offers a sustained defence of employing categories, such as capitalism and class, as well as for the continued relevance of Marxism.

6 In Boltvinik's background paper (see Chapter 1, section 3), there is a short discussion of the features of peasant family units.

7 Marc Edelman's 2013 briefing paper on conceptualising the peasantry provides an especially instructive overview of the ways in which peasants have been defined historically, in the social sciences, normatively, and as activist political movements. We draw from his analysis below.

References

Alavi, H. and T. Shanin (1988) 'Introduction' in K. Kautsky, *The Agrarian Question: Peasantry and capitalism*. English edition. 2 volumes. London: Zwan Publications.

Araghi, F. (1995) 'Global depeasantisation, 1945–1990', *Sociological Quarterly* 36 (2) (Spring): 339–40.

Balbus, I. (1982) *Marxism and Domination: A neo-Hegelian, feminist, psychoanalytic theory of sexual, political, and technological liberation*. Princeton NJ: Princeton University Press.

Bartra, A. (2006) *El capital en su laberinto. De la renta de la tierra a la renta de la vida*. Mexico City: Ítaca.

Bebbington, A. (1999) 'Capital and capabilities: a framework for analyzing peasant viability, rural livelihoods and poverty', *World Development* 27 (12): 2021–44.

Bernstein, H. (2010) *Class Dynamics of Agrarian Change*. Halifax: Fernwood Publishing.

Borras Jr., S. M. (2004) 'La Vía Campesina: an evolving transnational social movement'. TNI Briefing Series no. 2004/6. Amsterdam: Transnational Institute (TNI).

Buttel, F., O. Larson and G. Gillespie (1989) *The Sociology of Agriculture*. New York NY: Greenwood Press.

Chayanov, A. V. (1966 [1925]) *The Theory of Peasant Economy*. Edited by D. Thorner, B. Kerblay and R. E. F. Smith. Homewood IL: Irwin.

Chibber, V. (2013) *Postcolonial Theory and the Specter of Capital*. London: Verso.

Contreras, A. J. (1977) 'Límites de la producción capitalista en la agricultura', *Revista Mexicana de Sociología* 39 (3): 885–9.

Deere, C. D. and A. de Janvry (1979) 'A conceptual framework for the empirical analysis of peasants', *American Journal of Agricultural Economics* 61 (4): 601–11.

Dirlik, A. (1997) 'The postcolonial aura: Third World criticism in the age of global capitalism' in A. McClintock, A. Mufti and E. Shoat (eds), *Dangerous Liaisons: Gender, nation, and postcolonial perspectives*. Minneapolis MN: University of Minnesota Press, pp. 501–28.

Durkheim, E. (1960 [1893]) *Division of Labour in Society*. Glencoe IL: Free Press.

Eagleton, T. (2003) *After Theory*. New York NY: Basic Books.

Edelman, M. (2013) 'What is a peasant? What are peasantries? A briefing paper on issues of definition'. Paper presented at the Intergovernmental Working Group on a United Nations Declaration on the Rights of

Peasants and Other People Working in Rural Areas, Geneva, 15–19 July.

Engels, F. (1972 [1884]) *The Origin of the Family Private Property and the State*. New York NY: International Publishers.

Fanon, F. (1967 [1961]) *The Wretched of the Earth*. New York NY: Penguin Books.

FAO (2011) 'The role of women in agriculture'. ESA Working Paper no. 11-02. Rome: Agricultural Development Economics (ESA), Food and Agriculture Organization of the United Nations (FAO).

Figes, O. (1987) 'V. P. Danilov on the analytical distinction between peasants and farmers' in T. Shanin, *Peasant and Peasant Societies*. Second edition. Oxford: Basil Blackwell, pp. 121–4.

Gosse, V. (2005) *Rethinking the New Left: An interpretative history*. New York NY: Palgrave Macmillan.

Hammel, E. A. and A. Gullickson (2004) 'Kinship structures and survival', *Population Studies: A Journal of Demography* 58 (2): 145–59.

Hartmann, H. (1981) 'The unhappy marriage of Marxism and feminism: towards a more progressive union' in L. Sargent (ed.), *Women and Revolution: A discussion of the unhappy marriage of Marxism and feminism*. Cambridge MA: South End Press, pp. 1–42.

Harvey, D. (2007 [2005]) *A Brief History of Neoliberalism*. London: Oxford University Press.

Hilferding, R. (2007 [1910]) *Finance Capital: A study of the latest stage of capitalist development*. London: Routledge.

IFAD (2010) *Rural Poverty Report 2011. New realities, new challenges: new opportunities for tomorrow's generation*. Rome: International Fund for Agricultural Development (IFAD).

Kautsky, K. (1988 [1899]) *The Agrarian Question*. Volume I. London: Zwan Publications.

Kearney, M. (1996) *Reconceptualizing the Peasantry: Anthropology in global perspective*. Boulder CO: Westview Press.

Lenin, V. I. (1967 [1899]) *The Development of Capitalism in Russia*. Moscow: Progress.

— (1996 [1917]) *Imperialism: The highest stage of capitalism*. London: Pluto Press.

Leys, C. and B. Harriss-White (2012) 'Commodification: the essence of our time'. *openDemocracyUK*, 2 April. Available at www. opendemocracy.net/ourkingdom/ colin-leys-barbara-harriss-white/ commodification-essence-of-our-time (accessed July 2013).

Ludden, D. (2002) *Reading Subaltern Studies: Critical history, contested meaning and the globalisation of south Asia*. London: Anthem/ Wimbledon Press.

Mallon, F. (1987) 'Patriarchy in the transition to capitalism', *Feminist Studies* 13 (2): 379–407.

Mann, S. A. (2012) *Doing Feminist Theory: From modernity to postmodernity*. New York NY: Oxford University Press.

Mann, S. A. and J. Dickinson (1978) 'Obstacles to the development of a capitalist agriculture', *Journal of Peasant Studies* 5 (4): 466–81.

Martínez-Torres, M. E. and P. Rosset (2010) 'La Vía Campesina: the evolution of a transnational movement', *Journal of Peasant Studies* 37 (1): 149–75.

Marx, K. (1970 [1848]) 'The communist manifesto' in *Selected Works in One Volume*. New York NY: International Publishers.

— (1986 [1882]) *Ethnological Notebooks of Karl Marx*. New York NY: L. Krader.

Mbembe, A. (2001) *On the Postcolony*. Berkeley CA: University of California Press.

McMichael, P. (1996) *Development and Social Change: A global perspective*. Thousand Oaks CA: Pine Forge Press.

— (2008) 'Peasants make their own history, but not just as they please ...', *Journal of Agrarian Change* 8 (2/3): 205–28.

Mintz, S. (1973) 'A note on the definition of peasants', *Journal of Peasant Studies* 1 (1): 91–106.

Mohanty, C. T. (1984) 'Under Western eyes: feminist scholarship and colonial discourses', *Boundary* 2 (3): 333–58.

— (2006) *Feminism Without Borders: Decolonising theory, practicing solidarity*. Durham NC: Duke University Press.

Patel, R. (2006) 'International agrarian restructuring and the practical ethics of peasant movement solidarity', *Journal of Asian and African Studies* 41 (1/2): 71–93.

— (2013) 'The role of power, gender, and the right to food in food sovereignty', *Mundo Siglo XXI* 32.

Pogge, T. (2010) 'Poor thought: challenging the dominant narratives of poverty research'. Lecture given at the University of Bergen, 12 May.

Rodríguez, I. (2001) *The Latin American Subaltern Studies Reader*. Durham NC: Duke University Press.

Rowntree, B. S. (2000 [1901]) *Poverty: A study of town life*. London: Macmillan.

Scott, J. C. (1977) *The Moral Economy of the Peasant: Rebellion and subsistence in Southeast Asia*. New Haven CT: Yale University Press.

Sen, A. K. (1981) *Poverty and Famines: An essay on entitlement and deprivation*. Oxford: Clarendon Press.

Shanin, T. (ed.) (1971) *Peasants and Peasant Societies*. Harmondsworth, UK: Penguin Books.

— (1972) *The Awkward Class: Political sociology of peasantry in a developing society, Russia 1910–1925*. Oxford: Clarendon Press.

— (1973) 'The nature and logic of the peasant economy: a generalization', *Journal of Peasant Studies* 1 (1): 63–80.

Shiva, V. (1989) *Staying Alive: Women, ecology and development*. London: Zed Books.

Spicker, P., S. Álvarez Leguizamón and D. Gordon (eds) (2007) *Poverty: An international glossary*. Second edition. London: CROP/Zed Books.

Spivak, G. C. (1988) 'Can the subaltern speak?' in C. Nelson and L. Grossberg (eds), *Marxism and the Interpretation of Culture*. Urbana IL: University of Illinois Press, pp. 271–316.

Spurlin, W. (2006) *Imperialism Within the Margins: Queer representation and the politics of culture in South Africa*. New York NY: Palgrave Macmillan.

Townsend, P. (1979) *Poverty in the United Kingdom: A survey of household resources and standard of living*. Harmondsworth, UK: Penguin Books.

Van der Ploeg, J. D. (2008) *The New Peasantries: Struggles for autonomy and sustainability in an era of empire and globalization*. London: Earthscan.

Vogel, L. (1983 [1973]) *Marxism and the Oppression of Women: Towards a unitary theory*. New Brunswick NJ: Rutgers University Press.

Weber, M. (1978 [1922]) *Economy and Society*. Berkeley CA: University of California Press.

Welty, G. (2012) 'Contribución a la crítica de Chayanov: la teoría de la unidad laboral familiar', *Mundo Siglo XXI* 28.

Wolf, E. (1969) *Peasant Wars of the*

Twentieth Century. New York NY: Harper & Row.

World Bank (2008) *World Development Report 2008: Agriculture for development.* Washington DC: World Bank.

SECOND PART: PAPERS

SESSION ONE
THEORETICAL PERSPECTIVES ON PEASANT POVERTY AND PERSISTENCE

1 | POVERTY AND PERSISTENCE OF THE PEASANTRY: BACKGROUND PAPER[1]

Julio Boltvinik

1. Introduction: agricultural capitalism needs peasants

We know that most of the world's rural inhabitants are poor.[2] We have to explain why *the vast majority of the inhabitants of rural settings (who live in households headed by peasants or rural day labourers) are poor.* Conventional answers revolve around the severe limitations of peasants' resources and technology, which translate into low production levels and therefore low income, and/or the fact that peasants are subject to various forms of exploitation (surplus extraction).[3] However, these conventional explanations would find it hard to explain why '1.7 of the 2.6 million farms existing in the USA *had inadequate incomes for an acceptable living standard,* while their survival obviously depended on their access to income from other sources' (Mann 1990: 142, emphasis added). Moreover, these peasants and poor farmers have defied predictions from writers of both the left and the right that they would disappear off the face of the earth:

> The classical conception of the development of capitalism in agriculture is that, as in industry, the agrarian class-structure will tend to polarise; the petty commodity producer will tend to disappear: *a capitalist relation of production will develop* ... the agrarian future would be one of big estates, managed by capitalist farmers ... employing landless labourers. Close to a hundred years later, history has apparently falsified this notion: In Europe, the big estates have decreased in importance. *The typical unit today is the family farm.* The rural proletariat has decreased, not only in absolute size, but as part of the rural labour force. In the six original countries of the EEC [European Economic Community] in 1966–7, for example, only 14 percent of the labour force was 'non-family'. In the US the percentage

of hired labour to total farm employment has fluctuated around 25 percent since 1910 ... the modern rural proletariat is largely part-time ... drawn into agriculture during certain peak-periods ... The group of full-time agricultural labourers is surprisingly small. (Djurfeldt 1982: 139)

These are two of the issues I propose to deal with in this paper on poverty and the survival of family units: two phenomena that raise fundamental conceptual and practical challenges. To this end, I will review the appropriate international bibliography.

My theoretical position is that peasant poverty is determined by the seasonality of agriculture expressed in varying labour demands throughout the year and concentrated in sowing and harvest periods, and by the fact that, in capitalism, prices incorporate (as costs) only the wages of days that have effectively been worked and paid for. Since peasant producers act as price takers in the same markets as capitalist firms, the prices of their products can reward them only for the days that have been effectively worked. In other words, *the social cost of seasonality is absorbed by peasants, who then have to live in permanent poverty*, which makes them errant proletarians in search of additional income.

During a debate with Armando Bartra recounted in section 7 below, I discovered that the theory I had formulated to explain peasant poverty also accounted for the persistence of the peasantry, which led me to the thesis that capitalism cannot exist in a pure form in agriculture: *without the peasants' supply of cheap seasonal labour, capitalist agriculture would be impossible. There would be (virtually) no one prepared to work only during the sowing and harvesting periods.* The permanence of peasant agriculture therefore makes agro-capitalism possible. In other words, *peasant agriculture is not only functional but indispensable to the existence of capitalist agricultural firms.* But a peasant is obliged to sell his labour seasonally (and is willing to sell it cheaply) *only if he is poor*: rich farmers in the USA can (and do) spend the periods when there is no farm work in idleness. In other words, *agricultural capitalism can only exist in symbiosis with poor peasants who are ready to (and urged to) sell their labour some days a year.*

A theory that explains peasant survival must also explain their poverty. This is, however, asymmetrical: although agricultural capitalist firms could not thrive without peasants, the latter would be much better off without agricultural capitalists. This is because, as mentioned, when capitalist firms are present in the market, farm product prices reflect only the costs of labour power effectively paid for. For capital, labour power is a *variable cost*: it pays only for the days it hires the labour force. Conversely, for the peasant family economy, it is a *fixed cost*: it always has to provide for the reproduction of the whole family. In an agricultural market in which all suppliers of goods were family units (or cooperatives with a moral responsibility for the lives of their members and families), agricultural prices would reflect the year-round cost of the reproduction of labour power and would therefore be much higher than current prices. The most widespread cause of peasant poverty in the world would have disappeared.

2. The nature of agricultural production: its contrast with industrial production

The training of economists is such that the majority are incapable of properly answering the question about the essential economic differences between agriculture and industry (agricultural economists are the exception). One must begin by pointing out that agriculture works with living material: agricultural production basically consists in *taking care of and stimulating the natural biological process of plant growth*. By contrast, in industry the objects in the work process are (mostly) inert materials. Plants have a biological cycle – a period of growth – and grow in the earth. Therefore, work processes in agriculture must be carried out according to the plant's stage of growth and must be carried out where the plant is. In other words, the biological process imposes both temporal and spatial rules on man's activities. Conversely, in industry, where one works (mostly) with fibres, metals, wood, plastics or harvested grains, the work process is not constrained either spatially or temporally. The speed of the process (except for some chemical reactions) and the place in which it is carried out are dictated by man.

These differences can be summarised as follows. Firstly, whereas in industry processes can be *continuous* (24 hours a day, 365 days a year), in agriculture they are *seasonal* (for example, the harvest is concentrated in a few weeks of the year). Secondly, whereas in industry all the production activities may be *simultaneous* (one unit of clothing may be being cut out while another is being sewn and a third packed), in agriculture they are necessarily *sequential*. Thirdly, whereas in industry the material is usually transferred to the operator or the machine, in agriculture the operator or the machine must move to the place where the plant[4] is.

A fourth difference derives from the *uncertainty factors* associated with the biological nature of agricultural production, which do not exist in industrial (or service) activities. The variability of rainfall in zones without irrigation systems, the presence of pests and so on determine the risk of partial or total crop loss. The risks of industrial production loss are lower and, except for disasters, are not associated with natural phenomena beyond the producer's control. This difference can be summarised by saying that, whereas in agriculture *productive uncertainty* prevails, in industry *productive certainty* predominates.

A fifth difference results from the *perishable nature* of agricultural products, which contrasts with the *non-perishable nature* of industrial products. Although cereals are much less perishable than fruit and vegetables, they cannot be stored permanently as, in principle, most industrial products can.

Some of the consequences of these differences are obvious, others less so.

3. The specific character of the peasantry[5]

Leaving aside the question of whether the peasant economy constitutes a specific mode of production, the concept is applicable to smallholders who work individual plots of land as their principal source of income, based mainly on family work; however, it can also be applied to communities where certain activities are carried out collectively. Here, I follow Chayanov (1966), for whom 'peasant family farm work' or the 'family farm' is characterised by being based solely on family work and not employing wage labour.

It is unclear whether the concept of the peasantry should or should not include those smallholders whose main income comes from the sale of their labour force, while income derived from the plot complements this. Empirically, at least in Mexico, this is a very important group (on this, see R. Bartra 1974: 30).

Some features of *peasant family units* are as follows:

- The peasant unit is an organic structure, so changes in one of its elements affect the rest. Activities are interdependent because they compete for the same resources – sometimes the by-products of one activity serve as inputs for another – and due to competitiveness or biological complementarities.

- Unlike a capitalist firm, which is exclusively a production unit, the peasant family is both a production and a consumption unit. The dominant pole determining the objectives of the unit is the set of family needs, or the family as a consumer unit. For most of the world's peasants, the main objective is survival. Decisions about what to grow and with what intensity are influenced not only by their resource endowment and relative prices, as would be the case in a capitalist unit, but also by the number and age/sex composition of family members.

- Family security plays an essential role in any decision. The consequences of crop failure for a poor family go beyond financial difficulties. The larger the cash transactions, the greater the risks, so, for the same level of income and work, peasants prefer alternatives that involve a lower volume of monetary transactions.

- Peasant units are subject to various restrictions simultaneously: on land and on 'capital', as well as on peak seasonal labour. Since the resource endowment varies from unit to unit, the valuation of resources (their 'shadow price') also differs. Likewise, this valuation will vary within each unit according to the mixture of crops sown.

- Many cultivation practices, such as mixed crops and sowing distributed over time, are different from those of modern agriculture and little known in farming sciences.[6]

- The family goal, maximising well-being, is achieved through a flexible process that allows reviews and requires frequent decisions.

Even though there is no single theory on peasant behaviour, it is generally accepted that it cannot be explained using the capitalist rules of profit maximisation. According to some authors, the categories of 'profit' and 'wage' cannot be applied to family units. In 'On non-capitalist modes of production' (1996: 25), Chayanov attempted to define the economic categories applicable to a broad range of modes of production.

In any case, both Chayanov's theory and the discussions of those who have studied peasant behaviour in depth can be summarised by saying that the optimum sought by peasants is an optimum of well-being – or, as Chayanov would say, a work–consumption equilibrium.

4. Seasonality and rural poverty

Agricultural seasonality is expressed in unequal *labour requirements* throughout the year. In industry (with the exception of those branches that rely on a seasonal supply), labour requirements are, in principle, constant throughout the year. This well-known fact leads to consequences that have barely been analysed. The most important one is linked to the following question: *Who pays for the cost of reproduction of the agricultural worker – and his family – during periods of little or no agricultural activity?* This question can be reformulated as follows: *What labour costs are relevant to the setting of agricultural prices?* Only the cost of days worked? Or the year-round cost of reproduction of the producer and his family? This dilemma does not occur in industry: insofar as one works throughout the year, salaries are associated with maintaining the wage earner and his family year round. *The presence of this dilemma in agriculture explains the enormous variety of forms of production present within it. Each form of production is a particular way of solving this dilemma.*

In a classic essay, John W. Brewster, regarded as the 'philosopher of American agriculture', opens his argument thus:

> It has been said that because of mechanisation, 'A family farm in agriculture makes as little sense as a family factory in industry.' Is this so? Evidently not. Family units of production are unthinkable in car and steel manufacture, but *both* family and larger-than-family units are as common in agriculture after mechanisation as before. Why? (Brewster 1970 [1950]: 3, emphasis in original)

After arguing that 'neither hand nor machine techniques determine either family or larger-than-family farms', he asks what explains the 'dominance of the one or the other in various regions, both now and in the pre-machine era of American agriculture?' His reply is:

The answer seems to lie (1) in the degree to which a given farming area is more suitable for (approximately) single or multiple product farming, plus (2) *customs which free a larger-than-family operator from labour upkeep during periods of farm 'unemployment'.* (ibid.: 5)

He goes on to point out:

growing fewer and fewer products on a farm greatly lengthens unemployment periods between operations. Since most labour on family farms is family labour, this means that *family operators must pay (in the form of family living expenses) for their labour in both farm employment and unemployment periods. In other words, labour, for the most part, is a fixed cost for the family operator but not for the larger operator as he pays labour only for the time it is actually employed on his farm.* Were some custom available that would free the family as well as the larger operator from labour upkeep during the long unemployment periods between farm operations, it is highly questionable if the larger operator's managerial advantage would enable him to crowd out the family operator in even single product farming areas. (ibid.: 5–6, emphasis added)

The large agricultural units of the Latin American past, such as Mexican haciendas, solved the problem of maintaining the labour force during periods of unemployment intelligently – given their interests – by giving the peasant the right to work a plot of land for his family's consumption. This is a similar solution to that of feudal systems and sharecropping: by giving families the right to work the land, the landlords transfer to the peasant families the seasonal problem of agriculture, freeing the feudal lord or boss from the commitment to maintain the labour force all year.

In capitalist agriculture, the seasonal wage earner has to assume the responsibility of maintaining himself or herself (and their family) during periods of unemployment. *Price setting in capitalist agriculture is therefore determined only by the labour costs of days that have been effectively worked and paid for. Insofar as the family producer – whether he is a farmer or a peasant – takes part in the same markets as capitalist producers and acts in them as a price taker, it is also obvious that the price of his products can pay only for the days that have been effectively worked. However, the family has to assume responsibility for the year-round maintenance of its members.*

Given that the predominance of capitalism is not only economic but cultural, in a capitalist economy with a significant presence of capitalist firms in agriculture, peasant producers themselves will accept the capitalist way of calculating costs and will include only effectively worked days in their labour costs, rather than their year-round cost of reproduction. One way in which this cultural imposition occurs is through bank credit. Banks (public or private) will calculate crop costs in the same way for peasant as for capitalist units. This acceptance of the cultural imposition of the capitalist production mode explains why peasants are willing to produce and sell their products if they recover the costs of inputs and effectively worked time. *In effect, they internalise one of the factors of their own poverty.*

On the basis of the dominant paradigm, authors from the left and from the right have forecast the generalisation of the capitalist economy in agriculture: that is, the decomposition of the peasant economy. Who would take care of the labour force – and its families – during the periods of agricultural unemployment if this prediction came true? Can a generalised system of temporary wage labour be feasible? In 1912, Luis Cabrera said, on the subject of providing communities with *ejidos*,[7] that this would enable medium and large estates to have access to cheap, widely available labour power. Hence, he regarded capitalist agricultural firms and peasant family units as complementary.

Unlike these forms of production that transfer the problem of seasonality to peasants or wage earners, *the slave economy* in agriculture had to defray the cost of maintaining its slaves year round – as has to be done, in any productive form, with working animals. This must have reduced the slave economy's competitive capacity vis-à-vis the capitalist economy, which, as we have seen, pays only for days that have been worked. As the slave economy obtained adult slaves cheaply, this disadvantage was offset by the elimination of intergenerational reproduction costs. But, as Chayanov pointed out:

> As the sources for capture of slaves in war became exhausted by frequent attacks, the prime cost of acquiring slaves grew; their market price increased quickly and many slave uses that generated a small slave rent were no longer profitable and were

gradually dropped. As a result, the slave economy decreased in extent. ... an important factor in the decline of the ancient system of slavery was that in order to insure the supply of slaves, war and capture had to be abandoned for peaceful production by means of natural reproduction. Here, the ancient economic unit faced prime costs so high that they started to overtake the capitalised slave rent. (Chayanov 1966: 15–16)

Apparently, the only productive forms that assume the costs of reproducing the agricultural labour force year round are primitive communities, slavery and peasant units (including the family farmer). *If the peasant economy did not take part in the same markets as capitalist enterprises, competing with them, it could, in principle, transfer the costs of year-round family maintenance to the consumer, via prices. But insofar as this is not the case, it must assume the 'social cost' that the capitalist system imposes on agriculture*, with peasants having to seek employment as seasonal wage workers off their plot of land to complement their income. The human cost of this is extremely high – *separation from the family, often sub-human living conditions, and so on – while the economic result is permanent poverty*. Despite this, the peasant economy shows an enormous capacity for competition and resistance. The forecasted generalisation of the capitalist economy in the countryside does not occur partly because the capitalist firm needs the peasant economy, which supplies it with cheap labour, and partly because of the competitive advantage of the independent peasant, who appropriates all the added value and does not have to divide it between wages, profits and rents, as occurs in the capitalist economy.

Whether a family agricultural unit can live adequately from the working days invested in its plot of land, and therefore may or may not need to seek additional sources of income, obviously depends on factors that explain the productivity of agricultural work as well as the relative prices it faces. The objective situation of the 'American family farm' is evidently very different from that of the Latin American, African or Asian peasant.

To grasp the effects of the second and third differences between agriculture and industry (sequentiality versus simultaneity, and moveable material versus non-moveable material), I will follow Brewster's analysis of the different consequences of mechanisation in both:

In pre-machine times, farming and manufacture were alike in
that operations in both cases were normally done sequentially,
one after another; usually by the same individual or family.
The rise of the machine process has forced agriculture and
industry to become progressively different … For in substituting
machine for hand power and manipulations in agriculture
individuals in no way disturb their pre-machine habit of doing
their production steps one after another whereas in making the
same substitution in industry men thereby force themselves to
acquire increasingly the new habit of performing simultaneously
the many operations in a production process … the substitution
of machine power and manipulations in industry calls for a
corresponding revolution in the pre-machine social structure
whereas the contrary is true in agriculture … For in transforming
the older sequence of operations into the modern simultaneous
pattern, industrial mechanisation quickly multiplies the number
of concurrent operations in a production unit far beyond the
number of workers in a household. Hence, in adopting machine
techniques, men thereby force themselves to replace the older
society family production units with enormously larger units,
disciplined and guided by a hierarchy of bosses and managers. In
agriculture, however, machine methods remain as compatible as
hand techniques with either (1) family or (2) larger-than-family
units. Their compatibility with family units lies in the fact that
farm operations are as widely separated by time intervals after
mechanisation as before; hence, the number of things that must
be done at the same time on a farm remains as close as ever to
the number of workers in an ordinary family. (Brewster 1970
[1950]: 3–5)

Brewster also compares four associated consequences of
mechanisation in agriculture and industry:

First, such advance accelerates the functional and task forms
of specialisation in industry but not in agriculture. In working
simultaneously, manufacturing machines so multiply the
number of concurrent operations as to (1) wipe out the union
of the managerial, supervisory, and labour employments in the
same individual (or family) and re-establish them as full-time

occupations of different classes, and further (2) destroy a
similar union of labour operations ... For the absence of the
functional and task forms of specialisation in industry would
cause the worker to waste time in *going* from one operation
to another, while any marked degree of task specialisation in
agriculture would cause the workers to waste time in *waiting*
from one operation to another. To keep 'modern' in respect to
efficiency, farming must remain 'old-fashioned' in respect to
the 'higher forms' of specialisation. Second ... The relationship
that once prevailed in [agriculture and industry] was personal
identification of the worker with the product, as the sequential
pattern of operations in each case enabled him to guide materials
through one operation after another until the final product was
the embodiment of his planning and effort. This relationship
still holds in machine agriculture because the older sequence
of operations still remains. But in working simultaneously,
industrial machines have long since loosened the worker from
the product and tied him to the repetitive performance of a
particular operation ... Third, the machine ... [has left] farmers
undisturbed in their old standing as purposive (self-directing)
beings in their working activity while strongly tending to reduce
industrial workers to the status of machines. Fourth, not only
does machine agriculture conserve men as self-directing workers
... but it also conserves and expands the traditional human
satisfactions in work whereas the contrary is true in industry.
... machine farming remains even more in line with traditional
work-satisfaction than hand techniques. For in leaving unaltered
the product of farming as the expression of the farmers planning
and effort, machine agriculture likewise leaves the farmer in
possession of the old artisan's creative satisfactions ... because
it does not tear apart his management and labour activities.
Finally, machine agriculture expands these satisfactions of self-
directing and creative workmanship through releasing human
energies from the brute strain of operations into the larger life of
will and imagination on which farming so intimately depends.
(ibid.: 7–9)

The differences in the nature of the material (moveable or non-
moveable) mean that, in agriculture, machines must be moved to the

ground and plants; this contrasts with industry, where the object of work has to be moved to the machines, which are immobile. This difference places limits on the optimal economic size of agricultural units: the larger the unit, the higher the costs of moving the machinery to where it is needed. This limit means, among other things, that there are different market structures in agriculture and industry. As Brewster points out:

> The simultaneous pattern of operation makes possible such an expanded scale of production that the efficient utilisation of industry may require only one or at most a very few firms, each so large as to substantially influence the price at which it buys and sells. ... the guarantee of impersonal competitive forces, that the businessman will actually operate industry in line with the public interest, disappears ... Shift to machine methods has neither added to nor detracted from the primitive competitive character of American agriculture. (ibid.: 10–11)

The highly perishable nature of certain agricultural products is reflected in seasonal price variations; again, this contrasts with industry, which, in principle, maintains constant prices year round. However, when studying agricultural price setting, it is necessary to take other characteristics of agricultural production into account. Insofar as processes are not continuous, *neither is the production flow*. In general, the year's production can be concentrated into a few weeks. Unlike the industrial producer, the farmer cannot regulate his production flow on a daily basis. Whereas the former can adjust his production almost daily to the signs of the market, when the farmer makes the decision to sow – which, in principle, determines his volume of production several months later – he has to base this on his expectations of what the market situation will be at harvest.

One could say that, apart from the uncertainty (associated with natural risks) that characterises agriculture but not industry, there is another important difference: business risk in industry is concentrated in investment in *fixed* capital, whereas, in agriculture, risk is concentrated in investment in *circulating* capital (seeds, inputs, labour), and this investment must be made largely at the beginning of every agricultural cycle.

These differences have forced the development of specific theories of price setting for agriculture. One of the best known is the cobweb theorem, which, in essence, holds that the current price of an agricultural product is determined by the amount produced during the previous cycle, while this amount is determined by the price in the cycle before that.[8]

5. The debate on the persistence of peasantry

Frank Ellis identifies in Marxist theoretical work two opposite lines of reasoning regarding 'the persistence of peasant forms of production within the dominant mode of capitalist production'. On the one hand, there is the classic Marxist position put forward by V. I. Lenin (1967 [1899]):

> The pressures on peasants created by capitalist production
> relations must, inevitably, result in their disappearance as a
> distinct form of production … [Because of] *social differentiation*
> peasant communities are predicted to disintegrate into the
> two social classes of capitalist farmers and rural wage labour.
> The reasons this may happen … include such factors as …
> differential adoption of improved cultivation practices by
> different individual farmers, the enforced abandonment of their
> holdings by peasants unable to compete in the market … the
> foreclosure by creditors on farmers who have run into debt, and
> the increasing employment of wage labour by those farmers who
> are successful. (Ellis 1988: 51–2)

The opposite line of reasoning, says Ellis, is that the internal logic of family agricultural production enables it to withstand the pressure of capitalist production relations and reproduce itself indefinitely. This might be due to: 1) peasants' capacity, given their control over land, to provide for their needs for simple reproduction; 2) the social norms of peasant communities focusing on reciprocity rather than on the individual maximisation of profits (the 'moral economy' argument set out by James C. Scott); 3) demographic factors opposed to land concentration, given its subdivision in inheritance; 4) peasants' capacity to overcome the pressure of the market, by increasing the amount of work invested in production (peasants' self-exploitation); 5) natural or technical features specific to agriculture that make it unattractive to capital (such as the duration of the productive cycle, climate variability, the higher risk of production failure, and supervision difficulties); and 6) the functional advantages for capitalism of leaving agriculture in peasants' hands (cheaper foods, less risk, for example), linked to reasons 4 and 5 (ibid.: 52).

The model by the famous Russian populist Chayanov is one of the non-Marxist theories within this line of reasoning. Chayanov explains the absence of unequal accumulation among peasants, according to Ellis's account, by the fact that their motivation does not include accumulation, but is reduced to the satisfaction of family needs and therefore to simple reproduction. But Ellis also finds two reasons in Marxist thought for the persistence of the peasantry that are consistent with the logic of capitalism and the market. Firstly, non-accumulation in the peasant economy may occur not as a result of a lack of motivation among peasants, but because capitalist production relations continuously force peasants towards simple reproduction through the *capture* (through various mechanisms) *of any surplus value created* and by the devaluation of peasant work resulting from innovations that reduce the price of agricultural goods. Both factors can be described, following Henry Bernstein, as a 'squeeze towards simple reproduction' imposed by the market on peasants. Secondly:

> it has been argued that certain aspects of farm production are awkward for capitalist production relations and this discourages the advance of capitalism in agriculture. The principal factor is *the length of the farm production cycle compared to the time in which labour is productively employed.* This refers to the *seasonal pattern of labour use*, which in family production means that household labour is applied unevenly through the year. *For capitalist production this poses the problem either of paying for permanent wage labour when it is not needed all the time or depending on the uncertainties and social disruption of migrant labour.* (ibid.: 53–4[9])

Vergopoulos's conception of the family agricultural unit and its relations with capital is full of insights:

> Family farming is the most successful form of production for putting the maximum volume of surplus labour at the disposal of urban capitalism. It also constitutes the most efficient way of restraining the prices of agricultural products. The peasant

who is working for himself does not necessarily consider himself to be a capitalist, or an entrepreneur, whose activities depend on the ability to obtain a positive rate of profit. On the contrary, although the head of his agricultural concern, he sees himself, more often than not, as a plain worker who is entitled to a remuneration which will simply assure him his livelihood. Moreover, in the framework of domestic economy the problem of ground-rent does not arise ... For capitalists, contemporary family farming is not an economic space which has to be penetrated and conquered, but an 'exotic' whole which has to be subdued as such. (Vergopoulos 1978)

Harriss questions the general validity of family modes of production by noting that, in Asia and Latin America, most family units are *marginal agricultural units*, which he defines as units that are unsuitable for supporting the families that operate them. The same phenomenon happens in Mexico, where, in 1970, so-called *infrasubsistence peasants*, who are equivalent to Harriss's marginalised units, represented almost two-thirds of all peasant productive units, according to Cepal (1982: 113). Harriss (1982: 120) adds that these marginal units can continue existing and that they provide the basis for the deep entrenchment of commercial and usury capital. The reader should note that, in defining marginal units without explaining why they exist, Harriss begs the question on the persistence of the peasantry. Precisely because of this, I hold that poverty and the persistence of the peasantry must be explained together.

6. Djurfeldt's virtual debate with Kautsky

Djurfeldt (1982) claims that the non-fulfilment of the classic Marxist prediction that agriculture would become totally capitalistic should not be regarded as a fatal blow to a non-mechanistic, non-deterministic version of historical materialism. However, it is unlikely that Marx sustained this unfulfilled prediction (see Kautsky's quote from Marx at the end of this section).

The classic expectation about land concentration, he says, was based on the economies of scale supposedly present in large-scale agricultural units. This concentration would entail a revolution in productive forces that would expel peasants from production and turn them into wage workers. However, Djurfeldt argues that, since the late nineteenth century, large farms have become less important while medium-sized farms have increased in importance and small ones have been fragmented. To this, Djurfeldt adds another, very important, trend:

> there is a tendency for the big *latifundistas* to divide parts of their land into parcels, where they settle their workers; in this way they get their own labour-colonies. This process has a counterpart in many countries, for example the British Small-holding Act of 1892 ... *it is a way of decreasing the cost of labour in a capitalistic enterprise, which in more recent times also has been the specific aim of land reforms in many Latin American countries.* When they have their own land, labourers reproduce their labour-power on their land, and *thus the capitalists need not pay them the full value of their labour-power* (the value of labour-power is equal to its cost of reproduction) ... Stated in the most general way, we may say that one agrarian class, the poor peasants, who by definition own too little land to reproduce themselves, and who are thereby forced to take employment – are tied in exactly this way to the rich peasants or *latifundistas*. (ibid.: 141–2)[10]

This superb paragraph shows that *pure capitalism is impossible in agriculture* and that the seasonal nature of agricultural work is the implicit guiding thread of Djurfeldt's argument. He also shows how *capitalism needs poor peasants* to perform the function of suppliers of *cheap*, and one should add *seasonal*, labour power. Here, he would seem to coincide with the thesis I put forward above: *agricultural capitalism can exist only in symbiosis with poor peasants, ready to (and urged to) sell their labour some days a year.* However, arguing with Kautsky (who said that the problem for large farms is the shortage of labour), he states that the '*poor peasantry is not an integral part of the concept of the capitalist mode of production in agriculture,* but rather an indicator of a process of atypical reproduction' (ibid.: 142), which he attributes to the crisis in European agriculture unleashed by competition in the international grain market.

Let's examine some of Kautsky's statements in *The Agrarian Question* (1988 [1899]: 159–64), where he indeed (but implicitly) states that peasantry is an integral part of the capitalist mode of production in agriculture, albeit for demographic reasons:

The extension of the market, access to money, the necessary technical prerequisites – these in themselves are not enough for the creation of a large-scale capitalist enterprise: The most important thing is the *workers* ... In the older established nations, urban industry is not subject to any shortage of labour. *The proletariat multiplies,* and provides plentiful fresh labour-power for growing capital ... matters are quite different when we turn to agriculture. Working conditions in the towns render workers unfit for agricultural labour ... Under present day conditions, agriculture cannot supplement its labour supply from the urban, industrial proletariat. The problem for agriculture is that *the large agricultural enterprise is also unable to produce and retain the supply of wage-labourers it needs* ... Agriculture is still tied to the household. *No farm exists without a corresponding household.* And *there is no permanent household in the country without some form of agriculture* ... [In the countryside] a totally propertyless wage labourer, living in his own household, is a rarity ... Others with their own household are also usually independent farmers, on their own or rented land, *devoting only part of their time to wage-labour and the rest to working their own land* ... Such conditions *do not favour the reproduction of a class of rural propertyless workers.* House servants usually have no chance of marriage and the establishment of an independent household ... Conditions among the *Einlieger,* free day-labourers lacking their own household, are no more conducive to the raising of a new generation. *The best conditions for bringing up a plentiful supply of able-bodied labour are found amongst the owners (or tenants) of small farms on which an independent household is linked with independent farming.* Not only does this group supply labour-power for itself, but also turns out a surplus ... *These production sites for new labour-power progressively contract wherever the large-scale farm supplants the small. Clearing peasants off the land may release additional land for the large farm, but at the same time it reduces the number of people available to cultivate it. This in itself is sufficient to ensure that, despite its technical superiority, the large farm can never completely prevail within any given country* ... As long as the capitalist mode of production continues, there is no more reason to expect the end of the large-scale agricultural enterprise than that of the small. (ibid., emphasis added)

A propos of this, Kautsky cites an 1850 article by Marx in the *Rheinische Zeitung* in which he says that, 'As long as bourgeois relations subsist agriculture most move continuously in this cycle of land concentration and land splitting,' which might imply that Marx was not predicting the extinction of the peasantry.

7. Agricultural seasonality and peasant survival: a polemic with Armando Bartra

Reading Armando Bartra (2006), a compulsory reference in any analysis of the peasantry in Mexico, I became conscious that agricultural seasonality, on which I had based my theory of peasant poverty,[11] also explains the survival of the peasantry in almost all parts of the world, despite the generalised predictions of its imminent disappearance. As my answer to the question as to why peasants have not been crushed by all-powerful capitalism, I stated that capitalism could not function in a pure fashion in agriculture. In such a hypothetical case, there would be no one to provide the seasonal labour it requires. Capitalism in agriculture is only viable when it coexists with the peasant economy. Capitalism has to live in symbiosis with the peasantry if it is to function.

Conversely, Bartra's explanation of peasants' survival is based on *land rent*:

The primary rent is differential rent; moreover, absolute rent is actually differential rent, since it is paid in proportion to output. *Differential rent is unavoidable when the same goods produced with different costs are regularly sold at the same price.* These *cost disparities* originate in the diverse productive response of diverse natural resources. Obviously, this happens only when the level of demand … forces one to work in less productive conditions, since the higher costs of these additional harvests will be imposed as market regulating prices. This fact implies an overpayment or differential rent to producers operating in better conditions. Understood in this way, differential rent is consubstantial to capitalism and … favours those capitals controlling agricultural production in detriment of the remaining capitals. (ibid. 20–1)[12]

Bartra explains the alleged trend towards the disappearance of land rent by noting that the biotechnological revolution has transformed agricultural production in such a way that today, thanks to intensification and high yields, supply depends far less than before on harvests contributed by marginal areas, meaning that differential rent is subject to an irreversible declining trend (ibid.: 23). He adds: 'And it is there, in the perversions of rent, *that one of the structural reasons for the permanence and reproduction of the peasant economy in advanced capitalism lies: the fact that peasants can be forced to work at below average profits and on occasions, at the simple point of equilibrium*' (ibid.: 21). He makes his theory more explicit:

> In a hyper technified agriculture of productivities that tend towards homogeneity, small farmers capable of operating at a disadvantage and sacrificing profits become redundant. *Because if there is no differential rent, there are no peasants,* since insofar as *it is possible to supply demanded quantities without resorting to harvests with structurally unequal yields,* it will no longer be necessary to offset burdensome agricultural rents through non-capitalist commodity producers operating on the worst lands. (ibid.: 23)

The last two quotes clearly express Bartra's thesis: peasants are essential as a buffer mechanism for land rent. This is because peasants, as petty commodity producers, do not pursue profits and can therefore function and reproduce at lower prices than would be required by a capitalist unit on the same land, thereby reducing the amount of differential rent. This function of the peasant economy would explain its persistence.

Yet Bartra, unlike most authors, lucidly explores agricultural seasonality and the capitalism–peasant economy symbiosis that is derived from it:

> The contradiction between the discontinuity in farm work and the salaried reproduction of labour is *a problem that the absolute market system is incapable of overcoming, at least in an orthodox fashion.* The point is that *capitalism, which works well with specialised, continuous processes that make the use of means of production and labour profitable, falters when its consumption is syncopated by force as happens with agriculture, subject to natural cycles, where labour requirements are concentrated in sowing and harvests.* The entrepreneurs' strategy involves externalising the

contradiction by hiring temporary day labourers. But the system does not accept externalities and *if the direct employer does not pay more than the time worked, society as a whole would have to assume the costly integral reproduction of seasonal workers.* Luckily for global capital, the *domestic economy* [i.e. the peasant economy] is there to support part-time day labourers through production for self-consumption. By lowering the cost of commercial harvests, the self-supply economy that supports seasonal day workers not only benefits businessmen in the countryside but also solves a serious problem for the global capitalist system. (ibid.: 24–5)

Bartra opens his dialogue with me with the following statement (ibid.: 25): 'So important is the discontinuity of labour which characterises agriculture, that the economist Julio Boltvinik locates there part of the existing asymmetries between peasants and agro-businessmen, since whereas the former, he says, have to assume the costs of days not worked, the latter do not.' Bartra omits to point out that the ideas developed in this article are part of the outline of a theory of peasant poverty. There is an element that escapes his grasp: that the persistence of the peasant economy can be explained more by its function as provider of cheap, temporary (seasonal) labour, without which capitalism in agriculture is inconceivable, than by smoothing differential land rent.

Bartra places side by side the contradictions in the market of agricultural products, caused by the differential yields with which different portions of the same class of goods are produced (which gives rise to differential land rent), and the 'contradictions created in the labour market and in the conditions for reproduction of rural day labourers by the marked discontinuity of labour demand in virtually all crops' (A. Bartra 2006: 187). Bartra posits that, in pre-capitalist societies, the fluctuating, seasonal nature of work requirements, which is characteristic of activities subject to natural cycles, was dealt with through the diversification of economic activity; this contrasts with the fact that modern capitalist society requires specialisation.

From the point of view of the capitalist business production unit, there is nothing irrational about cyclically hiring and firing a large mass of workers, yet from a global perspective, part time use of the agricultural labour forces assumes a series of contradictions ... if the individual entrepreneur only pays for the days that have been worked, *society will somehow have to produce the rest of the income necessary for the subsistence of the seasonal employee.* (ibid.: 187)

Bartra conceives the peasantry as a class and calls it the *peasant class*, which 'has been defined on the basis of a double link with capital: petty commodity production and the reproduction of the partially salaried labour force' (ibid.: 188). He adds: 'Unlike the proletariat, the peasantry constitutes a class subjected to multiple, complex exploitation relations in which the extraction of the *surplus* through an unequal exchange in the market and the obtaining of *surplus value* through part-time wage labour are combined' (ibid.: 189). As we can see, Bartra considers that the performance of seasonal work is a constitutive element of the peasant class. He points out that the peasant sells part of his labour power because his income as a direct producer does not suffice to guarantee simple reproduction (ibid.: 266), *but he does not ask why this income is insufficient.* Conversely, he argues that, since the income the peasant seeks in wage labour is only a complement to his income from his plot of land, he is prepared to work for a salary below the value of his labour power. Thus, the *over-exploitation of peasant wage labour* can be sustained permanently, and therefore the peasant can subsidise the capitalist (ibid.: 270).

In my view, these different forms of peasant exploitation pale in comparison with the main form of exploitation, *which occurs through the peasantry absorbing the total cost of agricultural seasonality.* Even if there were no other forms of exploitation, the peasant would be condemned to permanent itinerant poverty.

My thesis in this fundamental point of the dialogue, as already stated, is this: *without the peasants' supply of seasonal labour, capitalist agriculture would be impossible.* There would be (virtually) no one prepared to work only during the harvests. *The persistence of peasant agriculture therefore makes agro-capitalism possible.* Given the rule of the game (you work, you get paid, and you leave), and given the formation of prices in markets in which peasant and capitalist farmers compete and in which the aforementioned rule prevails, only the days worked are incorporated into production costs and are therefore reflected in farm prices. The peasant farmer therefore obtains a net income from his plot of land that is approximately equal to the value of his labour power for the days effectively worked. Since he and his family have to eat every day, he is obliged to try to complement his income by becoming an *itinerant pauper. Pure capitalism, I conclude, is impossible in agriculture.*

I made public these ideas in my weekly column in the Mexican newspaper *La Jornada* (Boltvinik 2007a). In his reply, Bartra (A. Bartra 2007) made three comments. Firstly, he pointed out that peasants' exploitation is *polymorphous* while his existence is *plurifunctional.* He is exploited not only as he absorbs the costs of the seasonality of agricultural work (the central feature of my theory of peasant poverty) but also when he sells his labour power and when he migrates. These other forms of exploitation obviously cannot be denied. In a journal article in 2007, I held that:

> In Mexico, family agricultural producers live in abject poverty:
> 1) because their productivity levels are far below those of
> their competitors: Mexico's capitalist producers and US and
> Canadian producers; 2) because labour is undervalued in the
> country, particularly in rural settings; and 3) because the costs of
> seasonality are borne almost exclusively by peasants. (Boltvinik
> 2007b: 37)

There is one difference that should be stressed: when I say that peasants absorb the entire costs of seasonality, I do not mean that they are exploited in this way by capital but by society as a whole – everyone pays lower prices for food and therefore receives a subsidy from peasants. *Peasants are poor because they subsidise all of us.* If we subsidised peasants (and only them, since capitalist agriculture does not need these subsidies because it does not absorb the cost of seasonality), society as a whole would absorb this cost through taxes. If we intervened in price setting, we could make consumers absorb this cost in the form of relatively higher food prices, such as those that prevail in the First World.

Secondly, Bartra points out that the most important difference between his proposal and mine lies not in the diagnosis but in the solutions: whereas I propose the subsidy route, he holds that, although subsidies are not wrong, the real solution would be agricultural diversification. Bartra illustrates his argument with Cuba's virtually *monocrop* sugar economy. Plantations constitute an extreme case of monocropping agriculture and exacerbate the seasonality of the demand for labour. Additionally, typical plantation crops – particularly when they require an industrial process for transforming the product, such as sugar cane, cotton and coffee – exceed the scale of the family unit and involve serious difficulties in maintaining the autonomy of family agriculture. The sugar industry provides an example of the limits (or obstacles) that may be faced on the path of diversification. Since diversification is highly desirable for a peasant unit, one could ask why observed trends are going in the opposite direction. Why are peasant units increasingly *less* diversified? And why are the *milpa* fields (an ancient and highly diversified way of using land in Mexico) disappearing? Bartra is right: diversification not only entails the fullest use of human resources and often of land (such as the bean–maize combination in which the former fixes in the soil the nitrogen used by the latter), but also has enormous ecological advantages. Since Bartra does not reject the route of subsidies and I do not reject the advantages and benefits of diversification, the difference is only one of emphasis: my thesis is that the main policy instrument should be subsidies whereas Bartra focuses on diversification as the main solution. The real solution, however, is the eradication of capitalism, which is incompatible with rational agriculture.

Thirdly, Bartra points out that *capitalism believes that it has achieved its dream of transforming agriculture into another branch of industry*, where there is no land rent, or where land rent becomes irrelevant. Bartra also states that, by shifting from *latifundia* to transgenic crops from land rent to the rent of life through the appropriation of life as industrial property that can be patented, 'capitalism jeopardises human survival'.

I do not agree, however, with the minimisation of the importance of my thesis on rural poverty (as compared with the ecological dimension) with which Bartra's article ends: 'The fact that by operating in agriculture capitalism distorts the price setting mechanism is a minor issue.' It cannot be minor because this 'distortion' explains the poverty of billions of peasants. Capitalism does not only pillage nature; it brutally pillages human reproduction, and therefore it pillages the human species itself. In addition, it does so now on a global scale with more strength than ever. In other words, capitalism pillages subject and object, making its abolition an urgent task. Unfortunately, this will probably occur only after a long period of natural and social cataclysms whose monstrosity we cannot even imagine.

8. Obstacles to capitalist agriculture: the Mann–Dickinson thesis

As pointed out in section 5, Frank Ellis found two reasons for the persistence of the peasantry in the Marxist bibliography on peasants. One of the reasons is the difference, identified by Marx in Volume II of *Capital* (1978 [1885]), *between the duration of the agricultural productive cycle (production time) and the time when work is productively employed (working time)*; this refers to the seasonal pattern of the use of labour, a factor that constitutes the core of my theory on poverty and persistence of the peasantry. Concerning this reason, he cites only the Mann–Dickinson thesis, which I shall now examine (Mann and Dickinson (M&D) 1978). In a subsequent book (1990), Mann mentions that the position they hold is very similar to what Ariel José Contreras (Contreras 1977) had said a year earlier in a Mexican journal, although this article went largely unnoticed, given the dominance of the English language.

M&D acknowledge that the prediction about the generalisation of capitalism in world agriculture has not been fulfilled; even in the centres of industrial capitalism, farms based on family labour (family farms) are strikingly vital:

Thus, even in advanced capitalist countries, we are confronted with a significant anomaly: the persistence and co-existence of rural petty commodity production alongside a dominant capitalist mode of production. *Capitalist development appears to stop, as it were, at the farm gate.* (M&D 1978: 467, emphasis added)

They see this persistence as a challenge to Marx's notion of the universality of capitalism and aim to fill the gap about the unequal development of capitalism within advanced capitalist countries by analysing some of the reasons for the persistence of non-capitalist production units in agriculture. 'Far from arguing that this "anomaly" refutes or undermines Marx's analysis of the process of capitalist development, we intend to demonstrate that it is only with the use of Marxian categories that this "anomaly" itself can be adequately explained.' They discuss Marx's conception of the transitional nature of petty commodity production (PCP). Marx derived it from his analysis of the tendency towards the differentiation of classes within PCP, encouraged by market competition in which the price of commodities drops continuously as a result of capitalist innovations, destroying the old forms of production.

This prediction by Marx is intended to be universal, say M&D, and '[t]he demonstration that Marx's analysis could be generalised to the countryside was perhaps the essential achievement of Lenin's *Development of Capitalism in Russia*' (Lenin 1967 [1899]). They add that Plekhanov, Kautsky and Mao Zedong (M&D 1978: 469) shared this view of the instability of PCP.

They end by saying that several writers on rural development have interpreted the persistence of family farms as a refutation of Marx's prediction about the transitional nature of PCP, since, in fact, '*the family farm had managed to "capitalise" without becoming "capitalist"*' (ibid., emphasis added). In order to explain this persistence, many have resorted to non-Marxist theories, say M&D, who examine two groups of these theories. In the first group, they place Chayanov, who highlighted the fact that the family peasant unit does not seek to obtain profits and therefore continues producing even when it does not obtain the average rate of profit, which gives it a competitive advantage over capitalist units. Among criticisms levelled against this approach, they stress that it isolates the family unit from capitalist surroundings. However, the critique that I find most convincing is that *the argument about the general advantage of PCP cannot explain the disappearance of urban forms of PCP (artisan production)*. The second group, they say, involves a sort of technological determinism in which improved agricultural technology is the basis of the persistence of family farms. For example, threshing machines make it unnecessary to hire numerous workers. M&D argue that this group of theories does not explain why PCP and capitalist production coexist in the same production sphere and with similar technological conditions, or why more prosperous family firms do not continue expanding production until they reach and exceed the point at which they would need to hire non-family labour.[13] None of these approaches consider that Marx's theory offers an adequate explanation of the persistence of family farms, according to M&D, but 'we hold that a closer scrutiny of Marx's writings, particularly the *Grundrisse* and Volumes II and III of *Capital*, reveals a number of important insights' (ibid.: 471).

Like Ariel José Contreras, M&D in their thesis and Mann in her 1990 book focus their identification of obstacles to the development of capitalism in agriculture (which, for them, would explain the persistence of non-capitalist forms of agricultural production) on *the difference between working time and production time* (a conceptual distinction made by Marx in Volume II of *Capital*) and on other natural characteristics such as the perishable nature of the products.

M&D cite a key paragraph in Volume II of *Capital* in which Marx says that *working time is always production time* (defined as the time in which capital is trapped in the production process), *but not all production time is necessarily working time*. Marx explains this difference by pointing out that production time consists of two parts: a period in which work is applied to production and a second period *in which the unfinished commodity is abandoned to the influence of natural processes*. Although Marx provides various non-agricultural examples of this second stage (drying pottery, whitening cloth, fermentation, and so on), he highlights the fact that this phase is particularly important in agriculture and gives the example of cereals, where *there is a long period when working time is suspended while the seed matures in the earth*. Our authors state that 'the non-identity of production time and labour time establishes a whole series of obstacles to the capitalist penetration of certain spheres of agriculture' (ibid.: 473). They add that 'this becomes apparent when we look at its effect on the rate of profit' and at the process of circulation and realisation of value. Theirs is a partial, predominantly static analysis. For example, they state that, all other things being equal, the more rotations capital makes in a year, the higher the profit rate will be; this is obvious but does not lead to the conclusion that therefore 'capital will shy away from such areas of production' (ibid.: 474). This conclusion is similar to the one reached by Contreras: 'In addition to the greater length of time of agricultural capital rotation in relation to the length of industrial capital rotation, other factors contribute to *containing the development of capitalist production*' (Contreras 1977: 890).

In my opinion, these conclusions are based on a partial analysis that does not consider that the rate of profit effectively obtained by capital in any sector depends on prices of production rather than on exchange values, as Marx shows in Volume III of *Capital* when he analyses the tendency towards the equalisation of rates of profit between different branches of production. Just as production prices move away from values to compensate for the differences in the organic composition of capital and in order to equalise the profit rate, they will also do so to compensate for the length of production time and slow capital rotation. If this were not the case, the construction industry, for example, which often has longer production periods than the annual cycle of agriculture, could not be capitalistic. The most interesting part of M&D's article, in my view, is the last section. There, they point out that:

> *the seasonal hiring of wage labour,* which is a reflection of the non-identity of production time and labour time, *presents any capitalist with labour recruitment and management problems.* As the buyer of labour power, the capitalist must either attract and maintain his 'temporary' work force by offering high wages or *rely on the most desperate and marginal elements in society as in the use of rural migrant labour.* (ibid.: 477)

In the first sentence, the authors establish a link between the seasonality of work and the differences between working and production time. These are obviously two sides of the same coin, two ways of looking at the same phenomenon; therefore, the *starting point* of their explanation for the persistence of non-capitalist modes of production (family farms in their case) is the same as my explanation of the persistence of the peasantry. However, my answer to the question about why the peasantry persists is its symbiosis with agricultural capitalism. I think that the fundamental difference is that M&D are trying to analyse why *family farms* persist (which, as I have said, are not poor and spend the periods without work in idleness), whereas my question concerns the persistence of *peasant family units.* Their starting point is the excess of production time over working time in certain spheres of agriculture (the other side of the coin of seasonality) and their response is that, for capitalism, this represents an inefficient use of capital, lower profit rates and circulation problems, which means that these agricultural spheres *are not attractive to them.* In other words, family farms survive because capital is not interested in taking away their field of business, as opposed to what is forcibly argued by John Brewster, whose ideas were discussed above. M&D's merit (shared by Contreras) consists of having highlighted Marx's perception of the specific features of agriculture and their significance for capitalism.

9. Marx and his vision of agriculture

In exploring Marx's thoughts on the subject, I begin with M&D's and Contreras's references to Volumes II and III of *Capital* and to *Grundrisse*. Contreras says:

In industry, labour is nearly always used during the entire period of the production process, therefore working time and production time coincide. Conversely, in agriculture, *working time always includes a shorter period than production time* ... This is due to the fact that agricultural production goes through a phase of natural crop growth in which none or very little additional work is required. 'The lack of coincidence between production time and working time – says Marx [in *Grundrisse*] – can only be due to natural conditions ...' (Contreras 1977: 887–8; quoting Marx 1972 [written 1857–58; first published 1939]: 191)

M&D, who also refer to this passage, begin by citing the first paragraph of Chapter XIII of Volume II of *Capital*:

Working time is always production time, i.e. time during which capital is confined to the production sphere. But it is not true, conversely, that the entire time for which capital exists in the production process is necessarily therefore working time. (Marx 1978 [1885]: 316)

This passage continues as follows:

What is at issue here are not interruptions in the labour process conditioned by the natural limits of labour-power itself ... What is involved is rather ... an interruption conditioned by the *nature of the product* and its production, *during which the object of labour is subjected to natural processes of shorter or longer duration* ... while the labour process is either completely or partially suspended ... After grapes have been pressed, for instance, the wine must go through a period of fermentation, and then also rest for a while before it reaches a certain degree of readiness ... Winter corn needs nine months or so to ripen. Between seed-time and harvest, the labour process is almost completely interrupted ... In all these cases, additional labour is added only occasionally for a large part of the production time ... therefore, the production time of the capital advanced consists of two periods: *a period in which the capital exists in the labour process, and a second period in which its form of existence – that of an unfinished product – is handed over to the sway of natural processes, without being involved in the labour process.* (ibid.: 316–17)

M&D return to *Grundrisse* but fail to see a key sentence in the text from which they take certain phrases; this is a brief section called 'Difference between production time and working time – Storch' (Marx 1973 [written 1857–58; first published 1939]: Notebook VI, 668–70). Marx begins by eliminating the assumption of equality between working time and production time, exemplifying their lack of coincidence with agriculture, where work is interrupted during the productive phase. Marx clarifies the fact that if the problem were the greater length of working time in one case, it would not have been a special case. What makes it a special case (and a problem) is the interruption of work before the end of production time, since two different products (an agricultural and an industrial one, for example) could therefore incorporate the same working time, but the rotation of the capital cycle would be slower for the product with the longer production time (the agricultural one). Marx adds something to this (note the first phrase in italics, which shows what M&D failed to see, and which defeats their argument):

The fixed capital here allegedly acts quite by itself, without human labour, like e.g. the seed entrusted to the earth's womb ... The time required here for the product to reach maturity, the interruptions of work, here constitute conditions of production. Not-labour time constitutes a condition for labour time, in order to turn the latter really into production time. *The question obviously belongs only with the equalisation of the rate of profit.* Still, the ground must be cleared here. The slower return – this is the essential part – here arises not from circulation time, but rather from the conditions themselves in which labour becomes productive; it belongs with the technological conditions of the

production process ... *Value, hence also surplus value, is not =
to the time which the production phase lasts, but rather to the labour
time*, [both] *objectified and living, employed during this production
phase.* The living labour time alone ... can create surplus value,
because (it creates) surplus labour time. [Footnote: 'It is clear
that other aspects also enter in with the equalisation of the
rate of profit. Here, however, the issue is not the *distribution of
surplus value but its creation.*'] (Marx 1973 [written 1857–58; first
published 1939]: 668–9)

It is a central quote. On the one hand, it shows the untenability
of M&D's central argument that capitalism has not appropriated
agriculture *because it is not sufficiently profitable*, since this argument
forgets that, in capitalism, capital mobility between branches of
production leads to the equalisation of profit rates by means of the
differences between prices of production and values, redistributing
capital profits. They also seem to forget that profit rates and surplus
rates are extremely different.

On the other hand, *the second phrase in italics shows that, for Marx,
value is always equal to working time objectified in commodities, even in the
problematic case of agriculture.* Marx did not notice that interruptions
in work raise a far more serious problem for the worker: if he does
not work every day, where will he obtain the means of subsistence
to go on reproducing and be available for capital when it wants to
use him again? This in turn raises serious doubts about the theory
of value, since Marx does not seem to have resolved the problem of
the value of the agricultural labour force: is it the cost of its annual
reproduction or just what is required to reproduce labour during
the days in which the individual works effectively in agriculture? In
Volume I of *Capital*, in which he deals with the value of labour power,
Marx does not introduce the problem that emerges when work is
discontinuous. And in Volumes II and III, when he deals with the
special case of agriculture, he does not discuss the determination of
the value of labour power again.

10. Marx's theory of value disregards discontinuous labour processes

Marx clearly saw the seasonal nature of agricultural work but
he expressed this perception in *Capital* only in Volumes II and

III, not in Volume I where he develops the theory of the value of labour power. This is despite the fact that he was aware of the problem when writing Volume I, as shown by the quote from *Grundrisse* (written from 1857 to 1858, before *Capital*) included in the previous section. In the first five chapters of *Capital*, where he describes the essential features of his theory of value, he always assumes a *continuous process of work* and *equality between working time and production time*; these are both assumptions that Marx analysed in Volumes II and III, and found that they do not hold true in certain productive processes, particularly in agriculture. In this section, I review some of these early chapters, highlighting the work continuity assumption.

In Chapter I, Marx characterises commodities as useful objects or *use values*, which, as *crystallisations of abstract human work* (expenditure of labour power), are also *values* expressed in their *exchange values* vis-à-vis other commodities and whose *value magnitude* is determined by the socially necessary labour time required to produce them. However, whereas abstract human labour is the only source of value, he adds (quoting William Petty) that *work is the father and nature is the mother of material wealth*. Wealth (constituted by use values) increases when productive forces are developed, but the quantity of labour objectified in the commodities – their value – may remain the same or even be reduced.

In Chapter IV, Marx deals with the transformation of money into *capital* (money that increases its value). He has not yet worked out how this is possible, although he states that it cannot arise from circulation or money, but he resolves the enigma later by showing that the increase in value must be obtained from *the use of a commodity whose use value is a source of value: labour power*. Marx therefore sets out to undertake a detailed analysis of the peculiar commodity known as labour power, which, like all commodities, has a value. Marx asks how this value is determined. The answer, which is central to the theory of *surplus value*, leads Marx (in my opinion) to *force the concept of production* so that labour power can be conceived of as a *commodity that has been produced*. This answer only applies fully to continuous labour processes, where no interruptions are present during which the worker is left unpaid. My comments are in square brackets and I omit certain phrases, indicated by an ellipsis:

The value of labour-power is determined, as in the case of every other commodity, by the labour-time necessary for the production, and consequently also the reproduction, of this specific article. As far as it has value, it represents no more than a definitive quantity of the average social labour objectified in it. Labour-power exists only as a capacity of the living individual. Its production consequently presupposes his existence. Given the existence of the individual, the production of labour-power consists in his reproduction of himself or his maintenance. For his maintenance, he requires a certain quantity of the means of subsistence. Therefore, the labour-time necessary for the production of labour-power is the same as that necessary for the production of those means of subsistence; in other words, the value of labour-power is the value of the means of subsistence necessary for the maintenance of its owner. [This phrase is literally false because it does not include the worker's 'production', only his maintenance; neither does it include the production of his offspring, which Marx adds later.] However, labour-power becomes a reality only by being expressed; it is activated only through labour. But in the course of this activity, i.e. labour, a definite quantity of human muscle, nerve, brain, etc. is expended, and these things have to be replaced. Since more is expended, more must be received. If the owner of labour-power works today, tomorrow he must again be able to repeat the same process in the same conditions as regards health and strength. [In agriculture, *tomorrow's work* can be several months away from today's work, but Marx's text refers to a chronological today and tomorrow, assuming a continuous work process.] His means of subsistence must therefore be sufficient to maintain him in his normal state as a working individual ... The owner of labour-power is mortal. *If then his appearance in the market is to be continuous*, and the continuous transformation of money into capital assumes this, the seller of labour-power must perpetuate himself 'in the way that every living individual perpetuates himself, by procreation' [Marx quotes Petty here – although the term *continuous* refers here only to intergenerational continuity, it is evident that the whole argument is based on the assumption of all types of continuity, which, for that reason, leaves agriculture out.] The labour-power withdrawn from the market by wear and tear, and by death, must be continually replaced by, at the very least, an equal amount of fresh labour-power. Hence, the sum of means of subsistence necessary for the production of labour-power must include the means necessary for the worker's replacements, i.e. his children, in order that this race of peculiar commodity-owners may perpetuate its presence on the market. [Here Marx omits the means of subsistence of those who look after children and perform domestic chores, without which there is no production of labour power.] Some of the means of subsistence, such as food and fuel, are consumed *every day, and must therefore be replaced every day.* Others, such as clothes and furniture, last for longer periods and need to be replaced only at longer intervals. Articles of one kind must be bought or paid for every day, others every week, others every quarter or so on. But in whatever way the sum total of these outlays may be spread over the year, they must be covered by the average income, taking one day with another. [When Marx says *every day* he underlines the *continuous* nature of human consumption, but does not see any problem here, because he is also assuming a *continuous* labour process and *continuous* payment.] (Marx 1976 [1867]: 274–6)

What happens when the *reality of discontinuous work in agriculture* is introduced into this theory of the value of labour power? Since talking about the labour power commodity obviously entails talking about capitalism, we would have to formulate the answer in terms of an economy with a significant agricultural sector in which all production is carried out based on capitalist rules.

11. Towards a valid theory of value for discontinuous work processes

In Volume II of *Capital*, Marx deals with the 'process of circulation of capital' and introduces a distinction between *working time* and *production time*, which, in the case of agriculture, is the other side of the coin of the seasonality of work, which, as I hold, is the main cause of the poverty and persistence of the peasantry. Chapters 20 and 21 of Volume II develop the Simple Reproduction Scheme (SRS) and the Reproduction on an Expanded Scale Scheme. I will use the SRS to answer the question about what happens when discontinuous working time is introduced into the labour value theory. Although, in this scheme, Marx assumes the absence of capital accumulation – thereby ignoring an essential feature of capitalism – the scheme shows the basic logic of reproduction of the capitalist system.

In order to formulate the SRS, Marx divides the economy into two sectors: Sector I, the producer of means of production; and Sector II, the producer of means of consumption. In each of them, the total value of production obtained is equal to the sum of the capital employed and the surplus value created (S). Marx divides the capital used into constant (C) and variable (V) capital. C represents that part of capital that is invested in the means of production – machinery, buildings, raw and auxiliary materials – and whose value is transferred only to the product; this explains why he calls it *constant*. For its part, V is the amount invested in hiring labour power; Marx calls this component of capital *variable* because *labour power is a commodity whose use value is the source of value* and, in the technical conditions of capitalism, of greater value than that which the labour power itself contains. Therefore, the total value (W_1) of the product in Sector I is equal to $C_1 + V_1 + S_1$, and that of Sector II is $W_2 = C_2 + V_2 + S_2$. W is therefore the sum of W_1 and W_2, C the sum of C_1 and C_2, and similarly for V and S. Every letter has a double meaning. On the one hand, it expresses part of the value of the product (meaning that, from this perspective, W *is the total supply*) and, on the other, it expresses the income of someone (V for the workers, S for the capitalists, while C is the income used to replace capital that has been worn out or used). In other words, in this sense, W *expresses the total demand*. Note that, by definition, total supply and demand are the same, as in national accounting, in which the national income is equal to the sum of consumption and investment. Marx assumes, in the SRS, that both workers and capitalists dedicate their entire income ($V + S$) to purchase the means of consumption and that the income represented by C is used entirely to replace the use or wear and tear on C. The system is therefore in a state of equilibrium and the production of value remains constant over time. Moreover, so that there is no disproportionality between the two sectors of production, C_2 must be the same as the sum of V_1 and S_1 ($C_2 = V_1 + S_1$),[14] since Sector II of the means of consumption needs to buy from Sector I of the means of production what it needs to replace the wear and tear on its means of production (C_2), while the capitalists and workers in Sector I need to buy means of consumption from Sector II for a sum equivalent to their income $(V_1 + S_1)$.

Despite the arguments about how alien the SRS is to capitalism, it shows *how capital is reproduced*. However, *it does not show how labour power is reproduced*. Human beings must satisfy their needs, whether or not they work. That is why, as I showed in the previous section with the long quote from Chapter IV of Volume I of *Capital*, reproduction not only includes those who work in exchange for a wage but also their children (and their spouses who look after the children and perform domestic work, although in the passage mentioned Marx forgets them). However, in principle, *if labour power is paid for according to its value and if work is continuous* (a person works all year, except for one day a week and other holidays, *which, however, are paid for without that person having to work*), *capital reproduction also entails that of the labour power* (and its families). But if work is not continuous, as in agriculture, the reproduction of capital does not entail that of labour power. If agriculture is capitalist, as it has to be in the SRS (which is a scheme in which capitalism is the only mode of production), the value of labour power in Sector II (means of consumption) – which is where we will place agriculture – will not be sufficient for the reproduction of the labour power. It will not be possible to achieve what Marx says: 'If the owner of labour power has worked *today*, he must work *tomorrow* to repeat the same process under the same conditions of vigour and health.' If we replace *today* with *during sowing time*, and *tomorrow* with *during the harvest*, we will see that seasonal work does not meet this condition, since at the end of the sowing time, the owner of labour power will lack the means to be able to subsist until harvest time. There will therefore be no available labour power for this task: the person who did the sowing will have died.

The SRS requires a third equation that will establish the condition for the year-round reproduction of the labour force and their families (365 days) in terms of the annual value of the means of subsistence for the number of workers and their families (N) in each sector, N_1 and N_2. Let us call the daily value of the labour force v. So V is equal to the product of v multiplied by 365 days and multiplied by N: $V = V_1 + V_2 = v365N$. *This third equation, which is necessary for the capitalist to find someone to exploit* in each productive cycle, *negates the theory of value* that states that the value of a commodity is equal to the socially necessary work incorporated in it. In other words, *the third, necessary equation is also impossible.* *This impossibility appears as the collapse of the theory of value,* which would be incapable of taking into account the reality of seasonal work in agriculture unless we modify it in such a way that the working time incorporated into the commodity is not just the live work incorporated by the worker during the days he works but also the value of his labour power during the days when he does not work each year. During the days when he does not work, he does not produce any new value but he transfers the value of the livelihood he consumes to the commodity he produces when he works, acting in a similar way to constant capital, like a machine or draught animal.

12. Towards a general theory of value

By divine mandate, stipulated in the Ten Commandments, virtually all over the world people work for six days yet are paid for seven; this was maintained even during the worst moments of over-exploitation of labour at the beginning of industrial capitalism. This is stipulated in Article 123 of the Mexican Constitution, which also establishes other days of compulsory rest and holidays. A significant portion of those who work today do so for five days a week and receive a salary (wage) for seven. School teachers receive a salary for twelve months of the year although they only work ten. Public university professors, in many countries, also enjoy a sabbatical year (after six years of work) during which they do not work and receive their full salary. These are discontinuities in work imposed by religious or social traditions or by trade union and political achievements. At the same time, no one works twenty-four hours a day, since the initial limit on a working day for any system of exploitation of another person's work is a natural, biological limit: human beings, like any animal, need to rest. However, the body continues to expend energy even when it is resting.[15] *Work is discontinuous but payment is continuous* in all the cases mentioned above. But wage workers in discontinuous work processes such as agriculture receive *discontinuous payment for their discontinuous work,* despite the fact that this discontinuity *is imposed by nature:* the biological process of plants, *which creates a radical asymmetry.*

Towards the end of the previous section, I showed that introducing an additional equation into Marx's Simple Reproduction Scheme to guarantee not only the reproduction of capital but also that of labour power and to consider discontinuous labour processes apparently destroys Marx's theory of value. The solution to this problem involves considering that, in addition to incorporating live work and therefore value, *labour power transfers to commodities the value of its labour power during the days when it does not work each year*. In this case, it does not create new value, but, when work starts up again, live labour transmits to the commodity being produced not only the value of the livelihood consumed during working days but also of the means consumed during days without work. In other words, during the 100 days of annual work, the agricultural worker transfers the value of his and his family's livelihood for 365 days a year. By denoting the agricultural sector with A and separating the value of labour power into two parts – the number of days worked (V_{AL}) and the number of those not worked (V_{AR}) – Marx's original expression for agriculture would be $W_A = C_A + V_{AL} + S_A$. With the proposed change, it would be $W_A + V_{AR} = C_A + (V_{AL} + V_{AR}) + S_A$. In other words, the capitalist pays additional wages V_{AR}, but sells the commodities produced at a value that has also been increased by V_{AR}. Surplus value (S_A) is not modified.

In areas with a continuous work process, V_{AR} is equal to zero and we are back to Marx's equations. The previous formula has therefore made it easier to shift from the theory of value for continuous work processes to a *general theory of value* that is valid for both continuous and discontinuous processes, one in which the reproduction equations not only express the conditions of the reproduction of capital but also those of labour power in a capitalist mode of production in which agriculture exists. One can infer from this that the only way for pure capitalism to prevail in agriculture is for capital to pay for the cost of the reproduction of labour power for the entire year and transfer this additional cost to consumers.

Can we really think that the worker transfers the value of his means of subsistence to the commodities he produces, like a machine or the raw materials incorporated into the labour process? If the answer is yes, can we think that the value of consumption for several days without work can be transferred to the commodity when work begins again? In section 9, I quoted the passage in which Marx sets out his theoretical explanation of the value of labour power. There we found expressions such as: production and reproduction (or maintenance) of labour power; the value of labour power represents only a set amount of average socially necessary labour objectified within it; during the work process, a person uses up a set amount of human muscle, nerves and brain that must be replaced; and the *continuous* presence of labour power is required in the market, which is why the sum of the means of subsistence includes those necessary for the substitutes (children) of the mortal worker. But can we speak of *production of labour power as a commodity*?[16] Even if we say yes, we cannot fail to note that, whereas soaps are produced in capitalist factories as commodities for sale with the aim of obtaining profits, labour power, which cannot be separated from its bearers – human beings – is not produced for sale. Instead, human beings procreate other human beings as a similar socio-biological process to that of other species. That is why continuing to speak of the *production of labour power* requires reference to the life process of individuals, to the satisfaction of needs, to couple formation and to the procreation and raising of offspring. We have to be aware *that the production of labour power is the other side of the family consumption of means of subsistence.* In the famous 'Introduction' to the *Grundrisse*, Marx says:

> Consumption is also immediately production, just as in nature the consumption of the elements and chemical substances is the production of the plant. It is clear that in taking in food, for example, which is a form of consumption, the human being produces his own body. But this is also true of every kind of consumption which in one way or another produces human beings in some particular aspect. *Consumptive production.*
> (Marx 1973 [written 1857–58; first published 1939]: 90–1)

What Marx says in this passage about use values, and about the link between human beings and nature, he takes up again in *Capital* as his theory of the value of labour power, as social relations. It is thus understandable that he writes about the *production of the value of the labour power commodity.*

13. Subsidies and poverty in peasant economies

In the everyday reality of peasants, the unequal labour requirements throughout the year in markets in which capitalist firms and peasants concur force peasant producers to complement the income from their plots of land with off-farm income in order to be able to fulfil their mission of reproducing the labour force. In some cases, this off-farm income accounts for over 50 per cent of their income (for example, in the state of Puebla, Mexico, or the north-western tableland of Guatemala) (de Janvry 1991: Table 10).

The numerical importance of peasants in Latin America (the number of units nationwide tends to be hundreds of thousands or, in some countries, millions) and their key role in production, particularly of basic foodstuffs, reflects the competitive structure of agricultural production. The deterioration of the terms of exchange between agriculture and urban sectors (national and international) contributes to (and exacerbates) a structural tendency towards extremely low agricultural relative prices in Latin America, compared with the prevailing ones in developed countries.

There seem to be three factors that explain the low relative prices of agricultural products in Latin American compared with those of the First World, both today and many decades ago: 1) the low effective protection of agriculture – in relation to industry – during the prolonged period of industrial import substitution; 2) the abrupt trade liberalisation of the 1980s and 1990s, which has led to the mass import of subsidised agricultural products from rich countries, which further depresses the general price level of agricultural products; and 3) the fact – centrally analysed in this paper – that peasants assume the year-round cost of labour reproduction, and are able to transfer to the prices of agricultural products only the labour cost of effectively worked days.

Regarding this last point, it seems obvious that, unlike Latin American peasants, family farmers in Europe, the United States and Japan (some of them are called peasants), insofar as their respective governments protect their agriculture from outside competition and/or grant them large subsidies, obtain sufficient income from the value added of their agricultural units for the reproduction of their families all year round, without being obliged to sell their labour in a temporary, itinerant and undignified manner. This could be interpreted as the fact that *their societies acknowledge family farmers' right to a minimum standard of living without the need to degrade their status by temporarily hiring out their labour*. These conditions, given the resources and technology, can be achieved only if the prices of their products are protected and/or subsidised, given the price-setting logic in markets where the peasant (and family farm) economy concurs with capitalist firms, which assume only the cost of labour effectively used. *When this right is not acknowledged, as happens in all Third World countries, peasants are condemned to permanent poverty.* A hypothetical numerical example might clarify the argument. Let us assume, for the sake of simplicity, that labour is used in maize production for a third of the days in a year (i.e. 122 days). Let us also assume that maize is the only crop and that both family and capitalist farmers use the same technological package. The only difference is that capitalist units hire wage labour per day while family producers perform all the tasks using family labour. Let us also assume that the salaries paid in agriculture are enough for the 'satisfaction of the material and cultural needs of the worker and his family and enable him/her to pay for his children's education' (as the Mexican Constitution defines minimum wages): in other words, that minimum wages are equal to the poverty line for an average-sized household. The cost of labour (by hectare) in the first case (where it is a fixed cost) would be three times higher than in capitalist agriculture. Since capitalist and family farmers coincide in the same market (let us first think of a closed market), the price is determined by the price at which the former are prepared to sell. Since the former pay for only the 122 days worked, they are prepared to sell the production of each hectare at $110 ($40 for input costs, $60 for labour and $10 of profits).[17] So family farmers are also forced to sell at $110, as if their labour were a third ($60 instead of $180 for labour, $40 for inputs and $10 of 'profits'), rather than $230 ($40 for the cost of inputs, $180 for the costs of maintaining labour and $10 of profits). They would sell at half their total cost. If only family producers took part in the maize market, then production would be sold at $220 (with no profit, which is unnecessary in family production), twice what they would obtain when they compete with capitalists. Since the poverty line is $180, by selling at $110 the family would be very poor. By selling at $220, the family would obtain a net income of $180 (discounting the $40 for input costs) and would be exactly on the poverty line. It would not be poor.

Through the hypothetical example above, I have shown that even if we eliminate (through assumptions) the other poverty factors of peasant producers (lower productivity than their capitalist competitors and labour valuation below the cost of satisfaction of basic needs), peasant families *will continue to be poor in a market where price levels are determined by the operating logic of capitalist firms.*

Although the assumptions that eliminate the other factors of peasant poverty are false in countries from the 'South', they are not in most of the developed world, including the countries of the then European Common Market when the Common Agricultural Policy (CAP) was implemented.

The enormous agricultural subsidies of the First World, which some have calculated at $360 billion annually, manage to prevent (most of) the poverty into which family farmers would be plunged without them. This poverty would not come from their low productivity or from an undervaluation of the work in their societies but solely from the seasonality of the productive process in agriculture. Without subsidies, European or Japanese peasants (and even American farmers) would have to seek off-farm work in cities or abroad, for many months of the year, to complete the income necessary for survival and reproduction. They would experience the itinerant poverty of Third World peasants.

One of the goals that the CAP sought to achieve was precisely to avoid farmers' poverty. According to the Buckwell Report (Buckwell 1997),[18] in most European Union (EU) countries agricultural producers' incomes *are on a par with the average income of urban households.*

With a series of enormous technological and financial obstacles to face international competition, peasants in Third World countries also face large differences in the support and subsidies they receive from their respective governments vis-à-vis farmers in the First World. Let's examine the Farm Security and Rural Investment Act (the Farm Bill of 2002), which expired in 2008. That Act replaced the Federal Agriculture Improvement and Reform Act of 1996 (the Fair Act of 1996), which was in force from 1996 to 2002.[19] These US laws are in fact multi-annual budget allocation mechanisms. The 2002 Act established subsidy programmes for specific products, international trade and conservation programmes, among others. The subsidy programme includes a 70 per cent to 80 per cent increase over the previous one.

The central component of this Act was anti-cyclical, meaning that American farmers were compensated for market fluctuations, so that they continued to receive high prices although prices may have slumped, which might have led to over-production. The international consensus, which led Mexico to eliminate guaranteed prices for farm products, is to eliminate farm subsidies that create incentives for over-production.

The 2002 Act included three types of subsidies:

1. *Fixed payments* per farmer for each eligible crop. Soya bean and certain oilseeds were added. Payments were higher than under the previous Act.
2. *Compensation payments* when the market price is lower than a price set by government. These are called loan rates, apparently because prices are set when the farm receives credits to sow crops. This countercyclical subsidy already existed in the previous Act but was increased by approximately 5 per cent and a few pulses were added to the list of eligible crops.
3. *New countercyclical subsidies*, which were paid when farmers' total income (the sum of what they obtained through the market plus the two previous subsidies) failed to achieve a predetermined level. Although the previous Act did not have a similar stipulation, the US government had introduced emergency packages in response to the drop in prices since 1998.

'What is wrong with countercyclical subsidies?,' asks the EU's electronic bulletin. First of all, it answers with a crucial statement in terms of the theory outlined here:

> *These payments guarantee the American farmer a certain level of income.* As its income is now guaranteed, the farmer does not need to follow the market signals, particularly in times of low prices. As guaranteed income means guaranteed profitability in almost every crop, farmers will expand production in marginal lands without worrying if the crop will find a market at a good price. The additional production will flood the market and prices will be further reduced (while income will be protected by growing subsidies of types 2 and 3). This is why the most important American commentators describe this policy as ultimately self-destructive.

With NAFTA (the North American Free Trade Agreement), which allows the US to export to Mexico as though it were in its own country, with no tariffs, exports to Mexico can obviously increase enormously without US farmers worrying about the price at which those exports are sold. They can sell at the same price as in the US. Of all the developing countries, Mexico is the most severely affected. In short, this Act meant that Mexico's US farm imports increased while its exports to the US decreased. It could potentially lead to the bankruptcy of many small, medium and large productive units. This would occur simply as a result of the play of market forces. However, the Act increased financing for programmes for the creation, expansion and maintenance of overseas markets for US farm products. The US export credits and the US subsidy programme for exports remain. The Organisation for Economic Co-operation and Development (OECD) has identified these subsidies as the source of 97 per cent of the world's farm subsidies and they have been condemned by the World Trade Organization as illegal, which has obviously not prevented their continued use.

In Mexico (and elsewhere in the Third World), peasant families live in abject poverty because: 1) their productivity levels are far below those of their competitors, namely Mexico's capitalist producers and US and Canadian producers; 2) labour power is undervalued in the country, particularly in rural settings; and 3) the cost of seasonality is paid almost exclusively by peasants. In order to overcome the poverty of family farmers, these three factors must be overcome. The productivity disadvantage can be offset through a combination of trade protection measures and the promotion of technological development. Manuel Díaz, an outstanding expert on agriculture in Mexico, points out that there is virtually no applied research on agricultural practices in Latin America, and that 'we only buy and misuse what is done in other countries' (personal communication). This was not the case in Mexico in the 1960s and 1970s. Whereas at that time there was a growing development of agricultural research, an agricultural advisory service (*extensionism*) and a protected agricultural market, conditions have been reversed.

The three central factors explaining the undervaluation of labour power in Mexico are: 1) the forces of globalisation that have reduced trade unions' coverage and power; 2) wage repression policy, which uses wages as an anchor for inflation; and 3) the slow growth of the economy and jobs in the modern economy. It is possible to implement significant changes that would reverse the tendencies of these three factors: a new wage policy, a reform of the Federal Labour Law to strengthen independent trade unionism, and an economic policy to encourage economic growth instead of the current one, obsessed as it is with inflation control.

Lastly, farmers must be subsidised and protected from external competition. In order to prevent resources allocated to subsidies from boosting the income of the most privileged farmers, family farmers must receive the total amount of subsidies designed to offset the cost of seasonality. Conversely, capitalist farmers would require only subsidies to deal with the asymmetry of international competition, and these subsidies would be common to all producers. Subsidies and trade protection must be complementary. The less protection there is, the more subsidies are required.

In a unified world market (which does not actually exist), without protectionist systems or subsidies, agricultural prices (and those of inputs and machinery) would be the same worldwide, while peasants' and farmers' income would be a function of the product generated. Income differences between peasants in the First and Third World would only be equal to the differences in productivity per man employed. However, the theory outlined here predicts – and this would have to be proved empirically – that income differences are much greater due to the fact that, whereas the economic policy of the *First World leads society as a whole to assume the cost of the seasonality of farm labour, that of the Third World continues to insist that this cost must be assumed by peasants only, thereby keeping them in poverty.*

The correct policy for Third World countries, if they wish to reduce rural poverty substantially, is therefore not to combat the agricultural subsidies of First World countries but to subsidise their peasants as well and to protect them from low foreign prices.

Notes

1 For space reasons, the original background paper has been abridged slightly.

2 See section 2 of the Introduction for a critical appraisal of the World Bank's and International Fund for Agricultural Development's estimates of world and rural poverty respectively.

3 The exploitation of peasants has been emphasised by, among others, Henry Bernstein (1982), who has coined the expression 'simple reproduction squeeze'.

4 It is very significant that both in English and Spanish a living vegetable and a factory are called by the same name – *plant* – a term that denotes a given location in both cases.

5 This section is limited to the economic perspective and does not

attempt to review the vast existing
literature. For such a review, see Teodor
Shanin (1973).

6 Although very little research
has been undertaken to evaluate the
common agricultural practice of mixed
crops, the research that has been
conducted favours the practice (see
Belshaw and Hall 1972: 20).

7 For an explanation of what *ejido*
means, see note 4 in Damián and
Pacheco's chapter in this book
(Chapter 6).

8 For a detailed analysis of this
theory, see Frederick V. Waugh (1970:
89–106).

9 Here Ellis cites the Mann–
Dickinson thesis, which I shall discuss
later on (Mann and Dickinson 1978).

10 Here Djurfeldt uses, probably by
mistake, neither the plural English word
latifundia nor the Spanish plural word
latifundios. Probably he wanted to use
the synonym of rich farmers in Spanish,
which is *latifundistas*. As this makes
more sense, I have changed it.

11 This theory, presented in section
4 above, had been conceived decades
ago. The first published version of this
approach was Boltvinik (1991).

12 Whereas absolute land rent is
the portion of rent that corresponds to
any unit, differential rent is associated
with differential agricultural yields
determined by the varying degrees of
land fertility. Insofar as these differences
cannot be overcome, sale prices must be
fixed at a level that makes production
in less fertile lands profitable, thereby
producing differential rent. Conversely,
productivity differentials in industry are
attributable to technological differences
which, while they last, produce
extraordinary surplus value, which
will disappear once more productive
technology becomes more widespread.
If agricultural producers in the best lands
are also the landowners, differential rent

will appear to them as a higher rate of
profit, higher than the one obtained by
capital in other branches, and thereby
interfering with the tendency towards
equalisation of the rates of profit
between capitals. Perhaps because of
this, Bartra says that this privilege of
agricultural capitals harms the remaining
capitals.

13 They cite two authors on this
but omit perhaps the most important
one – John Brewster – whose classic
article on the process of the machine in
agriculture and industry (1970 [1950]) I
have examined in section 5 above. He
argues that mechanised methods are as
compatible as manual techniques with
family or multifamily units.

14 Paul M. Sweezy (1970 [1942]:
76–7) derives this condition from two
obvious equations of equilibrium. First,
in order for all the production of means
of consumption to be sold, given the
assumption that capitalists and workers
spend all their income on consumption,
the total value of Sector II must be equal
to the income of capitalists and workers
from both sectors. In other words: $C_2 +
V_2 + S_2 = V_1 + S_1 + V_2 + S_2$. Second, in order
to only and exactly replace the capital
worn out or used in production, $(C_1 + C_2)$
must be equal to the value of production
in Sector I $(C_1 + V_1 + S_1)$. In other words,
$C_1 + C_2 = C_1 + V_1 + S_1$. Eliminating the terms
repeated on both sides of the equal
sign from both equations, one arrives at
the same result, and only the condition
mentioned in the text is required.

15 During sleep, our bodies operate
at the basal metabolic rate (BMR). The
daily expenditure of a 'dependent,
totally passive person' is equivalent to
1.27 times BMR, a value known as *survival
forecast*; this represents approximately
60 per cent of the energy expenditure
of someone performing a high-intensity
job and 80 per cent of that of someone
performing a low-intensity job.

16 Karl Polanyi (2001 [1944]: 75) defines commodities as objects produced for sale on the market. He says that 'work, land and money are not obviously commodities'. On work, he says that this 'is another name for the human activity that accompanies life itself and is produced for entirely different reasons'.

17 These figures are in fictitious units.

18 Available at http://ec.europa.eu/agriculture/publi/buck_en/index.htm.

19 This law was replaced in June 2008 by the Food, Conservation, and Energy Act of 2008, also known as the 2008 US Farm Bill. The law maintains the logic of agricultural subsidies of the previous law.

References

Bartra, A. (2006) *El Capital en su laberinto. De la renta de la tierra a la renta de la vida*. Mexico City: Itaca.

— (2007) 'El campesino en su laberinto', *La Jornada* (Mexico), 20 July.

Bartra, R. (1974) *Estructura agraria y clases sociales en México*. Mexico City: Ediciones Era.

Belshaw, D. and M. Hall (1972) 'The analysis and use of agricultural experimental data in tropical Africa', *East African Journal of Rural Development* 5 (1–2): 39–71.

Bernstein, H. (1982) 'Notes on capital and peasantry' in J. Harriss (ed.), *Rural Development: Theories of peasant economy and agrarian change*. London: Routledge, pp. 160–77.

Boltvinik, J. (1991) 'Presentación' in *Economía popular. Una vía para el desarrollo sin pobreza en América latina*. Regional Project to Overcome Poverty in Latin America. Bogotá: United Nations Development Programme, pp. vii–lv.

— (2007a) 'El capital en su laberinto', Columna Economía Moral, *La Jornada* (Mexico), 16 March.

— (2007b) 'Hacia una teoría de la pobreza campesina', *Papeles de Población* 13 (54): 23–38.

Brewster, J. (1970 [1950]) 'The machine process in agriculture and industry' in K. Fox and D. G. Johnson (eds), *Readings in the Economics of Agriculture*. London: Allen & Unwin.

Originally published in *Journal of Farm Economics* XXXII (1): 69–81.

Buckwell, A. (1997) 'Towards a common agricultural and rural policy for Europe'. Brussels: European Commission. Available at http://ec.europa.eu/agriculture/publi/buck_en/cover.htm.

Cepal (1982) *Economía campesina y agricultura empresarial. Tipología de productores del agro mexicano*. Mexico City: Siglo XXI Editores for Comisión Económica para América Latina y el Caribe (Cepal).

Chayanov, A. (1966) *The Theory of Peasant Economy*. Edited by D. Thorner et al. Chicago IL: Homewood Publishing.

Contreras, A. (1977) 'Límites de la producción capitalista en la agricultura', *Revista Mexicana de Sociología* 39 (3): 885–9.

de Janvry, A. (1991) 'El caso latinoamericano' in *Campesinos y desarrollo en América Latina*. Bogotá: Tercer Mundo Editores.

Djurfeldt, G. (1982) 'Classical discussions of capital and peasantry: a critique' in J. Harriss (ed.), *Rural Development: Theories of peasant economy and agrarian change*. London: Routledge, pp. 139–59.

Ellis, F. (1988) *Peasant Economics: Farm households and agrarian development*. Cambridge: Cambridge University Press.

Fox, K. and D. G. Johnson (eds) (1970) *Readings in the Economics of Agriculture.* London: Allen & Unwin.

Harriss, J. (ed.) (1982) *Rural Development: Theories of peasant economy and agrarian change.* London: Routledge.

Kautsky, K. (1988 [1899]) *The Agrarian Question.* 2 volumes. London: Zwan Publications. In Spanish: *La cuestión agraria.* Mexico City: Ediciones de Cultura Popular (1974).

Lenin, V. (1967 [1899]) *The Development of Capitalism in Russia.* Moscow: Progress Publishers.

Mann, S. A. (1990) *Agrarian Capitalism in Theory and Practice.* Chapel Hill NC: University of North Carolina Press.

Mann, S. A. and J. Dickinson (1978) 'Obstacles to the development of a capitalist agriculture', *Journal of Peasant Studies* 5 (4): 466–81.

Marx, K. (1972 [written 1857–58; first published 1939]) *Elementos fundamentales para la crítica de la economía política (Grundrisse) 1857–1858.* Volume 2. Mexico City: Siglo XXI Editores.

— (1973 [written 1857–58; first published 1939]) *Grundrisse: Introduction to the critique of political economy.* Harmondsworth, UK: Penguin Books.

— (1976 [1867]) *Capital: A critique of political economy.* Volume I. Harmondsworth, UK: Penguin Books.

— (1978 [1885]) *Capital: A critique of political economy.* Volume II. Harmondsworth, UK: Penguin Books.

Polanyi, K. (2001 [1944]) *The Great Transformation.* Boston MA: Beacon Press.

Shanin, T. (1973) 'The nature and logic of the peasant economy' (two articles), *Journal of Peasant Studies* 1 (1 & 2): 63–80, 186–206.

Sweezy, P. (1970 [1942]) *The Theory of Capitalist Development.* New York NY: Monthly Review.

Vergopoulos, K. (1978) 'Capitalism and peasant productivity', *Journal of Peasant Studies* 5 (4): 446–65.

Waugh, F. (1970) 'Cobweb models' in K. Fox and D. G. Johnson (eds), *Readings in the Economics of Agriculture.* London: Allen & Unwin.

2 | RETHINKING RUSTIC ISSUES: CONTRIBUTIONS TO A THEORY OF CONTEMPORARY PEASANTRY

Armando Bartra

1. Introduction

Modernity has always tried to rid itself of its strange bedfellow – the stubborn peasant world. It has attempted to do so in two ways: by eroding rustic spheres demographically and socio-economically and by celebrating the supposed remission of rural barbarity at the level of discourse.

I will not retell the well-known story of how the urban-industrial sphere expanded at the expense of the rural agrarian and how industrial agriculture gradually replaced family farms.[1] At the discourse level, however, it does not hurt to recall the praise of de-ruralisation in that hymn to modernity, Karl Marx and Friedrich Engels' *Communist Manifesto*:

> The bourgeoisie has subjected the country to the rule of the towns. It has created enormous cities, has greatly increased the urban population as compared with the rural, and has thus rescued a considerable part of the population from the idiocy of rural life. Just as it has made the country dependent on the towns, so it has made barbarian and semi-barbarian countries dependent on the civilised ones, nations of peasants on nations of bourgeois, the East on the West. (Marx and Engels n.d. [1848]: 39)

Conversely, a century and a half later, the World Bank, the spokesperson for global capitalism, called for the reactivation of agricultural production and the return of peasants:

> Structural adjustment in the 1980s dismantled the elaborate system of public agencies that provided farmers with access to land, credit, insurance, inputs, and cooperative organisations. The

expectation was that removing the state would free the market for private actors to take over these functions – reducing their costs, improving their quality, and eliminating their regressive bias. Too often, that didn't happen. In some places the state's withdrawal was tentative at best, limiting private entry. Elsewhere, the private sector emerged only slowly and partially – mainly serving commercial farmers but leaving many smallholders exposed to extensive market failures, high transaction costs and risks, and service gaps. Incomplete markets and institutional gaps impose huge costs in forgone growth and welfare losses for smallholders, threatening their competitiveness and, in many cases, their survival. (World Development Report 2008: 138)

A prosperous smallholder sector is one of the cornerstones of an agriculture-for-development strategy. (ibid.: 153)

In the origin of the lack of coincidence between the expectations of two such conspicuous agents of modernisation as the founders of 'scientific socialism' and the 'global banker' of capitalism lies the fact that the latter speaks from the vantage point of the Great Crisis. Not merely the economic recession that started in 2008 but the multidimensional debacle that includes climate change, energy astringency, food dearth and revolutions ...

It is the depth of a collapse that is turning out to be epochal, that brings the agricultural sphere and smallholders who, until recently, had resisted in the shadows back to the fore. Some of the solutions to the lack of environmental sustainability – the agro-ecological and food crisis, the depletion of petroleum, social necrosis and the disrepute of short-sighted rationalism – require a reappraisal of the countryside and peasants as to their productive potential, their role as a moral reserve and a civilising inspiration.

At the present historical crossroads, I think it is useful to rethink rustic issues in a comprehensive fashion in regard to their many, interwoven dimensions. I differentiate between these aspects only for exposition purposes.

2. Peasants and technology: creating the *milpa* (maize mixed field)

In *El hombre de hierro* (Bartra 2008) and other texts, I have questioned the Prometheism shared for over two centuries by the apologists of capitalism and most of its critics; not their legitimate attempt to humanise nature but the idea that history is a single, fatal, rising course we take, driven by the always progressive 'development of productive forces'. This questioning, which is not new, is relevant because the debacle of modernity includes the plausible disrepute of short-sighted rationalism and instrumental thought, of the techno-science based on them, as well as the unsustainable patterns of profit-driven production and consumption supported by the reductionist paradigms of much modern science. The importance of this questioning increases when we realise that the multifaceted collapse of civilisations at the turn of the millennium is, in essence, a scarcity crisis expressed in the rarefaction of the natural and social premises on which human life depends.

It is precisely the scientific and technological dimension of the Great Crisis that leads me to reappraise the virtues of the theoretical and practical holism of peasant production, whose strategies are integral, extremely plastic and diversified in time and space. I am certainly not suggesting an impossible technological regression to the Neolithic era. Conversely, I do propose the recovery of certain models of production and consumption developed by the great agricultural cultures that might be inspirational for the replacement paradigms demanded by the evidence that the universalisation of the recipes for industrial agriculture is unsustainable. Thus, in the Mesoamerican *milpa* or maize field, the Caribbean *conuco* or smallholding, and the vertical 'management' of the agro-ecological floors of the Andes, among other examples of mixed cropping, I find a paradigm that is not only agro-ecological but also civilising.

Mesoamericans do not sow corn, we create *milpas*.[2] These are different things because maize is a plant, the *milpa* a lifestyle: the *milpa* is the matrix of Mesoamerican civilisation. Planted alone, maize is monotony, while the *milpa* is variety: in it, maize, beans, peas, broad beans, squash, chilli, vegetable pears, wild tomatoes, amaranth, fruit trees, nopal, century plants and the varied fauna that accompany them all intermingle. What distinguishes equinoctial regions from countries with cold or cool climates is that the latter plant seeds, whereas we create *milpas*. They produce their food in homogeneous plantations whereas we, when they let us continue our agro-ecological vocation, harvest them in baroque gardens.

From another perspective, the *milpa* farmer appears as an anti-systemic paradigm, since capitalism is synonymous with specialisation and homogeneity, as well as with the separation between the countryside and the city. In short, capitalism is industrial development at the expense of agriculture. Moreover, subjected to the market and purely profit-driven, big money is obsessed with increasing productivity through standardised technologies that are always being rapidly renewed. In contrast, the *milpa* field is the stronghold of natural and social diversity that is always resistant to the standardising model of industrial agriculture.

It is true that single crops have had some success in large, cool, easily mechanised plains, but success turns to failure when the northern paradigm bursts into equinoctial regions where the lack of climatic fluctuation encourages a wide variety of ecosystems, meaning that extreme specialisation is disruptive and eventually suicidal. Creating *milpas* is culture. But it is a cultural fact derived from natural conditioning.

The strength of the *milpa* lies not in the individual productivity of each of the plants comprising it but rather in the synergetic harmony of the whole. Its effectiveness comes not from its parts but from its interconnections, from its haphazard symbiosis. It draws its strength from its diverse solidarity, a crucial resource at times of anthropogenic climate change, when uncertainty is the only certainty.

Unlimited, extravagant, excessive, baroque: this is how the *milpa* is perceived from the simplistic classicism of single cropping, which sees confusion where complexity prevails. In a more profound sense, the *milpa* is baroque in that, although its parts are heterogeneous, they are inseparable from the whole. It is also baroque because, like the aesthetic paradigm from which the concept is taken, it is not uniform but adopts different modalities according to places and times. And like Latin American baroque, the *milpa* is syncretic, polluted and hybrid, a mestizo agrosystem into which agricultural species and practices of different origins have been incorporated.

Maize can be planted alone or with other plants, on newly broken ground or on ploughed land ready for sowing. It can be planted on a slope or on terraced land, and it can be found in sophisticated irrigation systems such as the *chinampa* or in the high-yield *calmil* fertilised with household waste. This multiplicity of ways of planting this graminaceous plant is part of the virtuous, intermingled diversity

I call *milpa*. Since this broad concept is not reduced to plots of land, it can include large maize fields and other specialised sown fields, if they are articulated into a diverse, holistic, sustainable whole where pluralistic forms of cultivation are adapted to agro-ecological conditions and meet socio-cultural needs.

A plausible productive strategy, the *milpa* and its kin are also a paradigm of good life shared by many farming peoples precisely because the way livelihoods are obtained translates into a worldview, and, in Mesoamerican and Andean cultures, the *milpa*, the *conuco* and ecological floors planted with crops are idiosyncratic spaces.

Old Mesoamerica was undoubtedly no paradise – the Mexica, for example, were openly imperialistic. But they were also respectful of the cultural diversity of tributary peoples and even adopted some of their gods, meaning that, on the arrival of the Spaniards, they found it easy to accept that they had another religion, but not that they should wish to impose it. Alonso de Zurita writes about this in his *Breve y sumaria relación de los señores de la Nueva España* (quoted in Katz 1966: 148): 'the Mexica kings ... in all the provinces they conquered ... allowed the lords to remain in their domains ... and allowed them to continue their habits and forms of government'. Why should one not assume that the *milpa* paradigm lies behind the pluralistic and tolerant features of pre-Colombian tributary despotism?

'The worldview,' as López Austin said in 'El núcleo duro, la cosmovisión y la tradición mesoamericana', 'derives primarily from everyday activities ... of the group, which, in its management of nature and its social dealings, integrates collective representations and creates patterns of behaviour' (López 2001: 62). And in *Tamoachan y Tlalolcan*, he expands the concept:

> On the agricultural nucleus of a worldview, it is possible to create other constructions ... resulting from individualised ... reflexive intellectual effort. However, the main principles, the basic logic of the complex always lay in agricultural activity, which is one of the reasons why the traditional worldview is so powerful today. (López 1995: 16)

The knowledge and practices that have their roots in tradition are a 'science of the concrete', as Lévi-Strauss would say in the *Savage Mind*, an 'early' rather than a 'primitive' science, no less penetrating than conventional academic disciplines: a 'wild' reflection which, according to the famous ethnologist, 'continues to be the substrate of our civilisation' and is now 'liberating' in that it shows the limits of positivist science (Lévi-Strauss 1972: 43).

For over 500 years, the *milpa* paradigm as a traditional worldview has resisted Western rationalism based on analytical decomposition, linear causality and specialised strategies, due, above all, to the fact that the thinking of original peoples operates within a different sphere to that of the invader. Whereas positivist rationalism is a scientific discourse transmitted through abstractions, the profound worldview is both myth and rite, alternative discourse and practice, produced and reproduced on the basis of everyday experience and productive work.

The words of the grandson of Netzahualcoyotl and the chieftain of Texcoco, Carlos Ometchtzin, are an intercultural declaration that is still valid nearly five centuries later:

> And so each of our ancestors had their gods and their costumes and their way of sacrificing and making offerings and we must have them and follow them as our ancestors ... See that friars and clerics have their own manner each ... The same was true of those who preserved our gods, because those of Mexico have a particular way of dressing and praying and offering and fasting and other peoples had another ... Let us follow what our ancestors had and followed and let us live as they did. (quoted in González 2009: 74–5)

Because of his subversive expressions of multiculturalism, inspired perhaps by the virtuous diversity of the *milpa*, Carlos Ometochtzin, also known as Chichimecatecuhtli, was subjected to an auto-da-fé and burned alive on 30 November 1539.

3. Peasants and economy: the return of differential rent

The economic facet of the Great Crisis reflects the enormous speculative-rentier irrationality of a capitalism that treats man, nature and money as commodities – which they are not – in an extreme form of commodification that in one case erodes productive capital and in another society and ecosystems. This ominous, catastrophic depredation calls to seek a different, less self-destructive productive rationality, a virtuous logic which, despite the wear and tear to which it has historically been subjected, persists in rustic ecology and in the moral economy of certain agrarian communities. However, the constant calls to bring back domestic production do not respond to its socio-environmental sustainability but rather to its capacity to survive at a disadvantage.

A few years ago, I showed that one of the reasons for the persistence and reproduction of small and medium peasant agriculture in capitalism was that the diverse and climatically voluble natural base of agricultural production produced large differential rents that substantially increased the total cost that the rest of capital had to pay for harvests (Bartra 2006: 95–132). This fact created a distortion in the distribution of surplus value that was attenuated or reversed if the part of production with the highest costs was taken to market by family producers whose harvests could be systematically underpaid, since their suppliers continued producing even without profits in order to obtain a subsistence income. If it is true, this thesis would explain why, during the second half of the twentieth century, the reduction of differential rents resulting from the increase in the supply of intensive agriculture based on the trend towards homogeneous industrial agriculture led to the consistent regression of peasant agriculture. Conversely, the return of differential rent at the start of the twenty-first century, resulting from the impetuous expansion of the agricultural frontier in order to increase the agricultural supply, which is being reached by demand, suggests that one can expect a new expansion – restricted to certain areas and products – of small and medium family production.

I will now return to my previous line of argument. I think that this approach has hardly been explored, just as the implications of territorial rent, discussed by several authors during the early stages of capitalism, have only barely been dealt with. The different yields that involve an equal investment of labour in agriculture, in which the productive process is more prolonged than the labour process and results in the discontinuity of the latter, along with the difficulties of speeding up an activity that is subject to natural climatic and biological cycles, reveal the existing tensions between capitalist rationality and the behaviour of nature, which, when properly examined, demonstrate the ultimate incompatibility between capitalism and nature. However, a man as concerned with environmental issues as John Bellamy Foster (2004: 224–9; Foster and Magdoff 2000: 48) underestimates the importance of differential rent by assuming the old hypothesis of James Anderson (1859), in the sense that progressive agricultural investments would even out productivity, eliminating differential rent; this is equivalent to saying that natural diversity ends up surrendering to technological uniformity. I find Susan Archer Mann's approach more sophisticated (1990: 28–46). She correctly links the productive diversity expressed in rent to the limitations faced by capitalism in agriculture in attaining what Karl Marx called the 'real subsumption' of labour by capital. However, I think that, in order to understand peasants' insertion into the system of big money, one must distinguish between what I have called 'a material subsumption', which involves the technological shaping of the productive process to adapt it to the logic of capital, which may be achieved while formally maintaining the independence of the direct producer, from what Marx calls 'real subsumption', which involves both formal and material (technological) subordination of labour to capital.

★ ★ ★

During the second half of the twentieth century, the historical tendency towards increasing food production and the consequent drop in prices was linked to the generalisation of the technological package associated with the 'Green Revolution'. Irrigation, mechanisation, improved seeds, fertilisers, herbicides and pesticides increase technical and economic yields. Since they are oriented towards replacing agro-ecological potentialities with inputs of industrial origin, they reduce the productivity differential associated with the varying quality of natural resources (soil fertility, quantity and regularity of rain, water availability, climate, etc.).

By reducing the differences between the average cost of a crop and the higher costs involved in harvesting the amounts required by markets, this increase in productivity also erodes the economic basis of differential rent. This derives precisely from the differences in productivity coexisting within the same crop and is expressed in the requirement that investment in land with lower yields (and higher cost per unit of product) has to be profitable as well, which, in free market and purely entrepreneurial supply conditions, raises the prices of agricultural products in direct proportion to these differences in productivity. This extra payment to agriculture, captured by capitals with agro-ecological advantages, may by offset by different means, such as underpaying the most expensive production, often undertaken by family producers with a subsistence orientation rather than a business approach. But regardless of whether this overpayment to agriculture is neutralised or not, the economic basis for differential rent lies in the cost differentials that must be assumed to fully meet demand.

From this perspective, the trend towards an increase in production and agricultural productivity with yields that, if not homogeneous, were less diverse (whereby agriculture was progressively assimilated into the industrial model based on manufactured means of production, barely subjected to the diversity and variability of natural resources) worked in the direction of reducing and – in the last instance of eliminating differential rent – making agriculture a conventional branch of production.

In recent years, however, the historical tendency of agricultural food production has been modified and we now have growing prices and potential conditions of scarcity. This is the case of wheat, maize, rice and oilseed prices, which in turn affect meat and dairy prices. This new situation goes beyond the current circumstances, since it originates in the combination of various deep-rooted tendencies: on the one hand, the constant loss of fertility, and the shifting of the agricultural frontier towards uncultivated lands with lower potential and less water availability; on the other, by a consistent increase in demand, driven not only by demographic growth but by the change in eating habits towards meat and dairy products. This change leads to an increase in the use of grain for forage but is also caused by the rapid increase in the industrial use of harvests, particularly in agrofuel production.

Unlike what happened a few decades ago, these practices promote a rapid increase in the amount of land under cultivation. Consequently, high yields in places whose agro-ecological conditions are optimal are accompanied by the persistence and expansion of crop fields with lower yields in land that is difficult to manage and has low natural fertility. All this is expressed in a growing production cost differential in different portions of the same product, which expands the economic base of differential rent.

Without being exceptional, the case of Mexico is paradigmatic as, based on the assumption that peasants are naturally inefficient and that from the perspective of comparative advantages the country does not have a vocation as a cereal producer, successive government policies since the 1980s have insisted on dismantling the institutional apparatus that just about made the rain-fed small and medium production of basic grains feasible. The result was a shift from food self-sufficiency to dependence, which in recent years has totalled 67.9 per cent in rice, 42.8 per cent in wheat, 8.2 per cent in beans and 31.9 per cent in maize. Maize imports would be even larger if it were not for the fact that a group of agrobusinessmen in the north-east with irrigated land and public subsidies use intensive technology and high yields to produce nearly 30 per cent of the white maize for human consumption.

The global food price increases that have existed since 2007 with fluctuations, particularly during the severe drought and early frosts Mexico faced in 2011, aggravated the problems of basic grain production and supply, lending credence to the proposals that, from various spheres, raised the need to reactivate and expand peasant production of cereals and pulses in the south-east. Antonio Turrent, a National Emeritus Researcher affiliated to the National Institute of Forestry, Agricultural and Livestock Research (INIFAP), declares that there are enough resources in the country to be able to overcome the food shortage:

> Approximately 9 million ha [hectares] of agricultural quality land in ... in the southeast ...; there is also freshwater that has not been used for irrigation, in quantities that virtually double the current capacity of all the reservoirs in the country ...; genetic diversity of native crops ...; an exceptional climate and a majority peasant sector whose productive potential has been gratuitously and unjustifiably excluded from promotion programs. (Turrent 2012)

The same has been said by Víctor Manuel Villalobos, Director of the Inter-American Institute for Cooperation on Agriculture (IICA): 'The future lies in the south and southeast of the country, where there is an abundance of water and fertile soil. It is no longer possible to make large investments in the north ... We have our backs to the wall because ... small-scale agriculture has been ignored' (quoted in Pérez 2012).

However, restoring food security by reactivating regions, forms of production and types of producers who have been marginalised by betting on the industrial agriculture of the north and north-east also means expanding the range of yields and production costs required to meet demand, thereby increasing differential rents and, on this base, speculative rents. The only way to prevent the growing productive diversity entailed by the expansion of the agricultural border from further increasing prices and increasing the already enormous super-profits obtained by privileged producers is to encourage peasant agriculture, both family and associative, and the state regulation of production and marketing. This might lead one to expect similar scenarios to those seen in Latin America during the time of the Alliance for Progress. I will deal with this issue in the following section.

* * *

The economist José Antonio Rojas Nieto (2011) has explored the issue of the rents generated in primary activities such as agriculture:

> In the market in the midst of the process of obtaining an average profit, transfers of value within branches ... tend to be lower. This is not true of production derived from the exploitation of natural resources, since the spread of technology in agricultural, mining, fishing, forest and petroleum production, among others, does not eliminate the essential influence of fertility and location.

This economist goes on to exemplify the enormous differences in productivity that exist between the wheat produced by France, Egypt and the United Kingdom and the wheat harvested in China, India and the United States. He also notes the case of rice, where the difference in yield between its two largest producers, China and India, is 100 per cent. He ends by describing the well-known differences in oil productivity that favour countries in the Persian Gulf. 'These enormous differences explain the rents,' sustains Rojas, 'which reflect significant international transfers from industrial spheres to those of primary products' (ibid.).

As David Ricardo well knew, the key to rent is scarcity. 'The labour of nature is paid not because it yields much but because it yields little,' he said in his *Principles of Political Economy*. 'In proportion as nature becomes niggardly in her gifts, she exacts a greater payment for her work' (Ricardo 1959 [1817]: 70). And as a scarcity crisis, the great civilising debacle is the best of all possible worlds for a Neronian rentier capitalism, which earns more the worse the disaster and the greater the natural and social rarefaction, which it causes itself.

★ ★ ★

In short: the historical tendency towards the growing production of foods at falling prices, in addition to the fact that the increase in yields was originated in technological resources relatively independent of agro-ecological diversity, pointed to a consistent reduction of differential rent, since the difference between average and maximum costs tended to shrink. However, the increase in demand due to food needs – but also because of fodder and industrial needs – together with the loss of fertility and pressure on the land and water point to a recovery of differential rent, since land with lower yields will be cultivated and the difference between average and maximum costs will tend to increase.

Two scenarios could lead to the recovery of the cost differential. Either prices are set at the high cost level and producers with lower costs obtain super-profits, which assumes that society as a consumer is obliged to make an extra payment which the capitals that participate in the sector appropriate in an unequal fashion. Or, more likely, the cost differential becomes the basis of a bargaining for increased profits, as a result of which consumers have to pay more, but over-profit does not reach primary production. Rather, the oligopsony that buys, transforms and markets agricultural products divides up the profits, excluding small and medium farmers.

4. The place of peasants in the development model: 'bimodal agriculture' again?

If territorial rent increases and threatens to be triggered by the Great Crisis (since, as Ricardo knew, rents flourish when scarcity prevails), we can expect a re-emergence of alternatives vis-à-vis a serious overpayment that will pillage society as a whole, including capitals not linked to agricultural business.

It is no coincidence, then, that even in the discourse of multilateral organisations, state intervention in food production should be under discussion once again. In addition, as happened over half a century ago, emphasis is being placed on the technological and economic updating of peasant production.

The point is that, unlike agribusiness, which can push successfully for a price rise, small and medium family producers that operate using the logic of subsistence could be forced to work on marginal lands and unprofitable crops: in other words, with low or no profits. Because of their agro-ecological knowledge and knowledge of polycrops, they have an almost miraculous ability to overcome losses due to natural disasters, an extremely useful skill during times of climate change and environmental uncertainty. If that were not enough, they are able to use income diversification strategies to absorb the idle time characteristic of agricultural activity (Bartra 2006: 120–3).

At first sight, we would seem to be faced with two mutually exclusive, opposing strategies. Indeed, one might think that the neo-peasant strategy of multilateral organisations and the practice of monopolising lands – a practice in which countries, transnational companies and investment funds are deeply involved – are pointing in different directions. The latter involves the essentially rentier, predatory, untenable model characteristic of industrial agriculture based on single crop farming, agrochemicals and transgenic seeds. The former involves diversified small and medium peasant production based on the family, the agrarian community and associative enterprises that use environmental, sustainable technologies and are supported by the state through promotion policies.

However, rather than alternative, incompatible methods, we are faced with the possibility that a dual agricultural model will once again be configured – a bimodal agricultural model by 'developmentalism' (*desarrollismo*), such as the one promoted in the subcontinent during the second half of the twentieth century by the Economic Commission for Latin America and the Caribbean (ECLAC), sheltered by the Alliance for Progress and implemented through agrarian reforms, agricultural extension and the promotion of the Green Revolution technological package.

But despite the dominant discourse of that time favouring family agriculture, it did not in fact try to promote a peasant path of rural development; rather, it encouraged the expansion of private agribusiness in highly profitable land and crops destined for global markets, and promoted small and medium agriculture devoted to national and local markets only on marginalised lands and with less profitable crops.

In an order dominated by the accumulation of capital, the preservation and even promotion of a peasant sector of agricultural production does not indicate social sensitivity, nor is it a political concession, but rather a cold, economic calculation. It has been proven that small and medium agriculture restricted to certain spheres of production may be functional to big money. Its advantages for the system lie in its unusual capacity to cope with climatic and economic uncertainty and endure the worst drops in prices, and its ability to continue operating in conditions of scarcity and to be particularly efficient when forced to work with fragile resources. Moreover, mixed cropping and productive diversification make it possible to take full advantage of families' natural and labour resources. The peasant mode of production is particularly suitable for operating in agro-ecological and economic conditions that would be unfavourable for intensive agribusiness: marginalised environments where families can not only produce for personal consumption but also create large surpluses of food products – and also, through some types of agriculture by contract, raw materials designed for the globalised agro-industry and agro-food trade.

Common until a few decades ago, a peasant sector like the one described, which by definition is subject to mechanisms of unequal exchange on the market, is always on the verge of decapitalisation and ruin. That is why its preservation is a state responsibility. By promoting peasant production, particularly food production for the internal market, it will cheaply and efficiently resolve the difficulties posed by permanent food shortages for the non-agricultural sectors of capital.

In essence, the fact that the functionality of such a bimodal agriculture – with an agribusiness operating on the land with the greatest potential and in the most attractive products, and a peasant sector located on marginalised land with unprofitable crops – should be preserved or reconstituted is based on the disparity between productivity levels caused by the diverse, scarce nature of the natural resources required in agriculture. At the bottom of conservative *neocampesinismo* is differential rent.

A dual or bimodal agriculture in which modern and traditional peasant agribusinesses coexist may be more desirable for everybody

– including myself – than a rurality in which smallholders and communities have been totally eliminated. But, in any case, it is essential to acknowledge the fact that it is an asymmetric, unfair duality that reproduces internal colonialism. There is the risk of the solidification of a perverse combination of leasing latifundia, engaged in intensive single cropping destined for the external market, with family agriculture that promotes diversified, small-scale production for the internal market. A perverse combination of predatory, ecocidal agribusinesses with sustainable, agro-ecological peasants. A rural freak where, in asymmetrical symbiosis, large, globally run, profit-driven capitals, focusing on cost–benefits and sponsored by megacorporations, coexist with community peasants locally managed, motivated by the *buen vivir* ('good living') ideal, respectful of the Pachamama (Mother Land) and protected by 'cooperation'.

It may be that the call by multilateral organisations to promote small and medium production is purely discursive or that it feeds into a tributary current which is barely marginal within the foreseeable agricultural expansion led by transnational companies and agribusiness. But no less of a threat is posed by the fact that history may repeat itself and peasants may once more be yoked to a modernising model dominated by the logic of capital, as happened in the mid-twentieth century in Latin America. This track has already made evident its limits and costs.

The World Bank, the International Monetary Fund and Food and Agriculture Organization of the United Nations have said that the state must promote the necessary agricultural recovery, with emphasis to be placed on small and medium producers. However, the solution to the food problem and progress towards an economically fairer society cannot be achieved only by relaunching the social sector of production. Rather, the results depend on how this sector is linked to the entrepreneurial economy and the public sector, agents that, due to their hegemonising nature, tend to subsume, instrumentalise and exploit peasants.

In the paradigm promoted by Cepal (ECLAC: the United Nations Economic Commission for Latin America and the Caribbean) during the second half of the twentieth century, there was room for family agriculture that produced consumer goods destined for the internal market and raw materials for agro-industry and export. But its development was at the service of the accumulation of industrial capital: a strategic sector to which it was obliged to contribute cheap food and raw materials and to which it was forced to transfer trained labour, and which it was obliged to serve as a market. All this took place within a scheme of modernisation in which industry imposed itself over agriculture and the city over the countryside.

Small and medium mercantile peasant production (simple commodity production) has already been promoted in the past but with an iniquitous model that should not be repeated. And in order to avoid this, one would have to alter the paradigms of agricultural development in a metamorphosis that involves broader concepts and entails the critical review of 'developmentalism' (*desarrollismo*) as an ideology and of the concept of development itself.

In fact, this is already happening in countries such as Bolivia, where the new Constitution speaks of a 'plural' economy in which large-scale private enterprises based on a capitalist logic coexists with family and community production whose rationality is well-being and with a state sector that must pave the way for post-neoliberal development whose aim is the construction of an unprecedented 'community socialism' based on the paradigm of *buen vivir*.

The social subjects behind this project are the peasant Indians (*campesindios*), and what will determine the course of events is their capacity – or otherwise – to make the shift from resistance in local forms of sociality and economies to the construction of a new kind of national economy and an unprecedented multinational state. This is a challenge that peasants and their communities have never faced in their long history: experts in surviving the exactions of iniquitous, expansive systems, but whose *ethos* has so far been of a regional scope and never – not even as a project – a world system of globalising vocation.

5. The peasant in his labyrinth: a polemic

In 'Outline of a theory of poverty and the survival of the peasantry. Polemic with Armando Bartra', Julio Boltvinik (2009) takes up a debate in which we engaged in *La Jornada* newspaper in March and April 2008. What follows is a summary of my positions at the time as well as the development – in a controversial way – of the reasoning explained in the previous paragraphs regarding the current persistence of family agriculture.

* * *

The possibility of exploiting peasants – understood in the economic sense as rural workers whose survival strategy includes, to a certain extent, self-employment – lies in the qualitative disadvantage with which they are inserted into the market. Since they are not soulless free capital but rather passionate social cells, they buy and sell in order to subsist and, if possible, progress, not only in order to obtain profits. Their difference from labourers, who have to sell their labour in order to live, which is where the labourer is 'strung up', lies in the fact that peasants also purchase inputs and sell products in addition to being employed as day workers, and in all these exchanges the peasant is 'strung up'. In short, the exploitation of the peasant is polymorphous in the same way as his existence is pluri-functional.

I agree, then, with Julio: the fact that the peasant/day worker absorbs the costs of the seasonality of agricultural work, both by working temporarily in agribusiness and because the price he receives for his harvests does not make up for idle time, is a substantial aspect of exploitation. I do not, however, agree that it is 'the fundamental aspect of his exploitation' or that peasant survival can be explained 'more' by this function than by others.

But the difference between us lies less in the diagnosis than in the medicine, since Julio considers that, '[t]he correct policy for Third World countries' includes subsidising peasants, so that 'family farmers will receive all the subsidies designed to offset the cost of seasonality'. In contrast, I believe that subsidies are not bad but that the fundamental solution does not lie in compensating for idle time, which is derived not only from natural cycles but also from specialisation and single cropping, but in returning to the diversified strategies whereby all earlier agrarian societies coped both with the discontinuous demand for labour in plant raising and with the need to make full use of the diversity of available natural and human resources.

I wrote the following:

> The fundamental solution (*to the problem of the seasonality of work*) lies in the diversified use of land that enables peasants to rationalise the use of both natural resources and their capacity for work ... The multiplicity of technologies and the interconnected diversity of uses – are imposed both by the plurality of ecosystems and by time and space limits of labour capacity. (Bartra 2006: 26)

For example, the fundamental solution to the labour problem posed by the enormous Cuban sugar cane production was not to support cane cutters all year long, or to replace some of them with voluntary workers, or to partially replace them with machinery. The true remedy was to do away with the economically, socially and environmentally predatory single cropping imposed in the Caribbean as a result of the Conquest. In this respect, the real Cuban Revolution did not start in 1959 or 1961 but nearly half a century later when the colonial agro-export model eventually began to be dismantled.

To return to the beginning, in the introduction to *Capital in its Labyrinth* (Bartra 2006), I do not say that differential rent disappeared and, with it, peasants' reason for existence. I do say that with innovations such as genetic engineering and nanotechnology, capitalism *believes* it has achieved its dream of turning agriculture into another branch of industry. And I also sustain that this is not so, but that by moving from latifundia to transgenics – in other words, from land rent to life rent – capitalism places human survival at risk.

And this leads me to extend the debate to 'ecological arguments', which Julio has ignored for the moment, since, in my view, the 'persistence of peasants' as a living legacy, as capitalist re-creation and as a utopia does not refer as much to derived economic phenomena – such as land rent and the cost of seasonally hired labour – as it does to the radical contradiction between big money and the reproduction of nature: a terminal antagonism pointed out by Marx in *Capital* (1964 [1867, 1885, 1894]), taken up by Polanyi in *The Great Transformation* (2003 [1944]) and emphasised by modern ecologists such as James O'Connor in *Natural Causes* (2001), to mention a few authors.

The fact that when capitalism operates in agriculture it distorts the price formation mechanism, is a comparatively minor issue. The big problem is that the frenzied pace and the technological homogeneity imposed by mercantile absolutism 'upset the social metabolism' (Marx) and are environmentally untenable. So peasants are much more than a means of lowering rents and reducing labour costs – they reveal the need to modify the patterns of the relationship between society and nature and prefigure an environmentally sustainable and socially fair order, where, rather than trying to even it out at all costs, the preserved natural diversity gives rise to technological, economic, societal and cultural diversity.

For the sake of simplicity, I will summarise the three, not antagonistic, differences between Julio's positions and mine: the causes of the poverty or exploitation of peasants; the implications of differential rent; and the role of agricultural diversification.

Keys to exploitation. My research focuses on the causes of *exploitation* rather than *poverty*, which are not the same. The fact that the price of his harvests does not compensate the peasant for his idle time impoverishes him but it does not mean that his non-executed work is exploited (in the same way that an unemployed person is not exploited, even though he may also be entitled to unemployment benefits). Conversely, if we examine the entire set of peasants' activities, we will conclude that peasants are poor because they are exploited and the key to their exploitation lies in the fact that, as social beings in which capacities and needs have not been split and where a subjective factor – well-being – is the mediation between production and consumption (Chayanov 1974), they participate in the capitalist market where only profit counts. While capital invests in order to profit, peasants work to live, which is their *handicap*.

The worker sells his labour *for what it is worth* and he is exploited when his labour is consumed. Conversely, the peasant – who, in this immediate context, is self-employed – is exploited when he sells his product *for less than what it is worth*, but also when he pays extortionate interest, buys overvalued inputs and consumer goods, and is employed for short periods as a day worker on below subsistence wages. Peasants say that this is the Law of St Neep: *buy dear and sell cheap*. They are right, because, in their case, the multifaceted, all-enveloping unequal exchange is the means of exploitation and poverty.

Elucidating the key to a form of exploitation that does not have its *premise* in the labour market and its *consummation* in the capitalist productive process – such as the workers' process – and instead has its *premise* in production through self-employment and its *consummation* in the market of goods, services and seasonal labour is crucial to the rigorous criticism of a system that, instead of leading to direct universal proletarianisation, which Marx foresaw, is growing old in the midst of an increasingly extensive world of precarious, part-time or self-employed workers, of which modern peasant domestic production subsumed in capital is the paradigm.

Significance of differential rent. Peasants – whose primary resource is family labour – experience difficulties not only in externalising the discontinuity of agrarian work, but also in cultivating land that is usually bad and uneven, thus producing at higher costs. But peasants are not the ones who, with the addition of the average rate of profit, determine price trends (as would happen in a market where all the suppliers were capitalists), because those who produce to subsist will maintain themselves in the furrows even though they do not obtain profits and sometimes operate at a loss (which translates into the erosion of man and the environment). This reduces, annuls or inverts the differential rent that would be paid by society if prices were set on the basis of higher costs, while the over-profits of wealthier farmers decline without disappearing.

I think that Julio would agree with this view – which I formulated in an essay in 1979 also included in *El capital en su laberinto* (Bartra 2006: 193–208) – since, for him, the 'rule' of prices in markets where peasants and capitalists concur is that only the days worked are incorporated as costs, which impoverishes the peasant who has to sell seasonally his labour force to agrobusinessmen, a mechanism that features prominently in my model and that my model tries to explain. I also think that his thesis is not 'counterposed', as he says, with my thesis that peasants would disappear – God forbid – when differential rent was eliminated: in other words, when agriculture was the continuous, intensive process independent from nature of which transgenicists and nanotechnologists dream. Nor does it contradict it, since in this case there would be no idle time or seasonal work, which is the basis, for Julio, of the persistence of the peasantry.

The advantages of diversification. But not only would there not be peasants, there would not be anyone, since in times of global warming, peasants' proverbial, diversified, sustainable, multiple management would give way to the radical levelling required by the mass production of agrofuels and other peremptory requirements of crepuscular capitalism. Human life itself would be jeopardised.

Mixed cropping and agricultural diversification in general face 'obstacles', and it is true that peasants practise them less and less. This is all the more reason to revindicate the familial, regional and national advantages of multiple uses, whose ecological and labour advantages are highlighted by Julio and to which one should add cultural ones. It is in the face of the risk posed by technological uniformity to ecosystems – a matter on which we agree – that I think that the distortion in the price mechanism is a 'minor affair' and that offsetting it by socially compensating for the number of days worked is at best a provisional remedy and deeply counterindicated.

In other words, using subsidies to compensate single-cropping peasants whose idle time is not compensated for by prices does not discourage the use of this specialised model – on the contrary, it encourages it. So if the point is to subsidise, let us subsidise diversification and sustainable management instead. Which is essentially not a subsidy but rather payment for environmental, social and cultural contributions.

★ ★ ★

In the article entitled 'Teoría del valor del trabajo en el laberinto campesino' (Boltvinik 2007), Julio focuses on my argument on the keys to the pillaging of peasants. A propos of this, he holds that the 'causes of peasant poverty/exploitation' lie in the fact that the prices paid for their harvests include only the 'effectively invested' days, which 'entails a subsidy … for society … and … constitutes a form of exploitation'. The measure of this exaction is the unpaid cost of unworked days due to agricultural seasonality (305 days each year are unworked in the case of maize). According to this curious theory, the less a peasant works, the more he is exploited.

I repeat my fundamental points of agreement: in an order of commodification and continuous, intensive consumption of labour, the fact that the burden of agricultural seasonality is transferred to peasants – who cannot externalise it as capital does – as well as the spatial-temporal differences and fluctuations in yield due to natural factors, are injustices of the system that must be corrected – against the system. This can be done by compensating for the additional efforts of those who work in close cooperation with varied, unhurried and voluble Nature – particularly if they do so with good peasant habits: diversified, holistic, sustainable strategies.

I also confirm my disagreements: I did not say that 'there is no exploitation in the 60 days paid for labour which requires means of subsistence for 365', as Julio maintains in the article cited. What I do say is that peasant exploitation *does* exist even if the payment for harvests coincides with its entrepreneurial *cost* (means of production consumed plus effectively paid wages), since, in order for exploitation *not* to exist, its *price* should be paid (cost plus average profits). There *is* peasant exploitation when smallholders, with income generated through their work, pay a high price for loans, supplies and livelihoods; there *is* obviously peasant exploitation when they are forced to hire themselves temporarily for a wage; and, lastly, there *is* exploitation of Mexican peasant communities when the US economy appropriates the youth labour force of rural migrants who were raised and supported by their families during their pre-productive life. Exploitation of 'effectively invested' work (it could hardly be otherwise), which, according to the Marxist classics, is expressed and measured in its surplus value: in other words, the difference between the magnitude of the value created by work and the measure of the value contained in the livelihood required to reproduce it.

Exploitation – which assumes several forms in the case of peasants – whose *historical premise* is expropriation from the means required for autonomous reproduction (but peasants were left with or given little or bad land) and whose *economic consummation* has two moments: production through self-employment, which is its base (surplus is created), and a series of structurally iniquitous commercial exchanges, which are their *culmination* (surplus is transferred). These last operations include the sale of labour force at a price that may be, and is, lower than its real cost, since sustaining it uses self-generated goods and services for which salaries pay the cost but not the price. (This mechanism, in fact, also explains the surreptitious exploitation of traditionally female domestic work, which produces goods and services in which the well-known 'expense' pays for the cost of reproduction but not the full value.)

Unlike those that flow between national economies or branches of production, the chronic, unequal exchanges that affect a rural smallholder condemned to 'buy dear and sell cheap' are *both* economic expressions of relations of exploitation, in that the peasant is not a fairly fortunate businessman in the always unequal distribution of profits but a *direct producer*, who, by being fleeced as a *purchaser* and as a *seller*, is fleeced as a *worker* – in other words, he is exploited.

All that remains is for me to explain why, in the turbulent scenario of 'free concurrence' in which you win some and you lose some, the peasant always loses. It is not because of his small size, weakness and poverty – which, although in a historical sense they are a premise, in structural terms they are a recurring result. These all count, but the key to disadvantage is not quantitative but qualitative. His Achilles heel – as I have said in *El capital en su laberinto* (Bartra 2006: 247–80) – is that, unlike the businessman who buys and sells only to make a profit, the main objective of the peasant is to subsist. Although he would like to earn – retaining a surplus that would enable him to improve his quality of life and boost his production – he has to continue buying and selling even if he does not obtain profits, and often without even covering his costs, since, unlike the fluid, opportunistic capital, the peasant fights for his life by hanging on to the few resources and skills that are his assets.

Although he cannot suppress the structural bases of his exploitation other than by changing the system, the peasant not only can but needs to organise and mobilise to negotiate the terms and rates of exploitation, since otherwise the stupid, blind forces of capitalism would do away with him, as they would have done with the proletariat if it had not fought for the working day, a salary and working conditions. This struggle will eventually enable farm workers to reduce the need to engage in day work and migration, a need that is caused by the ruinous prices they obtain for their harvests. I think that the fact that the advance in the correlation of social forces makes it possible for the maize grower to work 60 days and charge for 365 (or a similar proportion in other crops), which means that he would no longer have to be employed for a salary, is a generous but speculative proposal in an order which, by definition, tends to turn all available labour capacity into a commodity, so as to have it as a 'reserve army'. I think a more feasible strategy is the struggle in which field workers are currently engaged for better prices, decent wages and, in general, viable options for productively exercising their working capacity, not in the exhausting, monotonous conditions imposed by single crops but in the polyphonous, pleasurable modalities encouraged by multi-activity.

By way of an example: in the early nineteenth century, when threshing machines became widespread, leaving day workers unemployed during the winter, they did not claim the degrading Poor Law subsidy designed to compensate for their unemployment; instead, they organised to destroy the machines that had displaced them. These were, in fact, economically inefficient contraptions, since the threshing machines were employed for short periods and replaced a resource such as the labour force which, in addition to being abundant, also had to be supported during the winter – whether or not it worked – since it would be necessary for sowing and harvesting. The struggle of the legendary 'Captain Swing' and his followers against machines and for decent jobs kept threshing machines out of the fields for a long time, in part because the strategy of specialisation and mechanisation at all costs is irrational even for capitalist logic when it is imposed in a seasonal, not totally mechanisable activity such as agriculture (Hobsbawm and Rudé 1978).

★ ★ ★

The anomie of a modernity whose teleology and values are questioned calls for the resignification of the social fabric and the restoration of its density – and for doing this by using a collective solidarity approach that, for reasons of survival, has endured on the natural and social banks of capitalism, on the periphery of what is both the reservoir and the garbage dump of the system and the sphere of reproduction and resistance of those who are excluded. This constitutes an ethos that is both subsumed and not subsumed – both devoured and excreted by big money – where alternative forms of sociality survive and are occasionally strengthened in unexpected ways, such as those of peasants and indigenous people.

'Progress' is already dead. The abundance resulting from the development of productive forces – a promise shared by capitalism and socialism – leads us to a scenario in which there is not only inequality in the division of goods and opportunities but also an omnipresent scarcity: the rarefying of the natural and social conditions on which human existence depends. And since both opulence with individual freedom and opulence with social equality proved to be illusions, then one will have to reconcile oneself with scarcity and perhaps acknowledge it as the ontological limit of human existence. In any case, austerity is our immediate future ... if we are to survive. And agrarian communities are skilled at handling this, since they are more concerned with always having enough than with having more and more. In this line, and in the line of revindicating both the past and the future, both the myth and the utopia, advance – albeit falteringly – the Amazonian, Andean revolutions that are underway: changes led by the indigenous people and peasants, by the Indian peasants of a colonised continent.

Notes

1 This and other issues related to the revitalisation of peasant-based agrarian alternatives are explored by some authors in Magdoff et al. (2000).

2 Maize is equivalent to *milpa*, since these graminaceous plants are the soul of numerous agricultural combinations and the nucleus of the various *milpas*. And this is the case because it is a cereal with an exceptional yield per unit of area and even more so by planted seed. This generosity is made possible by its ample foliage, which receives abundant sunlight for photosynthesis, and an extensive root that captures a large amount of moisture and nutrients. This means that it has a low density on the ground in comparison with other cereals, which can be sown by scattering seeds, whereas maize must be planted individually. Conversely, this practice enables it to be cultivated on steep slopes and in stony soil, in the kind of land predominant in equinoctial America, since it does not need to be rotated and can be planted using a pointed stick to deposit the seeds. The required distance between plants is fortunate for a baroque imagination that rejects empty spaces, since the spaces can be used to develop other species which – properly selected – not only do not compete with maize but contribute to its healthy growth by fixing nitrogen (beans and other legumes), preserving moisture and preventing the growth of weeds (squash) and repelling certain insects (chilli), and so on. In addition to permitting or encouraging the presence of wild grasses such as *quelites*, which are edible and also fix nitrogen, the *milpa* also allows the growth of plants such as century plants, nopales and various fruit trees that delimit plots of land, filter water and provide protection from wind, while reducing erosion.

References

Anderson, J. (1859) *Observations of the Means of Exciting a Spirit of National Industry*. London: Walton and Mabery.

Bartra, A. (2006) *El capital en su laberinto. De la renta de la tierra a la renta de la vida*. Mexico City: Ítaca.

— (2008) *El hombre de hierro. Los límites naturales y sociales del capital*. Mexico City: Universidad Autónoma Metropolitana (UAM), Universidad Autónoma de la Ciudad de México (UACM) and Ítaca.

Boltvinik, J. (2007) 'Teoría del valor del trabajo en el laberinto campesino', *La Jornada* (Mexico), 23 May.

— (2009) 'Esbozo de una teoría de la pobreza y la sobrevivencia del campesinado. Polémica con Armando Bartra', *Mundo Siglo XXI* 18.

Chayanov, A. (1974) *La organización de la unidad económica campesina*. Buenos Aires: Nueva Visión.

Foster, J. B. (2004) *La ecología de Marx, Marxismo y naturaleza*. Barcelona: El Viejo Topo. Originally published in 2000 as *Marx's Ecology: Materialism and nature*. New York NY: Monthly Review Press.

Foster, J. B. and F. Magdoff (2000) 'Marx and the depletion of soil fertility: relevance for today's agriculture' in F. Magdoff, J. B. Foster and F. Buttel (eds), *Hungry for Profit: The agribusiness threat to farmers, food and environment*. New York NY: Monthly Review Press.

González, L. (2009) 'Paleografía y nota preliminar' in *Proceso inquisitorial del cacique de Tetzcoco*. Mexico City: Cultura DF.

Hobsbawm, E. and G. Rudé (1978) *Revolución industrial y revuelta agraria. El capitán Swing*. Mexico City: Siglo XXI.

Katz, F. (1966) *Situación económica social de los aztecas*. Mexico City: Universidad Nacional Autónoma de México (UNAM).

Lévi-Strauss, C. (1972) *El pensamiento salvaje*. (*The Savage Mind*.) Mexico City: Fondo de Cultura Económica.

López, A. (1995) *Tamoanchan y Tlalocan*. Mexico City: Fondo de Cultura Económica.

— (2001) 'El núcleo duro, la cosmovisión y la tradición mesoamericana' in J. Broda and F. Báez (eds), *Cosmovisión, ritual e identidad de los pueblos indígenas de México*. Mexico City: Centro Nacional de la Cultura y las Artes (CNCA) and Fondo de Cultura Económica.

Magdoff, F., J. B. Foster and F. H. Buttel (2000) *Hungry for Profit: The agribusiness threat to farmers, food and the environment*. New York NY: Monthly Review Press.

Mann, S. A. (1990) *Agrarian Capitalism in Theory and Practice*. Chapel Hill NC: University of North Carolina Press.

Marx, K. (1964 [1867, 1885, 1894]) *El capital*. Mexico City: Fondo de Cultura Económica.

Marx, K. and F. Engels (n.d. [1848]) *Communist Party Manifesto*. Moscow: Foreign Language Editions.

O'Connor, J. (2001) *Causas naturales. Ensayos de marxismo ecológico*. Mexico City: Siglo XXI.

Pérez, M. (2012) 'Con el actual modelo agrícola habrá escasez, dicen expertos', *La Jornada* (Mexico), 27 February.

Polanyi, K. (2003 [1944]) *La gran transformación*. Mexico City: Fondo de Cultura Económica.

Ricardo, D. (1959 [1817]) *Principios de economía política y tributación*. Mexico City: Fondo de Cultura Económica.

Rojas, J. A. (2011) 'El precio de los productos primarios', *La Jornada* (Mexico), 1 February.

Turrent, A. (2012) '¿Cambio climático y última opción para el campo?', *La Jornada* (Mexico), 25 February.

World Development Report (2008) *Agriculture for Development*. Washington DC: International Bank for Reconstruction and Development.

3 | FROM FIELD TO FORK: LABOUR POWER, ITS REPRODUCTION, AND THE PERSISTENCE OF PEASANT POVERTY

Gordon Welty, Susan Mann, James Dickinson and Emily Blumenfeld

1. Introduction

In this essay we revisit our earlier writings on several topics including obstacles to the development of a capitalist agriculture (Mann and Dickinson 1978; Mann 1990a), A. V. Chayanov's theory of the peasant economy (Welty 2012), and the production and reproduction of labour power (Blumenfeld and Mann 1980; Dickinson and Russell 1986). The Mann–Dickinson thesis originally examined uneven capitalist development in agriculture from the vantage point of *capital*, arguing that a non-congruence of production time and labour time impeded or even prohibited the articulation of full-blown capitalist relations of production in agriculture. At present, we sustain that this thesis, despite the criticisms received, is a valid reply to the question on the persistence of the peasantry, given its focus on natural and socio-historical obstacles to capitalist development. Here, however, we explore uneven development from the point of view of *labour*, looking at peculiarities in the production and reproduction of labour power that have implications for the structuration of global poverty. If our earlier work highlighted obstacles to a successful capitalist transition from field to factory, we now examine obstacles to capitalist development from field to fork.[1] Accordingly, the central question we address is why the production and reproduction of labour power, like peasant production itself, remains largely non-capitalist even in the current era of late capitalism, and how this enigma might throw light on the persistence of global rural poverty: that is, to many observers, it is indeed an enigma or contradiction that capitalism's most valuable commodity – surplus value producing labour power – is not produced capitalistically.

We begin with a critique of the theoretical framework advanced by Julio Boltvinik to explain peasant poverty in the background paper presented to the 2012 CROP conference, which now forms the opening chapter of this volume. We then consider the reproduction of labour from a gendered perspective, emphasising the role of unpaid work by women in peasant and proletarian households. Noting capitalism's reliance on non-capitalist forms of production, we look at neoliberal policies of structural adjustment and the expansion of the informal sector as factors contributing to the immiseration of rural populations. We conclude with a critique of farm subsidies as a possible solution to peasant poverty.

2. Problems with Boltvinik's analysis of peasant poverty

Boltvinik identifies a number of differential features between agriculture and industry that help explain the social relations of production in agriculture, including seasonal (or discontinuous) versus continuous production; sequential versus simultaneous production; the perishable versus non-perishable nature of the commodities produced; and the different modes of deployment of machines in each sector (machines must be constantly moved in agriculture, whereas they can remain fixed in place in industry). His major contention is that the seasonality of agricultural production (a function of the biological cycle of living things and its relation to seasonal climate variation) contrasts sharply with the continuous production processes permitted by the lifeless, inert qualities of the materials used in industrial production. For Boltvinik, this seasonality of agricultural production underpins the persistence of rural poverty and of the peasantry.

Because many of the features identified by Boltvinik were discussed in the Mann–Dickinson thesis (1978) and in Mann's *Agrarian Capitalism in Theory and Practice* (1990a) as 'obstacles' to the capitalist development of agriculture, it would appear as if there is much common ground between our respective arguments. However, there is also contested terrain. To begin with, we take issue with Boltvinik's ontology of industry and agriculture which rests on an essentialist view of agriculture drawn from the writings of John Brewster, especially the latter's 'The machine process in agriculture and industry' (Brewster 1950). An essentialist argument generally claims that there are natural or inherent traits that characterise a particular group or category and that these irreducible traits constitute its very being, but this type of essentialism has been called into question by a number of critics of modernist thought (Fuss 1989). For Brewster, the 'fundamental difference between machine industry and agriculture stems from the contrasting nature of materials handled in each case' (1950: 70, note 1). Following Brewster, Boltvinik argues that 'agriculture works with living material … By contrast, in industry the objects in the work process are inert materials' (Boltvinik 2011: 3). Boltvinik concludes that agricultural production is essentially seasonal, thus contrasting sharply with the continuous nature of production permitted by the use of lifeless, inert materials in industry.

Yet, to say that the production of many agricultural commodities reflects the confluence of these natural features is not the same as saying that all agricultural commodities are subject to the same logic and to the same degree. We recall Georg Lukács' critique of the attempt to translate the concretely historical into supra-historical essences (Lukács 1981: 594).[2] Many branches of agricultural production have been successfully penetrated by capitalism and by pure forms of wage labour, and some non-agricultural industries are themselves based on the manipulation of living materials (Mann and Dickinson 1978: 472–3; Mann 1990a: 48–50). The fact that brewing relies on the activity of micro-organisms to convert sugars into alcohol has not prevented this industry from developing along capitalist lines. The same can be said for the commercial production of fermented foodstuffs such as bread, cheese, kefir, kimchi, pickles, sauerkraut and yoghurt, and the biopharmaceutical production of various vaccines. Indeed, hydroponic plant production, industrially scaled cattle feedlot operations and the combined horrors of modern factory farming – to give but a few examples – all undermine essentialist arguments about agriculture.

We thus question Boltvinik's contention that the distinction between inorganic and organic features of production accounts for differences between industry and agriculture. Our major point is that essentialist, ontological distinctions between agriculture and industry cannot account on their own for structural differences in these spheres. In contrast, we hold that *historically specific and commodity-specific analyses* are always preferable to an explanatory framework based on an essentialist ontology; only such an approach, we argue, can help unravel the thorny issue of natural obstacles, impediments or barriers to capitalist development and give guidance to political action.

Boltvinik's analysis is also problematic in that it blurs the distinction between the use value of labour power (its productivity in production) and its exchange value (its wage or price in the labour market). For example, he treats the wage as a value that directly corresponds to the hours worked or the time that labour power is set to work in production. From his point of view, peasants, as seasonal producers, necessarily earn relatively little because they work relatively few days per year. That is, as petty commodity producers competing with capitalist firms, peasants receive little for their crops since 'they only include [in commodity prices] effectively worked days in their labour costs, rather than their year-round cost of reproduction' (Boltvinik 2011: 7). With such meagre economic returns, how then is the year-round reproduction of labour power possible? According to Boltvinik, the peasantry absorbs the 'social cost that capitalist forms impose on agriculture by seeking employment as wage workers off the plot of land or undertaking other activities ... to supplement their income' (ibid.: 8). Consequently, he holds that agricultural seasonality immiserates rural producers and results in persistent poverty, the lengthy separation of workers from their families, and sparse, sub-human living conditions.

Boltvinik's analysis here is problematic for several reasons. First, he passes over the fact that under capitalism (until the rise of state-sponsored welfare, social insurance and other programmes) the maintenance and reproduction of labour power are almost entirely privatised. As Marx pointed out, 'free' wage labour is 'free' to undertake its own reproduction in households and families that lack any 'social means of subsistence and of production' (Marx 1996 [1867]: 179, 181, 705). Indeed, the lengthy struggle of organised labour for the family wage – a wage sufficient for one worker (the male) to be able to support an entire family (ibid.: 182) – reflects the working class's concern over this precarious aspect of capitalist reproduction.

Second, we think that more emphasis needs to be placed on the variable character of both labour power and the value of the wage. On the one hand, the value produced by labour power in capitalist production is variable. Labour productivity varies in relation to the extension of the division of labour and employment of machinery. Thus, capitalist accumulation is not a function of the congruence of production time and labour time per se, but is made possible by the discrepancy between the use value of labour power (its productivity) and its exchange value (wages). For example, despite the seasonal nature of cotton production, the use of mechanical cotton harvesters by the US farmers in the post-World War II era so enhanced the productivity of their labour that they were able to compete successfully on the world cotton market with Pakistani cotton farmers who earned incomes fifteen times lower than their American counterparts (Mann 1990a: 112–13).

On the other hand, the wage is variable in the way it represents a historically and socially constructed subsistence level. This aspect is discussed by Boltvinik in his earlier paper on poverty measurements, where he quotes Marx to the effect that 'there enters into the determination of the value of labour-power a historical and moral element' (Marx 1996: 181; as quoted in Boltvinik 2001: 6). Further, as Boltvinik and other theorists of peasant economy argue, 'outrage over these moral assumptions', quite apart from absolute physical deprivation, has often triggered peasant revolts and food riots (Boltvinik 2001: 7; Thompson 1993: 188; Scott 1976). Again, within a given country or region, as well as at different historical junctures, wages reflect broader inequities associated with the demographic composition of the labour force, including age, race, ethnicity and gender, as well as its degree of organisation or unionisation.

Generally, we find that Boltvinik's analysis of the reproduction of petty producers falls short, especially with respect to the implications for women's unpaid domestic labour. It is to the questions of gender, domestic labour and reproduction that we now turn.

3. The production and reproduction of labour power

To understand uneven capitalist development from the vantage point of labour requires a focus on the production and reproduction of labour power. All societies are necessarily founded on three interrelated production processes: the production of the means of production (tools and raw materials), the production of the means of subsistence (food, shelter, clothing), and the production of human labour power (Seccombe 1992: 11). To sustain themselves over time, societies must establish a robust cycle of production, distribution, exchange and consumption that secures both the short- and long-term (day-to-day and intergenerational) reproduction of the population. Of course, historically not all societies have succeeded in this; many have collapsed, even disappeared, as they failed to produce and consume in a manner commensurate with reproduction (Diamond 2011).

In market societies where labour power necessarily appears as a commodity, reproduction takes on special characteristics. For Marx, labour power has both a use value and an exchange value. Its exchange value is determined in the same way as it is for other commodities: by the amount of socially necessary labour time which is needed to produce and (in the case of labour power) reproduce it. However, labour power's usefulness to capital is something quite different, consisting in no less than its ability to produce (under appropriate working conditions) more value during the course of the working day than its own value. Indeed, for Marx, this discrepancy is the original source of surplus value.

But labour power is also special in its mode of production and reproduction. As Marx notes, as labour power is productively consumed at the point of production, its use value is rapidly used up; as he put it, during work 'a definite quantity of human muscle, nerve, brain, etc. is wasted and these require to be restored' (Marx 1996 [1867]: 181). Additionally, for Marx, the reproduction process must encompass the long-term or intergenerational replacement of human beings. Addressing this point, Marx writes: 'Hence the sum of the means of subsistence necessary for the production of labour-power must include the means necessary for the labourer's substitutes, i.e., his children, in order that this race of peculiar [labour-power] commodity-owners may perpetuate its appearance in the market' (ibid.: 182). Thus the wage must be sufficient to cover not only socially necessary costs needed to secure the day-to-day reproduction of the adult worker, but also the domestic labour that is socially necessary to secure the next generation of workers.

For many years scholars approached the reproduction of labour power simply as a *consumption issue*: what can the wages of proletarians or the income earned by petty commodity producers buy in the marketplace and what does this mean for their subsistence or poverty level? Even Marxist accounts gave short shrift to the production and reproduction of labour power, largely passing over a chance to analyse the daily restoration and generational replacement of labour power. This omission is especially ironic given the status of labour power in Marx's theory as the source of all value. Not until the 1970s was this lacuna finally taken up in a systematic way by Marxist and socialist feminist writers in the so-called 'domestic labour debates' (Vogel 1973; 1981; Seccombe 1973; Fox 1980). Collectively, this work highlighted gender aspects, pointing to the centrality of women's unpaid domestic work in the reproduction process.

What this literature establishes is that the production and reproduction of labour power are antithetical to capitalist methods of production and rely heavily on women's unpaid domestic work in the home. Indeed, as Blumenfeld and Mann (1980) argued, the inseparability of labour power from living human beings presents major obstacles to the socialisation of reproductive labour. With respect to daily reproduction, many activities such as shopping, cooking and cleaning are inordinately labour intensive and lack congruence between production and labour time (the cook remains 'unemployed', as it were, while the cake bakes in the oven). Moreover, housework is sporadic by nature and done intermittently rather than continuously, as, for example, with laundry or cooking. The spatial dispersal of work among separate households also precludes the efficient capitalist substitution of constant capital (machinery) for variable capital (labour) (ibid.: 270, 290–6). It is critical, then, to acknowledge that women's unpaid labour in the household absorbs the 'costs' of producing and reproducing the commodity labour power that capitalism itself is unable to undertake (ibid.: 289).

These obstacles are even more apparent in long-term, intergenerational reproduction through childbearing and socialisation. Many years of labour-intensive, emotionally intimate and face-to-face interactions are necessary to secure the physical, cognitive and social development of children into socially useful adults (ibid.: 295–7). Indeed, the emotional, personal and expressive character of much nurturing and childcare labour conflicts sharply with the rational, impersonal, instrumental aspects of capitalist production epitomised by its substitution of living labour with machines, mass assembly-line production and the stockpiling of parts and inventory (ibid.: 296 ff.). As Kathleen Lynch has similarly theorised, the sphere of primary care relations necessarily involves a set of human relations that fundamentally resists commodification (Lynch 2007: 557–61, 565–6).

At a minimum, then, the autarkic nature of domestic labour and the psychosocial processes at the heart of human socialisation preclude the capitalist production of the commodity labour power.

At the household level, any number of factors may disrupt the formation of robust peasant or proletarian households. Peasants may lose access to land, hence their ability to produce subsistence goods directly, or they may face such stiff price competition from other producers that they are unable to sell their produce. Working-class households may fail to sufficiently valorise labour power on account of unemployment, sickness and disability or old age, or because of wages so low and exploitation so high that they have insufficient resources (income, time) to set up and maintain a domestic sphere able to secure day-to-day – let alone intergenerational – reproduction. Such challenges, as Marx observed, compelled the early bourgeois state to intervene with regulatory relief on behalf of the interests of capital in general, passing legislation to limit the length of the working day and to exclude children from the industrial labour force, and later implementing unemployment, health and pension insurance schemes to regulate the uncertainties of industrial life. In this way, the individual wage is augmented by means of social welfare legislation into a social or 'citizen' wage sufficient to secure the reproduction of labour at a collective or class level (Dickinson and Russell 1986). While such a development adds a historical and moral element to the value of labour power, as is implicit in Marx's narrative of national capitalist development as moving from absolute to relative surplus value extraction, neoliberal global capitalism today reverses the trend, contributing significantly to the absolute immiseration of both workers and peasants from the core to the periphery.

4. The invisibility of domestic labour in theory and practice

Analyses of domestic labour show that it is a category of labour and work like no other. For one thing it appears as never-ending, cyclical, mundane toil, much like the 'torture of Sisyphus' – clean clothes and floors get dirty again and full stomachs soon become empty (de Beauvoir 1970: 425). Moreover, such work falls for the most part to women, although they represent but half of the potential domestic labour force. Indeed, although more and more women today work outside the home in both the developed and developing worlds, the domestic realm remains their primary ground, shaping their life courses and anchoring their relationships with others. Again, domestic or reproductive work is unpaid labour (a housekeeping allowance is an informal payment that may cover the costs of needed commodities but rarely, if ever, amounts to wages for housework). Thus wages paid to employed workers can be that much lower since the wage need only cover commodified aspects of reproduction. In peasant farming and other types of petty commodity production, where food and clothing production as well as home building may be a significant part of such unpaid 'domestic labour', incomes paid to those working outside the home can be correspondingly lower.

In addition, women in both peasant and proletarian households are often expected to stretch available money income by making preserves or sewing clothes at home; alternatively, they may take on additional domestic chores for which they get paid, for example taking in laundry or adding lodgers to the household (Seccombe 1992; Rubin 1976). Studies show how poor women not only work longer hours than their male counterparts, but also are more likely to devote time or income to the well-being of children as opposed to their own benefit. Similar patterns have been found in studies of the working hours of slave women in the US (Mann 1990b), as well as in gender differences in the use of income garnered in the informal economy (Ward 1990) and from micro-credit (Lairap-Fonderson 2002).

Moreover, because domestic labour is unpaid and hidden in the household, its vital and necessary contributions to the reproduction of labour power remain socially obscured. Indeed, women's unpaid work in the household not only frees men from systematic participation in these tasks, but also, the more successfully women perform the concrete work of reproducing everyday life, the more invisible the domestic realm appears to men, and the less culturally valued and appreciated it is as a distinct form of socially necessary labour. As Simone de Beauvoir put it over half a century ago, 'order and neatness' appear to 'come of their own accord' (de Beauvoir 1970: 428–9).

Additionally, as Dorothy Smith points out, the category of domestic labour is generally less visible to conventional social science, where objectivised forms of knowledge produced by men typically fail to understand women's role in the reproduction of labour power and everyday life (Smith 1990: 19). According to Smith, this is another example of how objectified or abstracted modes of knowledge favour the constructed realities of privileged groups and experts over the lived realities of their subjects. Such conceptual strategies, she claims, when applied to the world of domestic labour, 'obliterate women as active agents' and ignore the 'standpoint of women' (Smith 1987: 164).

At an earlier historical juncture, Alexander V. Chayanov (1966 [1925]) clearly passed over the chance to explore the value of a gendered standpoint when he wrote of 'self-exploitation' in the reproduction of the peasant economy. His analysis of the economy of small rural producers essentially obscured how the peasant household is the locus of domestic patriarchy (Welty 2012: 13–14; Mallon 1987; Hammel and Gullickson 2004). Historically, domestic patriarchy has been buttressed by marriage laws (such as the doctrine of coverture in the US)[3] that explicitly recognised the male head of the household's control over family income and property, as well as his right to chastise or punish his wife and children. In short, the peasant household was never the equitable institution Chayanov supposed; rather, family dependants were vulnerable to abuse and exploitation by the male head, oftentimes supported and reinforced by traditional mores and religion. Despite these shortcomings, agrarian analysts continue to revive Chayanov's gender-blind work today.

5. Women and global development

What do these remarks mean for women in developing societies? Recent data compiled by the United Nation's Food and Agriculture Organization (FAO) estimate that women comprise just over 40 per cent of the agricultural labour force in the developing world, ranging from 20 per cent in the Americas to almost 50 per cent in East and Southeast Asia and Africa. Indeed, in several of these regions agriculture is a greater source of employment for women than for men. The FAO data also reveal that women are over-represented in unpaid, in seasonal and in part-time work. And, when they are paid, they are paid less than men for the same work (FAO 2011: 1–3). Despite such data, analysts all too often ignore how gender and gender relations play a central role in the reproduction of petty commodity production and the persistence of peasant poverty.

Building on Rosa Luxemburg's claim that capitalist development is predicated on the perpetuation of non-capitalist forms of production

(1951 [1913]), some contemporary authors have compared women's non-wage, domestic labour to peasant labour. As the authors of *Women: The last colony* (Mies et al. 1988) document, women across the globe are held responsible for non-wage housework and childcare, whether or not they work for wages outside the home. They also point to how many Third World workers (men as well as women) are engaged in non-wage forms of production such as subsistence agriculture or petty commodity production, forming an 'army of male and female so-called "marginalised" people' (ibid.: 14–15).

These authors are primarily concerned with how gender is intertwined with the uneven development of global capitalism. Discussing the impact of uneven development on Indian women, they conclude that, while:

> capitalist penetration leads to the pauperisation and marginalisation of large masses of subsistence producers ... women are more affected by these processes than men, who may still be partly absorbed into the actual wage labour force ... [Capitalist development] ... far from bringing about more equality between men and women ... has, in fact introduced new elements of patriarchalism and sexism. (ibid.: 40–1)

Moreover, they point out how, with rising gender inequality and the feminisation of poverty, violence against women increases as their position deteriorates relative to men. As global development advances, families effectively break up as pauperised men migrate to the cities in search of wage work while wives and children remain in local villages doing subsistence farming or being forced into prostitution to make ends meet (ibid.: 42–3).

In particular, the feminisation of migration that has characterised recent decades weaves together class, gender, race and ethnicity issues (Castles and Miller 1993). For example, wealthy families around the world hire poor, often migrant, women not only as domestic servants but as nannies who undertake the emotional labour of childrearing and socialisation. Studies point to an increasing flow of women from poor countries to rich ones, where they work as nannies and maids in private homes, or as caregivers in institutional settings such as hospitals, hospices, childcare centres and nursing homes. Whereas men constituted the vast majority of global migrant labourers up until the late 1970s, since the 1980s women have contributed an ever greater share. By the beginning of the twenty-first century, over half of the world's estimated 120 million migrant workers were thought to be women (Ehrenreich and Hochschild 2004: 5–6).

The development of this global female migrant labour force coincides with First World de-industrialisation. Between 1965 and 1985, employment in industrial manufacturing in the US dropped from 60 per cent to 26 per cent of the labour force, while employment in service jobs rose from 40 per cent to 74 per cent (Stacey 1991: 18). Yet, the growth of the service sector did not compensate for the loss of blue-collar manufacturing jobs, since many of these new jobs, especially in retail, health services and the food industry, were paid little and lacked pension, medical and other benefits. In fact, real male wages fell between 1965 and 1985 – a steep and unusual decline given that per capita gross domestic product (GDP) was increasing (Thurow 1996: 224). As a consequence of this wage erosion, the demographic profile of the US labour force began to change as more women, especially women with small children, entered the labour force in an attempt to buttress their household incomes. Whereas in the 1950s only 15 per cent of mothers with children under the age of 6 were employed, by 2002 that number had increased to 65 per cent (Ehrenreich and Hochschild 2004: 8).

As US women began to enter the paid labour force in record numbers, capitalism worked assiduously where it could to transform unpaid domestic labour into profitable commodity production. This is particularly evident in the area of food preparation, where fast food restaurants, frozen dinners, prepared foods and the like, in conjunction with microwave ovens and other domestic appliances, generally speed up and simplify domestic food preparation, albeit often at the cost of affordable, nutritious diets (Blumenfeld and Mann 1980: 293–5). Although the 'outsourcing' of intimate life has become the subject of serious study in recent years (Hochschild 2012), much domestic labour still remains privatised, non-wage labour.

While Boltvinik argues that capitalist agriculture cannot exist without a pauperised peasantry, we broaden this point by suggesting that capitalism continually creates and relies on non-capitalist forms to secure accumulation in both industry and agriculture. Further, we argue that global capitalism cannot provide – indeed, it has no interest in providing – a livelihood for many of those systematically dispossessed in the course of its development. Let us now turn to these issues.

6. Impure capitalism and its peculiar forms of production

Capitalism, despite its desire to do so, is generally unable to create a world entirely in its own image. From its earliest stirrings to its latest global manifestations, the accumulation process has consistently relied on economic arrangements that deviate from pure commodity production. Recall, for example, capitalism's midwife, primitive accumulation, as well as our discussion above of peculiarities in the reproduction of labour power. Non-capitalist forms of production continue to be integral to industries otherwise dominated by capitalist production methods. For example, in the poultry industry, independent contract farmers typically undertake riskier stages of production (the production of day-old chicks) while the more predictable, less risky stages (intensive feeding to market weight) are organised capitalistically (Mann 1990a: Appendix 1). The same arrangement is evident in the livestock industry, where the breeding and weaning of cattle are left to small-scale ranchers and feedlot operations take on aspects of continuous-process factory production (Schlosser 2012). Similarly, transnational corporations often subcontract parts or all of the production process to smaller local enterprises operating in export-processing zones, which manage labour recruitment, worker discipline and other issues. As one study noted: 'Subcontracting means that the so-called manufacturer [transnational corporation] need not employ any production workers, run the risk of unionisation or wage pressures, or be concerned with layoffs resulting from changes in product demand' (Appelbaum and Gereffi in Bonacich et al. 1994). Subcontracting is a major feature of the global assembly line, allowing the geographic dispersal and decentralisation of production while at the same time concentrating wealth and power in select core locations.

Large-scale capitalist agriculture, as Boltvinik argues, not only recruits 'underemployed' peasant farmers as seasonal wage workers but often goes further, maintaining a more or less permanent migrant labour force to harvest crops. In the US, this rural labour force not only is pauperised but is significantly isolated from the mainstream by issues of race, ethnicity and legal status, leading in recent years to nativist demands for punitive laws to limit or control the immigration of undocumented workers. In Alabama, for example, one result of legislative efforts to restrict undocumented workers is that employers must now check the immigration status of workers or face fines and penalties. Not surprisingly, large-scale fruit and vegetable farmers have been at the forefront of efforts to repeal such laws, many claiming that they risk losing their farms under their provisions. One farmer even tried to replace migrant labour with convict labour drawn from the state's burgeoning prison population, but found the cost too high and the quality of work too low (Allen 2011).

Again, large-scale capitalist firms that, in the past, typically provided in-house all needed services from janitorial and food catering to payroll and accounting, now more frequently use temporary or short-term contract workers to perform such tasks, or outsource entire functions in order to reduce labour costs and avoid paying medical and pension benefits. Even some skilled white-collar work is fundamentally seasonal, as is the case with the annual ritual of tax form preparation. As some scholars have noted, the 'trend toward a permatemp world has been developing for years' and 'has been good for corporate profits' (Coy et al. 2010).

Our point here is that capitalist agriculture is not alone in its reliance on seasonal labour recruited from the peasant economy, but that capitalist producers in other areas often utilise, or even rely on, non-capitalist and petty forms of production to reduce risk and enhance flexibility and profits. In this way, both industry and agriculture in their use of contingent and seasonal labour are complicit in the ongoing pauperisation of working populations around the world.

In terms of peasant poverty, our more orthodox approach to the labour theory of value suggests that in the highly commoditised markets that exist today – both locally and globally – peasants are impoverished because of their low labour productivity. Accordingly, social differentiation renders the poorest peasants either landless or forced to find additional forms of income to survive. In highly commoditised markets, time is money. Capital utilises its larger scale and mass volume production, along with investments in labour-saving technology and transforming the division of labour to reduce labour time, in ways that are not possible for petty commodity producers, such as peasants, who rely on family labour. While Chayanov highlighted some market advantages of family labour and contemporary writers have pointed to peasants' small ecological footprint, more attention must be paid to the limitations of family labour, as well as to the gender inequalities entailed in unpaid domestic labour, to better understand peasant political economy.

Given the relatively low labour productivity of peasants, neoliberal, globalised capitalism undercuts any prices peasants garner in markets for locally produced goods compared with imports of industrialised agri-commodities, and it also converts local, small-scale, poly-culture into large-scale, cash and/or monocrop production – an argument similar to Mike Davis's 'planet of slums' thesis (Davis 2004). In short, the persistence of non-capitalist forms of production today is less an atavistic hangover from a pre-modern past, and more an essential feature of contemporary global accumulation.

7. The informal sector and global poverty

Increasingly the success of global capitalism is associated with the expansion of what some call the 'informal sector' – unregulated income-producing work marked by an absence of formal contracts, low or irregular wages, and generally poor working conditions. As such, the informal sector is extremely heterogeneous and is made up of small-scale, often illegal work in mineral and precious metal extraction, various kinds of agricultural and pastoral production, small-scale workshops and trade, subcontracting to home-based producers, trash recycling, and the semi-legal or clandestine world of sweatshop industries, as well as a range of personal services including prostitution and the sex trade.

Gender is a significant feature of the informal sector, something earlier scholars of the global economy too often ignored or downplayed (Truelove 1987). As Kathryn Ward argues, one of the major features of global restructuring over the last half century has been a marked increase in female workers in the informal sector (Ward 1990: 2). Here, women workers typically make less money than their male counterparts and seldom have the opportunity to fill management or supervisory positions, which are largely monopolised by men. Ward also suggests that when scholars focus primarily on women's formal work experiences, they fail to appreciate how boundaries between women's formal work, informal work and housework overlap in ways that are quite distinct from men's work (ibid.: 7).

In 'Planet of slums' (2004), Mike Davis sounds the alarm about increased global poverty as a consequence of the inexorable expansion of the informal sector in the global capitalist system. Much informal labour today, he argues, is qualitatively different from nineteenth-century conceptions of an immiserated but productive proletariat (the Manchester model) and is more akin to urban poverty experienced in cities such as Dublin or Naples, which were more weakly integrated into national systems of capitalist growth and development at the time. He writes that the informal sector today 'is not the pettiest of petty bourgeoisie, neither is it a "labour reserve army" or a "lumpen proletariat" in any obsolete nineteenth century sense' (ibid.: 26). Its growth in many parts of the world signifies, therefore, not the emergence of a new working class, which is poor relative to the wealth it creates, but rather an eruption of absolute poverty, the creation of a mass of 'surplus humanity' essentially superfluous to the needs of global accumulation. For Davis, it is no accident that this catastrophe of injustice unfolds in the Third World, where globalisation, brutally implemented via 'structural adjustment' programmes insisted on by development agencies such as the World Bank and the International Monetary Fund (IMF), have more or less destroyed the subsistence peasantries of Asia, Africa and Latin America without providing adequate opportunities for wage work as an alternative subsistence strategy (ibid.: 23).

From Davis's perspective, then, globalisation and 'structural adjustments' have essentially turned the world's peasantry into desperately poor rural workers or city migrants crammed into the slums and *favelas* of the exploding cities of the developing world. He estimates that, 'while the countryside will for a short period still contain the majority of the world's poor, that doubtful title will pass to urban slums by 2035' (ibid.: 17).

8. Farm subsidies: a perishable, no longer ripe idea

In regard to Boltvinik's claim that agricultural subsidies can be an effective solution to peasant poverty, we argue that prospects for success here would appear to be slight, especially given the current influence of neoliberal ideas and policy making. As an official state ideology, neoliberalism arose in the late 1970s and 1980s in response to the twin crises of economic recession and stagnation in core countries and a looming debt crisis in many parts of the developing world. Neoliberals hold that only through a return to unfettered free markets and competitive, unregulated capitalism can stalled development and national indebtedness be overcome. Generally speaking, neoliberals call for deregulation and privatisation of the economy and an opening up of local markets to unfettered free trade; not surprisingly, they oppose government subsidies to the poor in both developed and developing countries, claiming that such policies introduce distortions and inefficiencies into national and global markets. A brief look at agricultural subsidies in the US, as well as neoliberal-inspired 'structural adjustment' programmes in the Third World, clearly suggests the limitations of subsidies with respect to moderating rural inequality and poverty.

Although government support for agriculture in the US goes back to the nineteenth century, it was only with the passage of the Agricultural Adjustment Act of 1933 as part of the New Deal that commodity price supports and production limits, marketing orders to limit competition, import barriers and crop insurance programmes were introduced. Indeed, Chris Edwards has shown that, although details of farm subsidy legislation may have changed over time, its overall purpose of supporting farm prices and protecting farmers from competition has not. The US Department of Agriculture, depending on the overall strength of agricultural prices, distributes between $10 billion and $30 billion annually as cash subsidies to farmers and to owners of farmland. In turn, the Farm Credit System – a fifty-state network of financial cooperatives – boasted assets of $90 billion in 2009 (Edwards 2009: 1).

Even though the proportion of the US workforce directly engaged in agriculture is now less than 5 per cent, the farm lobby remains strong. For one thing, sparsely populated agricultural and western states continue to elect two Senate members each, perpetually skewing a bicameral legislative process in favour of issues of importance to rural America. Whereas New Deal farm legislation was originally concerned with saving the family farm, after World War II national security issues became more persuasive with respect to pursuing US food independence. Later, farm state legislators teamed up with urban legislators in mutual support of farm subsidies and anti-poverty programmes such as food stamps. In turn, ideological support for the family farm as the moral backbone of an independent nation has proved quite enduring despite overwhelming historical evidence that farm subsidies heavily favour large capitalist producers over smaller family enterprises (Schnittker 1970; Frundt 1975; Gilbert and Howe 1991). Farm subsidies do little to support small farmers: by 2009, more than half of the recipients of direct farm payments had incomes above $100,000 (Edwards 2009: 1). This detail alone should give pause to the idea that farm subsidies might be a way to deal with peasant poverty. Indeed, as many suggest, even should the agrarian welfare state in the US be dismantled, such a development would actually benefit the global North's increasingly transnational agribusiness in other ways (McMichael 2005; Friedmann 2005; Araghi 2009).

In developing countries, where agricultural tariffs and food subsidies have supported peasant producers and have provided price stability for important subsistence goods, neoliberals have often successfully introduced punishing programmes of economic reform ostensibly to correct for extravagant national development policies that have resulted in crippling indebtedness. As Philip McMichael and others have pointed out, this neoliberal-inspired agenda helped create a new direction for the world capitalist system, often referred to as the 'globalisation project', in which the scale and power of transnational banks and corporations benefited relative to, and at the expense of, nation states (McMichael 2008: 189–90). As such, the globalisation project assigns communities, regions and countries within its orbit to new specialised niches within the global economy, a goal dependent on opening up local or national markets to global competition through policies of 'structural adjustment' and implementation of free trade agreements. In this way, new agencies such as the World Trade Organization wield forms of authority, discipline and regulation that increasingly supersede the institutional powers of previously autonomous, even democratic, nation states.

For several decades beginning in the early 1980s, the World Bank and the IMF required developing countries seeking debt refinancing to cut government expenditures, end food and other subsidies, slash spending on health, education and welfare programmes, foster the production and export of commodities and cash crops, and devalue local currencies. The effects of such neoliberal, structural adjustment policies in many countries – especially in the countryside – have been enormous, where the massive growth of the informal sector and a reserve army of migrant labour have coincided with opportunities for transnational agribusiness interests to introduce large-scale, export-oriented agriculture in place of peasant farms (McMichael 2008; Araghi 2009).

Additionally, neoliberal policies impact women and the reproduction of labour power particularly hard. As Chang summarises:

SAPs [structural adjustment programmes] strike women in these [Third World] nations the hardest and render them most vulnerable to exploitation both at home and in the global labour market. When wages and food subsidies are cut, wives and mothers must adjust household budgets, often at the expense of their own and their children's nutrition. As public healthcare and education vanishes, women suffer from a lack of prenatal care and become nurses to ill family members at home, while girls are the first to be kept from school to help at home or go to work. When export-oriented agriculture is encouraged ... peasant families are evicted from their lands to make room for corporate farms and women become seasonal workers in the fields or in processing areas. (Chang 1997: 132)

Given the influence of neoliberalism in the globalisation project, we see little chance for the implementation of agricultural subsidies as a way to alleviate peasant poverty. Rather, under current political conditions that everywhere seem to favour capital over labour, the expectation is that pauperised, unemployed and disposable people will become ever more numerous at the same time as they appear more invisible to elites in an increasingly flexible and transnational global capitalist system.

9. What is to be done?

The global advance of neoliberalism threatens populations worldwide, intensifying inequality in core countries as well as increasing poverty and pauperisation among rural and urban inhabitants in the developing world. Indeed, as we have noted, the development project is no longer predicated on the transformation of previously self-sufficient producers into wage workers (with all the attendant risks and uncertainties associated with such a transformation), but now creates a vast mass of surplus humanity who are socially located off the grid of the new regime of wealth accumulation. This surplus population, written off by mainstream politicians everywhere, struggles to survive in the informal sector and on the dwindling resources not under capital's control.

We certainly do not have any easy solutions to address these new and expanding forms of rural and urban poverty. Nonetheless, we conclude by noting several objectives that must be part of any programme of progressive change designed to strengthen and improve the lives of the global poor.

First, the well-being of women and children, no less than that of men, must be pursued in rural areas, including the eradication of all forms of violence against women and children. This goal depends on an explicit recognition of the need for gender analysis in any explanation of rising poverty as well as gender equality in any programme of change.

Next, a comprehensive prohibition against environmental and ecological degradation must be a priority. Safe working conditions must be established and maintained for rural dwellers, especially with respect to the careful control and regulation of herbicides, pesticides, toxic chemicals and genetically modified organisms in commercial monocrop agriculture. Also, securing clean air and clean drinking water is a precondition for improving public health in rural and urban areas.

Third, the ruinous grip of neoliberal capitalism on rural development must be countered with a comprehensive programme that prevents the destruction of small farmers, promotes widespread land reform, maintains the viability of local food production (including mixed cropping), and increases food security and sustainable development for rural as well as urban populations. The global struggle against neoliberal capitalism must be pursued in the countryside and in the cities.

Finally, there must be a progressive integration of the local and the global, including resistance to the atomising of the peasantry.

Such policies can be enacted by progressive social movements, as they have been earlier in the movements led by Emiliano Zapata, V. I. Lenin, Mao Zedong, Ho Chi Minh and Fidel Castro. More recent movements continue this struggle, such as Jean-Bertrand Aristide's *Fanmi Lavalas*, the Zapatistas of Chiapas, the Brazilian Landless Workers' Movement (Movimento dos Trabalhadores Rurais Sem Terra or MST), the peasant movements in India celebrated by Vandana Shiva and Arundhati Roy, and the governments of Evo

Morales, Rafael Correa and Nicolás Maduro. Many address the major sources of peasant grievances, including disputes over land, labour practices and environmental pollution by international capital. The power of these multifaceted peasant mobilisations is enhanced when they can connect with similar movements for change emanating from urban areas, thus bringing together the landless poor, the working class, the environmental movement and the women's movement into a powerful movement for change.

Notes

1 The phrase 'from field to fork' is borrowed with permission from an unpublished paper by Harriet Friedmann.

2 We also recall Lukács' further point that such binary thinking serves the purposes of quietism – why struggle against capitalism if the obstacles are essentialistic? (1981: 596)

3 The doctrine of coverture governed marriage laws across most of the United States in the nineteenth century. This doctrine held that once a man and woman were married, they were one in the eyes of the law. This 'one' was the man and he not only controlled the property and income of the household but also had the legal right to chastise or punish his wife and children (Mann 2012: 37).

References

Allen, M. (2011) 'Alabama farmers may replace migrant farmers with prisoners', OpposingViews.com, 6 December. Available at www.opposingviews.com/i/money/jobs-and-careers/alabama-farmers-may-replace-migrant-workers-prisoners (accessed 7 September 2012).

Araghi, F. (2009) 'The invisible hand and the visible foot' in A. H. Akram-Lodhi and C. Kay (eds), Peasants and Globalisation. New York NY: Routledge.

Blumenfeld, E. and S. Mann (1980) 'Domestic labour and the reproduction of labour power: towards an analysis of women, the family, and class' in B. Fox (ed.), Hidden in the Household: Women's domestic labour under capitalism. Toronto: Women's Press, pp. 267–307.

Boltvinik, J. (2001) 'Poverty measurement methods: an overview'. Poverty Reduction Series Working Paper no. 3. New York NY: United Nations Development Programme (UNDP).

— (2011) 'Poverty and persistence of the peasantry'. Background paper for the International Workshop on Peasant's Poverty and Persistence, Comparative Research Programme on Poverty (CROP) and El Colegio de México, Mexico City, 13–15 March 2012.

Bonacich, E., L. Cheng, N. Chinchilla, N. Hamilton and P. Ong (eds) (1994) Global Production: The apparel industry in the Pacific Rim. Philadelphia PA: Temple University Press.

Brewster, J. M. (1950) 'The machine process in agriculture and industry', Journal of Farm Economics 32 (1): 69–81.

Castles, S. and M. J. Miller (1993) The Age of Migration: International population movements and the modern world. Basingstoke, UK: Macmillan.

Chang, G. (1997) 'The global trade in Filipina workers' in S. Shah (ed.), *Dragon Ladies: Asian American feminists breathe fire*. Cambridge MA: South End Press, pp. 132–52.

Chayanov, A. V. (1966 [1925]) *The Theory of Peasant Economy*. Edited by D. Thorner, B. Kerblay and R. E. F. Smith. Homewood IL: Irwin.

Coy, P., M. Conlin and M. Herbst (2010) 'The disposable worker', *Bloomberg Business Week*, 7 January.

Davis, M. (2004) 'Planet of slums: urban involution and the informal proletariat', *New Left Review* 26 (March–April): 5–34.

de Beauvoir, S. (1970) *The Second Sex*. New York NY: Knopf.

Diamond, J. (2011) *Collapse: How societies choose to fail or survive*. New York NY: Penguin Books.

Dickinson, J. and B. Russell (eds) (1986) *Family, Economy and State: The social reproduction process under capitalism*. London: Croom Helm.

Edwards, C. (2009) 'Agricultural subsidies.' Washington DC: Cato Institute (June).

Ehrenreich, B. and A. R. Hochschild (eds) (2004) *Global Woman: Nannies, maids, and sex workers in the new economy*. New York NY: Metropolitan.

FAO (2011) 'The role of women in agriculture'. ESA Working Paper no. 11-02. Rome: Food and Agriculture Organization of the United Nations (FAO).

Fox, B. (ed.) (1980) *Hidden in the Household: Women's domestic labour under capitalism*. Toronto: Women's Press.

Friedmann, H. (2005) 'From colonialism to green capitalism: social movements and emergence of food regimes' in F. Buttel and P.

McMichael (eds), *New Directions in the Sociology of Global Development: Research in rural sociology and development*. Volume 11. Oxford: Elsevier, pp. 277–64.

Frundt, H. J. (1975) 'American agribusiness and U.S. foreign agricultural policy'. PhD thesis, Rutgers University, New Brunswick, NJ.

Fuss, D. (1989) *Essentially Speaking: Feminism, nature, and difference*. New York NY: Routledge.

Gilbert, J. and C. Howe (1991) 'Beyond state vs. society: theories of the state and New Deal agricultural policies', *American Sociological Review* 56 (April): 204–20.

Hammel, E. A. and A. Gullickson (2004) 'Kinship structures and survival', *Population Studies: A Journal of Demography* 58 (2): 145–59.

Hochschild, A. R. (2012) *The Outsourced Self: Intimate life in market times*. New York NY: Henry Holt and Company.

Lairap-Fonderson, J. (2002) 'The disciplinary power of micro credit: examples from Kenya and Cameroon' in J. Parpart, S. Rai, and K. Staudt (eds), *Rethinking Empowerment: Gender and development in a global/local world*. New York NY: Routledge.

Lukács, G. (1981) *The Destruction of Reason*. London: Merlin.

Luxemburg, R. (1951 [1913]) *The Accumulation of Capital*. New Haven CT: Yale University Press.

Lynch, K. (2007) 'Love labour as a distinct and non-commodifiable form of care labour', *Sociological Review* 55 (3): 550–70.

Mallon, F. (1987) 'Patriarchy in the transition to capitalism', *Feminist Studies* 13 (2): 379–407.

Mann, S. A. (1990a) *Agrarian Capitalism in Theory and Practice*. Chapel Hill NC: University of North Carolina Press.

— (1990b) 'Common grounds and crossroads: slavery, sharecropping, and sexual inequality', *Signs: Journal of Women in Culture and Society* 14 (4): 77498.

— (2012) *Doing Feminist Theory: From modernity to postmodernity*. New York NY: Oxford University Press.

Mann, S. A. and J. M. Dickinson (1978) 'Obstacles to the development of a capitalist agriculture', *Journal of Peasant Studies* 5 (4): 466–81.

Marx, K. (1996 [1867]) *Capital*. Volume I in *Marx/Engels Collected Works*, Volume 35. New York NY: International Publishers.

McMichael, P. (2005) 'Global development and the corporate food regime' in F. Buttel and P. McMichael (eds), *New Directions in the Sociology of Global Development: Research in rural sociology and development*. Volume 11. Oxford: Elsevier, pp. 265–99.

— (2008) *Development and Social Change*. Thousand Oaks CA: Pine Forge Press.

Mies, M., V. Bennholdt-Thomsen and C. Von Werlhof (1988) *Women: The last colony*. London: Zed Books.

Rubin, L. (1976) *Worlds of Pain*. New York NY: Basic Books.

Schlosser, E. (2012) *Fast Food Nation*. Boston MA: Mariner Books.

Schnittker, J. A. (1970) 'Distribution of benefits from existing and prospective farm programs' in E. O. Heady (ed.), *Benefits and Burdens of Rural Development*. Ames IA: Iowa State University Centre for Agricultural and Economic Development, Iowa State University Press, pp. 89–104.

Scott, J. C. (1976) *The Moral Economy of the Peasant: Rebellion and subsistence in southeast Asia*. New Haven CT: Yale University Press.

Seccombe, W. (1973) 'The housewife and her labour under capitalism', *New Left Review* 83 (January–February): 3–24.

— (1992) *A Millennium of Family Change: Feudalism to capitalism in northern Europe*. London: Verso.

Smith, D. E. (1987) *The Everyday World as Problematic: A feminist sociology*. Boston MA: Northeastern University Press.

— (1990) *The Conceptual Practices of Power: A feminist sociology of knowledge*. Boston MA: Northeastern University Press.

Stacey, J. (1991) *Brave New Families*. New York NY: Basic Books.

Thompson, E. P. (1993) 'The moral economy of the English crowd in the eighteenth century', in *Customs in Common*. New York NY: Penguin Books.

Thurow, L. C. (1996) *The Future of Capitalism: How today's economic forces shape tomorrow's world*. New York NY: William Morrow.

Truelove, C. (1987) 'The informal sector revisited: the case of the Colombian mini-maquilas' in R. Tardanico (ed.), *Crises in the Caribbean Basin: Past and present*. Beverly Hills CA: Sage, pp. 95–110.

Vogel, L. (1981) 'Marxism and socialist-feminist theory: a decade of debate', *Current Perspectives in Social Theory* 2: 209–31.

— (1983) *Marxism and the Oppression of Women: Towards a unitary theory*. New Brunswick NJ: Rutgers University Press.

Ward, K. (ed.) (1990) *Women Workers and Global Restructuring*. Cornell International Industrial and Labour Relations (ILR) Report no. 17. Ithaca NY: ILR Press, Cornell University Press.

Welty, G. (2012) 'Contribución a la crítica de Chayanov: la teoría de la unidad laboral familiar', *Mundo Siglo XXI* VIII (28): 5–17.

4 | BAROQUE MODERNITY AND PEASANT POVERTY IN THE TWENTY-FIRST CENTURY

Luis Arizmendi

1. Epochal crisis of capitalism and peasant poverty

Peasant poverty constitutes a complex tragedy in which the various dimensions of the epochal *crisis of twenty-first-century capitalism* are intertwined and combined: in one way or another, the mundialisation of poverty,[1] the world food crisis, the global financial crisis, the new crisis of overproduction and the globalised environmental crisis (Arizmendi 2013) all converge and have an impact on peasant poverty. The peasant poverty of our time is a window onto the epochal crisis of twenty-first-century capitalism and the complexity of crossroads that make of this age a time of transition.

Without doubt, the twenty-first century is the time of the most radical ambivalence in the history of capitalist modernity. It is the century that reveals, in the most glaring way, how far capitalism has already carried forward the schizophrenic and dangerous combination that defines and characterises the essence of its configuration of modernity: the combination of progress and devastation. Although this is the time of the greatest technological progress in the history of modernity, contradictorily, and in tandem, a new era has begun: the *mundialisation of poverty*.[2] Previously, poverty was not worldwide, but by the turn of the present century capitalism had made it a planetary phenomenon. In conjunction with the mundialisation of poverty, the current global warming process – which is not simply synonymous with 'climate change' but rather represents a *truly global environmental collapse* – is at the core of the epochal crisis of twenty-first-century capitalism: the most radical combination of progress and devastation in the history of modern capitalism.

What may be defined as the *epochal crisis of capitalism* is a crisis that calls into question capitalism *in toto*. A crisis that is indeed epochal because it began several decades ago and will last for many decades to come in contemporary history. In addition to the combination of the *globalised environmental crisis* – whose beginnings date back to the 1970s – and the *mundialisation of poverty* – which, given its potential for political destabilisation, was acknowledged by the World Bank for the first time as a strategic problem in its 1990 *World Development Report* – the second half of the new century's first decade saw the juxtaposition of the *first great crisis of worldwide overproduction* and the emergence of the *world food crisis*. Crises of different orders intersect and complicate each other, together forming the current multidimensional but unitary crisis, the worst in the history of capitalist mundialisation. Neither the Long Depression of the late nineteenth century (1871–93) nor the Great Depression of the twentieth century (1929–44) were crises with such gigantic historical impacts. While an epochal crisis is not synonymous with inevitable collapse, this is indeed a possibility – to the extent that the globalised environmental crisis is the main threat to the future of modernity (Arizmendi 2014a). Capitalism is confronted with the challenge of undergoing a metamorphosis – of redefining its very historical configuration – if it is to continue.

In this context, 2011 has been registered as a highly idiosyncratic year in the advance of the epochal crisis of twenty-first-century capitalism. Alongside the energy industry, referred to in Wall Street as the 'mother of all markets', the agro-industrial food chain has positioned itself as one of the largest sales channels in the global accumulation of capital. At the same time, as an incontrovertible expression of the schizophrenic character of capitalist modernity, while the agro-industrial food circuit became one of the most lucrative businesses on the planet, a food crisis exploded that was the most severe not only in the history of modernity but in the history of humanity. Never before have so many human beings – more than 1 billion – been immersed in the limit situation of starving.

Questioning the hunger measurement method employed by the Food and Agriculture Organization of the United Nations (FAO), Thomas Pogge has emphasised that, far from moving forward to achieve the first Millennium Development Goal by 2015, which proposed to halve the 1996 numbers for global hunger, the total number of hungry people is now more than 50 per cent above the FAO's estimate. The FAO adopts as a threshold the calorie intake required for a sedentary lifestyle; if instead it used the intake needed for hard manual labour – which is the calorie intake predominantly needed by the poor – the result would be that, during the last decade, hunger would have displayed a drastic upward trend rather than decreasing. Thus, the real number of undernourished human beings in 2012 would be more than 1.33 billion instead of the 800 million acknowledged by the FAO (Pogge et al. 2013: 3).

There is a double connection between this positioning of agro-industry in the global economy and the mundialisation of poverty: in relation to consumption, the spread of hunger around the world; and in relation to agricultural production, the dramatic persistence of peasant poverty. Peasants not only suffer the most intense poverty in the era of the mundialisation of poverty, but their grave situation persists despite the growing productive capacity of the world food economy, precisely because we are entering a period of high food prices and agribusiness has become one of the foremost channels for the global accumulation of capital.

After the undeniable failure of all the predictions relating to the alleged unstoppable tendency towards the disappearance of the peasant economy during the twentieth century – to be replaced by large-scale capitalist agriculture with the mundialisation of modern technology – and even more so now that this mundialisation has taken place, within the framework of the world food crisis it is becoming increasingly important that small rural producers continue to exist in order to confront this crisis. In this scenario, the controversy over the complex relationship between capitalism and the peasantry – and between the process of reconfiguring modernity in the twenty-first century and the peasantry – has become a matter of the utmost importance.

2. The controversy over peasant poverty within capitalism

The main limit in this controversy has arisen from the impact of the myth of progress: that is, from the illusion that capitalism is synonymous with a purely positive lineal history of political and economic progress for everyone.

The controversy on the peasant economy within capitalism has encompassed a range of diverse positions. Three of them are highly relevant.

The first, conventional position that derives from the myth of progress attributes peasant poverty to the *persistence of pre-modern, pre-capitalist forms of production*. This line of thought views the peasantry as being outside the trajectory of progress, and regards its destiny as being absorbed and extinguished by capitalism. This perspective is unable to decipher the relation between the peasantry and capitalism. It fails to acknowledge *capitalist domination over peasant labour as the foundation of peasant poverty.*

The second position is one that foregrounds the relation between the peasantry and capitalism, but immediately reduces the sphere of this relation to simple commodity production, thereby disregarding capitalist domination of peasant labour, as does the first position. Within the framework of international influence of the Althusserian controversy about the 'articulation of modes of production' or the 'social-economic formation', this position interpreted peasant poverty through the illusion of a historically non-existent 'peasant mode of production' (Rey 1973; Palerm 1980).

In both cases, the persistence of pre-capitalist forms of production would presumably be the basis of the poverty experienced by the peasantry (or what we call *campesindios* in some regions of Latin America). Pre-modernity is viewed as the cause of peasant poverty.

Progressivist Marxism – the name corresponds to a Marxism that is trapped and defeated by the myth of progress – is unable to decipher peasant poverty.

Lastly, the third position assumes that, in effect, the capitalist economy deploys different forms of domination over the peasant economy, but considers it essential – in order to decipher the different historical configurations of capitalist domination of peasant labour – to develop the perspective of critical Marxism. As opposed to progressivist Marxism, *critical Marxism* refuses to look at the history of capitalist modernity as the unstoppable march of progress. It does not read the history of capitalism as a linear path, but as an extremely complex process in which the development of capitalist domination may well resort to the coexistence and the criss-crossing of different and even opposing historical configurations.

3. The specific formal subsumption of agricultural labour by capital, and seasonal time wages

Julio Boltvinik has accurately highlighted that, despite the advance of the capitalist configuration of agriculture, capitalism has enabled the peasantry to persist because of the asymmetry between the discontinuous requirement of labour in agriculture and the need for the continuous reproduction of the labour force. By stating the problem in these terms – by placing emphasis on the seasonal nature of agriculture as the basis for discontinuous labour and pointing out that capitalism does not absorb the costs of the annual reproduction of the peasant labour force, in contrast to the case in major industrial branches where labour is continuous – Boltvinik places the discussion in the extremely prolific terrain of *use value*: that is, within the framework of the qualitative legality of the social–natural metabolism. In this sense, the concrete peculiarity of the agricultural labour process, in which nature and its cycles are decisive, determines a particular type of relation of labour power and capitalism.

He points out that the reproduction schemes of capital, formulated by Marx in Volume II of *Capital: A Critique of Political Economy*, are adequate only for continuous processes of production; when applied to non-continuous processes such as those of agriculture, the labour force would be unable to reproduce. If one corrects this by incorporating payment for 365 days of wages in the agricultural labour force, a discrepancy arises, since the commodities produced by the agricultural sector contain solely the value generated in the working days in which this discontinuous labour is carried out (in this example, 100 days per year). This underscores the fact that the peculiarity of the agricultural labour process, in terms of its use value, has an ineluctable impact on the dimension of value and on the reproduction of the labour force. He focuses on a genuine problem that is not solved by questioning the Critical Theory of Value in order to redefine it, as Boltvinik does. Rather, this problem makes it necessary to decipher the way in which capitalism uses and abuses the law of value, alternating between complying with it and violating it, depending on what is deemed necessary for the functioning of its system of domination.

The premise that the value of labour power must invariably be equivalent to the satisfaction of needs, thus guaranteeing the process of social reproduction of the worker (proletarian or peasant), disregards the unavoidable violence contained and unleashed by the commodification of human labour power. The case of peasant labour is perhaps the most radical case of violence involved in the violation of the law of value in the relationship between capital and labour.

The commodification of the labour force involves historical violence that is unleashed at different levels. At the foundation of an anonymous economic violence that takes many forms is the general violence that is implied in placing the subject worker in danger of death in order to impose the commodification of the labour force by means of the expropriation of the means of production.

The commodification of the labour force constitutes a historical form with a profound contradiction: although its configuration introduces an abstract legalism that begins with equivalence, it always contains the potential and effective threat of 'inequivalence', or, in other words, of the violation of the law of value in the capital–labour relation. In his theory on wages, in Part 6 of Volume I of *Capital*, Marx demonstrates that the commodification of the labour force has the permanent potential to radicalise the violence on which it is founded, with a disruption of the equivalence between the value of the labour force and the historical-moral element that determines the necessary requirements of its social reproduction (Marx 1976 [1867]: 275, 675 ff.). In its concrete dimension, labour power is a subjective force endowed with capacities and needs that must be satisfied; however, in its abstract dimension it is a value that may always be fragmented to fit the needs of capital.

Equivalence may be violated not only through an *extension of the labour workday* in which the corresponding exertion is not acknowledged with an increase in wages, but also through a *reduction in the working day (or period)* that justifies not covering the total value of the labour force: this takes place when wages are configured as time wages (Marx 1976 [1867]: 675 ff.).

From this perspective, it may be said that capitalist domination over agricultural dayworkers (whether peasants or proletarians) establishes and constitutes a particular form of wages that I refer to as *seasonal time wages*. This is a peculiar form that, based on the unavoidable configuration of working time as seasonal working time, imposes and justifies a fragmentation of the value of the labour force which determines that wages will not be adequate for the annual reproduction of that labour force. The discontinuous labour of the dayworker in agriculture results in a specific form of time wages. This signifies that the rule for agricultural dayworkers is in violation of the law of value in the capital–labour relation, as wages paid to rural seasonal workers will never be adequate for satisfying their needs.

Stated more broadly, in the rural context, the formal subsumption of the labour process under capital structurally acquires an extremely peculiar configuration in which the burden of seasonal labour is placed on the subject, violating permanently the law of value in the capital–labour relation.

Formal subsumption of the labour process to capital is a critical concept in the economic structure of capitalism, and not just a phase of modern economic history. There is no capitalism without formal subsumption (Marx 1976: 1019 ff.). *Subsumption is almost synonymous with domination. But the meaning of subsumption is a combination of subordination and inclusion,* as explained by Pedro Scaron in his translation to Spanish of 'Resultate des Unmittelbaren Producktionsprozesses' (1971: xv). The term emphasises that the abstract legality of capital penetrates and alters the concrete legality of the labour process. Capital seeks the refunctionalisation and absorption of what it dominates.

The subsumption of the *form* of the labour process – that is, of the relationship between the subject worker and the means of production – corresponds to the domination that capital imposes by forcing the subject to admit the commodification of his/her labour power. Expropriation of the means of production generates expropriation of the means of consumption, therefore establishing the threat of a structural crisis in the process of life reproduction of the worker and the worker's family. The subject internalises what begins as an external violence, as the danger of death, when he or she accepts the commodification of his or her labour power as a survival strategy. In this sense, a simulation of peace – or rather a state of *pax*: anonymous economic violence as the foundation of *specific formal subsumption* – is the permanent platform of capitalism.

Through its regular and continuous functioning, the formal subsumption of labour by capital imposes the commodification of the workforce and an abstract productivism that incessantly extracts surplus value, and does not need to violate the law of value in the capital–labour relation. But the formal subsumption of agricultural labour by capital is highly peculiar: it constitutes a historical domination that imposes this violation as a permanent rule. The capitalist formal subsumption of the relationship of the peasant with nature inevitably transfers to the worker the impact of the seasonality of agricultural labour. Therefore, the *specific formal subsumption* of agricultural labour by capital is characterised by seasonal time wages.

In the previous phase of the world food economy, which was characterised by the capacity of many nations to produce their own food requirements, the functionality of the formal subsumption of wage peasant labour for capital accumulation was twofold: on the one hand, it brought an effective saving in the amount of wages paid for the agricultural labour force; and, on the other, it allowed an effective transfer of value from the rural context to urban and national industrial capital, by decreasing the costs of food and fibres. In both cases, a domino effect was provoked by the reduction in wage costs (as fibre, and especially food, represent a substantial part of the cost of reproduction of the national labour force).

Only through a political intervention by the state in the rural setting would it be possible to apply monetary transfers to compensate for the violence accompanying the violation of the law of value for wage agricultural labour. However, this is not the way the state functions in peripheral capitalism. In fact, this is not the case in metropolitan capitalism either, where agro-capitalism tends to hire a migrant labour force in order to impose this violence. The agricultural labour power of peripheral capitalism, whether working in the South or in the North, receives a wage that does not cover the value of that labour power.

4. Cynical or brutal overexploitation

Given the power structure of the world economy, the states of peripheral capitalisms are unable to duplicate the practices of metropolitan states. Through unequal exchange, they must pay the tribute of technological rent to metropolitan capitalism due to the instrumental supremacy of the latter. Therefore, peripheral capitalisms repeatedly impose a violation of the law of value in the capital–labour relation within their nations, as an ongoing attempt to compensate for their losses on the world market (Marini 1973). And the place where this violation is established most severely is in the *formal subsumption of agricultural* labour by capital. For this reason, modernity's penetration into agriculture – consolidating the *specific formal subsumption of the agricultural labour force* – in no way generates prosperity for peasants.

Overexploitation is a concept that does not necessarily mean that there is a very high rate of surplus value. Rather, it indicates that, in addition to the *exploitation* of surplus value – but different from it – another mechanism is installed and imposed in order to extract value from workers: the mechanism of *expropriation* of value, which is bound originally to the social consumption fund as payment of wages and is re-channelled to the capitalist accumulation fund. Overexploitation, which indicates not only obtaining surplus value but also the expropriation of a certain percentage of the value of labour power, is imposed. Although they are formally different, both the extension and the reduction of working time, when there is no equivalence between the value of labour power and wages, are effective ways to impose labour overexploitation.

In the history of capitalist overexploitation of labour power, three periods can be distinguished (Arizmendi 2010: 35–7). The first is the *period of overexploitation of labour power concentrated in the metropolis*. This period spans approximately from 1740 to 1880, during the genesis of modern technology within large-scale industry in the West. This technology was used as a weapon that allowed capitalism to systematically set the reserve army of workers against the army of active workers, in order to increase surplus value in all its modalities, and to promote an aggressive violation of the law of value in the capital–labour relation.

The second, from approximately 1880 to 1970 or 1980, is a period in which the capitalist mundialisation counteracted the overexploitation of workers in the metropolises of Europe and the US, increasing their living standards in order to boost internal markets and national accumulation processes; this was not the case, obviously, for migrant labour power from peripheral countries. Meanwhile, peripheral capitalisms offset the tribute paid to metropolitan capitalisms by violating the law of value in capital–labour internal relations in order to obtain a *spurious* surplus value. We could call this the *period of labour overexploitation concentrated in the periphery*. At this stage, the superexploitation of the metropolis was transferred to the periphery, and one of its expressions was the overexploitation of migrant labour in the metropolis.

The third period – the period *of mundialisation of labour overexploitation*, which emerged in the 1980s – has dramatically highlighted the dominance of planetary technology in the service of capitalist accumulation. The peculiarity about this stage is that the segments of capital holding the monopoly of cutting-edge technology have adopted the leading role in the expansion and intensification of the super-exploitation of labour throughout the planet. Based on the computerisation of the labour process, offshoring has given metropolitan capitals the greatest mobility in their history to move from one country to another, undercutting wages everywhere. The information revolution has generated, in addition to the largest international reserve army in modern economic history, the globalisation of competition and confrontation among the various national portions of world labour power, despite maintaining a formally non-globalised labour market. Even without emigrating from their countries, workers in the peripheral states are pitted one against the other to accept ever lower wages and thus attract transnational investment.

In this new period, overexploitation of the labour force has widened: it is now imposed not only by peripheral capital but also by metropolitan transnational capital, and even by capital controlling the most advanced technologies.

Although suggestive, the term 'redoubled overexploitation' (Osorio 2009) is not the most appropriate term to describe this phenomenon. *Brutal or cynical overexploitation* seems more adequate, to the extent that it identifies an increasingly violent capitalism that overexploits the labour force, which belongs to the active working army, leaving its basic needs unsatisfied.

When overexploitation is imposed by peripheral capital to pay tribute to metropolitan capital, it is an *extraordinary indirect profit*; and when cynical overexploitation is imposed by metropolitan capital, especially if it is applied to large numbers of workers, as happens with peasants, it becomes a source of *direct extraordinary profit*.

5. Baroque modernity and the non-specific formal subsumption of peasant labour by capital

Because they are obliged to invent necessarily mixed strategies for vital reproduction, the social units of peasant labour power have found it necessary to interlink two lines of reproduction in order to survive: 1) their commodification as labour force; and 2) the baroque persistence of ecological and communitarian social forms, such as self-production and self-consumption processes adapted specifically to scarcity.

Baroque modernity is an innovative concept created by Bolívar Echeverría – one of the most erudite critical thinkers of the last half century – to define the complexity of the historical configuration of modernity and capitalism in Latin America, and more generally in peripheral nations. Its historical peculiarity lies precisely in the extremely extravagant combination of pre-modern and modern social forms (Echeverría 2011). In baroque modernity, two different historical times coexist as one: pre-capitalist and capitalist forms are interlinked, since the social subject can resist adversity and danger through this configuration (Arizmendi 2014b: 45–58). With an *unstable combination of resistance and integration*, baroque modernity creates a survival strategy in capitalist modernity, a strategy that tries to make liveable the unliveable character of capitalism (Echeverría 1998: 173–84).

For all readings of the persistence of peasant poverty based on the myth of progress, it is simply impossible to understand the complexity of baroque modernity. Such readings are incapable of understanding peasant poverty as a result of modern domination. They cannot understand that *peasant labour (during the capitalist era) has never been outside the orbit of capitalist subsumption, although, of course, it is not reduced to it.*

In Latin America, critical Marxism, contrary to the viewpoint of the progressivist discourse, has investigated the connection between the peasant economy and the capitalist economy, not in terms of a relation of exteriority, and not as the contact between two forms that are articulated from the outside, but rather as a relationship of domination in which the capitalist economy absorbs and penetrates the peasant economy, placing it at its service, while the peasant economy attempts to survive. Thereby, the persistence of pre-capitalist forms can be conceptualised not only as a result of *resistance* but, paradoxically, also as a result of *a necessity of capitalism*. However, it can also be conceptualised the other way round: not only as a result of *a necessity of capitalism*, but as a result of an *effective historical resistance*.

The pioneering contributions of Bolívar Echeverría and Armando Bartra opened up new perspectives in the search for routes to decipher the peculiarity of the relationship between capitalism and non-capitalism. These contrast with the simplified versions of subsumption theory based on a unilinear reading of economic history, as developed by Roger Bartra and Guillermo Foladori. If the myth of progress absorbs subsumption theory, its innovative potential is diluted.

Roger Bartra (1979) explored the complex relationship between peasant labour and formal capitalist subsumption, but without the necessary mediations. He ends up confounding the definition of the peasant economy as simple commodity production with capitalist commodity production; in the latter, peasants would presumably be simultaneously their own bosses and their own workers. His attempt to apply subsumption theory to rural areas fails precisely because it is impossible for the peasant to be subject and object of an exploitation of himself by himself. All relations of exploitation require a split: a polarity between exploiters and exploited. In this sense, his intervention is suggestive for opening up a problem that it fails to resolve: that of the complex relation between peasant labour and capitalist subsumption.

Later, Foladori (1986) advanced a step forward and included some mediations, when, in his critique of Roger Bartra, he used the content but not the term *hybrid forms* of subsumption created by Marx in Chapter 16 of Volume I of *Capital*. These are forms in which the producer is not exploited directly, but through the circulation of capital. Nonetheless, Foladori does not manage to move beyond Roger Bartra's perspective in relation to the subsumption theory. Both of them conceive of formal subsumption and real subsumption merely as *successive phases* in the unstoppable, linear march of capitalist history. It could be said, therefore, that the greater possibilities of the subsumption theory were absorbed and defeated by the myth of progress, by a progressivist and linear reading of modern history.

When Bolívar Echeverría translated into Spanish selected passages from Marx's *Manuscripts of 1861–63* (Marx 1983),[3] he also formulated a complex conception in which formal subsumption and real subsumption of labour by capital are not merely successive phases in the development of capitalism. He argued that real subsumption – that is, the capitalist domination that alters the technological network, stamping it with the schizophrenic legality of progress and devastation of capitalist modernity – emerges as a stage following the formal subsumption of labour by capital. However, it may well be that highly advanced configurations of capitalist real subsumption could require an evolving process that re-edits the *formal subsumption* of labour by capital as a form of domination or leads to its persistence. Rather than simply preceding it, formal subsumption may *coexist* alongside real subsumption as a *complementary form*. In his presentation of this translation, Bolívar Echeverría (1983: 2) outlined an innovative theoretical programme, pointing out that a complex conception of the forms of capitalist subsumption has a very important role to play in the reconceptualisation of Latin America's history.

Armando Bartra (1979) proposed, from a different perspective, his formulation of the parallel coexistence of formal subsumption as a form of domination that is different from, but functional and complementary to, capitalist real subsumption of labour. In the framework of debate relating to the rural ambit, this is one of his most significant contributions to classic Marxism in Latin America.

From a perspective that explores the relationship between Marxism and peasantism (*campesinismo*), he argues that the persistence of non-capitalist forms in rural areas, without constituting the full formal subsumption of labour by capital, does not leave peasant labour outside capitalist domination in any way. In this sense, peasant labour is effectively an object of exploitation, but inserted within a very particular configuration of capitalist domination, one that is conceptualised by Armando Bartra as *restricted formal subsumption* (2006: 227).

Two elements lead to the shaping of this peculiar configuration of capitalist domination of peasant labour. First, its uniqueness as a productive process in which it is more difficult to 'substitute natural processes with technological processes' (ibid.: 225), so that restricted formal subsumption 'adapts better to the relative backwardness of agricultural labour processes' (ibid.: 228). And, second, global capital's need to counteract the transfer of value as ground rent, which, if the full formal subsumption of labour were to be established broadly and exclusively in agriculture, would necessarily have to occur from non-agricultural activities to capitalist agriculture. Therefore, establishing the restricted formal subsumption of agricultural labour by capital – in other words, allowing and even encouraging the persistence of peasant labour – is highly functional for capitalism because it leads to a certain kind of 'reversed rent', or a transfer of value from peasant agriculture to capitalism.

The relationship between peasants and capitalism cannot be reduced to unequal exchange. The importance of the concept of restricted formal subsumption is shown in the fact that, without the personification of the capitalist and the wage worker within rural production, capital effectively dominates peasant labour. Initially it exercises this dominion via the process of circulation, and from there it enters into the labour process, constituting a type of *indirect subsumption*.

Paradoxically, this historical configuration of capitalist domination makes it possible to exploit surplus value without commodifying the labour force. Armando Bartra thoroughly deciphers this in the following terms:

> Paraphrasing Marx, we might say that the solution to the mystery of the exploitation suffered by the peasant cannot emerge from an analysis of circulation, nor, however, does the key lie outside it ... In the case of the wage worker, the possibility condition of exploitation is located in the market with the appearance of labour power as a commodity, but the exploitation process is consummated in production ... In the case of exploitation of the peasantry, the articulation between the two aspects is equally strong but inverted: the possibility condition of exploitation is located in the production process ... but the exploitation is consummated in the market, where peasants transfer their surplus through an unequal exchange. (ibid.: 249)

The complexity of the unequal exchange in the relationship between the peasantry and capitalism consists in the fact that it configures a path for the effective exploitation of peasant labour by capital.

But Armando Bartra also develops the concept of the *general subsumption of labour in capital*:

> concepts of formal and real subsumption should be developed to refer them to global social capital ... If we refer to the process of production in a broad sense – that is, to the process of production–circulation of global capital – it seems evident that there can be no domination of the capitalist mode of production without the real subsumption of labour to [global] capital ... The domination of the capitalist mode of production, and therefore real subsumption, take place in the degree that capital

takes hold of – or develops – the key branches of industry, and therefore appropriates the decisive segment of the means of production and proletarianises the fundamental sector of the labour force. This is enough to put the rest of the units of production and branches at the service of capital ... It is thus possible to conclude that, in formations where productive processes subsist in which real subsumption, and occasionally also formal subsumption, have not taken place as *particular forms*, it is the *general subsumption of labour in capital* that always takes place. (ibid.: 222–4)

Applying this theoretical development to agriculture, he argues that non-capitalist forms of production in rural areas are not outside capitalist domination, even though full formal subsumption of labour by capital is not configured. The *general subsumption of agriculture* occurs:

through a *restricted formal subsumption*, or, which is the same, an agriculture in which a more or less extended sector of units of production, which in themselves are non-capitalist, ... subsist. In this way, paradoxically, the logic of the general subsumption of agricultural work in capital imposes itself through the form of restricting particular subsumption, and the needs of global social capital manifest themselves in the reproduction of non-capitalist units of production. The existence of the peasantry in the capitalist mode of production is manifested as a result of the reproduction needs of this mode of production. (ibid.: 227–8)

From the content of the 'specifically capitalist' concept that Marx used to define the 'specifically capitalist mode of production' (to qualify a historical configuration of capitalism that destroys all remnants of pre-capitalism), I formulated the concept of *non-specific formal subsumption* of labour by capital. It is a concept that examines the relation of capitalism to non-capitalism from the perspective of the domination of the latter by the former. Although the terms *restricted formal subsumption* and *non-specific formal subsumption* are synonymous, I prefer the latter.

While restricted formal subsumption is a term that highlights the fact that exploitation is consummated in the market, *non-specific formal subsumption* is an expression that emphasises capital's domination of the labour process by refunctionalising those non-capitalist forms that have not been overthrown. In this sense, and to complement the concept of the 'specifically capitalist', we could state that the 'non-specifically capitalist' corresponds to the combination of capitalist and pre-capitalist relations of production. It is precisely this peculiarity to which Marx refers when he constructs his complex concept of '*hybrid forms*' of formal subsumption of labour by capital (Marx 1976: 645). It could be said that, even though the non-specific formal subsumption precedes the specifically capitalist mode of production (in the framework of primitive accumulation), *the specifically capitalist mode of production itself generates spaces of non-specific formal subsumption* in order to dominate certain productive processes, first of all in rural settings.

This exploitation, consummated in the market in the case of peasants, not only transfers surplus value through an unequal exchange, but expropriates the value of the wage fund of consumption as well. However, despite these multiple violations of the law of value in the capital–labour relation, the global validity of the law of value in capitalism is not cancelled out. Violation of the law of value is always followed by its subsequent compliance. It makes sense for capital to violate the law of value in the capital–labour relation only if it subsequently makes the law of value effective for converting this expropriated value into money. Not paying the full value of peasant products makes sense if, when selling the final goods for which they serve as raw materials or when reselling the same products, the capitalist converts into money the value expropriated from peasants. Therefore, this violation of the law of value is a weapon of *restricted or non-specific formal subsumption* of peasant labour by capital.

From this viewpoint, it can be stated that in Latin America, where capitalism necessarily acquired the historical configuration of baroque modernity, there were two bases on which the persistence of peasant labour non-specifically formally subsumed to capital was generated.

On the one hand, as stated above, Latin American capitalism counterbalances technological rents paid abroad by compensating for its losses on the world market through the establishment of wages that stop short of satisfying the historical moral reproduction of the labour force. Thus Latin American capitalism has been obliged not only to allow the persistence of mixed strategies of social reproduction that combine the commodification of the labour force with the continuity of pre-capitalist forms of production. It has made the *mixed strategies of social reproduction a structurally positive condition for the functioning of capitalist accumulation*, which otherwise would be unable to achieve the reproduction of the national labour force.

Baroque modernity has not only been an *epochal resistance* but has simultaneously been an *epochal necessity* of Latin American capitalism. However, at the same time, *the baroque is irreducible to its functionality for capitalism because its self-management and ecological resilience contain an effective and hopeful transcapitalist power*. In this sense, baroque modernity combines resistance and integration.

On the other hand, because of the peculiarity of the *use value* that constitutes the object of domination in agriculture – nature and its seasonal cycles – the non-specific formal subsumption of labour by capital, while slowing down the development of real subsumption without blocking it, constitutes an ad hoc modality for capitalist domination over agriculture in baroque modernity. Capitalism always tends to externalise costs. It thus consistently externalises environmental costs – letting the future pay for the environmental devastation produced by capitalist modernity here and now – and the costs that agricultural seasonality imposes on the annual reproduction of the labour force. Within the specific formal subsumption of agricultural labour by capital, this externalisation takes place through the establishment of seasonal time wages as its structural form of wages. Within the non-specific formal subsumption of labour by capital, this is carried out through the unequal exchange that enables the overexploitation of peasant labour. Both are ways of overexploiting labour.

In Latin American baroque modernity, real subsumption as the general form of the economy – in other words, industrial capitalist modernisation – has been accompanied and complemented by both the specific formal subsumption and the non-specific formal subsumption of agricultural labour by capital. The combination of capitalist and pre-capitalist forms in agriculture, and the persistence of peasant labour, reveals its functionality for baroque modernity as a form of capitalism.

6. The interaction of the non-specific and specific configurations of formal subsumption with the real subsumption of agricultural labour by capital in the twenty-first century

The explosion of the world food crisis, a crucial element in the multidimensional structure of the epochal crisis of twenty-first-century capitalism, is confronting capitalism with the need for its reconfiguration. It is not the extinction of peasant labour that is being promoted, but rather its persistence (at least to a certain degree), together with a tendency to interweave it with more developed forms of capitalist subsumption.

In the history of the world food economy, three phases can be distinguished during the last century.

1. The *food sovereignty phase* revolved around the capacity of many nations to provide for their own food requirements. At the end of the 1930s, Western Europe was the world's only cereal-importing region. The amount of cereals exported by Latin America was practically twice the amount exported by North America and Eastern Europe (including the Soviet Union).

2. The *increasing artificial food dependency phase* was brought about by the wrongly named 'neoliberal' globalisation beginning in the 1970s. The reordering of the world economy based on 'free trade' drove a strategic de-financing with which the 'neoliberal' state weakened agriculture in practically all peripheral countries. At the same time, a strategic concentration of cereal production controlled by powerful transnational corporations was promoted, primarily in the United States. Africa was the continent where what can be called the cynical domination of the food production and consumption chain was first tested. As a result of the mundialisation of this cynical domination, the majority of nations that previously enjoyed food sovereignty have lost that status. Latin America, Eastern Europe, Asia and Africa are now increasingly importing cereals, while approximately 70 per cent of peripheral nations are net food importers.

3. The *phase of global food crisis of the twenty-first century* means that the promise made by capitalist modernity – the promise that the progress from modern technology would leave agricultural crises and famines behind, as phenomena linked to the economic

backwardness of the *ancien régime* – is heading for its most radical collapse in history. A new transition is beginning, driving the reconfiguration of the world food economy in the context of different and conflicting projects for capitalism and modernity.[4]

Without doubt, the global food crisis is not synonymous with an unstoppable breakdown of capitalism. Rather, it represents a challenge to capitalism that calls for its metamorphosis – something it has undertaken countless times throughout its history – in order to shore up its power. But history is not destiny. Complex and contradictory tendencies are vying for the upper hand in defining the path to be taken by mundialisation.

An initial crossroads in response to the collapse resulting from the cynical configuration of the world food economy can be found in the confrontation between the advocates of a genuinely liberal (in the political sense) reconfiguration of capitalism and those of a neo-authoritarian tendency, who are not willing to give up the advantages achieved by cynical capitalism and are attempting to take it even further.

A number of states – not for philanthropic reasons but rather with the aim of configuring the strategic management of class struggle – have begun to implement policies for controlling their markets to safeguard their food security: China, Russia, Argentina, India, the Ukraine, Kazakhstan, Vietnam, Egypt and Cambodia have all reduced or cancelled their grain exports. The outcomes, scopes and rhythms of this new transition are still to be defined, but what cannot be denied is that the current global food crisis is shattering the social limits towards which cynical capitalism has been pushing the reproduction of the labour force in many nations and regions (FAO 2009).

With the aim of achieving or restoring food sovereignty in many nations – and even more so in light of the historical need to nearly double the world's food production in the next four decades to match population growth – the project of a genuine liberal capitalism in the twenty-first century is already announcing its intention of expanding the area under cultivation by millions of hectares, and making extensive use of peasant labour. It is not by accident that a new pro-peasantry project is emerging in the discourse of various international organisations.

If this tendency in the reconfiguration of world capitalism triumphs, peasant labour will be far from extinct in this century. However, this is in no way synonymous with achieving an end to peasant poverty. The unfolding of capitalist domination, with its interaction of real subsumption, operating in urban industry and in the agro-industry that monopolises land with the greatest fertility, and non-specific formal subsumption of peasant labour by capital, launched to operate in marginal lands, will guarantee the continuity of the exploitation of peasant workers by capital and the continuity of their poverty.

This unfolding, however, tends to involve a complex interweaving, not seen before in the history of capitalist domination, between the non-specific formal subsumption of peasant labour by capital and its real subsumption. The complexity of this interweaving lies in the fact that peasant economic units – without the direct personification of the capitalist or the wage worker, and despite their persistence – are now being contracted to apply genetic engineering innovations that imply real capitalist subsumption of peasant work, as capital dominates the materiality of modern technology, materiality that embodies the schizophrenic capitalist legality combining progress and devastation.

With the objective of confronting the environmental crisis of global warming, PepsiCo has developed potatoes and sunflowers – necessary for producing potato chips – that are resistant to drought and that are being grown by farmers and peasants in China and Mexico. This company states that it is currently working with 25,000 peasants around the world. Nestlé is subcontracting 500,000 farmers to produce certain crops and milk products. SABMiller, one of the world's most powerful beer corporations, works with 28,000 peasants (19,000 of them in Africa) to grow genetically modified grains (ETC Group 2012).

The persistence of non-specific formal subsumption in the twenty-first century seeks to combine a form of capitalist domination of discontinuous labour, which allows capital to avoid assuming the annual reproduction of the labour force, with a condition that places on the shoulders of the *campesindios* not the ecological rebalancing of the planet but rather the externalities produced by both global warming and experimentation with genetic engineering.

Stated in another way, the new pro-peasantry project that international organisations are beginning to formulate does not constitute a return to the past. Rather, it seeks to promote new forms of the subsumption of peasant labour by capital in the era of climatic chaos and playing God with modern biotechnology.

On the other hand, the extremely aggressive neo-authoritarian tendency refuses to back down or dismantle the cynical configuration of the world food economy, and applies pressure in order to continue obtaining extraordinary profits despite the mass proliferation of hunger. This is taking place during a time in which capitalism, due to its technological development, may be willing to let die enormous segments of the international reserve army. This neo-authoritarian tendency points towards using the current frenzied purchasing of land by transnational corporations in peripheral countries as a platform for expanding and consolidating specific formal subsumption of labour by capital in agriculture, with the corresponding seasonal time wages.

This tendency is aimed particularly at diminishing peasant labour and promoting its metamorphosis into seasonal time-wage labour. Of course, the expansion of the specific formal subsumption of agricultural labour under capital will serve to increasingly incorporate the real subsumption of agriculture, including the anti-ecological innovations of genetic engineering (Ritterman 2015).

As we can see, in the context of a process in which the outcome is yet to be defined, both the trend towards a liberal reconfiguration of capitalism and the trend towards a neo-authoritarian reconfiguration of capitalism – by way of different paths – will lead to the development of the capitalist domination of agricultural labour. In this sense, given the peasant poverty of the twentieth century, the response of twenty-first-century capitalism is to point towards its reconfiguration, in one way or another, but clearly not towards overcoming peasant poverty. A genuine alternative for fighting peasant poverty requires policies for national sovereignty and projects for transcapitalist modernity.

7. Food crisis, post-baroque modernity and transcapitalism

The crossroads emerging from the epochal crisis of twenty-first-century capitalism is extremely complex. Comprehending this complexity demands questioning the perspective of historical determinism, which assumes that the future is predetermined. The history of mundialisation is not destiny. It is an open process in which various pathways are possible. The feasibility of the breakdown of capitalism does not mean that global capitalism is incapable of reconfiguring itself in order to re-establish its planetary power. Until now, great crises have historically operated as schizophrenic mechanisms, whereby capitalism has been destabilised yet has ended up refunctionalising itself, assimilating this destabilisation as an effective means of historical metamorphosis to shore up its power. The challenge we face is to overcome this schizophrenic legality of crises in order to transcend them.

Although times of crises are inevitably times of danger, they also constitute times of unprecedented opportunity. Along with the epochal crisis of capitalism there has also emerged a crossroads of another order, one that is different from and opposed to the one in which various configurations of capitalism vie to reconfigure the world system. It is, in fact, a crossroads marked by the confrontation of capitalism versus transcapitalism. Post-capitalist societies imply alternative modernities that could emerge from the convergence between the struggles for counter-hegemonic political sovereignty and for anti-capitalist and socio-natural-ecological self-management.

The construction of alternatives must assume the multidimensional character of the epochal crisis of twenty-first-century capitalism. The globalised environmental crisis and the mundialisation of poverty, with the global food crisis, are potentially the most explosive dimensions of the epochal crisis of twenty-first-century capitalism. Whereas trends leading to the collapse of capitalism derive from the global environmental crisis – if, as is currently happening, the transition to post-fossil fuel patterns of technology and energy is blocked – the global food crisis, rather than the mundialisation of poverty in general, points to potential political explosions on a grand scale. Kostas Vergopoulos (2012: 8), citing the historian Harold James (2011), has shown that 'sharp, brutal increases in food prices have often triggered social revolutions'; this is borne out by the French Revolution (1789), the Russian Revolution (1917) and the Chinese Revolution (1949), and to these one could add the juxtaposition of higher food prices and the social unrest of the Mexican Revolution (1910).

In Latin America, baroque modernity, characterised by the impossible attempt to reconcile resistance and subordination to capitalism, contains within the lengthy persistence of ecological-communitarian forms of contact with nature a set of first order proposals for coping with food and environmental crises. The historical need to counteract the cynical configuration of the global food economy within the context of an environmental crisis requires the convergence of the struggle for food sovereignty and the promotion of the mixed cropping or polyculture of the Andes, the Caribbean and Mesoamerica, which provide an agro-ecological alternative. In scenarios of extreme weather variability, polyculture offers significant strategies for agro-ecological resistance. If a seed variety does not survive, others will. In this sense, the new Constitution of the Plurinational State of Bolivia provides historical lessons for the twenty-first century because it links indigenous councillism and food sovereignty. Beyond the vision of the new pro-peasantry projects of liberal capitalism, the fight against peasant poverty could open up a window of opportunity linking projects for food sovereignty with projects for mixed cropping, within the framework of the strategic development of national sovereignty and respect for indigenous sovereignty.

However, defending the secular lessons of the ecological-communitarian forms that have subsisted within Latin American baroque modernity should not be equated with rejecting alternative projects for modernity. Nor should it mean accepting peasant poverty because it allegedly constitutes an agro-ecological-communitarian strategy that seeks to neutralise the effects of scarcity by first accepting it as historically insurmountable.

In other words, an alternative modernity could not possibly be a reconfiguration of baroque modernity. The alternative modernities must take up the challenge of producing necessarily *post-baroque modernities* (Echeverría 2003: 106). Because in a world or society where scarcity prevails, the antagonistic society becomes unavoidable. Saying farewell to modernity can only lead to an endless *bellum omnium contra omnes*.

Projects for transcapitalist modernity include those that propose paths for the development of alternative modern technologies that respond to the assertion of human life, and which, on the basis of a pluralistic polity, explore possible points of consensus between pre-capitalist and post-capitalist forms of sociality as an eco-communitarian alternative for the future. With all the complexity involved, these are projects that must face the challenge of building bridges of communication and alliance between the struggles for eco-communitarian self-management and the counter-hegemonic struggles for national sovereignty.

The complexity of the multidimensional crisis that is currently underway requires post-fossil energy sources and eco-technological restructuring projects that will deal not only with the *non-functional but cynical form of depredation of nature* through the use of fossil fuels that has characterised capitalist accumulation since the twentieth century, but also with the *new form of depredation – increasingly programmed but necessarily unstable* – that twenty-first-century capitalism is bringing about, above all with genetic engineering and nuclear energy (Arizmendi 2014a: 257–65).

At the end of the twentieth century, the hegemony of postmodern political culture has brought about a peculiar quid pro quo that identifies the schizophrenic legality of capitalist modernity with modernity in general. Progress and devastation are not the immanent legality of all projects of modernity; they correspond to capitalism as a schizophrenic configuration of modernity. Post-Marxism is lost in the same quid pro quo, and for that reason has sought refuge in Heidegger (2000), in a critique of modernity that fails to acknowledge the *differentia specifica* between capitalism and modernity (Echeverría 1997: 138–40). Because of its disenchantment with the Marxist critique of capitalist modernity, post-Marxism is unable to conceptualise projects of modernity without the devastation of the social and natural world (Leff 2004).[5] Its main limitations are revealed in the discussion of strategic policy. It is certainly inappropriate to propose to poor countries, within the framework of a world food crisis, that they should forget economic growth and technological modernisation. In the twenty-first century, poor countries need strategic projects of alternative modernities, sovereign projects of post-baroque modernities.

Insofar as we live in the era of the greatest technological progress in the history of civilisations, the mundialisation of modern techniques provides technological capacity with a presence that, by stripping it from the hegemonic trajectories of capitalist accumulation, in an entirely accessible way, could be channelled in another direction by creating anti-crisis strategies based on principles of human security in order to guarantee the vital reproduction of nations. Contemporary hunger is the result of a spurious scarcity imposed by historical cynicism, rather than of an unavoidable technological scarcity; the mundialisation of poverty constitutes a state of artificial scarcity rather than an inevitable fate. At the beginning of this century, historical necessity and technological capacity are coming together and calling for the development of political capacity and social sovereignty, on which the ability of this potentiality to spread around the world depends. A historical period such as the twenty-first century, marked by danger, calls for the consistent deciphering of the epochal opportunity for transcapitalist projects of modernity that lie dormant in its folds.

Notes

1 Globalisation is a highly problematic term. It confuses the *conceptual analysis of the world history of capitalism* and what could be called the *myth of globalisation.* This myth reads history in an inverted way and propagates the illusion that capitalism only became global with the fall of the Berlin Wall and the USSR, and sees it as the globalisation of wealth and democracy. The critique of the myth of globalisation is facilitated through the use of the term *mundialisation*, which opens a new horizon of intellection, by putting forth the principle that there is no capitalism without mundialisation. Capitalism gave birth to mundialisation from its origins in the sixteenth century, and since then it has been developing it. Capitalism and mundialisation constitute an inseparable binomial unit. *Mundialisation* is a term that invites a reconceptualisation of the dialectic relationship between capitalism and world history.

2 A panoramic perspective of the genesis of the mundialisation of poverty as a peculiarity of our era suggests that its historical foundations are: 1) the trend towards the victory of technological rent as a weapon of metropolitan capitalisms against peripheral states; 2) the information revolution as a foundation of the mundialisation of overexploitation of labour; and 3) the farewell to the liberal state caused by the trend towards mundialisation of the authoritarian state (Arizmendi and Boltvinik 2007).

3 Echeverría points out that most of Marx's references in these *Manuscripts* to the concept of subsumption are also reproduced in 'Results of the immediate process of production' (Chapter VI of the manuscript of 1865), known as *Resultate.* The *Resultate* have been published in English as an Appendix to Volume I of *Capital* in the Penguin Classics edition (Marx 1976, reprinted 1990). Whenever possible, I will quote from this source.

4 'There are many Somalias in the developing world: the economic reform package is similar in over a hundred countries ... *Hunger is not the result of food scarcity.* On the contrary, *famines are triggered by a global oversupply of grains.* Since the 1980s, the grain market has been deregulated, under the supervision of the World Bank, while US grain surplus has been systematically used to destroy the peasantry and destabilise national agriculture' (Chossudovsky 2002: 119–20).

5 In stark contrast to the post-Marxist perspective of 'environmental rationality' (Leff 2004: 137–41), the

'ecological critique of political economy', founded by Elmar Altvater, shows not only the epistemological viability but the contemporary need to realise a specific convergence between the thinking of Marx and that of Georgescu-Roegen, i.e. between the critique of capitalist modernity from use value as its foundation and the entropic economy (Altvater 1993: 181–233).

References

Altvater, E. (1993) 'Towards an ecological critique of political economy' in *The Future of the Market*. London: Verso.

Arizmendi, L. (2010) 'Concepciones de la pobreza en la fase del colapso del capitalismo neoliberal', *Mundo Siglo XXI* VI (21): 31–7.

— (2013) 'Crisis epocal del capitalismo, encrucijadas y desafíos del transcapitalismo en el siglo XXI' in *Nuestra América y EU: Desafíos del Siglo XXI*. Buenos Aires: Facultad de Ciencias Económicas de la Universidad Central de Ecuador e Instituto de Estudios de América/CIIEP-PIA.

— (2014a) 'Crisis ambiental mundializada y encrucijadas civilizatorias' in *Crisis global y encrucijadas civilizatorias*. Mexico City: Fundación Heberto Castillo.

— (2014b) 'La trascendencia de la lectura de *El Capital* de Bolívar Echeverría para América Latina' in L. Arizmendi, J. Peña y Lillo E. and E. Piñeiro (eds), *Bolívar Echeverría: trascendencia e impacto para América Latina en el siglo XXI*. Quito, Ecuador: Instituto de Altos Estudios Nacionales (IAEN).

Arizmendi, L. and J. Boltvinik (2007) 'Autodeterminación como condición de desarrollo en la era de mundialización de la pobreza', *Mundo Siglo XXI* III (9): 35–43.

Bartra, A. (1979) *La explotación del trabajo campesino por el capital*. Mexico City: Macehual.

— (2006) *El Capital en su laberinto*. Mexico City: Itaca.

Bartra, R. (1979) *El poder despótico burgués*. Mexico City: Era.

Chossudovsky, M. (2002) *Globalización de la pobreza*. Mexico City: Siglo XXI.

Echeverría, B. (1983) 'Editorial', *Cuadernos Políticos* no. 37. Mexico City: Era, pp. 2–3.

— (1997) *Las ilusiones de la modernidad*. Mexico City: Ed. El Equilibrista and Universidad Nacional Autónoma de México (UNAM).

— (1998) *La modernidad de lo barroco*. Mexico City: Era.

— (2003) 'Barroco y Modernidad Alternativa. Diálogo con Bolívar Echeverría', *Iconos* no. 17. Quito: Facultad Latinoamericana de Ciencias Sociales (FLACSO), pp. 102–13.

— (2011) 'Meditaciones sobre el barroquismo' in *Discurso crítico y modernidad*. Bogotá: Ediciones desde abajo.

ETC Group (2012) 'La revolución verde dólar'. Comuniqué no. 108, January/February. Ottawa: ETC Group, pp. 3–4.

FAO (2009) 'More people than ever are victims of hunger'. Rome: Food and Agriculture Organization of the United Nations (FAO). Available at www.fao.org/fileadmin/user_upload/newsroom/docs/Press%20orelease%20june-en.pdf.

Foladori, G. (1986) *Proletarios y campesinos*. Mexico City: Universidad Veracruzana.

Heidegger, M. (2000) *Carta sobre el humanismo*. Madrid: Alianza Editorial.

James, H. (2011) 'Food and revolution', *Project Syndicate*, 2 June. Available at www.project-syndicate.org/commentary/food-for-revolution.

Leff, E. (2004) *Racionalidad ambiental*. Mexico City: Siglo XXI.

Marini, R. M. (1973) *Dialéctica de la dependencia*. Mexico City: Era.

Marx, K. (1976 [1867]) *Capital*, Volume I. Reprinted 1990. London: Penguin Classics.

— (1983) 'Subsunción formal y subsunción real del proceso de trabajo al proceso de valorización', *Cuadernos Políticos* no. 37. Mexico City: Era.

Osorio, J. (2009) *Explotación redoblada y actualidad de la revolución. Refundación societal, rearticulación popular y nuevo autoritarismo.* Mexico City: UAM and Itaca.

Palerm, A. (1980) *Antropología v Marxismo*. Mexico City: CIS-INAH and Nueva Imagen.

Pogge, T. et al. (2013) 'How we count hunger matters', *Ethics & International Affairs* 27 (3): 1–9.

Ritterman, J. (2015) 'América Latina y Monsanto', *Mundo Siglo XXI* X (35): 5–20.

Rey, P. (1973) *Les Alliances de classes: sur l'articulation des modes de production.* Textes à l'appui no. 77. Paris: François Maspero.

Scaron, P. (1971) 'Advertencia del traductor' in K. Marx, *El Capital Capítulo VI (Inédito)*. Buenos Aires: Ediciones Signos, pp. xiii–xvi.

Vergopoulos, K. (2012) 'La crisis alimentaria. La Tierra tiembla', *Mundo Siglo XXI* VII (26): 5–9.

World Bank (1990) *World Development Report 1990: Poverty*. New York NY: Oxford University Press.

SESSION TWO

HISTORICAL AND EMPIRICAL APPROACHES

5 | AGRICULTURE/INDUSTRY, RURAL/ URBAN, PEASANTS/WORKERS: SOME REFLECTIONS ON POVERTY, PERSISTENCE AND CHANGE

Henry Bernstein

1. Boltvinik's argument

This article responds to Julio Boltvinik's stimulating paper in this volume (Chapter 1). It does so by suggesting some of the difficulties inherent in three of the key pairs of concepts or binaries central to our constructions of modernity and how we understand its trajectories: agriculture/industry, rural/urban, and peasants/workers. There are ways of historicising these fundamental terms, and hence problematising them, that in some respects are critical of Boltvinik's argument, and in other respects complement his theoretical approach. An alternative view is sketched of how 'peasants' are integrated in modern capitalism, the nature of petty commodity production in farming, and tendencies to class differentiation in the countryside.

Boltvinik's stimulating and unusual paper first makes a strong claim to theorise and explain the structural basis of the persistence of 'peasants' or 'family farmers'[1] and their poverty; second, it does so on the basis of Marxian value theory – and, indeed, proposes a reformulation of value theory.

There are three principal elements of Boltvinik's argument. First is a systematic contrast of the conditions of production in agriculture and industry, summarised in Table 5.1.[2]

Of these contrasts, the most fundamental is the *seasonality* of agricultural production, which Boltvinik emphasises throughout and which is the key link with the second element of his argument: the difference between capitalist and peasant farming.

The dynamic of capitalist farming for Boltvinik (following Marx) is investment to achieve profits on the basis of exploitation of labour or the appropriation of surplus value, hence expanded reproduction or accumulation. This necessitates paying wages only for the days

TABLE 5.1 Conditions of production in agriculture and industry

	Agriculture	Industry
Production process 1	Discontinuous, determined by seasonality	Continuous
Production process 2	Activities necessarily sequential	Activities can be simultaneous or synchronised
Locus of production	Fixed by location of land under cultivation (fields), to which workers and machines have to move	Not fixed; materials moved to where workers and machines are located (factories)
Materials of production	Biological uncertainties as constraints (author's note: direct appropriation of nature)	No such uncertainties (materials already appropriated from nature)
Products	Often perishable	Can be stored for long periods

of labour power used in production, limited by the seasonality of agricultural labour processes, and not paying wages adequate to reproduce workers on an annual basis (as in industry).

The dynamic of peasant, or family, farming (following Chayanov) is simple reproduction based on the use of household labour. This means that the income (in kind and cash) from days worked in farming seasons has to be stretched over the annual cycle for maintenance of the household and its generational reproduction (but see note 14 below). If peasants or family farmers are unable to achieve this from their own production, then they have to seek additional – that is, off-farm – income.

As farmers, peasants are price takers in markets for agricultural commodities, where prices are set by capitalist farmers who pay wages only for days worked. Other things being equal, this tends to set the prices that peasants receive for the same commodities at levels that compel them to engage in wage labour for part of the year in order to meet the full costs of their social reproduction: 'the social cost of seasonality is absorbed by peasants, who then have to live in permanent poverty'; 'capitalism cannot exist in a pure form in agriculture: without the peasants' supply of cheap seasonal labour, capitalist agriculture would be impossible' (see Chaper 1, section 1).[3]

The third element of the argument, and its policy conclusion in section 13 of Boltvinik's chapter, is that removing the inbuilt tendency towards 'permanent poverty' to enable viable peasant livelihoods through their own farming requires subsidies to, and protection of, family farmers in the global South, similar to those enjoyed by their counterparts in North America, the European Union (EU) and Japan.

One of the virtues of Boltvinik's paper is its focus on the reproduction of rural households that combine *both* petty commodity production in farming *and* (seasonal) wage labour. In this respect, it broadens often capital-centric arguments about the uneven development of capitalism in agriculture ('obstacles to capitalist agriculture', and so on), in which peasant 'persistence' is a kind of residual.

The paper also has the following problematic features. First, it is highly abstract. It proceeds via: 1) the series of contrasts between labour processes in farming and industry, and between capitalist and peasant/family farming, outlined; 2) critical engagement with other scholars who have attempted to apply Marxian value theory to explain 'peasant persistence';[4] and 3) (re-)readings of Marx's *Capital* (Chapter 1, sections 9 and 10) and a reformulation of Marx's theory of value (Chapter 1, section 11). The abstract analysis, moreover, centres on *the interrelation of two forms of production in farming, with almost no reference to the wider capitalist economy.*

Second, Boltvinik's salutary move of going back to Marx's *Capital* (and his attempt to reformulate value theory) is not matched by a movement forward from *Capital* to periodise and explore 'the development of agriculture in capitalist society'.[5] In short, the kinds of abstractions deployed are not grounded in 'theory as history' (Banaji 2010; though see note 6 below).

Third, there is little in the way of empirical illustration, especially an exploration of *patterns* and dynamics of rural class relations and poverty and the challenges of investigating them – a matter of putting the theoretical account to empirical use (and thereby testing it). This may be noted, *inter alia*, in relation to two issues: firstly, the assumption of *generalised* persistent/'permanent' rural poverty, which gives no analytical purchase on such questions as: why are some farmers/rural people *not* poor? Which, and why? What are the trends of rural poverty? And, secondly, does (all) capitalist farming depend on seasonal labour *from peasants* to be viable? Where does the migration of rural workers to non-agricultural sectors fit in? Is cheap migrant labour similarly 'functional' to the whole capitalist economy?

Fourth, the notion of a 'pure' capitalist agriculture (as a particular kind of theoretical abstraction) confronts the great diversity of historical and actually existing forms of capitalist farming, and their explanation (Banaji 2010).[6]

Finally, I wonder how accurate some of Boltvinik's observations are about current realities, in the (mostly) timeless world of his abstractions, for example, concerning the 'numerical importance of peasants in Latin America ... and their key role in production, particularly of basic foodstuffs' (Chapter 1, section 13). Again, one might ask: who exactly are peasants in Latin America? What are the trends in their numbers over, say, the last forty years?[7] What is the size of their contributions (and the trend of those contributions) to total aggregate food staple production?

Are there significant differences in the answers to such questions in different countries and regions of the continent? If so, what explains them?

The point is not to suggest that one paper can cover everything, of course, but rather to enquire whether the analytical framework deployed provides the means for investigating the kinds of questions noted. A more detailed critique of Boltvinik's argument, especially his use of value theory, is not appropriate for this volume. I concentrate rather on proposing aspects of an approach to issues of 'the development of agriculture in capitalist society' as an alternative to that of Boltvinik, and in some instances partly complementary to it. For this, I borrow from a series of articles written over several decades, and recently synthesised and summarised in *Class Dynamics of Agrarian Change*, which aims to be accessible to a wide audience.[8]

2. Agriculture and industry, rural and urban

A first step, or a necessary preliminary, is to distinguish 'farming' and 'agriculture'. So far I have used these terms interchangeably, as is common practice, and Boltvinik's paper, which focuses on forms of production in *farming*, refers to 'agriculture' throughout. The distinction I propose has a substantive theoretical and historical purpose to it: it is not merely semantic.

Subject to important qualifications (noted elsewhere), in agrarian societies before the advent of capitalism – both in its European heartlands and in colonial conditions – farming was what most people did, and did on very local scales. Farmers connected with non-farmers to some degree – through the exactions of rents and taxes, and through typically localised exchange – but the impact on farming of wider divisions of labour, processes of technical change, and market dynamics was very limited relative to the formation of 'the agricultural sector' in capitalism.[9]

The notion of 'agriculture' or the 'agricultural sector' in the social division of labour, and as an object of policy and politics, was invented and applied in the development of capitalism. Marx noted that social divisions of labour between agriculture and industry, and between countryside and town (as well as between mental and manual labour), emerged as characteristic features of capitalism. It only made sense to distinguish an agricultural sector when an industrial sector was rising to prominence in the North, and subsequently when industrialisation became the main economic objective of (state) socialist construction in the USSR and China, and not least in 'national development' in the countries of the South following their independence from colonial rule.

By 'agriculture' or 'the agricultural sector' in modern (capitalist) economies, I mean farming *together with* all those economic interests, and their specialised institutions and activities, 'upstream' and 'downstream' of farming that affect the activities and reproduction of farmers. 'Upstream' of farming refers to the ways in which the conditions of production are secured before farming itself can begin, including the supply of instruments of labour or 'inputs' – tools, fertilisers, seeds – as well as markets for land, labour, and credit. 'Downstream' of farming refers to what happens to crops and animals when they leave the farm – their marketing, processing and distribution – and how those activities affect farmers' incomes, which are necessary to reproduce themselves. Powerful agents upstream and downstream of farming in capitalist agriculture today are exemplified by 'agri-input' capital and 'agro-food' capital respectively, in the terms used by Weis (2007).

Agriculture in this sense was not given immediately by the origins of capitalism (from, say, the fourteenth or fifteenth century[10]), but rather *emerged* in the subsequent course of the development of capitalism on a world scale. I suggest that *a systemic shift from farming to agriculture was consolidated from the 1870s.* Its markers include:

1. the emergence of the 'second industrial revolution', based in steel, chemicals, electricity and petroleum (the first was based in iron, coal and steam power), which vastly accelerated the development of the productive forces in farming, as well as in food processing, storage, transport, and so on;

2. the first international food regime (IFR) from 1870 to 1914, based in wheat: 'the first price-governed [international] market in an essential means of life' (Friedmann 2004: 125); and

3. the sources of supply of the first IFR in vast frontiers of mostly virgin land, sparsely populated and little cultivated previously – in Argentina, Australia, Canada and the USA – now dedicated to the specialised production of 'essential means of life' for export to a rapidly industrialising and urbanising Europe. In this conjuncture, Chicago and its agrarian hinterland became the key locus of emergent agribusiness and its institutional innovations, both upstream and downstream of farming, for example futures markets (Cronon 1991).

A global division of labour in agricultural production and trade emerged from the 1870s. This comprised:

1. new zones of grain and meat production in the 'neo-Europes' (Crosby 1986) established by settler colonialism in the temperate Americas, as well as in parts of Southern Africa, Australia and New Zealand;

2. more diversified patterns of farming in parts of Europe itself (together with accelerating rural out-migration); and

3. specialisation in tropical export crops in colonial Asia and Africa and the tropical zones of the former colonies of Latin America (whether grown on peasant or capitalist farms or industrial plantations).[11]

Thus, while debate of agrarian 'transitions from feudalism to capitalism' is rooted in the historical experiences of 'old' Europe (England, France, Germany, the Low Countries) from the fifteenth century onwards (see note 10), and was then extended to other countries and regions such as Russia (Lenin 1964 [1899]) and India following independence (Byres 1981), the formation of modern capitalist agriculture is rooted in developments in the world economy from the last third of the nineteenth century – the moment of modern imperialism, in Lenin's analysis (1964 [1916]).

Concerning the emergence of agriculture as an object of policy and politics, here are several illustrations. On the supply side, in the second half of the nineteenth century, '[s]pecialised commodity production ... [was] actively promoted by settler states [author's note: this was the basis of the first IFR] via land and immigration policy, and the establishment of social infrastructure, mainly railways and credit facilities' (Friedmann and McMichael 1989: 101). We can also note that, after World War II, the strategic practice of US wheat exports under PL480 formed the basis of the second IFR, in Friedmann's compelling account (1982). Currently, and of great concern to Mexico (as noted by Boltvinik), there are the effects of the North American Free Trade Agreement (NAFTA). On the demand side, the way to a (relatively) free trade order was prepared by the 1846 repeal of the Corn Laws in Britain; these had protected British farmers and landowners, and their commercial rents, from (cheaper) imported grain.[12] This occurred before my suggested historical watershed of the 1870s, but, significantly, it did so in the most industrialised capitalist country of the time, and anticipated that watershed, during which Britain imposed 'free trade' in food staples on other European states (Winders 2009).

In short, *one cannot conceive of the emergence and functioning of agriculture in modern capitalism without the centrality and reconfigurations of new sets of dynamics linking agriculture and industry, and the rural and urban* (and indeed the local, national and global). Of course, much could be added to amplify this thesis, including:

1. the vast exodus from European countrysides to populate Europe's *and* North and Latin America's growing cities and classes of labour;
2. the way in which industrialisation and other sources of demand for labour (such as mining) generated capital's search for cheaper food staples to reduce the costs of labour (variable capital)[13] – a typically brutal process that drove the development of the productive forces in farming, at the same time as factory production destroyed the value of rural handicrafts and artisanal production;[14]
3. peasants' growing use over time of industrially manufactured

instruments of labour in their farming (and of industrially manufactured means of consumption);

4. the extension and intensification of peasant seasonal wage labour, not only on capitalist farms but also in mines, factories, construction, and so on; and

5. the historical and contemporary evidence of diverse ways in which households and wider family groupings organise themselves in combinations of rural and urban residences, own-account farming and off-farm employment (including self-employment in the urban informal economy), in order to meet the needs of simple reproduction.

3. Peasants

In however schematic a fashion, I propose the following theoretical-cum-historical theses.

Thesis 1. By the time of independence from colonial rule in Asia and Africa, the economies of these former colonial territories were permeated (like those of Latin America) by generalised commodity production: that is, capitalist social relations of production and reproduction.

To elaborate: first, by commodification I mean the process through which the elements of production and social reproduction are produced for, and obtained from, market exchange and subjected to its disciplines and compulsions. In capitalism, this process is premised on the historical emergence and formation of a fundamental social relation between capital and wage labour. The historical driving force for peasants was the 'commodification of subsistence' (Brenner 2001). Often (but not always) this required initially 'forced' commercialisation by colonial states through taxation and other means (Bharadwaj 1985) until peasants were subject to 'the dull compulsion of economic forces' in Marx's famous phrase.

Second, the central tendency of capitalism towards generalised commodity production does not mean that all elements of social existence are immediately, necessarily or comprehensively commodified. Rather, the commodification of subsistence signifies that *reproduction cannot take place outside commodity relations* and the disciplines they impose.[15]

Thesis 2. Generalised commodity production includes both: 1) the internalisation of capitalist social relations in the organisation of economic activity (including 'peasant' production); and 2) how economies are located in international divisions of labour, markets, and circuits of capital and commodities.

Aspects of the second point were sketched above; the first is strategic here and requires elaboration. The argument is that peasants in modern capitalism are *petty commodity producers*.[16] Petty commodity production in capitalism *internalises* and combines the class 'places' or locations of both capital and labour: in farming, capital in the form of land, tools, seeds, fertilisers and other chemicals, and labour in the form of families or households (Gibbon and Neocosmos 1985).[17] It is a 'contradictory unity' of class places, for several reasons. First, the class places are not distributed evenly within farming households, especially given gender divisions of property, labour, income and spending.[18] Second, and most fundamentally, there is a contradiction between reproducing the means of production (capital) and the producer (labour): that is, allocating income (including from borrowing) between, on the one hand, the replacement fund and fund of rent, and, on the other, the funds for consumption and generational reproduction – a distribution that is typically also strongly gendered. Third, the contradictory combination of class places is the source of differentiation of petty commodity enterprises, which I come back to below.

Thesis 3. Agrarian capital – that is, capital invested in farming – can have a range of sources beyond the countryside and its 'original' (precapitalist), localised (indigenous) rural classes of landed property and peasantry; the range of non-agrarian, non-indigenous sources of agrarian capital is likely to expand and diversify, and the significance of those sources to increase, over the history of capitalism. We can signify this as '*agrarian capital beyond the countryside*', just as the previous section proposed '*agriculture beyond the farm*'.

Thesis 4. As indicated above, different types of agrarian capital (in capitalist and petty commodity production, among different peasant classes) are increasingly likely to be combined or articulated with forms of activity and income in non-agricultural sectors, or spaces in social divisions of labour, with (variant) effects for the specific forms of organisation, scale, economic performance, and simple or expanded reproduction of farming enterprises.

Thesis 5. Following on from the above, there are similar tendencies to the decomposition of (notionally) once 'pure' classes of agrarian labour (including agrarian labour combined with capital in petty commodity production) that have to diversify their forms, and spaces, of employment (and self-employment) to meet their simple reproduction needs as labour ('survival'), and, in the case of petty commodity producers, as capital too (the replacement fund and fund of rent).

* * *

This approach contrasts with Chayanovian views of an essential – hence historically transcendent – internal logic of peasant production (Bernstein 2009) and the misleading assumption, if less common today than in the past, that small farmers in the Third World are 'subsistence' cultivators whose primary objective is to supply their food needs from their own farming. The alternative position proposed here is that *once farming households are integrated into capitalist commodity relations, they are subject to the dynamics and compulsions of commodification that are internalised in their relations and practices.* If they farm only for their own consumption, then this is because they are integrated in commodity relations in other ways, usually through the sale of their labour power. In this case, it is common for 'subsistence' production to be funded from wages, which are also used to buy food when their own production from farming is inadequate to supply household needs, whether on a regular basis or in bad harvest years. In effect, then, the extent to which peasants can satisfy their food needs from their own production is shaped by the ways in which they are integrated in commodity relations rather than the other way round.

The view of petty commodity production proposed generates a method of theorising the tendencies of peasant differentiation into classes that Lenin (1964 [1899]) termed rich, middle and poor peasants:

1. Those able to accumulate productive assets and reproduce themselves as capital on a larger scale, engaging in *expanded*

reproduction, are emergent capitalist farmers, corresponding to Lenin's 'rich peasants'.

2. Those able to reproduce themselves as capital on the same scale of production, and as labour on the same scale of consumption (and generationally) – simple reproduction – are medium farmers, corresponding to 'middle peasants'.

3. Those struggling to reproduce themselves as capital, hence struggling to reproduce themselves as labour from their own farming and subject to what I term a simple reproduction squeeze, are poor farmers, corresponding to Lenin's 'poor peasants'.

Emergent capitalist farmers tend to employ (more) wage labour in addition to, or in place of, family labour. Medium farmers, especially those who are relatively stable petty commodity producers, are of special interest, not least because they are dear to the heart of agrarian populism, which often assumes that the 'middle peasant' condition was the norm in pre-capitalist rural communities, which are regarded, rather romantically, as intrinsically egalitarian. Consequently, the emergence of rich and poor peasants is seen as an unfortunate deviation, a kind of fall from grace caused by malevolent forces (capital and states) that are external to peasant communities. The theoretical schema here recommends a different view: that *medium farmers are also produced by class differentiation*. That is, processes of commodification: 1) raise the 'entry' costs and reproduction costs of capital in farming, and the risks associated with those higher costs; and 2) increase competition for land and/or the labour to work it. Thus, even 'medium' family farmers establish their commodity enterprises at the expense of their neighbours, who are poorer farmers unable to meet those costs or bear their risks, and who lose out to those who can. These poorer farmers are likely to be forced out of farming, or, if they can obtain credit, become highly indebted and slide towards marginal farming.

Marginal farmers or those 'too poor to farm' do not always or necessarily lack access to land, but they lack one or more of the following to be able to reproduce themselves through their own farming: enough land of good enough quality; the capacity to buy other necessary means of production, such as tools and seeds; and the capacity to command adequate labour, often an effect of gender relations that prevent women farmers from commanding the labour of men.

An often neglected aspect of class differentiation in the countryside is that rural labour markets are a critical condition of petty commodity production in farming, however common it is to overlook the employment of wage labour by even 'small' farmers. In the contemporary European context, for example, Shelley (2007: 1) observes that 'France prides itself on its self-sufficient peasant agriculture, yet without Moroccan field workers many farmers would struggle'.[19] And in an excellent study of rural Costa Rica in the 1980s, Marc Edelman refers to 'peasant' hiring of labourers or *peones* (2002: 122, 123, 167) and reports that small farmers complained about their lack of cash to hire *peones* (ibid.: 126), although he does not say who those *peones* were nor where they came from in the rural class structure.

Connecting with the fourth and fifth 'theses' above, rural 'livelihood diversification' suggests tendencies to class differentiation, which it might intensify or impede, according to circumstances. Emergent capitalist farmers often invest in activities ancillary to farming, such as crop trading and processing, rural retail trade and transport, and advancing credit, as well as renting out draught animals and tractors or selling irrigation water. They also invest in urban activities, education for their sons and good marriages for their daughters, alliances with government officials and in political processes, and influence more generally. In short, they engage in 'diversification for accumulation' (Hart 1994).

Medium-scale farming typically depends on combining farming with 'off-farm' activities, including labour migration, as sources of income to invest in farm production, especially when its costs of reproduction are rising. It also rests, as just noted, on the capacity to hire wage labour, which is provided by landless workers or marginal farmers (who are often migrants). Wage labour may be hired to replace family labour that is engaged in other 'off-farm' activities or to augment family labour at moments of peak demand in the farming calendar, including weeding and harvesting.

A further factor that complicates, or destabilises, class formation is the way in which precarious conditions of much small-scale farming in the global South exert pressures on the reproduction of farming households. Medium farmers are often pushed into the ranks of poor farmers because of their vulnerability to 'shocks' such as drought or flood, and to deteriorating terms of exchange between what they need to buy and what they are able to sell – a typical expression of the 'simple reproduction squeeze'. They can buy fewer 'inputs', less food and less labour power when they earn less from their farming. They may earn less because of reduced harvests – due to adverse weather, crop diseases, pest infestations, not enough fertiliser or shortages of labour – or when prices for the commodities they sell decline, or when they have to repay debts. Precariousness is also registered in the vulnerability to 'shocks' of *individual* households, for example the illness or death of a key household member, or of a valued draught animal, either of which might mean crossing the precarious threshold between 'getting by' and 'going under'.

Like the patterns of commodification of small-scale farming (noted above), patterns of differentiation also display massive variation. The *tendency* to differentiation that can be identified theoretically from the contradictory unity of class places in petty commodity production is not – and cannot be – evident in identical *trends*, mechanisms, rhythms or forms of class differentiation everywhere. This is because 'many determinations' mediate between the tendency and particular concrete circumstances and local dynamics.[20]

I have indicated some of those determinations, which might appear paradoxical. For example, the centrality of off-farm income and hiring wage labour to the reproduction of medium-scale farmers disturbs their idealised image as the *'independent'* family farmer, 'middle peasant' or sturdy yeoman.[21] Similarly, the sale of their labour power by the poor can help some of them cling onto a piece of land, however marginal. They often make considerable sacrifices to do so, because that land represents an element of security, and perhaps hope, in the 'economic struggle for existence'[22] that they confront, as well as a marker of cultural value and identity.

Depending on circumstances, there can also be limits to the expansion of their farming by richer peasant farmers. Harriss (1987) studied a village in south-east India, where households farmed an average of 1.2 hectares of irrigated rice and groundnuts. There was inequality between households but it was not increasing in terms of the distribution of land and scale of farming because of resistance to richer farmers acquiring more land in this densely populated and intensively cultivated area, and due to inheritance practices of dividing family land between sons. Richer farmers diversified into rice trading, which was more feasible and more profitable, rather than trying to expand the scale of their farming.

By contrast, in the very different conditions of northern Uganda in the 1980s, a local (village) capitalist told Mahmood Mamdani (1987: 208) that 'what helped us [to accumulate] was the famine of 1980. People were hungry and they sold us things cheaply [including land and cattle]. That is when we really started buying.' In effect, as always in capitalism, the crises of some present opportunities to others, a dynamic that permeates the often intricate and fluid contours of class formation in the countryside.

The kinds of ideas proposed in this section, and their illustrations, point to an opening up of questions about patterns and distributions of rural poverty, *and their shifts*, beyond Boltvinik's stylised peasant 'persistence' and (generalised) *'permanent* poverty'. I come back to issues of poverty below. For the moment, it is high time to consider whether poor and marginal peasants should be considered 'peasants' or farmers at all, or whether they are indeed better understood as workers, as a particular (and large) formation within 'classes of labour' in the Third World.

4. ... and workers (classes of labour)?

Poor farmers experience most acutely the contradiction of reproducing themselves as petty commodity producers, as both labour and capital, and may reduce their consumption to extreme levels in order to retain possession of a small piece of land or a cow, to buy seeds, or to repay debts – and, as Boltvinik suggests, are likely to accept the most arduous, precarious and dangerous work for the lowest wages (albeit, *pace* Boltvinik, not exclusively, or even mostly, on capitalist farms). Following from the designations of 'agriculture beyond the farm' and 'agrarian capital beyond the countryside' above, I suggest here a notion of *rural labour beyond the farm*, supplied not only by fully 'proletarianised' rural workers who are landless, and hence unable to farm on their own account, but also by marginal farmers or those too poor to farm as a major component of their livelihood and reproduction. Both categories of labour, which typically have very fluid social boundaries, can be employed locally on the farms of neighbours (capitalist and petty commodity producers), or seasonally in more distant zones of capitalist farming and well-established petty commodity production – sometimes in other countries, or in towns and cities within their own countries or, again, internationally. 'Footloose labour', in the term of Jan Breman

(1996), is a massive fact of social life in the rural zones of today's global South, and expresses the ways in which their types of farming are differentiated by class dynamics. What I term here 'classes of labour' comprise 'the growing numbers … who now depend – directly *and indirectly* – on the sale of their labour power for their own daily reproduction' (Panitch and Leys 2000: ix, emphasis added). They have to pursue their reproduction in conditions of growing income insecurity (and 'pauperisation') as well as employment insecurity and the downward pressures exerted by the neoliberal erosion of social provisions for those in 'standard' wage employment; this latter group is shrinking as a proportion of classes of labour in most regions of the global South, and in some instances in absolute terms as well.[23] Pressures on reproduction have even more serious consequences for the growing numbers of what Davis (2006: 178) calls 'the global informal working class', which 'is about one billion strong, making it the fastest-growing, and most unprecedented, social class on earth', and what Standing (2011) calls the precariat ('the new dangerous class'). Both authors refer primarily to the urban component of this class, but poor and marginal farmers in the Third World also form a significant part. They might not be dispossessed of *all* means of reproducing themselves, recalling Lenin's warning against 'too stereotyped an understanding of the theoretical proposition that capitalism requires the free, landless worker' (1964 [1899]: 181), but nor do most of them possess *sufficient* means to reproduce themselves, which marks the limits of their viability as petty commodity producers.[24]

The working poor of the global South have to pursue their reproduction through insecure and oppressive – and typically increasingly scarce – wage employment and/or a range of similarly precarious small-scale and insecure 'informal economy' ('survival') activities, including marginal farming in many instances. In effect, livelihoods are pursued through various and complex *combinations* of wage employment and self-employment.[25] Additionally, many pursue their means of reproduction across different sites of the social division of labour: urban and rural, agricultural and non-agricultural, as well as wage employment and (marginal) self-employment. The social locations and identities that the working poor inhabit, combine and move between make for ever more fluid boundaries, and defy inherited assumptions of fixed, and uniform, notions of 'worker', 'farmer', (petty) 'trader', 'urban', 'rural', 'employed' and 'self-employed'.

Moreover, relative success or failure in labour markets, salaried employment and other branches of activity is typically key to the viability (reproduction) of agricultural petty commodity production, but is not distributed equally across those who farm or otherwise have an interest in farming and access to land. In turn, this has effects for those in classes of labour who combine self-employment in farming and/or other branches of ('informal economy') activity with wage labour. And as small-scale farmers they inhabit a social world of 'relentless micro-capitalism' (Davis 2006: 181).

That poor or marginal farmers engage in 'survival' activities to reproduce themselves, primarily through the sale of their labour power, is now acknowledged, however belatedly, by organisations such as the International Fund for Agricultural Development (IFAD) and the World Bank. IFAD's *Rural Poverty Report 2001* noted that the rural poor 'live mainly by selling their labour-power' (IFAD 2001: 230), while Table 5.2 is adapted from the *World Development Report 2008* (World Bank 2007: 205).[26]

While such highly aggregated ('jumbo') statistics have to be treated with considerable caution, their broad indications are suggestive. The table suggests that own-account farming is the primary economic activity for more than half the adult rural population *only* in sub-Saharan Africa. However, even there, a strong trend of 'de-agrarianisation' or 'de-peasantisation' (Bryceson 1999) has been argued, manifested

TABLE 5.2 The share of the adult rural population with own-account farming as its primary economic activity (percentage)

Region	Men	Women
Sub-Saharan Africa	56.6	53.5
South Asia	33.1	12.7
East Asia and Pacific (excluding China[1])	46.8	38.4
Middle East and North Africa	24.6	38.6
Europe and Central Asia	8.5	6.9
Latin America and the Caribbean	38.4	22.8

Note: [1] For China, best 'guesstimates' are that the proportion of the total labour force employed in agriculture has declined from about 71 per cent in 1978 to about 45 per cent today, some 400 million people.

in the growing proportion of rural incomes derived from non-farm sources. Moreover, the comprehensive economic crisis that has gripped most of sub-Saharan Africa in recent decades puts additional pressures on reproduction through longstanding combinations of farming and labour migration (of 'hoe and wage', in the term used by Cordell et al. (1996)), of the kind emphasised by Boltvinik. This is because opportunities in urban employment (including 'informal' employment and self-employment), which can provide sources of support to farming in the countryside, have declined at the same time as pressures on reproduction have increased, in large part as a result of neoliberal globalisation.

5. Poverty, persistence and change

How adequate is it to take a 'ball-park' figure of 1 billion (plus) rural poor from IFAD (2011) and use it as a stylised empirical launch pad for theorising mutually constitutive peasant 'persistence' and 'permanent' rural poverty, as Boltvinik does? To identify, in however rough and ready a manner, *who* are 'peasants', *who* are 'rural', and *who* are the poor, as well as to attempt to count them, and to assess (and explain) trends in *their numbers over time* are activities of far greater complexity than Boltvinik's paper allows. This is because of the conceptual challenges attached to such categories of social analysis, some of which have been indicated – the blurred distinctions between 'peasants' and classes of labour (applicable to many 'peasants', or to most in some places today), and between rural and urban[27] – as well as shifting fashions in technologies (in the Foucauldian sense) of defining poverty as a condition and measuring the numbers of the poor: those who inhabit that condition (Gupta 2012).

The problems involved can be illustrated here, although they can hardly be resolved. As far as the 'jumbo' figures are concerned, the standard estimate, derived from the Food and Agriculture Organization of the United Nations (FAO), is that today 'agriculture provides employment for 1.3 billion people worldwide, 97 percent of them in developing countries' (World Bank 2007: 77).[28] Some of those 1.3 billion qualify as 'farmers', subject to many variations of what types of farmers they are, where, and *when*. During peak moments of the annual agricultural calendar? In good or bad rainfall years? Good or bad market years? In other words, not all farmers are farmers all the time. Many rural people may not qualify as 'farmers' in any strong sense, perhaps a majority in some countrysides at some times, and over time – because they are 'too poor to farm', engaged in only 'marginal' farming. Hazell et al. (2007: 1) define marginal farming as 'incapable of providing enough work or income to be the main livelihood of the household'. They point out that in India, for example, the term 'marginal farm' is used for farms of less than 1 hectare, which make up 62 per cent of all landholdings but occupy only 17 per cent of all farmed land in what are predominantly (class-differentiated) 'peasant' countrysides.

Table 5.3 presents data from IFAD (2011) suggesting that, while agricultural employment grew for all regions of the South from 1998 to 2007 (with the exceptions of Southern Africa and South America) – principally as an effect of population growth – the *share* of agricultural employment in total employment *declined* for all regions.

Table 5.4 is more striking for the concerns of this volume, given the emphasis of the IFAD report on rural poverty – and *even* allowing for

TABLE 5.3 Agricultural employment by region, 1998–2007

	1998 (millions)	2007 (millions)	Growth (%)	1998 (% of all employment)	2007 (% of all employment)
East Asia[1]	478.36	512.3	7.1	64.9	53.1
South Asia	300.7	377.86	26.6	46.8	36.7
Southeast Asia	116.72	141.72	22.8	47.7	37.6
Eastern Africa	54.23	105.55	39.9	74.7	62.5
Southern Africa	2.48	2.29	–3.6	11.5	6.6
Middle Africa	21.34	26.28	35.4	60.6	45.0
Western Africa	44.10	55.94	31.3	50.7	35.5
Caribbean	3.89	3.84	1.9	24.3	20.0
Central America	12.35	13.02	6.2	20.8	14.0
South America	28.23	25.79	–6.4	17.1	10.3
Middle East	17.40	20.97	24.3	31.3	24.3
North Africa	21.11	24.97	20.3	28.8	19.9

Source: IFAD (2011: 256).

Note: [1] East Asia in this table is heavily weighted by China, of course. Other sources give even lower estimates for agriculture's share of total employment in China in 2010: for example, 44 per cent (Fan et al. 2010) and 39.6 per cent (FAO 2012).

TABLE 5.4 Rural poverty trends by region, 1988–2008

	East Asia	South Asia	SE Asia	SSA	LA	MENA	Total South
Rural population (millions)							
1988	827	837	293	333	129	124	2,548
1998	828	984	311	412	128	143	2,812
2008	863	1,112	307	497	122	161	2,968
Incidence of rural poverty < US$2/day (%)							
1988	98.4	85.2	76.5	75.2	42.4	32.7	83.2
1998	76.1	86.8	87.7	86.7	44.3	30.7	78.6
2008	34.8	80.4	62.0	87.2	19.9	11.7	60.9
Rural poverty as a percentage of total extreme poverty < US$1.25/day (%)							
1988	86.8	79.4	76.6	71.8	57.6	99.0	80.5
1998	84.0	86.5	94.2	76.6	51.9	61.3	82.9
2008	54.3	80.7	74.5	75.0	26.5	40.1	71.6

Source: IFAD (2011: 233; see also technical notes 234–5).

Note: SE Asia = Southeast Asia; SSA = Sub-Saharan Africa; LA = Latin America and Caribbean; MENA = Middle East and North Africa.

the problems of possible (or likely) undercounting that Boltvinik and others suggest for a number of important reasons, both technical and ideological (and how they interact). The figures in the table, although highly problematic, suggest relatively little difference in rural poverty in South Asia, Southeast Asia and sub-Saharan Africa over the period 1988–2008, while the incidence of rural poverty (income of below $2 per day) and the rural share of the total extreme poor (income of less than $1.25 per day) have *more than halved* overall in Latin America and the Middle East and North Africa, and the first indicator in East Asia.

Here are some very preliminary observations and hypotheses that could serve to frame an investigation into the trends suggested by the IFAD data.

Of the regions with the most marked, extreme and apparently persistent rural poverty, South Asia (in which India is heavily weighted) is a zone of pervasive rural class differentiation and 'marginal' farming, with many (most?) rural people in classes of labour and 'footloose' too – migrants in search of waged work. There is relatively little capitalist farming on a Latin American scale (of farm size and degree of capitalisation), but there are certainly extensive rural labour markets that supply the needs of capitalist and rich peasant farmers. The current hype about India as an emerging economic 'giant' (by analogy with China) ignores the fact that the dynamic centres of urban accumulation generate virtually no stimuli, backward and forward linkages, with the economies and classes of the countryside. Sub-Saharan Africa has its own distinctive agrarian histories (Bernstein 2004; 2005), but, as in South Asia, there is relatively little large-scale capitalist farming outside South Africa and pockets of continuing (or new) plantation and settler production, including from inward investment. Sub-Saharan Africa's peasants or rural classes of labour are also 'footloose' across shorter and longer distances, and their migration supplies labour to capitalist *and* (so-called) 'family farming' in southern Italy and Spain. The data for Southeast Asia – like the others, a region of great variation – suggest a pattern of increasing rural poverty, especially extreme poverty, from 1988 to 1998 (manifesting the immediate effects of the Asian financial crisis of the 1990s; see Breman 2001) and then a relative decline ('recovery') from 1998 to 2008. Southeast Asia is also a key region in accounts of contemporary 'land grabbing' (Hall et al. 2011; Borras and Franco 2012).

What of the regions where there has been a marked decline in rural poverty, according to Table 5.4? China's path of capitalist development is almost *sui generis*, not only because of its extraordinary economic growth centred on industrialisation and urbanisation, but also because of the usually less remarked but strategic importance of government-led *rural industrialisation* (Bramall 2007), and the diversification of the rural economy in small-scale manufacturing, construction and other services stimulated by migrant worker remittances and the skills returning workers bring with them (Murphy 2002). Latin America exhibits the full range – from key zones of large-scale capitalist farming through 'capitalised family farms' (Llambi 1988) to 'sub-subsistence' peasants. I would hypothesise here, *pace* Boltvinik, that poor 'peasant' households may no longer be the primary source of cheap seasonal labour for capitalist farms, and that rural labour migration – local, national and international – to other sectors of the capitalist economy now far outstrips the supply to capitalist farming. The Middle East and North Africa (MENA) lacks the extent of large-scale capitalist farming found in many parts of Latin America and may be the most evident case (along with Latin America) of the 'displacement' or 'transfer' of rural poverty via permanent out-migration in a global 'planet of slums' (Davis 2006). Long-distance migration is a marked feature of classes of labour in the region, including the supply of labour to farmers in southern Europe and France ('family farmers' among them, as remarked above of West African migrants to southern Europe).

The effect of these observations, together with the rest of my exposition, is to direct investigation and debate away from Boltvinik's 'two sector' model of capitalist and peasant farming and its use to explain both the 'persistence' of peasantry and 'permanent' rural poverty. My alternative approach is to consider the *more general conditions of existence, and struggles for reproduction, of (fragmented) classes of labour*, including Davis's 'global informal working class' and Standing's 'precariat' (see above), in today's neoliberal globalisation. What has changed, and continues to change, in capitalist *agriculture* is the vast diversity of types of *farming* it encompasses, and in the diverse countrysides of the global South, it is, of course, a key element of that bigger story. However, while my theoretical starting point remains the 'classic' materialist texts (Marx, Engels, Lenin, Kautsky) on capitalism qua mode of production and historical epoch, and on the forms of the agrarian question and paths of agrarian transition or development within that epoch (Bernstein 1996), my emphasis is *more on change than 'persistence'*. In the last several centuries of industrial capitalism, 'all that is solid melts into air' indeed.[29] And if I had to emphasise only one aspect of the remarkable trajectories of capitalist farming over the last 150 years (and accelerating in the last sixty or seventy years), it would be its remarkable *development of the productive forces*, of the productivity of labour, in farming. Boltvinik acknowledges but does not explore this systemic tendency of capitalism, with its crucial corollary of labour displacement – including in conditions of rising farm labour costs and wages and/or labour struggles even when there is massive rural 'surplus labour' (or a reserve army of labour). This, of course, reminds us that capitalist farming finds various means of dealing with labour recruitment and costs – which vary a great deal in different branches of farming in different places at different times – and is not necessarily structurally dependent on cheap seasonal labour supplied by peasants, the central proposition in Boltvinik's theoretical model.[30]

What then of policy measures to overcome rural poverty, which usually links so closely to urban poverty for the reasons sketched here, not least in the movements of 'footloose labour' between countryside and town? Boltvinik's main proposal is that:

> farmers must be subsidised and protected from external competition. In order to prevent resources allocated to subsidies from boosting the income of the most privileged farmers, family farmers must receive the total amount of subsidies designed to offset the cost of seasonality. Conversely, capitalist farmers would require only subsidies to deal with the asymmetry of international competition, and these subsidies would be common to all producers. Subsidies and trade protection must be complementary. The less protection there is, the more subsidies are required. (Chapter 1, section 13)

This follows from his theoretical model of peasant 'persistence' or 'permanent' rural poverty, and its principal and secondary arguments: respectively, seasonality of farm production and subsidies to farmers in the global North that are denied to at least small farmers in the global South. According to the logic of Boltvinik's model, this would mean inter alia that capitalist farming in the global South would disappear once it no longer enjoyed a supply of cheap seasonal labour provided by peasant households. It also implies *redistribution* on a major scale within the government budget. How such redistribution would be paid for is not spelled out. Is it implied that this would be achieved by higher consumer prices for food and other agricultural products?[31] If so, what would be the effects for wider classes of labour engaged in continuous daily struggles to reproduce themselves, including those in the countryside who are net purchasers of staple foods?[32]

Several further observations. First, it is striking that Boltvinik does not mention other redistributive measures that would strengthen the viability of small-scale farming, including redistributive land reform with its world-historical resonance in the making of modern societies (Bernstein 2002), not least in Mexico, of course.[33]

Second, there is the matter of feeding a world population of 7 billion or so, over half of which is urban (in the global South as a whole, approximately 45 per cent is urban), and whether the productive forces in small-scale farming can be developed to undertake that task without (even greater) food price inflation,[34] and in an ecologically sustainable manner.[35]

This points immediately to a third question, bound up with the issues of *who* are the small farmers: what *types* of farmers are they? It is always a critical question in redistributive land reforms, and agrarian reform more broadly, whether *all* 'beneficiaries' can establish themselves as viable small-scale farmers – that is, are they able to reproduce themselves principally through their farming activities? I am highly sceptical that reinforcing the material basis of small-scale farming (not least by fiscal and financial means) can overcome the kinds of rural poverty experienced in today's global South. I would speculate that such measures, even if politically possible and varying greatly with specific conditions of farming – ecological, social, in terms of branches of production and markets – could succeed for more than, say, between 10 and 40 per cent of those in very different environments who engage in one or other degree and scale of farming; very large numbers of rural-based (and 'footloose') members of classes of labour would remain and they would continue to struggle for their reproduction.[36]

This suggests that the key question, transcending Boltvinik's principal focus on the seasonality of farm production, labour and wages, is the *broader struggle over employment and real wage levels*, for a 'living wage' and 'decent work' (in the words of the International Labour Organization or ILO), and how much those ideals can be supported or supplemented by a 'social wage' paid through the public provision of basic services – another redistributive 'transfer', of course, that neoliberal policies aim to reduce and, if possible, eliminate.[37]

I conclude with two possibilities for combinations of own-account small-scale farming with wage labour that were implied earlier and might be considered more 'positive'. One is the hope, at least, that access to even 'sub-subsistence' plots, and cultivation of them, can boost the 'reserve price' of labour power, thereby giving the rural poor some flexibility, however constrained, in the sale of their labour power (see, for example, Cousins 2011 on South Africa). The other is more expansive (and noted above in relation to the dynamics of 'middle peasant' production and reproduction): namely that savings from labour migration can be beneficially invested in improving small-scale farm production and its role as a source of livelihood or reproduction.[38] This case is made for Mexico by Barkin (2002), with strong claims that, using savings from migrant labour, a 'modern' peasantry is reconstructing itself and, moreover, is doing so as a collective project driven by its desire for autonomy and cultural integrity,[39] albeit without strong evidence to support such claims. Certainly, Elizabeth Fitting (2011) presents an analysis of much more contradictory social dynamics in her ethnography of Tehuacán, which subvert simple and unitary notions of rural 'community' close to the heart of agrarian populism.

Notes

1 The quotation marks here indicate my dissatisfaction with such terms, explained below. Hereafter, I mostly drop the quotation marks, which become tedious. One common problem of notions of family farms/farming is that they conflate family-owned, family-managed and family-worked farms. While the last (the use of family labour) follows the tradition of Chayanov (1966 [1925]) and provides the most potent meaning of 'family farm', both analytically and ideologically, many so-called 'family farms' are family owned, and sometimes family managed, without being worked with household labour.

2 Derived from Brewster (1970). Strictly speaking, in Marxist terms, these contrasts concern the *labour processes* of agriculture and industry, rather than their production processes.

3 All quotes from Boltvinik are taken from Chapter 1 unless otherwise noted.

4 In particular Djurfeldt (1981; Boltvinik, Chapter 1, section 6), whose analysis is commended; Armando Bartra (Chapter 2, section 5); and Mann and Dickinson (1978: 466–81).

5 'The development of agriculture in capitalist society' is the title of Part I of Kautsky's *Agrarian Question* (1988 [1899]).

6 Occasionally Boltvinik points towards the historical political economy advocated here. For example:

What labour costs are relevant to the setting of agricultural prices? Only the cost of days worked? Or the year-round cost of reproduction of the producer and his family? This dilemma does not occur in industry: insofar as one works throughout the year, salaries are associated with maintaining the wage earner and his family year round. *The presence of this dilemma in agriculture explains the enormous variety of forms of production present within it. Each form of production is a particular way of solving this dilemma.* (Chapter 1, section 4, emphasis in original)

The last two sentences are, in effect, deductive and thus presented as assertions or generalisations, but they could be reformulated to provide the kinds of theoretico-historical hypotheses for investigation that I suggest below.

7 For example, Pechlaner and Otero (2010: 201) report that 'while Mexico's employed labor force increased by 9.8 percent between 1998 and 2007, it decreased in agriculture by 23.97 percent, from 7.5 million people to only 5.7 million', and that agricultural liberalisation induced by NAFTA has caused 'the greatest rural population exodus that the country has experienced in its history' (ibid.: 202).

8 See Bernstein (2010), the first in a series of 'little books on big ideas' in *Agrarian Change and Peasant Studies*, established by Saturnino M. Borras Jr. The book has appeared in Bahasa, Chinese, Japanese, Portuguese, Spanish and Turkish editions, with French and Thai translations forthcoming. In the interests of exposition in this chapter, I provide a lot of notes so as not to burden the main text unduly.

9 The localism of small-scale ('peasant') farming has provided one of the enduring attractions, and tropes, of *agrarian populism* since the advent and impact of industrial capitalism. By agrarian populism I mean the defence of peasant or family farmers against the threats to their reproduction by capitalism and its class agents – from merchants and banks to capitalist landed property, agrarian capital and agribusiness – and by projects of state-led 'national development' in all their capitalist, nationalist and (once) socialist variants.

10 Schematically, there are two main approaches in Marxist and *Marxisant* debates on the origin of capitalism. One locates it in the emergence of a 'world system' from the fifteenth or sixteenth centuries, as argued, among others, by Gunder Frank (1969), Wallerstein (1974; 1980; 1989), Arrighi (1994), Banaji (2010) and Moore (2012a; 2010b; 2010c). The other approach is that of the transition from feudalism to capitalism in north-west Europe from the fifteenth century or so; this is the object of Dobb's *Studies in the Development of Capitalism* (1963 [1946]) and the celebrated debate it stimulated (Dobb et al. 1954; Hilton et al. 1976). A central element of that debate was the search for the 'prime mover' in the transition, subsequently treated in an original way in Brenner's seminal essay (1976; Aston and Philpin 1985). Byres (1991; 1996) fits into the latter approach but

(re-)introduced the centrality of agrarian transitions to capitalism to subsequent industrialisation.

11 Adapted from Friedmann and McMichael (1989). The new 'industrial plantation' of this period provides a tropical and colonial counterpart to the shift from farming to agriculture pioneered by the American Midwest. What distinguished the 'industrial plantation' from earlier forms of plantation (typically worked with slaves and other forms of coerced labour) were the connections between its organisation and methods of production, its ownership structures, and its close linkages with finance capital, shipping, industrial processing and manufacturing – aspects of a 'worldwide shift towards agribusiness in the late nineteenth century', as remarked by Stoler (1985: 17) in her study of plantations in Sumatra. Banaji (2010: 333) similarly suggests that: 'The late nineteenth century was the watershed of agrarian capitalism, the first age of discernibly modern forms of agriculture and their rapid evolution'. Like the prairies of the 'temperate grain-livestock complex', many zones of industrial plantation production were also new agricultural frontiers, in this case established by clearing vast areas of tropical forest.

12 'Corn' here was wheat, not 'corn' in the sense of maize. De Janvry's stimulating class-analytic comparative essay on why governments do what they do in terms of food price policy takes off from the emblematic instance of Corn Law repeal in Britain (de Janvry 1983).

13 Earlier transitions to industrial capitalism, and the contributions to them of agriculture, occurred when prices for agricultural commodities were generally much higher in real terms than they are now: the international terms of trade 'moved in favour of agriculture ... through the nineteenth

century and indeed up to the First World War, whereas since the 1940s they mostly turned sharply against agricultural commodities and in favour of manufactured goods for the first time since the industrial revolution' (Kitching 2001: 154–5). We can add that the promotion of exports of tropical agricultural commodities, in the moment of developmentalism in the South and beyond in the current era of neoliberal globalisation, tends to generate systematic overproduction, which depresses their prices in international markets (coffee is perhaps the best-known example). Kitching (ibid.) also reminds us that today's richest countries had much smaller populations and rates of population growth at the time of their industrial take-off than the principal countries of the South today. Also, industrial technologies were generally more labour-intensive than they are now, hence industry needed, and was better able to absorb, the labour of migrants from rural areas displaced by primitive accumulation and the development of capitalist farming.

14 This is another pressure on peasant reproduction that can be added to Boltvinik's account. He assumes that periods outside the working calendar of farming, imposed by its seasonality, are 'idle time'. This is not always or necessarily so, as activities such as spinning and weaving were often vital sources of non-farming income or the reproduction of peasant households; there are also the activities of preparation for the next cycle of cultivation, and the raising of livestock, during cropping 'down' seasons. Marx, of course, remarked on the destruction of peasant handicrafts in the British context as well as considering rural household production in the context of 'putting out' organised by merchant capital before the advent of 'machinofacture'.

Bagchi (2009) suggests that the impact of colonialism in India was to *increase* 'ruralisation' and 'peasantisation': that is, an economically more narrow existence in the countryside.

15 Gibbon and Neocosmos state:

to suggest that a social formation is capitalist by virtue of being founded on the contradiction of capital and wage-labour is not to assert that all – or even the majority of – enterprises in this social formation will conform to a 'type' in which capitalists and wage-labourers are present, and which constitutes the measure in relation to which all other forms deviate. What makes enterprises, and more generally social formations, capitalist or not, is not their supposed essential features but *the relations which structurally and historically explain their existence.* (1985: 169, emphasis added)

Also apposite here is Balibar's observation that, across the social worlds of capitalism, class relations are '*one determining* structure, covering *all* social practices, without being the *only* one' (quoted in Therborn 2007: 88, emphasis in original). In sum, commodity or class relations are *universal but not exclusive* determinations of social practices in capitalism. They intersect and combine with other social differences and divisions, of which gender is the most widespread but which can also include oppressive and exclusionary relations of race and ethnicity, religion and caste.

16 Boltvinik sometimes uses the term 'petty commodity producers' (for example in his discussion of Armando Bartra; Chapter 1, section 7), but as a descriptive synonym for peasants or family farmers rather than as a theoretically defined category.

17 Much of the political economy literature on peasants centres on their (incomplete) integration into capitalist markets (see, for example, Friedmann 1980), but relatively little has addressed how capitalist social relations are internalised in peasant production through the 'commodification of subsistence' and 'dull compulsion of economic forces'. I am struck that Boltvinik's only reference in this respect is to peasants' 'acceptance of the cultural imposition of the capitalist production mode ... *In effect, they internalise one of the factors of their own poverty*' (Chapter 1, section 4, emphasis in original).

18 Again, I am struck that this is the only time when Boltvinik refers to 'contradictions in the ... peasant unit' (household), and this is in connection with his sole reference to gender relations (Boltvinik 2011: 5, note 11).

19 'Self-sufficient peasant agriculture' is a strange description of ('family') farming in France today. Shelley is referring to a particular national, and populist, myth, in which hired labour, especially immigrant labour, vanishes from sight.

20 In 'The method of political economy', which is a section of the Introduction to the *Grundrisse*, Marx (1973: 101) famously suggested that '[t]he concrete ... is the concentration of many determinations'.

21 In recent decades, 'pluri-activity' – that is, combining own-account farming with other farm-related or off-farm income-earning activities – has become a major trope in academic and policy discussion of European (family) farming (see Losch 2004).

22 '[I]n the course of the most ferocious economic struggle for existence, the ... [small farmer] who knows how to starve is the one who is best adapted' (Chayanov 1991 [1927]: 40).

23 And their wages often support wider networks of kin – urban and rural.

24 The issue here is acknowledged but not confronted by Boltvinik, who says 'It is unclear whether the concept of the peasantry should or should not include those *smallholders whose main income comes from the sale of their labour force*, while income derived from the plot complements this' (Chapter 1, section 3, emphasis added). In his original paper he then cites Roger Bartra's view on Mexico in 1960, when '1,240,000 peasants were classified as possessing below subsistence plots of land. These peasants, who account for 50% of the total, must complement their income with wage labour (it might be more accurate to say that they are *proletarians who complement their income with agriculture*)' (Boltvinik 2011, emphasis added). Later, Boltvinik refers to Harriss's view (1992 [1982]) that most family units in Asia and Latin America are marginal agricultural units, and observes that 'without explaining why they exist, Harriss begs the question on the persistence of the peasantry' (Chapter 1, section 5). I am confident that Harriss's response or answer would follow broadly similar lines of argument to those presented here concerning peasant class differentiation and the formation of (rural) classes of labour (see Harriss 2011; see also Lerche 2010; 2011 on India).

25 Concepts of 'self-employment' are highly problematic, and are often misleadingly applied to those who are 'wage workers in thin disguise' (Harriss-White and Gooptu 2000: 96).

26 This is not to say that the *World Development Report 2008* is a consistent or coherent document (see the symposium in the *Journal of Agrarian Change*, vol. 9, no. 2 (2009) with contributions by Carlos Oya, Philip McMichael, Kojo Amanor, Philip

Woodhouse and Matteo Rizzo). Note too IFAD (2011: 16): 'The livelihoods of poor rural households are diverse across regions and countries, and within countries. Livelihoods are derived, to varying degrees, from smallholder farming – including livestock production and artisanal fisheries – agricultural wage labour, wage or self-employment in the rural non-farm economy and migration.' (See also ibid.: 52–7; Annex 3: 281–2.)

27 In addition, there are issues of how 'rural' and 'urban' population is defined in different countries for census purposes, and how well they are counted (IFAD 2001: 17–18). It is also important to note tendencies in the other direction, so to speak: that is, to the peri-urbanisation of some rural areas. This can be witnessed widely in China, for example, and Fitting (2011) suggests that it is also the case in the Tehuacán valley of Mexico.

28 The greatest concentrations of 'small farmers' are in South Asia, China and sub-Saharan Africa. Numbers of 'peasants' or 'small farmers' in the global South are often exaggerated, sometimes greatly so, by those 'taking the part of peasants': for example, Martínez-Alier (2002) and Samir Amin (2003) give figures of 2 billion and 3 billion respectively. The latter, in fact, is close to the standard aggregate of *total* rural population used in IFAD (2011).

29 In the famous words of the *Communist Manifesto*, which provide the title of Berman's classic work (1982).

30 Boltvinik notes the importance of labour productivity in passing:

Whether a family agricultural unit can live adequately from the working days invested in its plot of land, and therefore may or may not need to seek additional sources of income, obviously depends on factors that explain the *productivity of agricultural work* as well as the relative prices it faces. The objective situation of the 'American family farm' is evidently very different from that of the Latin American, African or Asian peasant. (Chapter 1, section 4, emphasis added)

Indeed it is, and this observation, together with other factors, undermines the tendency to bracket 'family' farmers in North America and the EU with those in the global South (for example, Boltvinik, Chapter 1, section 1). By 2000, according to the French radical agronomists Mazoyer and Roudart (2006: 11), average labour productivity in US grain production was *2,000 times* that of sub-Saharan Africa, which remained predominantly dependent on hoe cultivation. Another illustration: IFAD (2011: 32) reports that, since the world food price spike of mid-2007 to mid-2008, developed countries have expanded cereal output by over 13 per cent while developing countries have increased theirs by only 2 per cent. It is notable that prominent scholars critical of capitalist agriculture seem to converge in the view that neoliberal globalisation spells the (final) demise of the peasantry (and thus its 'functions' for capitalism): for example, 'relative depeasantisation' has given way to 'absolute depeasantisation and displacement' through a wave of 'global enclosure' (Araghi 2009: 133–4); globalisation represents a 'massive assault on the remaining peasant formations of the world' that builds on previous waves of assault (Friedmann 2006: 462); and, for McMichael (2006: 476), the globalising 'corporate food regime … dispossess[es] farmers as a condition for the consolidation of corporate agriculture'.

31

[W]hen I say that peasants absorb the entire costs of seasonality, I do not mean that they are *exploited* in this way by capital but *by society as a whole* – everyone pays lower prices for food and therefore receives a subsidy from peasants. *Peasants are poor because they subsidise all of us.* (Boltvinik, Chapter 1, section 7, some emphasis added)

32 Boltvinik's proposal for subsidies ('transfers') is redistributive from food consumers to producers: in effect, a market-oriented intervention at a historical moment when any measure of significant social redistribution – from capital to labour, rich to poor – is ruled out by the ideological hegemony of neoliberalism and the policy frameworks it informs and permits. While IFAD's latest proposals to overcome rural poverty include some measures of investment – for example, in rural infrastructure, services, training and social protection – it does not envisage any significant redistributive policies (IFAD 2011: 23–4), as one might expect. Indeed, its proposals are framed within today's standard conventions of 'stimulating' markets to be pro-poor together with good 'governance' and institutions.

33 Land reform looms large in the politics of indigenous peoples, as elsewhere in Latin America (Otero and Jugenitz 2003). The case for redistributive land reform continues to be restated more generally; see, for example, Griffin et al. (2002), but see also its critique in Byres (2004), and the response by Griffin and his co-authors (2004).

34 The food price inflation that peaked in 2007–08 and has continued since, with severe effects for the food consumption of many in the global South, cannot be explained only, or even mostly, by production and supply conditions. Ghosh (2009), among others, draws attention to the role of speculation by finance capital in commodities markets.

35 The ecological effects of industrialised capitalist farming – its 'accelerating biophysical contradictions', in the terms of Weis's outstanding overview (2010) – are its Achilles heel, of course, and a threat to all (see also Moore 2010c).

36 The upper figure of 40 per cent is taken from the important study by Scoones et al. (2010) on the effects of Zimbabwe's 'Fast Track Land Resettlement Programme' (FTLRP), the world's most comprehensive (only?) state-sponsored redistributive land reform of the twenty-first century. Of those acquiring land whom the authors' research tracked over time in Masvingo province, about 40 per cent had established viable farms. A number of their findings resonate well with some of the dynamics emphasised in this paper: class differentiation (in three main strata) with emergent capitalist 'accumulation from below'; the importance of the supply and management of labour, especially wage labour, to relative success or failure; and the centrality of 'straddling' own-account farming and off-farm activities and sources of income (including through cross-border migration). The study is a salutary counter to five principal 'myths': that Zimbabwe's land reform is a total failure; its beneficiaries are mainly 'political cronies' of ZANU-PF (Mugabe's political party); there is no investment in the new settlements; agriculture is in complete ruins, creating chronic food insecurity; and the rural economy has collapsed.

37 Boltvinik (Chapter 1, section 13) points towards this in outlining 'three central factors explaining the

undervaluation of labour power in Mexico': reduction in trade unions' coverage and power; wage repression policies; and slow economic and employment growth.

38 This was the case, for example, even in conditions of extreme national oppression, for a minority of migrant mine workers from Mozambique to South Africa whose savings enabled them to invest in farm production – in effect, small-scale 'accumulation from below' (First 1983). By contrast, in her ethnography of three rural counties

of Jiangxi province in China, Murphy (2002) found that returning long-term labour migrants with skills, savings and entrepreneurial ambition invested in establishing small manufacturing and service enterprises. Their experiences reinforced their sense of what they aimed to avoid: to work for a 'boss' (a capitalist employer) again *and* to farm (to return to the peasant condition).

39 Barkin (2006: 133) further suggests that this is a '*response to the decline in opportunities in urban-industrial society*' (emphasis added).

References

Amin, S. (2003) 'World poverty, pauperisation and capital accumulation', *Monthly Review* 55 (5).

Araghi, F. (2009) 'The invisible hand and the visible foot: peasants, dispossession and globalisation' in A. H. Akram-Lodhi and C. Kay (eds), *Peasants and Globalisation: Political economy, rural transformation and the agrarian question*. London: Routledge.

Arrighi, G. (1994) *The Long Twentieth Century: Money, power and the origins of our times*. London: Verso.

Aston, T. H. and C. H. E. Philpin (eds) (1985) *The Brenner Debate: Agrarian class structure and economic development in pre-industrial Europe*. Cambridge: Cambridge University Press.

Bagchi, A. K. (2009) 'Nineteenth century imperialism and structural transformation in colonised countries' in A. H. Akram-Lodhi and C. Kay (eds), *Peasants and Globalisation: Political economy, rural transformation and the agrarian question*. London: Routledge.

Banaji, J. (2010) *Theory as History: Essays on modes of production and exploitation*. Leiden: Brill.

Barkin, D. (2002) 'The reconstruction of a modern Mexican peasantry', *Journal of Peasant Studies* 30 (1): 73–90.

— (2006) 'Building a future for rural Mexico', *Latin American Perspectives* 33 (2): 132–40.

Berman, M. (1982) *All That Is Solid Melts Into Air: The experience of modernity*. London: Verso.

Bernstein, H. (1996) 'Agrarian questions then and now' in H. Bernstein and T. Brass (eds), *Agrarian Questions: Essays in appreciation of T. J. Byres*. London: Frank Cass.

— (2002) 'Land reform: taking a long(er) view', *Journal of Agrarian Change* 2 (4): 433–63.

— (2004) 'Considering Africa's agrarian questions', *Historical Materialism* 12 (4): 115–44.

— (2005) 'Rural land and land conflicts in sub-Saharan Africa' in S. Moyo and P. Yeros (eds), *Reclaiming the Land: The resurgence of rural movements in Africa, Asia and Latin America*. London: Zed Books.

— (2009) 'V. I. Lenin and A. V. Chayanov: looking back, looking forward', *Journal of Peasant Studies* 36 (1): 55–81.

— (2010) *Class Dynamics of Agrarian Change*. Halifax, Canada: Fernwood.

Bharadwaj, K. (1985) 'A view on commercialisation in Indian agriculture and the development of capitalism', *Journal of Peasant Studies* 12 (4): 7–25.

Boltvinik, J. (2011) 'Poverty and persistence of the peasantry'. Background paper for the International Workshop on Peasant's Poverty and Persistence, CROP and El Colegio de México, Mexico City, 13–15 March 2012 (Chapter 1, this book).

Borras, S. M. Jr and J. C. Franco (2012) 'Global land grabbing and trajectories of agrarian change: a preliminary analysis', *Journal of Agrarian Change* 12 (1): 34–59.

Bramall, C. (2007) *The Industrialisation of Rural China*. Oxford: Oxford University Press.

Breman, J. (1996) *Footloose Labour: Working in India's informal economy*. Cambridge: Cambridge University Press.

— (2001) 'The impact of the Asian economic crisis on work and welfare in village Java', *Journal of Agrarian Change* 1 (2): 242–82.

Brenner, R. (1976) 'Agrarian class structure and economic development in pre-industrial Europe', *Past and Present* 70: 30–75.

Brenner, R. P. (2001) 'The Low Countries in the transition to capitalism', *Journal of Agrarian Change* 1 (2): 169–241.

Brewster, J. W. (1970) 'The machine process in agriculture and industry' in K. A. Fox and D. G. Johnson (eds), *Readings in the Economics of Agriculture*. London: George Allen & Unwin.

Bryceson, D. F. (1999) 'African rural labour, income diversification and livelihood approaches: a long-term development perspective', *Review of African Political Economy* 26 (80): 171–89.

Byres, T. J. (1981) 'The new technology, class formation and class action in the Indian countryside', *Journal of Peasant Studies* 8 (4): 405–54.

— (1991) 'The agrarian question and differing forms of capitalist transition: an essay with reference to Asia' in J. Breman and S. Mundle (eds), *Rural Transformation in Asia*. Delhi: Oxford University Press.

— (1996) *Capitalism From Above and Capitalism From Below: An essay in comparative political economy*. London: Macmillan.

— (ed.) (2004) *Redistributive Land Reform Today*. Special issue of *Journal of Agrarian Change* 4 (1–2).

Chayanov, A. V. (1966 [1925]) *The Theory of Peasant Economy*. Edited by D. Thorner, B. Kerblay and R. E. F. Smith. Homewood IL: Richard Irwin for the American Economic Association.

— (1991 [1927]) *The Theory of Peasant Co-operatives*. London: I. B. Tauris.

Cordell, D., J. W. Gregory and V. Piché (1996) *Hoe and Wage: A social history of a circular migration system in West Africa*. Boulder CO: Westview Press.

Cousins, B. (2011) 'What is a "smallholder"? Class-analytic perspectives on small-scale farming and agrarian reform in South Africa' in P. Hebinck and C. Shackleton (eds), *Reforming Land and Resource Use in South Africa*. London: Routledge.

Cronon, W. (1991) *Nature's Metropolis: Chicago and the Great West*. New York NY: W. W. Norton.

Crosby, A. W. (1986) *Ecological Imperialism: The biological expansion of Europe, 900–1900*. Cambridge: Cambridge University Press.

Davis, M. (2006) *Planet of Slums*. London: Verso.

de Janvry, A. (1983) 'Why do governments do what they do? The case of food price policy' in D. G. Johnson and E. G. Schuh (eds), *The Role of Markets in the World Food Economy*. Boulder CO: Westview Press.

Djurfeldt, G. (1981) 'What happened to the agrarian bourgeoisie and rural proletariat under monopoly capitalism? Some hypotheses derived from the classics of Marxism on the agrarian question', *Acta Sociologica* 24 (3): 167–91. Reprinted as 'Classic discussions of capital and peasantry: a critique' in Harriss (1992 [1982]), pp. 139–59.

Dobb, M. (1963 [1946]) *Studies in the Development of Capitalism*. London: Routledge & Kegan Paul.

Dobb, M. et al. (1954) *The Transition from Feudalism to Capitalism: A symposium*. With a foreword by M. Dobb and contributions by M. Dobb, P. M. Sweezy, H. K. Takahashi, R. Hilton and C. Hill. London: Fore Publications.

Edelman, M. (2002) *Peasants Against Globalisation: Rural social movements in Costa Rica*. Stanford CT: Stanford University Press.

Fan, S., B. Nestorova and T. Olofinbiyi1 (2010) 'China's agricultural and rural development: implications for Africa'. China-DAC Study Group on Agriculture, Food Security and Rural Development, Bamako, 27–28 April.

FAO (2012) *FAO Statistical Yearbook 2012*. Rome: Food and Agriculture Organization of the United Nations (FAO).

First, R. (1983) *The Mozambican Miner: Proletarian and peasant*. London: Macmillan.

Fitting, E. (2011) *The Struggle for Maize: Campesinos, workers, and transgenic corn in the Mexican countryside*. Durham NC: Duke University Press.

Frank, A. G. (1969) *Capitalism and Underdevelopment in Latin America*. New York NY: Monthly Review Press.

Friedmann, H. (1980) 'Household production and the national economy: concepts for the analysis of agrarian formations', *Journal of Peasant Studies* 7 (2): 158–84.

— (1982) 'The political economy of food: the rise and fall of the post-war international food order', *American Sociological Review* 88 (Supplement): S248–S286.

— (2004) 'Feeding the empire: the pathologies of globalised agriculture' in L. Panitch and C. Leys (eds), *The Socialist Register 2005*. London: Merlin Press.

— (2006) 'Focusing on agriculture: a comment on Henry Bernstein's "Is there an agrarian question in the 21st century?"', *Canadian Journal of Development Studies* 27 (4): 461–5.

Friedmann, H. and P. McMichael (1989) 'Agriculture and the state system: the rise and decline of national agricultures, 1870 to the present', *Sociologica Ruralis* 29 (2): 93–117.

Ghosh, J. (2009) 'The unnatural coupling: food and global finance', *Journal of Agrarian Change* 10 (1): 72–86. Symposium on *The 2007–08 World Food Crisis*.

Gibbon, P. and M. Neocosmos (1985) 'Some problems in the political economy of "African socialism"' in H. Bernstein and B. K. Campbell (eds), *Contradictions of Accumulation in Africa: Studies in economy and state*. Beverly Hills CA: Sage.

Griffin, K., A. R. Khan and A. Ickowitz (2002) 'Poverty and distribution of land', *Journal of Agrarian Change* 2 (3): 279–330.

— (2004) 'In defence of neo-classical neo-populism', *Journal of Agrarian Change* 4 (3): 361–86.

Gupta, A. (2012) *Red Tape: Bureaucracy, Structural Violence and Poverty in India*. Durham NC: Duke University Press.

Hall, D., P. Hirsch and T. Li (2011) *Powers of Exclusion: Land dilemmas in Southeast Asia*. Singapore: National University of Singapore Press.

Harriss, J. (1987) 'Capitalism and peasant production: the Green Revolution in India' in T. Shanin (ed.), *Peasants and Peasant Societies*. <edition>Second</edition> edition. Oxford: Blackwell.

— (ed.) (1992 [1982]) *Rural Development: Theories of peasant economy and agrarian change*. London: Routledge.

— (2011) 'Reflections on agrarian change in India since independence: does "landlordism" Still Matter?' Paper presented to the workshop 'Agrarian Transformation in India: Its Significance for Left Politics', Oxford, 13–14 July.

Harriss-White, B. and N. Gooptu (2000) 'Mapping India's world of unorganised labour' in L. Panitch and C. Leys (eds), *The Socialist Register 2001*. London: Merlin Press.

Hart, G. (1994) 'The dynamics of diversification in an Asian rice region' in B. Koppel, J. N. Hawkins and W. James (eds), *Development or Deterioration? Work in rural Asia*. Boulder CO: Lynne Rienner.

Hazell, P., C. Poulton, S. Wiggins and A. Dorward (2007) *The Future of Small Farms for Poverty Reduction and Growth*. 2020 Discussion Paper 42. Washington DC: International Food Policy Research Institute (IFPRI).

Hilton, R. et al. (1976) *The Transition from Feudalism to Capitalism*. With an introduction by R. Hilton, and contributions by P. Sweezy, M. Dobb, K. Takahashi, R. Hilton, C. Hill, G. Lefebvre, G. Procacci, E. Hobsbawm and J. Merrington. London: New Left Books.

IFAD (2001) *Rural Poverty Report 2001. The challenge of ending rural poverty*. Rome: International Fund for Agricultural Development (IFAD).

— (2011) *Rural Poverty Report 2001. New realities, new challenges: New opportunities for tomorrow's generation*. Rome: International Fund for Agricultural Development (IFAD).

Kautsky, K. (1988 [1899]) *The Agrarian Question*. 2 volumes. Translated by P. Burgess. London: Zwan.

Kitching, G. (2001) *Seeking Social Justice through Globalisation*. University Park PA: Pennsylvania State University Press.

Lenin, V. I. (1964 [1899]) *The Development of Capitalism in Russia: The process of the formation of a home market for large-scale industry*. In *Collected Works*, Volume 3. Moscow: Progress Publishers.

— (1964 [1916]) *Imperialism, The Highest Stage of Capitalism*. In *Collected Works*, Volume 22. Moscow: Progress Publishers.

Lerche, J. (2010) 'From "rural labour" to "classes of labour": class fragmentation, caste and class struggle at the bottom of the Indian labour hierarchy' in B. Harriss-White and J. Heyer (eds), *The Comparative Political Economy of Development: Africa and South Asia*. London: Routledge.

— (2011) 'Agrarian questions or labour questions? The agrarian question and its irrelevance for rural labour in a neo-liberal India'. Paper presented to the workshop 'Agrarian Transformation in India: Its Significance for Left Politics', Oxford, 13–14 July.

Llambi, L. (1988) 'Small modern farmers: neither peasants nor fully-fledged capitalists? A theoretical and historical discussion', *Journal of Peasant Studies* 15 (3): 350–72.

Losch, B. (2004) 'Debating the multifunctionality of agriculture: from trade negotiations to development policies by the South', *Journal of Agrarian Change* 4 (3): 336–60.

Mamdani, M. (1987) 'Extreme but not exceptional: towards an analysis of the agrarian question in Uganda', *Journal of Peasant Studies* 14 (2): 191–225.

Mann, S. A. and J. M. Dickinson (1978) 'Obstacles to the development of a capitalist agriculture', *Journal of Peasant Studies* 5 (4): 466–81.

Martínez-Alier, J. (2002) *The Environmentalism of the Poor.* Cheltenham: Edward Elgar.

Marx, K. (1973) *Grundrisse: Foundations of the Critique of Political Economy (Rough Draft).* Translated by M. Nicolaus. Harmondsworth, UK: Penguin Books.

Mazoyer, M. and L. Roudart (2006) *A History of World Agriculture from the Neolithic Age to the Current Crisis.* London: Earthscan.

McMichael, P. (2006) 'Reframing development: global peasant movements and the new agrarian question', *Canadian Journal of Development Studies* 27 (4): 471–83.

Moore, J. W. (2010a) '"Amsterdam is standing on Norway". Part I: The alchemy of capital, empire, and nature in the diaspora of silver, 1545–1648', *Journal of Agrarian Change* 10 (1): 33–68.

— (2010b) '"Amsterdam is standing on Norway". Part II: The global North Atlantic in the ecological revolution of seventeenth century capitalism', *Journal of Agrarian Change* 10 (2): 188–227.

— (2010c) 'The end of the road? Agricultural revolutions in the capitalist world-ecology, 1450–2010', *Journal of Agrarian Change* 10 (3): 389–413. Special issue on *Productive Forces in Capitalist Agriculture: Political Economy and Political Ecology,* edited by H. Bernstein and P. Woodhouse.

Murphy, R. (2002) *How Migrant Labour is Changing Rural China.* Cambridge: Cambridge University Press.

Otero, G. and H. A. Jugenitz (2003) 'Challenging national borders from within: the political-class formation of indigenous peasants in Latin America', *Canadian Review of Sociology and Anthropology* 40 (5): 503–24.

Panitch, L. and C. Leys (2000) 'Preface' in L. Panitch and C. Leys (eds), *The Socialist Register 2001.* London: Merlin Press.

Pechlaner, G. and G. Otero (2010) 'The neoliberal food regime: neoregulation and the new division of labour in North America', *Rural Sociology* 75 (2): 179–208.

Scoones, I., N. Marongwe, B. Mavedzenge, J. Mahenehene, F. Murimbarimba and C. Sukume (2010) *Zimbabwe's Land Reform: Myths and realities.* Woodbridge: James Currey.

Shelley, T. (2007) *Exploited: Migrant labour in the new global economy.* London: Zed Books.

Standing, G. (2011) *The Precariat: The new dangerous class.* London: Bloomsbury.

Stoler, A. L. (1985) *Capitalism and Confrontation in Sumatra's Plantation Belt, 1870–1979.* New Haven CT: Yale University Press.

Therborn, G. (2007) 'After dialectics: radical social theory in a post-communist world', *New Left Review* (NS) 43: 63–117.

Wallerstein, I. (1974) *The Modern World-System. I: Capitalist agriculture and the origins of the European World-economy in the sixteenth century.* New York NY: Academic Press.

— (1980) *The Modern World-System. II: Mercantilism and the consolidation of the European world-economy, 1600–1750.* New York NY: Academic Press.

— (1989) *The Modern World-System. III: The second era of great expansion of the capitalist world-economy, 1730–1840s.* New York NY: Academic Press.

Weis, T. (2007) *The Global Food Economy:* *The battle for the future of farming.* London: Zed Books.

— (2010) 'The accelerating biophysical contradictions of industrial capitalist agriculture', *Journal of Agrarian Change* 10 (3): 315–41. Special issue on *Productive Forces in Capitalist Agriculture: Political Economy and Political Ecology*, edited by H. Bernstein and P. Woodhouse.

Winders, B. (2009) 'The vanishing free market: the formation and spread of the British and US food regimes', *Journal of Agrarian Change* 9 (3): 315–44.

World Bank (2007) *World Development Report 2008: Agriculture for development.* Washington DC: World Bank.

6 | EMPLOYMENT AND RURAL POVERTY IN MEXICO

Araceli Damián and Edith Pacheco

This article seeks to contribute to the discussion of the link between poverty and the persistence of the peasantry in the current capitalist system. It provides empirical evidence of the socio-economic characteristics of the peasantry in Mexico and their links with agricultural production, focusing on the period from 1991 to 2003.[1] However, we shall refer to the living conditions of the peasantry up to 2010. We begin with a brief description of the socio-economic conditions that prevailed in the Mexican countryside after the Revolution of 1910. We will emphasise the public policies that shaped and/or exacerbated inequalities in forms of production and, therefore, in the lives of: 1) major agricultural producers, defined here as those who own medium and large-sized plots; 2) waged and/or salaried agricultural workers; and 3) peasants, identified as producers on small plots.

1. The Mexican countryside in the twentieth century

During the last century, the Mexican countryside underwent major transformations. On the one hand, the core of the agricultural economy was transformed from large haciendas producing for both national consumption and exports, to modern agricultural zones whose production was designed to ensure the development of national industry and the urban proletariat. Despite these changes, large contingents of peasants remained outside the benefits of development, with undeveloped means of production and land destined largely for subsistence.

In 1930, 70 per cent of the employed population of Mexico worked in rural areas,[2] and working conditions had not improved since pre-revolutionary times; company stores continued, workers were heavily indebted,[3] and their daily pay was insufficient to satisfy their basic needs (Tello 2010: 137). At the same time, the agricultural population became more dependent on monetary income while the importance of subsistence production declined.

Although agricultural land distribution was one of the main symbols of the 1910 Revolution, the agrarian reform was insufficient, since the land provided was largely non-arable (Table 6.1) and there was very little support given to the modernisation of smallholders' and farmers' production (see Hewitt de Alcántara 1978).

During the Cárdenas administration (1935–40), attempts were made to create a rural middle class. The proportion of the population that benefited from the agrarian reform rose from 31 per cent to 42 per cent of the total agricultural population, and the Banco Nacional de Crédito Ejidal (National Bank of Ejido Credit) was established, together with mutual insurance funds. Ejido funds were created and the profits used to build auditoriums and corn mills, among other facilities. Mass literacy campaigns were established, and regional agricultural schools created, together with women's organisations. Attempts to alleviate poverty did not entail emerging programmes to protect the poor from hunger but instead sought to involve them in productive programmes (ibid.: 186).[4]

Mass immunisation programmes reduced mortality rates in rural zones, which, according to Hewitt de Alcántara, produced rapid population growth and a sharp imbalance between arable land and demographic pressures. The rapid growth of industrial activity generated employment, permitting mass rural–urban migration.

Agricultural activity was functional to industrial and urban demands, providing cheap supply inputs for production and food, which led to a transfer of value from the agricultural to the industrial sector. The export of agricultural raw materials generated foreign currency to facilitate imports of capital and intermediate goods and to cover payments for the technology that fostered national industrialisation. Health services and education were established for the urban population, but were neglected in the countryside. As Hewitt de Alcántara (ibid.) suggests, the rural population became a reserve army for this nascent industrial development. Moreover, rural–urban migration accelerated in the 1940s, continuing at a high rate until 1980.

The abandonment of rural zones since the 1982 crisis and the subsequent change in the economic model of development – the adoption of neoliberalism – have exacerbated the decline of

TABLE 6.1 The distribution of agricultural land, 1915–70

President (period)	Hectares	Beneficiaries	Hectares per beneficiary	Type of agricultural land (%)		
				Irrigated land	Rain-fed land	Non-arable land
Carranza (1915–20)						
De la Huerta (1920)	381,949	77,203	4.9	2.5	42.8	54.7
Obregón (1921–24)	1,730,684	154,128	12.3	3.1	28.4	68.5
Calles (1925–28)	3,173,343	292,194	8.6	3.2	27.2	69.6
Portes Gil (1929–30)	1,436,203	187,203	7.7	2.9	22.4	74.7
Ortiz Rubio (1931–32)	910,261	56,884	16.0	2.4	18.8	78.8
Rodríguez (1933–34)	2,056,268	158,262	13.0	4.4	25.2	70.4
Cárdenas (1935–40)	20,107,044	763,009	26.4	4.9	21.1	74.0
Ávila Camacho (1941–46)	5,306,922	112,107	47.3	1.6	17.9	80.5
Alemán (1947–52)	4,210,478	91,054	46.2	1.5	19.7	78.8
Ruiz Cortines (1953–58)	3,563,847	195,699	18.2	1.2	24.8	74.0
López Mateos (1959–64)	7,935,476	255,283	31.1	0.8	18.2	81.0
Díaz Ordaz (1965–70)	24,491,000	396,700	65.9	0.5	8.2	91.3

Source: Hewitt de Alcántara (1978).

the agricultural sector. Today, only a few states have modern agricultural production, most of them located in northern Mexico (Sonora, Colima, Baja California and Baja California Sur).[5] At the other extreme are states that have more numerous, poorer, peasant populations (Quintana Roo, Yucatán, Chiapas, Tabasco, Guerrero, Veracruz, Oaxaca, Campeche, San Luis Potosí and Hidalgo). In these states, agricultural production is carried out with rudimentary technology, and a major proportion of peasants still use pre-capitalist techniques of production: animal traction and rudimentary tools (Florez 2012).

2. Demographic aspects of the rural population

In the twentieth century, Mexico was transformed from a predominantly rural to an urban country (Figure 6.1): whereas in 1910 the percentage of the rural population was 71 per cent, by 2010 it accounted for only 23.2 per cent. Moreover, as Pacheco and Sánchez (2012) have pointed out, the decrease in the proportion of the rural population was accompanied by territorial dispersion. Nevertheless, in absolute terms, the population living in rural zones continued growing (from 10.7 million in 1910 to 26.1 million in 2010).

In the early post-revolutionary years, the decrease in the proportion of rural population was relatively slow; as late as 1940, it accounted for

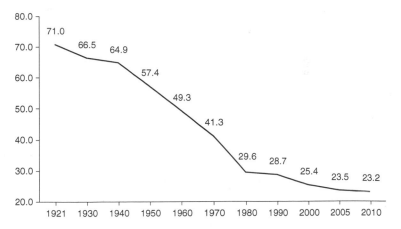

6.1 The rural population as a percentage of the total population, 1921–2010 (*source*: 1910–2000: Pacheco and Sánchez (2012: cuadro 1); 2010: Censo de Población y Vivienda (National Census) for 2010 (INEGI 2011)

two-thirds of the total population (64.9 per cent). That year marked the beginning of Mexico's greatest industrial development and country to city migration speeded up. According to certain authors, an important part of this migratory flow had a circular component. In other words, people returned to their place of origin for certain seasons, particularly in regions where the employment structure made it possible to combine various activities (Appendini 2008). This circularity, developed several decades ago, can be regarded as forming part of the mechanisms used by Mexican peasants to ensure their persistence. The fact that agricultural activities are seasonal provides a possible explanation for this circularity, an issue we will explore in greater depth below.

The reduction in employment opportunities in cities as a result of the exhaustion of the import substitution model of industrialisation coupled with the 1982 debt crisis reduced the possibilities of migration from rural zones. Since then, a considerable increase in migration towards northern Mexico and the United States has been observed, making remittances from this migration (especially from the US) an important source of income for rural families. Historically, there has been a strong link between the Mexican rural proletariat and capitalist forms of production in the United States. Formal links were established in the 1940s with the first Bracero programme, and although this programme was eliminated in the 1970s, there continues to be labour migration quotas together with large volumes of unauthorised migration. In 1999, according to the official US census, there were 650,000 Mexican workers in US agriculture, 7.6 per cent of the total US agricultural labour force, with the percentage higher among males (10.9 per cent). Although the number of Mexican workers in agriculture has now decreased considerably (in 2010, 323,000 Mexican workers were reported in this activity in the United States), this may be due to the fact that figures are underestimated. Not only is there a large number of unauthorised workers, but also the composition of Mexican labour in the United States has been transformed in recent years with a higher percentage now engaged in service activities. Nevertheless, remittances continue to be a significant source of income in certain rural areas.[6] Migration to the United States, therefore, constitutes a resource that contributes to the persistence of Mexican peasantry.[7]

The dynamic of migration to the US has been modified, partly as a result of stiffer control over Mexico's northern border but also as a result of the 2008 crisis. During the first decade of this century, it was calculated that the yearly number of emigrants to the United States fluctuated between 400,000 and 600,000. However, there is a dispute over the real amount of emigration to the US.[8]

As a result of national and international migration, there has been a depopulation of the working age population in rural zones, largely because of the lack of job opportunities. As a result, ancestral poverty is combined with a lack of human resources for engaging in economic activity in these zones. This situation can be observed in Figure 6.2, where the age structure in 2010 of the population in the most urbanised localities (with 100,000 or more inhabitants or metropolitan) is contrasted with that of rural villages (with fewer than 2,500 inhabitants). It is quite clear that rural areas have a lower proportion of the population between 20 and 60 years old than do

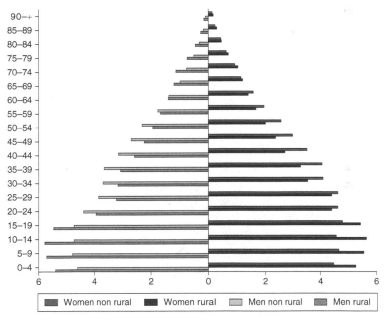

6.2 Population pyramid, 2010 (*source*: 1910–2000: Pacheco and Sánchez (2012: cuadro 1); 2010: Censo de Población y Vivienda (National Census) for 2010 (INEGI 2011). (source: INEGI (2011))

Note: Men are shown on the left side of the pyramid, women on the right.

metropolitan areas; and this contrast is even stronger for the population whose ages range from 25 to 35. Hence, there is a larger proportion of the population under the age of 15 and over 60 in rural zones. Migration, particularly international migration, means that children and youth are left in their localities of origin to care for the elderly. Pacheco and Sánchez (2012) point out that the higher proportion of the population of 60 years and over in rural localities may be explained by the fact that they are probably the owners of the land, which is why they remain there. But it also could mean that their age prohibits them from migrating, since travel might be arduous and, even if they migrated, employers would not hire them.

One possible hypothesis that arises from these findings is that the persistence of the peasantry in Mexico, despite migration, can be attributed to the ways in which peasant households are 'tied' to the land (partly as a result of the Agrarian Reform). Although these peasant households may be unproductive, the land constitutes a heritage that ensures the survival of the family nucleus through subsistence farming, the sale of agricultural products, or by obtaining rental income.

According to the Special Section on Agriculture (AM) of the National Employment Survey (ENE), in 2003, 26.4 per cent of the population in localities of up to 2,500 inhabitants lived in households in which some of their members stated that they were engaged in activities as peasant, farmer or *ejido* owners, which allows us to deduce that they own or possess land. This percentage is higher among households where income depends more on agricultural activity (Table 6.2). We can therefore assume that these types of households preserve peasant forms of production and that their members engage in wage work at certain periods of the year (for capitalist agricultural units or in other activities such as construction, commerce or services).

In other words, peasants in Mexico also depend on the existence of capitalist forms of production that enable them to complement their limited family resources through the sale of their labour power. Mexican peasants have therefore survived despite the fact that, since the mid-1980s, policy measures have been implemented that have benefited big business and have limited public investment in infrastructure for small farmers.

Medium and large landowners continued to receive federal government support through programmes such as PROCAMPO

TABLE 6.2 The percentage of the population distributed according to the proportion of total household income represented by agricultural income, 2003

Percentage that agricultural income represents of the total household income	Landless households (%)	Households owning land (%)	Total
100%	65.6	34.4	100.0
50% of income or more	61.4	38.6	100.0
Less than 50% of income	62.4	37.6	100.0
Non-agricultural income	100.0	0.0	100.0
Total	**73.6**	**26.4**	**100.00**

Source: Authors' calculations based on the AM of the ENE.
Note: Includes earnings from work only.

(Programa de Apoyos Directos al Campo, or Direct Support for the Countryside Programme)[9] and ASERCA (Agencia de Servicios a la Comercialización y Desarrollo de Mercados Agropecuarios, or Support and Services for Agricultural Commercialisation) (Yúnez Naude 2010), since they were designed to provide resources according to the number of hectares or tons produced. Smallholders, including Mexican peasants, were therefore relatively deprived of these benefits. Thus, in 2006, 23.9 per cent of those who received PROCAMPO had plots of land of up to 1 hectare[10] and received just 0.6 per cent of the transfers, whereas farmers with 5 hectares or more (22.5 per cent of the total number of production units) received 53.3 per cent of the transfers. The remaining subsidies were given to farmers with between 1 and 5 hectares of land (Merino 2010: Chart 2). Such inequality in the allocation of governmental transfers is also observed at state level. States with a low level of rural poverty (Sinaloa, Tamaulipas, Zacatecas and Jalisco) have received most of the benefits of ASERCA, PROCAMPO and the Target Income Programme[11] (ibid.).

3. Poverty in Mexico's rural setting

This section refers to poverty in rural areas calculated using the Integrated Poverty Measurement Method (IPMM)[12] to process micro-data from the National Household Income and Expenditure Survey (Encuesta Nacional de Ingresos y Gastos de los Hogares or ENIGH). This survey does not have enough information to analyse the work-employment strategies used by Mexican peasants in order to obtain the income that would enable them to survive for a period of more than one month. However, the agricultural module of the ENE does include this information. The ENIGH provides a broader view of the deprivation suffered by the population in rural zones in Mexico, since it contains more detailed information on well-being compared with the ENE, the main objective of which is to record information on people's economic activity. In turn, the ENIGH has information on all sources of income, not only labour income (as does the ENE), but also government transfers, remittances, presents, pensions, and so on. At the same time, the ENIGH provides a detailed account of housing conditions, water and drainage services, durable goods, consumption expenditures, including expenditures on education and health, and overall a larger number of variables than are included in the ENE. It should be pointed out that we will also present data on poverty using the ENE, but this data will refer only to labour income.[13]

Poverty in the rural areas in Mexico is extremely generalised. As one can see from Figure 6.3, in 2010 the incidence of poverty measured using the IPMM was nearly identical to that found in 1984: around 95 per cent of the population in rural areas. We should remember that this last year reflected the impact of the 1982 crisis, meaning that Mexico is facing the persistence not only of peasants but also of widespread, entrenched poverty.

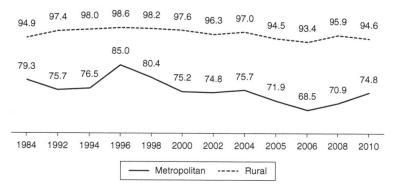

6.3 The percentage of people living in poverty in rural and metropolitan settlements (*source*: Boltvinik et al. (2012))

Note: Based on IPMM.

To illustrate the territorial inequalities in Mexico, we also included the level of poverty in the country's metropolitan zones (with over 100,000 inhabitants) in the graph. As one can see, in 2010, the distance between the two types of localities was nearly twenty percentage points. Moreover, although the difference tends to decrease during crises, in large, urban localities poverty has tended to decline, whereas in rural settings it has remained virtually constant.

It should be noted that, although the percentage of people in rural poverty has not declined in recent years, poverty is currently less intense. This is reflected in the fact that the indigent population (which meets fewer than 50 per cent of the thresholds used as criteria *not* to be poor) fell from 74 per cent of the total in 1984 to 57.8 per cent in 2010. Conversely, the stratum of people in intense poverty (which meets 50 per cent to 66.6 per cent of the criteria) nearly doubled: from 10.5 per cent to 19.9 per cent. Lastly, the population in moderate poverty (which meets over 66 per cent but under 100 per cent of the criteria) rose from 10.4 per cent to 16.9 per cent (Figure 6.4).

From a multidimensional perspective, so far we have seen that deprivation in the rural setting is extremely acute and generalised. Even considering the income variable only, poverty incidence is also extremely high. Although we will be mainly analysing income poverty as measured using the agricultural module (AM) of the ENE, for comparative purposes and to cover the years after 2003 (when the

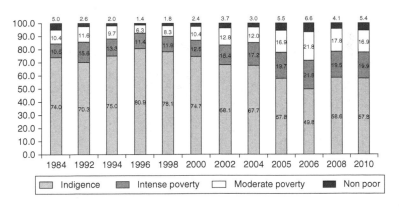

6.4 Rural population by poverty strata, 1984–2010 (*source*: Boltvinik et al. (2012))

Note: Based on IPMM.

last AM was applied), we also calculated income poverty in rural areas in 2004 and 2010 using the respective ENIGH databases. As shown in Table 6.3, although the percentage of income-poor people rose slightly (from 92.3 per cent to 94.7 per cent), poverty intensity (or the poverty gap) decreased, as reflected in the fall in the incidence of indigence from 71.6 per cent to 57.0 per cent.

Table 6.4 shows the results of labour income poverty measured using the ENE by settlement size. As one can see, labour income poverty in localities with fewer than 2,500 inhabitants is almost the same as in the following stratum by settlement size (2,500 to 14,999). However, as we shall see later on, both the number of workers in the agricultural sector and agricultural income are extremely low in this second class of localities. Labour income poverty in localities with 15,000 to 99,999 inhabitants drops significantly (64.5 per cent), which is similar to the findings using data from the ENIGH.

At this point, it is important to highlight the fact that the incidence of income poverty resulting from both surveys is quite different, as the available information and the procedures adopted to measure poverty differ. Using ENIGH data in 2004, 92.4 per cent of the population was identified as poor in localities with fewer than 2,500 inhabitants, whereas in 2003, using ENE data, we identified 79.6 per cent of the same population as poor (Tables 6.3 and 6.4). This

TABLE 6.3 Income poverty in rural areas (percentage of the total population), 2004 and 2010

Income poverty strata	2004	2010
Indigence	71.6	57.0
Intense poverty	10.4	20.4
Moderate poverty	10.2	17.2
Total poverty	**92.3**	**94.7**
Income satisfaction[1]	6.1	3.0
Middle class[2]	1.5	1.9
Upper class[3]	0.1	0.5
Non-poor	**7.7**	**5.3**

Source: Authors' calculations based on the ENIGH.

Notes: [1] Income between the poverty line (PL) and less than 1.1 times the PL; [2] Income between twice the PL and less than 1.5 times the PL; [3] Income 1.5 times the PL or more.

TABLE 6.4 Labour income poverty by settlement size (percentage of the total population), 2003

Poverty strata (LF)	15,000–99,999 inhabitants	2,500–14,999 inhabitants	Fewer than 2,500 inhabitants	Total
Indigence	20.2	43.5	45.5	42.8
Intense poverty	13.8	15.8	13.0	13.8
Moderate poverty	30.5	20.7	21.1	21.8
Total poverty	**64.5**	**80.0**	**79.6**	**70.9**
Income satisfaction	28.7	16.6	16.9	17.8
Middle class	5.8	3.3	3.2	3.5
Upper class	1.0	0.1	0.3	0.3
Non-poor	**35.5**	**20.0**	**20.4**	**29.1**

Source: Authors' calculations based on the ENE.

Note: 'Income' includes earnings from work only.

difference is largely due to the fact that the poverty line adopted to compare with income in the ENE is 22 per cent lower than the one adopted for the ENIGH. (This difference occurs because an adjustment was necessary to take into account the restricted nature of income measured by the ENE, where only income derived from working activities or labour income was counted.) However, as the adjustment relied on an average value (the percentage that labour income represented in total income in rural areas: 78 per cent), the procedure used underestimated poverty (by underestimating the poverty line) in households that depend only on labour income or depend on it more than the average, since the ENE does not show which households receive transfers, gifts, remittances, and so on. Calculations based on the ENE also show (as do those based on the ENIGH) that in rural areas indigence constitutes the largest poverty stratum (45.5 per cent), but they show moderate poverty as a larger percentage than intense poverty (21.1 per cent compared with 13.0 per cent), inverting the results based on the ENIGH.

Although the intensity of rural poverty has declined according to the ENIGH figures, there has been a relative reduction in the importance of income from wages in agricultural gross domestic product (GDP). According to Puyana and Romero (2008: 178, Graph 8.1), whereas in the period 1980–83 the proportion of income from agricultural wages was above 20 per cent, since 1984 a nearly constant fall has been observed and these wages now account for only 12 per cent of the total, whereas the share of capital has increased, representing almost 90 per cent of GDP. These authors also show that the share of rural households in the national household income total, which in 1989 was 20 per cent, had been reduced to 13 per cent by 2012 (ibid.: 182, Graph 8.2). They also show that income distribution has deteriorated in these zones, as the real household income of deciles one to nine declined between 1989 and 2002 while the income of the tenth decile increased significantly (ibid.: 194, Graph 8.5).

4. Activities in rural contexts and family composition

As mentioned earlier, the Statistics Institute of Mexico (Instituto Nacional de Estadística, Geografía e Informática or INEGI) applied an agricultural module (AM) in less urbanised zones (with fewer than 100,000 inhabitants) during the period 1991–2003 within the framework of the ENE. This source of information enabled us to find out more about the characteristics of agricultural workers. The AM asked whether workers had engaged in activities corresponding to the agricultural sector during the past six months, unlike the usual question in employment surveys that records information only on the previous week.

The change in the period of reference – from one week to six months – shows that the volume of work carried out in agriculture is inaccurately recorded when the period of reference is last week. For example, in 2003 the AM recorded 1.5 million additional workers in this sector (in relative terms, around 13 per cent of the agricultural labour power estimated using the AM) compared with those who would have been recorded if the information had referred to the week prior to the application of the survey. This result constitutes the first evidence of the high level of intersectoral occupational mobility of agricultural workers in Mexico, in a context in which the seasonality of production plays a central role.[14]

We should bear in mind the fact that, regardless of the greater or lesser under-registration of agricultural workers using periods of reference shorter than a year, there is a secular process of reduction in the number of agricultural workers. Particularly during the period of the strengthening of the North American Free Trade Agreement (NAFTA; 1995–2003), the proportion of agricultural workers in relation to the working age population at the national level dropped from 15 per cent to 10 per cent (Figure 6.5), which, in absolute terms, actually involved a reduction in the number of agricultural workers from 10.6 million to 7.7 million.[15]

It should be noted that the period on which the AM was carried out (1991–2003) included one of the greatest crises in Mexico (1995), and this affected the agricultural sector. Moreover, the entry into force of NAFTA (1994) affected the productive bases of all the economic sectors and therefore of agriculture.

The agricultural working population in Mexico is primarily male. As shown in Figure 6.5, the decrease in the proportion of working men is much greater than among women. This decrease occurred within the context of enormous difficulties in agricultural production, in conjunction with the increase in labour-saving processes.[16] Given these results, is it still possible to talk about the persistence of the peasantry?

Given that the agricultural module (AM) of the employment survey in Mexico was applied in the areas classified as less urbanised – localities with fewer than 100,000 inhabitants – we believe it is relevant to first determine the importance of agricultural labour by

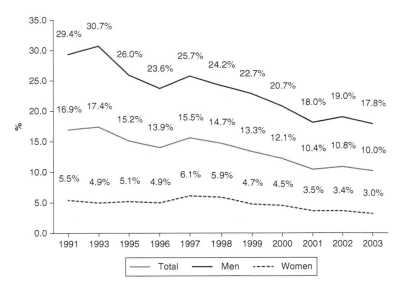

6.5 Share of agricultural workers in the working age population, 1991–2003 (*source*: Pacheco Gómez (2010))

settlement size. Based on the information in this module, we found that, in 2003, most of the population that worked in the agricultural sector was located in rural areas (localities with fewer than 2,500 inhabitants): 76.7 per cent (Table 6.5). In these localities, 59.1 per cent of the labour force was engaged in agricultural activities, whereas in the next two larger sizes of localities (2,500–14,999 and 15,000–99,999 inhabitants) the proportion was 23.7 per cent and 6.2 per cent respectively.

The pattern of spatial distribution of agricultural labour was very similar in 1991 (Pacheco Gómez 2010) and has remained virtually unchanged. In order to support this statement, since the AM contains information only up to 2003, we will use information from the 2010 population census. As can be seen in Table 6.6, agricultural activities, according to this source, were mainly carried out in rural localities, where agricultural workers still constituted practically half of the labour force, whereas in the next two larger locality sizes (2,500–14,999 and 15,000–99,999 inhabitants) the percentage drops to 19.0 per cent and 6.2 per cent respectively.[17]

At the household level, we observe different degrees of labour participation in agricultural activities. According to the AM, in 2003, 64.3 per cent of households in rural contexts (localities of fewer than 2,500 inhabitants) had household workers engaged in some

TABLE 6.5 Share of workers in agricultural activities by settlement size, 2003

Size of the locality (no. of inhabitants)	Non-agricultural workers	Agricultural workers	Total
Horizontal percentage			
15,000–99,999	93.6	6.4	100.0
2,500–14,999	76.3	23.7	100.0
Fewer than 2,500	40.9	59.1	100.0
Vertical percentage			
15,000–99,999	40.1	4.9	27.9
2,500–14,999	31.5	18.4	27.0
Fewer than 2,500	28.3	76.7	45.2
Total	**100.0**	**100.0**	**100.0**

Source: AM of the ENE, 2003.

Note: The reference period is the last six months.

TABLE 6.6 The percentage of workers in agricultural and non-agricultural activities by settlement size, 2010

Size of the locality (no. of inhabitants)	Non-agricultural workers	Agricultural workers	Total
Horizontal percentage			
15,000–99,999	93.8	6.2	100.0
2,500–14,999	81.0	19.0	100.0
Fewer than 2,500	50.6	49.4	100.0
Vertical percentage			
15,000–99,999	40.8	7.3	40.2
2,500–14,999	31.3	19.6	28.1
Fewer than 2,500	27.9	73.1	31.7
Total	**100.0**	**100.0**	**100.0**

Source: INEGI (2011).

agricultural activity (Table 6.7). Yet, very few rural households were able to live exclusively off the land, since only 8.3 per cent had *all* household workers engaged in agricultural activities. Nevertheless, this percentage is still high when compared with those observed in larger localities.

There was still a significant group of households (31.6 per cent) in rural localities with over 50 per cent of their family labour engaged in agricultural activities. Another 24.4 per cent of households had family labour that was more than 50 per cent non-agricultural but had some of their members engaged in agricultural activity. This broad participation in agricultural activity by households in rural contexts points to the 'persistence of the peasantry' and also to the insufficiency of income obtained from agriculture in most rural households.

However, we must understand the nature of this participation in order to more adequately answer one of the central questions in this book: is the seasonality of agriculture an aspect that contributes to understanding peasants' poverty? What are the forms of labour force participation of the rural population and what are the differences according to the type of household?

As we remarked at the beginning of this study, one factor that may explain families' continued engagement in agricultural activity is their access to land possession or ownership, either as part of

TABLE 6.7 Households according to the proportion of members engaged in agriculture (percentage by settlement size), 2003

	Settlement size (no. of inhabitants)			
	15,000–99,999	2,500–14,999	Fewer than 2,500	Total
Composition of the labour force at the household level				
All household workers engaged in agricultural activities	0.8	2.6	8.3	4.7
More than half of household workers engaged in agriculture	3.1	12.4	31.6	18.5
Less than half of household workers engaged in agriculture	5.2	14.6	24.4	16.4
All household workers engaged in non-agricultural activities	90.8	70.3	35.7	60.3
Total	**100.0**	**100.0**	**100.0**	**100.0**

Source: AM of the ENE, 2003.
Note: The figures consider household members' labour participation in the last six months.

an *ejido* or community, or as smallholders. Although the AM did not identify whether workers are landowners, we have considered farmers and *ejido* owners as an indirect indicator of land ownership or possession, and we have called them peasants. This assumption is based on the fact that the rural active population that does not own land is usually recorded as wage workers in the rural context (basically day workers or unpaid family workers). Peasants account for only 11.7 per cent of the working age rural population, but 22.9 per cent of the occupied population and 38.7 per cent of the agriculturally occupied, while wage agricultural workers represent 18.5 per cent (36.2 per cent and 61.3 per cent respectively), and non-agricultural workers represent 20.9 per cent of working age population and 40.9 per cent of occupied rural population (Table 6.8, vertical percentages; some figures given in the text are not shown in this table but can be calculated from it).

It is generally assumed that rural poverty is related to the low labour force participation rate (LFPR). This assumption is derived from the low LFPR calculated on the basis of the person's condition of activity in the previous week. Although in Mexico there is not much difference between the rural and urban LFPR (in 2003, 51.9

TABLE 6.8 Population of 12 years and over in rural areas by their work status and branch of activity, according to the proportion in which household workers are engaged in agricultural activities (percentage), 2003

	Household composition				
	All agric. workers	50% or more agric. workers	Less than 50% agric. workers	Non-agric. workers	Total
Type of worker	*Vertical percentages*				
Peasants	29.5	18.8	12.9	—	11.7
Wage agricultural workers	61.1	34.1	13.8	—	18.5
Non-agricultural workers	—	7.1	16.3	43.6	20.9
Unemployed	—	0.0	0.2	0.5	0.2
Inactive	—	34.9	54.5	55.9	45.9
Others	9.4	4.9	2.3	—	2.8
Total	100.0	100.0	100.0	100.0	100.0
	Horizontal percentages				
Peasants	13.9	49.6	36.5	—	100.0
Waged agricultural workers	18.2	56.9	24.8	—	100.0
Non-agricultural workers	—	10.5	25.9	63.5	100.0
Unemployed	—	6.0	25.9	68.1	100.0
Inactive	—	23.5	39.4	37.1	100.0
Others	18.4	54.2	27.5	—	100.0
Total	5.6	30.8	33.2	30.4	100.0
	Labour force participation rate				
Participation rate	100.0	65.1	45.5	44.1	53.5

Source: AM of the ENE, 2003.

Note: The figures consider household members' labour participation in the last six months.

per cent and 55.4 per cent respectively), when we take the past six months to estimate this rate, we can see that the rural rate comes closer to that observed in urban settings (53.5 per cent versus 55.4 per cent in 2003). The increase in the LFPR in rural areas might be explained by the characteristics of production, particularly the seasonality of agricultural activities. Moreover, the lower rate in rural areas, when it is calculated using the previous week, also shows the lack of employment opportunities in rural contexts during idle periods. This, in turn, contributes to the very high poverty level observed in rural localities.[18]

As Table 6.8 shows (horizontal percentages), only 5.6 per cent of the total population of 12 years and above lives in households in which all members of this age group are engaged in agricultural activities; however, they represented 13.9 per cent of peasant workers. This type of household is heavily dependent on wage work, since 61.1 per cent of their members belong to this category (Table 6.8, vertical percentage), and only 29.5 per cent belong properly to the peasant category; this shows that the majority cannot survive by producing only on their own land. It can also be seen that none of their members experienced unemployment, and that there is no inactive population. Indeed, their LFPR was 100 per cent, suggesting that adults in this type of household cannot afford not to work.

Table 6.8 also shows that 30.8 per cent of the population of 12 years and above in rural areas lives in households in which more than 50 per cent and less than 100 per cent of their working age members are engaged in agriculture. Most of the peasant and wage agricultural workers live in this type of household (49.6 per cent and 56.9 per cent respectively; Table 6.8, horizontal percentages). Compared with the previous type of household, this type depends less on wage agricultural work (34.1 per cent). Moreover, above a third of their working age population is inactive (vertical percentages). This shows that it is unlikely that these peasant households can devote themselves exclusively to production on their own land.

It can also be seen that, in households where most or all of their members are engaged in non-agricultural activities, there is a much higher proportion of inactive population. This might be explained by the fact that in non-agricultural activities wages tend to be higher on average than in agricultural activities.

The urgency of having to work when household income depends largely on agricultural activity is clearly expressed in the LFPR of individuals who belong to households where all workers are engaged in agriculture. As one can see in Figure 6.6, rates here are 100 per cent for all age groups and are much higher than in households in which the majority of members participate in the non-agricultural sector. Differences are even sharper in the groups at either end of the age range (children and senior citizens). In households that depend exclusively on agriculture, members are all forced to work at very young ages and they must continue working even into old age.

Households with less than 50 per cent of their labour in agricultural activities have a similar LFPR to households with no agricultural labour (Table 6.8). Participation rates by age are also similar between the two groups (Figure 6.6). Once again, we find data suggesting that poverty is more widespread among the population that relies most heavily on agricultural activity; this may explain why households in this group have a higher proportion of their members working throughout their lives.

When the composition of only the occupied population is analysed, we can see that more than a fifth (21.2 per cent; Table 6.9) of workers were peasants in 2003, and an additional 35.9 per cent were wage agricultural workers. The sum of both categories is 57.1 per cent, showing that the combination of peasant production with wage employment is an essential key to economic activity in rural areas.

In order to contribute to the discussion on the link between peasant poverty and peasant persistence, we classified the households in the AM of the ENE in such a way as to be able to locate the

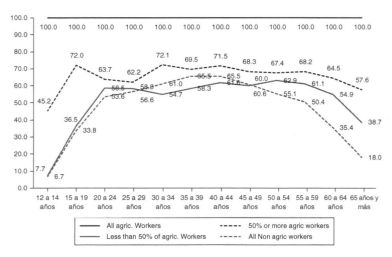

6.6 Labour force participation rate by age and household working structure (percentage of the working age population), 2003 (*source*: AM of the ENE, 2003)

TABLE 6.9 The percentage of occupied workers in rural areas by their working status and type of household composition (percentage of total workers), 2003

	Household composition				
	All agric. workers	**50% or more agric. workers**	**Less than 50% agric. workers**	**Non-agric. workers**	**Total**
Type of worker					
Peasants	2.9	10.5	7.7	0.0	21.2
Wage agricultural workers	5.5	21.0	9.3	0.0	35.9
Non-agricultural workers	0.0	6.9	13.5	22.5	42.9
Total	**8.4**	**38.5**	**30.6**	**22.5**	**100.0**

Source: AM of the ENE, 2003.

role of peasants within the work dynamic of rural contexts. This classification includes six categories:

1. peasant households: households comprising persons who reported being smallholders, occupants, lessees or sharecroppers and *ejido* owners, who mainly engage in farming on their own land and/or plant their backyards, for their own use or sale, and where family labour is crucial;
2. farmers (capitalist) households, which comprise those who mainly produce for sale (i.e. commodities) on land under irrigation and on medium-sized (50 to 100 hectares) and large (over 100 hectares) plots of land;
3. agricultural proletarian households: households comprising day workers, workers or employees in the agricultural sector;
4. non-agricultural proletarian households;
5. mixed proletarian households that include wage workers in both agricultural and non-agricultural activities); and
6. households comprising persons who do not engage in economic activities. In the following empirical analysis, the last category is excluded.

We can describe economic participation by these types of household for 2003 in rural areas, but we are not able to analyse how it changed between 1991 and 2003 specifically in rural areas (localities with fewer than 2,500 inhabitants), since the information from the AM in the 1990s was representative only for localities with fewer than 100,000 inhabitants as a whole. However, we can see the changes observed in this broader group of localities.

In localities with fewer than 100,000 inhabitants, the employed population of peasant households fell from 45.0 per cent to 29.6 per cent of the employed total between 1991 and 2003, whereas the percentage corresponding to non-agricultural proletarian households rose from 30.2 per cent to 52.3 per cent (Figure 6.7). This might suggest that there is a de-agriculturalisation of economic activity. However, the information for 2003 (which disaggregates rural areas from the group of localities with less than 100,000 inhabitants) suggests that this de-agriculturalisation might have occurred in localities with more than 2,500 inhabitants, while in rural localities the 'persistence of the peasantry' and the overwhelming importance of agriculture are maintained: the active population in peasant households accounted for 50 per cent, whereas it was only 24.6 per cent in non-agricultural households (Figure 6.7).

On the basis of this finding, let us examine the group of peasant households in rural contexts in order to determine the conditions and purpose (the destination of crops) of their production during the last year of the AM (2003).[19] First of all, most of the employed population located in peasant households declare that they produce for home consumption (80.7 per cent), whereas this crop use in capitalist agricultural households accounts for only 29.4 per cent

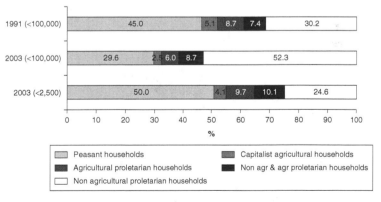

6.7 The distribution of the labour force by household type and by settlement size (percentage), 1991 and 2003 (*source*: AM of the ENE, 1991 and 2003)

of total production (Figure 6.8). The information shows that maize production represents an overwhelming proportion of crops cultivated for subsistence, even in the case of capitalist agricultural households (Figure 6.9).

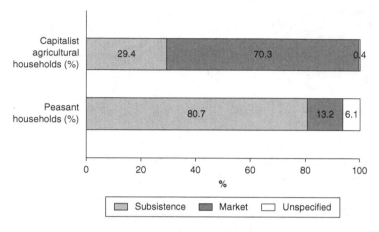

6.8 The labour force with land by household type and crop destination (percentage) (*source*: AM of the ENE, 2003)

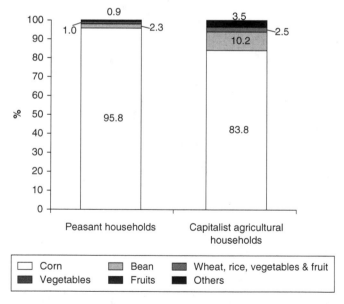

6.9 The labour force by crop cultivated for self-consumption in rural areas (percentage), 2003 (*source*: AM of the ENE, 2003)

Figure 6.8 also shows that capitalist agricultural households mainly produce for the market (70.3 per cent), whereas in the case of peasant households this accounts only for 13.2 per cent. This situation is closely linked to the type of land available to peasants and capitalist agricultural households. While peasants mainly have rain-fed land, capitalist agricultural households rely mostly on irrigated land (Figure 6.10).

Figure 6.11 shows the structure of labour occupation, by groups of crops, in different types of households. While two-thirds of the labour

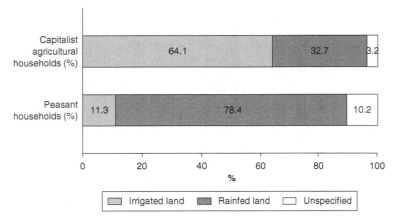

6.10 Labour force with land by type of unit and water source in rural localities (percentage), 2003 (*source*: AM of the ENE, 2003)

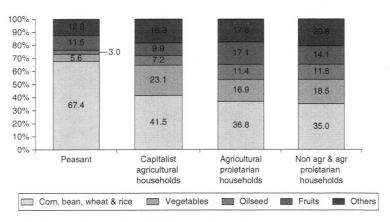

6.11 Labour force by household type and crop type in rural areas (percentage), 2003 (*source*: AM of the ENE, 2003)

force in peasant households are employed in the production of basic cereals (mainly maize) and beans, labour in capitalist households (a minority, if we recall that they represent only 5 per cent of the employed population) and in both types of proletarian households (agricultural and mixed) is distributed in a more diversified way. Basic cereals and pulses represent between 35.0 per cent and 41.5 per cent of labour occupation, while vegetables, fruits, oilseeds and other crops represent a high proportion.

It should also be noted that capitalists control market prices. According to Appendini (2001: 22):

> corporate maize farmers account for less than 1% of all the country's grain producers yet contribute 15% to 20% of production and determine the variations in supply on the basis of profitability. Conversely, it is estimated that 60% of the internal grain supply and 40% of the commercialised supply comes from what one could call peasant production units.

For her part, Rubio (2004: 42) states that:

> One of the characteristics of the current phase of production is that crops that occupy a smaller area and involve a lower number of producers become the leading crops and impose their operating logic on the aggregate of producers in the area. Whereas grains and oilseeds occupy 64.5% of the area, producing 49.9% of rural employment, 39.9% of value and 5.1% of foreign currency, fruit and vegetables, which only occupy 8.6% of the country's total area, but create 22.6% of rural employment, contributing 34.6% of value and 62.7% of foreign currency (Schwentesius and Gómez Cruz).

5. Labour intensity and 'multi-activity'

One of the aspects of peasant production continually mentioned in studies of rural areas is 'multi-activity'. In some studies, this phenomenon is framed from the perspective of occupational mobility (Ramírez 2005), whereas in others the focus is on the various labour combinations that may occur in a domestic unit (Guzmán Gómez and López 2005; Garay 2008). Still others frame the discussion from the perspective of the various sources of income produced in rural families

(Reardon and Berdegué 1999; Taylor and Yúnez-Naude n.d.; Carton de Grammont 2007; Yúnez and Meléndez-Martínez 2007).

In other words, the issue of 'multi-activity' can be seen from various perspectives. Individuals can engage in various occupations, whereas, within the household sphere, its labour members may be engaged in pluri-activity – a topic dealt with in the previous section – in order to have different sources of income. At the territorial scale, certain family members may work outside the country and/ or in different regions within the country. Some of them may send remittances, whereas other family members stay in the domestic unit and engage in agricultural and/or non-agricultural activities. We consider that this situation is largely due to the seasonal nature of agricultural work and, therefore, we first need to obtain information on the number of months in which people engage in a particular agricultural activity during the year, according to the answers given in the AM.[20] Second, the job itineraries of individuals over a period of six months are analysed. In addition to the information on the months in which people took part in agricultural activities, the module recorded the intensity (high, medium and low) with which they carried out their work. This provides us with elements to explore the proposal formulated by Boltvinik regarding the fact that:

> capitalism cannot exist in a pure form in agriculture: *without the peasants' supply of cheap seasonal labour, capitalist agriculture would be impossible. There would be (virtually) no one prepared to work only during the sowing and harvesting periods.* (Chapter 1, section 1)

The seasonal nature of agricultural activity is clearly reflected in Figure 6.12. It shows that, during the winter period (December, January and February), a higher percentage of workers report not having had any activity or that their activity was of very low intensity compared with the rest of the year. The intensity of agricultural work starts an upward trend in March at the beginning of spring; it becomes the highest (above medium intensity) in May and reaches a peak in June, with 47.8 per cent of those engaged in agriculture reporting a high intensity of work. This period corresponds to the sowing of maize and beans, activities that require intensive work. The figure shows that, during the months from October to November, the proportion of workers with intense productive activity (which had reached a minimum in September) increases again; this corresponds to the

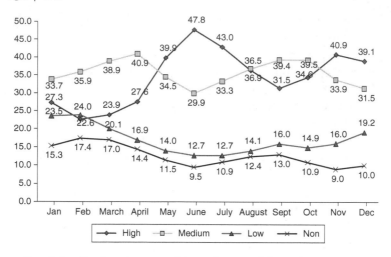

6.12 Intensity of work per month in settlements of fewer than 2,500 inhabitants (percentage of agricultural workers), 2003 (*source*: AM of the ENE, 2003)

harvest periods. The changes in the intensity of work at key points in agricultural production reflect the seasonality of agriculture.

Figure 6.12 also reflects that, throughout the year, there is a need to undertake a series of agricultural activities (weeding, spraying insecticides and fertilising, for instance) that may be associated with workers who report engaging in medium-intensity labour activities, the percentages of whom fluctuate just below and around 40 per cent of the total agricultural labour force during the months of August to October (during which the maize harvest begins). Lastly, the seasonality of agriculture is also reflected in the low intensity of work during the coldest months: January and February.

The seasonality of agricultural work is not recorded in traditional employment surveys, since, as we mentioned earlier, the period of reference for recording activity status is the previous week. Expanding this period to six months (as happened in the AM) showed that the total volume of workers in this activity increased substantially (by a million and a half workers in 2003). Moreover, when asked why they do not work the whole year, most workers declared that their work is seasonal (66 per cent in 2003, a percentage that did not change substantially during the period under study).

In order to answer the question about which activities are carried out in a context of fluctuating seasonal work requirements in agriculture, we will analyse the agricultural labour itineraries. The information refers to the changes observed in the worker's activity status (employed, unemployed or inactive) and occupational position (peasant or farmer with land, wage or unpaid worker) in three different moments: six months ago, three months ago and the previous week (Figure 6.13).[21] We have distinguished seventeen work itineraries. For example, these itineraries include having been a peasant or farmer in the three specific points in time[22] (a trajectory identified as P or F/P or F/P or F; see Figure 6.13), or just an agricultural worker (waged and/or unpaid) (AW/AW/AW), or having been a worker but being occupied in agricultural and then in non-agricultural activities (AW/AW/Non-agri). Twelve itineraries correspond to farmers and five to workers (Figure 6.13). With the information obtained from the AM, one could say that the number of peasants, farmers and agricultural workers recorded in this survey depended primarily on the period under study: the further back workers are asked about their participation in agricultural activities, the greater the likelihood of identifying peasants. It is important to note that this situation did not change substantially between 1993 and 2003.

In 2003, in rural areas 6.29 million respondents were defined as agricultural workers, out of a total of 17.9 million persons of working age. A total of 2.11 million said that they were peasants or farmers, while 3.68 million declared that they were agricultural wage or unpaid workers (Figure 6.13). Among the peasants or farmers, 1.03 million reported having had an itinerary without occupational mobility, accounting for 16.4 per cent of agricultural workers (P or F/P or F/P or F). There is a type of itinerary where a person remains in agricultural activities yet changes their work status: peasants or farmers who were wage (or unpaid) workers during the previous three months (0.510 million); most of them (0.416 million) had returned to their condition of peasants or farmers in the previous reference week. The rest had remained as agricultural wage workers (0.067 million) or had moved to non-agricultural wage activities (0.023 million). The third largest group corresponds to peasant or farmers who moved to off-farm activities (0.305 million). More than a third of them (0.117 million) had returned to being peasants or farmers in the previous reference week, while a larger proportion (0.187 million) had remained as non-agricultural workers.

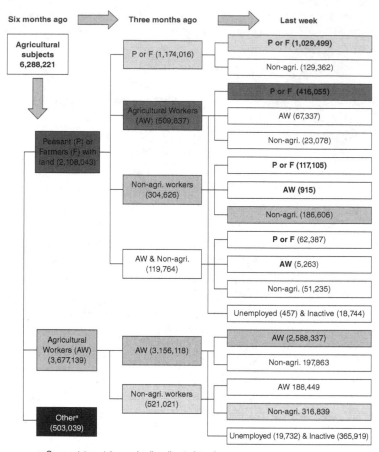

a: Occupant, tenant, lessee, landless livestock producers

6.13 Mobility itineraries of the agricultural labour force, 2003 (*source*: AM of the ENE, 2003)

Note: Includes occupants, tenants, lessees and landless livestock producers.

In the case of agricultural wage or unpaid workers, most of them reported having had an itinerary without agricultural mobility (2.59 million out of 3.68 million workers); they represent 41.2 per cent of the total who described themselves as agricultural subjects (AW/AW/AW). Additionally, 0.521 million became non-agricultural workers in the previous three months. In this case, the majority (0.317 million) had remained in non-agricultural work in the previous week, and the rest (0.188 million) had become agricultural workers again during that same time period.

Lastly, there are two groups of itineraries in which agricultural workers had become unemployed or inactive during the week of reference.

Because of the job mobility of workers in different moments of the year, we can state that the employment surveys that refer to activity during the previous week generate data that do not adequately reflect the actual numbers of those who depend on agricultural activities for their livelihood. As shown in Table 6.10, the percentage of peasants or farmers and agricultural workers is higher if the workers are asked about their occupational status and branch of activities in the six months prior to conducting the survey, compared with the percentage reported when they are asked about their position at work in the previous week. Thus, while 22.1 per cent of workers in rural areas declared that they were peasants or farmers six months ago, the percentage declined to 17.7 per cent when they were asked about their position at work during the previous week. In the case of wage (or unpaid) agricultural workers, 38.5 per cent described themselves as such when asked about their occupational status six months ago, compared with 31.1 per cent in the previous week. Taking together the two agricultural work positions, the six-month reference period gives a total of 60.6 per cent compared with only 48.8 per cent for last week (a difference of 20 per cent). Therefore, agricultural activities are greatly underestimated by traditional employment indicators used all over the world.

As we have seen, the unavoidable seasonality of agricultural activity causes fluctuations in the intensity of labour, the number of months worked, and the forms of participation in the labour force (agricultural,

TABLE 6.10 The percentage of workers in rural areas according to their position at work and branch of activity six months ago and in the last week, 2003

Work status	Period of reference	
	Last six months	**Last week**
Peasant or farmers	22.1	17.7
Wage agricultural workers	38.5	31.1
Non-agricultural workers	39.0	50.5
Unemployed	0.5	0.7
Total	**100.0**	**100.0**

Source: Authors' calculations based on the AM of the ENE, 2003.

non-agricultural and without activity). Agricultural workers and peasants have to use various work strategies to maintain a minimum income throughout the year; in 2003, they composed 60.6 per cent of the occupied population in rural areas. The rest of the active population recorded by the AM (39.4 per cent) had more stable itineraries as they were occupied in essentially non-seasonal activities. The mobility of the agricultural labour force shows that agricultural households need to diversify their sources of income. We must also consider the fact that the population recorded by the survey does not reflect the total mobility that is actually occurring for two reasons. The first is that it interviews only those who engaged in agricultural activity over the past six months, even though we saw how labour requirements vary throughout the year. At the same time, those who migrated at the time of the interview are not included in the analysis. We therefore assume that agricultural labour mobility is even greater than what the data show.

In addition to the need to diversify the sources of income in households that depend largely on agricultural activity, workers earn very low wages and face precarious labour conditions, as we shall see in the following section.

6. Working conditions of the rural population: a poor, persistent peasantry

As has been shown by Pacheco and Sánchez (2012), farm workers are poorer than non-farm workers in terms of income and social security. Wages for agricultural workers are noticeably lower than for non-agricultural workers. Women engaged in farm work earn almost a third less (29 per cent) than female non-farmer workers (Figure 6.14). According to Garay (2008) this difference is probably one of the factors that drove women in rural contexts towards growing participation in non-agricultural activities. However, wage differences are worse in the case of men. Thus, the mean wage for male agricultural workers represents only 46.7 per cent of the non-agricultural mean (Figure 6.14).

As shown in Figure 6.15, the same pattern is observed in terms of hourly wages. Thus, the mean wage for non-farm male workers was $2.12 an hour in 2003, while those engaged in agricultural activities had a mean of $1.03 per hour (less than half). While this comparison does not account for differences in qualifications between activities, the gap is wide enough to show how poorly paid jobs are in rural areas

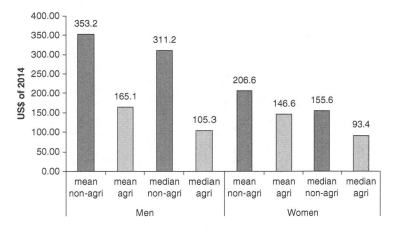

6.14 Wages and salary earnings per month in rural areas, 2003 (*source*: Sánchez and Pacheco (2012))

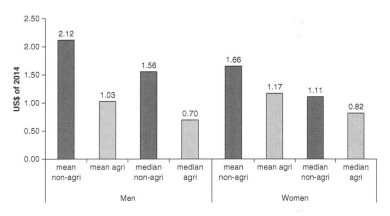

6.15 Wages and salary earnings per hour in rural areas, 2003 (*source*: Sánchez and Pacheco (2012))

and one of the major reasons for migration and the abandonment of agricultural activities.

Farm workers tend to report shorter working days on average than those reported by non-farm workers, which may translate into lower total income. However, they may also under-report the number of hours they actually work. Farm workers may also under-declare the days worked per week (David et al. 2001). Lastly, the deprivation of agricultural workers is particularly acute, since only 9.9 per cent

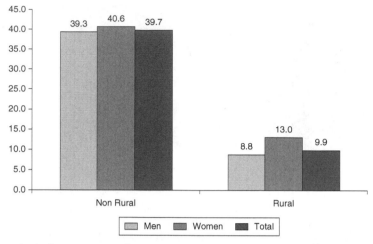

6.16 The percentage of workers in rural areas with access to health services as a social security benefit (IMSS and ISSSTE), 2003 (*source*: IMSS and ISSSTE; Pacheco and Sánchez (2012))

of these workers had access to social security in 2003, in contrast with 39.7 per cent for non-rural workers (Figure 6.16). Rural male workers are in a worse situation compared with rural women in terms of access to social security (which includes health services).

7. Some final reflections

Through the information provided by the agricultural module (AM) of the ENE, we found that the vast majority of Mexican peasants and agricultural workers who live mostly in rural localities (defined as those with fewer than 2,500 inhabitants) live in poverty. We also found that their poverty is closely linked both to the seasonal character of agricultural activity and to the prevalence of very low wage levels.

The enormous poverty suffered by peasants is observed throughout their lifecycle. We found that the poorest had high rates of labour participation, even among the populations aged 12 to 17 and 65 and over. These two age groups have lower LFPRs in family contexts and structures where poverty is lower. When there is less poverty, the first age group devotes its time primarily to education, while the second group can 'afford' to withdraw from the labour market. However, in poor peasant contexts, these population groups are forced to contribute their labour to guarantee the reproduction of the family nucleus.

At the same time, the results we obtained on poverty in rural contexts showed that the persistence of the peasantry requires poor households to adopt strategies to diversify their sources of income.

It can therefore be said that, in Mexico, there is evidence that the peasantry absorbs the economic and social costs of agricultural labour seasonality and instability of work, creating an ad hoc industrial reserve army.

Notes

1 The period of analysis is restricted, since these are the only years when the National Institute of Geography and Statistics (INEGI) included a special section on the agriculture sector in the National Employment Survey (Encuesta Nacional de Empleo or ENE).

2 We define rural areas as localities with fewer than 2,500 inhabitants. We are aware of the broad debate on the adequate threshold to identify rural settlements. However, later on, we will show that this particular threshold is appropriate for the purposes of this paper.

3 Company stores were supply stores belonging to the owners, who sold workers products whose cost (which was artificially inflated) was docked from their pay, forcing them to continue working for the same employer, and thus fostering a system of debt peonage.

4 The Agrarian Reform was stipulated in the national Constitution of 1917. It established land distribution through the division of latifundia; the development and protection of small property; and the allocation of land to new agricultural population centres or to those that lacked land in sufficient quantity, creating or restoring the *ejidos* and restoring communal land. The *ejidos* are a form of social organisation

with land allocated to them. Land was generally classified as land for collective uses and land for private family uses. The members of the *ejido* (*ejidatarios*) were given the right to make use of the land and to bequeath this possession to their heirs, although they did not own the land. In 1993, during the administration of Carlos Salinas de Gortari (1988–94), this law was reformed, enabling the *ejido* owners to sell individual plots.

5 Baja California is the only state with internationally competitive means of production; it is a state with low levels of poverty and a shortage of labour.

6 In 2008, 1.6 million households (out of 26.7 million) reported receiving remittances, which accounted for between 15 per cent and 44 per cent of their total income. Women-led households in rural areas have the highest percentage, since they are usually families in which the main provider has emigrated to the US (authors' calculations based on INEGI 2008).

7 Yúnez and Meléndez-Martínez (2007) note that international emigration significantly increases total household income and that most of this income is received through remittances.

8 According to Passel, the 2010 census shows that this volume was overestimated (Passel 2011). This author

suggests that the total population in Mexico was higher than what the National Population Council (CONAPO) had projected, but it is difficult to know whether the difference is due to emigration or, as has also been suggested, to the overestimation of the decrease in fertility rates. Boltvinik (2006), however, estimated that emigration during the years 2000–05 was 1.2 million per year.

9 Implemented in late 1993, it is a monetary transfer system where the amount is a function of the size of the cultivated land. It replaced a system of subsidies to inputs combined with a guaranteed price scheme for grains and oilseeds.

10 Five hectares are equivalent to 12.3 acres or 50,000 square metres.

11 Target income is the amount provided by the federal government to cover the difference between the market price and the minimum offered by the government for agricultural products (maize, wheat, sorghum, safflower, canola, cotton, rice, soya beans, and triticale and forage wheat).

12 The IPMM combines three dimensions to calculate poverty: income, basic needs and available or free time.

13 To this end, we calculated the average percentage that labour income represents in the total income of all households in the ENIGH, which resulted in 78 per cent. Thus, we compared labour income in the ENE with a 'reduced' poverty line representing this same percentage of the poverty line used in the ENIGH.

14 It also gives us a clue as to how large the underestimation of the labour force might be in other Third World countries, given that the measures used in most countries across the globe adopt 'last week' as a period of reference. Note that the correct procedure to estimate

participation in seasonal activities would be to ask about activities during the preceding year. Thus, the real underestimation is much greater and the AM still underestimates the agricultural labour force.

15 The survey uses the term 'farm subjects' to describe 'any individual who at any time during a period of six months, ending in the week the survey was taken, participated in obtaining products from the earth or livestock production, either directly as a worker or as an organiser or supervisor of the production process as a whole' (INEGI 2002: 182).

16 We do not ignore the fact that this period includes a spatial mobility dynamic of the working age population, on which we will reflect later.

17 Let us not forget that census data on labour matters are recorded using the previous week as the reference period. That is why the difference between 59.5 per cent and 49.4 per cent of the labour force dedicated to agriculture in 2003 and 2010 respectively is explained both by the secular decline trend of this type of worker and by the different periods of reference.

18 It should be noted that some studies based on the LFPR and that referred to the previous week claim that there is a low level of participation by women in rural contexts (see Pacheco and Sánchez 2012). However, it is likely that this is due, in part, to the seasonality of agricultural activity.

19 The threshold of fewer than 2,500 inhabitants turned out to be a very good selection. A table constructed but not included in this chapter shows that settlements with 2,500–14,999 inhabitants had a completely different pattern of labour force composition in 2003 compared with that of rural localities. In localities of 2,500–14,999 inhabitants, more than 60 per cent of

occupied persons belong to households with non-agricultural workers.

20 It should be noted that the INEGI recorded information only on those who participated in agricultural activity over the past six months, although they were asked about the characteristics of their participation in this activity throughout the year.

21 In the AM of the ENE, if the respondents gave a positive answer to the question of whether they had cultivated land and/or participated in agricultural or livestock activities over the past six months, they were then asked in which type of activity (agricultural or non-agricultural) they had engaged in the past three months. In order to construct the trajectories, this information was also compared with the answers given by agricultural farmers and workers on their economic activity during the week prior to the interview. Pacheco and Florez (2009) identified twenty-two work itineraries in the AM. They are different from the ones we present here.

22 Landowners, *ejido* owners, occupants and rentiers are called 'peasants or farmers'.

References

Appendini, K. (2001) *De la milpa a los tortibonos. La restructuración de la política alimentaria en México.* Mexico City: El Colegio de México and United Nations Research Institute for Social Development (UNRISD).

— (2008) 'La transformación de la vida rural en tres ejidos del centro de México' in K. Appendini and G. Torres (eds), *¿Ruralidad sin agricultura? Perspectivas multidisciplinaria de una realidad fragmentada.* Mexico City: El Colegio de México, pp. 27–58.

Boltvinik, J. (2006) 'Los fracasos de Fox /I', Columna Economía Moral, *La Jornada* (Mexico), 26 May.

Boltvinik, J., A. Damián et al. (2012) *Evolución de la pobreza y la estratificación social en México y el Distrito Federal 1992–2010. Valoración crítica de las de las metodologías de medición y las fuentes de información.* Available at www2.df.gob.mx/virtual/evaluadf/files/pdfs_sueltos/evo_pobreza_vfinal.pdf.

Carton de Grammont, H. C. (2007) 'La desagrarización del campo mexicano'. Lecture at the Congreso Encrucijadas del México Rural, ' *Contrastes regionales en un mundo desigual*', Asociación Mexicana de Estudios Rurales (AMER), Veracruz, 22–26 October.

David, M. B. de. A., C. Morales and M. Rodríguez (2001) 'Modernidad y heterogeneidad: estilo de desarrollo agrícola y rural en América Latina y el Caribe' in M. B. de A. David (ed.), *Desarrollo rural en América Latina y el Caribe.* Bogotá: Economic Commission for Latin America and the Caribbean and Alfaomega.

Florez, N. (2012) 'Trabajo y estructura productiva agrícola en México, desde finales del siglo XX, a inicios del siglo XXI'. PhD thesis, Economics Department, Universidad Nacional Autónoma de México (UNAM).

Garay, S. (2008) 'Trabajo rural femenino en México: tendencias recientes'. PhD thesis in population studies, Centro de Estudios Demográficos, Urbanos y Ambientales, El Colegio de México.

Guzmán Gómez, E. and A. L. López (2005) 'Multiactividad y migración campesina en el poniente de Morelos, México', *Política y Cultura* 23 (Spring): 103–20.

Hewitt de Alcántara, C. (1978) 'Ensayo sobre la satisfacción de las necesidades básicas en México' in M. Nerfin (ed.), *Hacia otro desarrollo. Enfoques y estrategias*. Mexico City: Siglo XXI Editores.

INEGI (2002) *Encuesta Nacional de Empleo 2002*. Mexico City: Instituto Nacional de Estadística, Geografía e Informática (INEGI).

— (2011) *Censo General de Población y Vivienda, 2010*. Mexico City: INEGI.

— (various years) *National Employment Survey (ENE)*. Databases. Mexico City: INEGI.

— (various years) *National Household Income and Expenditure Survey* (ENIGH). Databases. Mexico City: INEGI.

Merino, M. (2010) 'Los programas de subsidio al campo: las razones y las sinrazones de una política mal diseñada' in J. Fox and L. Haight (eds), *Subsidios para la desigualdad. Las políticas públicas del maíz en México a partir del libre comercio*. Santa Cruz CA: Woodrow Wilson International Center for Scholars, University of California and Centro de Investigación y Docencia Económicas (CIDE), pp. 55–72.

Pacheco, E. and N. Florez (2009) 'Having more than one job as a family strategy in rural Mexico'. Lecture at the XXVI International Union for the Scientific Study of Population (IUSSP) International Population Conference, Marrakesh, Morocco, 27 September–2 October.

Pacheco, E. and L. Sánchez (2012) 'Rural population trends in Mexico: demographic and labour changes' in L. J. Kulcsár and K. J. Curtis (eds), *International Handbook of Rural Demography*. Dordrecht and New York NY: Springer.

Pacheco Gómez, E. (2010) '¿Cómo ha evolucionado la población que labora en actividades agropecuarias en términos sociodemográficos?' in B. García and M. Ordorica (eds), *Población. Los grandes problemas de México*. Mexico City: El Colegio de México, pp. 393–429.

Passel, J. S. (2011) 'Flujos migratorios México-Estados Unidos de 1990 a 2010. Un análisis preliminar basado en las fuentes de información estadounidenses', *Coyuntura Demográfica* 1: 15–20.

Puyana, A. and J. Romero (2008) *El sector agropecuario mexicano: un decenio con el Tratado de Libre Comercio de América del Norte, Efectos económicos y sociales*. Mexico City: El Colegio de México.

Ramírez V., E. (2005) *Análisis de la Movilidad del Empleo Rural en Chile 1996–2001*. Debates y Temas Rurales no. 3. Santiago de Chile: Red Internacional de Metodología de Investigación de Sistemas de Producción (RIMISP) and Centro Latinoamericano para el Desarrollo Rural, pp. 1–26.

Reardon, T. and J. A. Berdegué (1999) 'Empleo e ingreso rural no agrícola en América Latina'. Mimeograph. Santiago de Chile: Red Internacional de Metodología de Investigación de Sistemas de Producción (RIMISP).

Rubio, B. (2004) 'El sector agropecuario mexicano en los años noventa: subordinación desestructurante y nueva fase productiva' in B. Rubio (ed.), *El sector agropecuario mexicano frente al nuevo milenio*. Mexico City: Universidad Nacional Autónoma de México (UNAM) and Plaza y Valdés Editores.

Taylor, J. E. and A. Yúnez-Naude (n.d.) 'Los impactos de las reformas internas y del TLCAN en la agricultura Mexicana'. Boletín Informativo no. 1. Mexico City: Programa de Estudios de Cambio Económico y la Sustentabilidad del Agro Mexicano (PRECESAM), El Colegio de México and University of California-Davis.

Tello, C. (2010) *Sobre Desigualdad en México*. Mexico City: Universidad Nacional Autónoma de México (UNAM).

Yúnez, A. and Á. Meléndez-Martínez (2007) 'Efectos de los activos familiares en la selección de actividades y en el ingreso de los hogares rurales de México', *Investigación Económica* LXVI (260, April–June): 49–80.

Yúnez Naude, A. (2010) 'Las políticas públicas dirigidas al sector rural: el carácter de las reformas para el cambio estructural' in *Los Grandes Problemas de México*, Volume 11. Mexico City: El Colegio de México.

ENVIRONMENT, FOOD CRISIS AND PEASANTS

7 | FROM THE PERSISTENCE OF THE PEASANTRY IN CAPITALISM TO THE ENVIRONMENTALISM OF INDIGENOUS PEOPLES AND THE SUSTAINABILITY OF LIFE

Enrique Leff

1. Stating the problem of peasants' poverty and persistence

Two related lines of inquiry convened this seminar: to provide a satisfactory explanation for peasant poverty and to understand the persistence of the peasantry in capitalism. In the background paper of the seminar, Julio Boltvinik (Chapter 1 in this volume) responds to this 'lack of knowledge' by postulating that both questions are functionally linked by their determination and submission to the functioning of agrarian capitalism. He draws his arguments from Marx to explain why peasants' poverty persists as a prerequisite for the possibility of capitalism in agriculture. If poverty is produced by capitalism, discursively the 'poorness of the poor' is constructed 'Marxistically'. The comprehension of the persistence of poor peasantry is 'locked in' to the persistence of Marxism, albeit in an extension of its orthodox approach that failed to account for the seasonality of the labour process in the overall capitalist agricultural productive process.

Once peasantry is defined as people living and producing 'outside' the capitalist system, differentiating them from rural proletarian workers – those who reproduce their labour force by earning a wage working in capitalistic agriculture – Boltvinik sees the persistence of the peasantry as a result of the functional interdependence of the peasantry – petty commodity producers – with the capitalist mode of production, disclosing entrenched relations that remain hidden in the articulation through simple commodity exchange (Fossaert 1977).

The corollary of this investigation into the determination of the persistence of poverty is the will to complete what is lacking in Marx's theory of value by offering a 'general theory of value'. In practical terms, this would be accomplished by adding to seasonal wage labour the required amount to complete the total annual cost of reproduction of the rural labour force. This might be done by increasing consumer prices through trade protection and/or by subsidising peasants' production – the way, it is argued, developed countries do. These pragmatic reforms to theory and to economic policy should contribute not only to explaining but also to solving the problem of persistent peasant poverty in the South.

I do not intend to contest Boltvinik's account of the functional interdependence of those two forms of production in terms of its more pragmatic and political reasons. I will rather challenge his proposal to reform value theory to incorporate the full cost of peasants' labour force reproduction – including its seasonal and often very long periods of non-laboured days – in order to offer a 'general theory of value' that would translate in practical terms to subsidies for peasants' traditional agriculture (see Chapter 1). As I will try to argue in what follows, we must explain the persistence of the peasantry not only because it is functional to capitalist agriculture, but because of other reasons, such as its social imaginaries, its cultural traditions and practices, and its attachment to the territory where it lives, adopting an ontological, historical, anthropological, social and ecological perspective that challenges the absolutism of economic reasoning, internal logic and structural determinism, and opens up a more complex understanding of human history in the face of the crisis of capitalism and the environmental question. This implies a shift from traditional Marxism to eco-Marxism, and to the perspectives opened up by political ecology and environmental rationality (Leff 1994; 2004; 2014).

2. The poverty of theory: the seasonality of labour and the historicity of Marxism

The functional articulation of the capitalist mode of production (CMP) with the peasants' simple commodity production explains why the capitalist does not have to pay the full reproduction cost of peasants' labour power, as its subsistence economy provides a substantial part of the basic means of survival – for their endosomatic consumption and physiological needs – that is, for the reproduction of available labour power to provide seasonal work for capitalist agriculture. The explanation of why peasants are forced to offer and sell their seasonal labour in the market is that their subsistence economy is insufficient. And the reason why it is insufficient is not because peasants are intrinsically and traditionally poor, but because colonialism, first, and then capitalism brought about an impoverishing process that entailed the pillaging of peasants' resources, the degradation and deterioration of the productivity of their ecosystems, the appropriation of their cultural patrimony of natural resources, the dispossession of their territories, and the colonisation of their knowledge. As a consequence, indigenous peoples and peasants have been displaced to less productive marginal lands, which would justify the prevalence of differential rent as an explanation for their persistence. In fact, the destruction of their means of production and subsistence goes beyond the state of survival in the most eroded fields due to population pressure and the degradation of their socio-environmental conditions. Their poverty is not fully explained by their functional interdependence with the CMP or by differential rent, but by a *historical process of entropic degradation of their environment and their livelihoods*. In this context, explaining the capitalistic determination of their present 'state of poverty' requires a historical analysis of this process of dispossession and a critical deconstruction of Marxist concepts in order to understand the condition of peasantry and of indigenous peoples – of that 'labour force' whose working conditions are interlinked with the workings of nature.

Thus, it is one thing to elucidate why peasants' seasonal work is functional and profitable, subsidising capitalist agriculture by merging with the unvalued forces of nature that contribute to the production process in the sequential or seasonal moments of the 'productive' labour process. It is quite another to extend this explanation to the causal reason for the poverty and persistence of the peasantry. *Toute proportion gardée*, it would be tantamount to justifying the persistence of nature because of its functionality in the agricultural productive process: that is, to circumscribe the ontology of nature to the theory of value.

Differential rent also does not offer a full explanation for the peasantry's poverty and persistence. Land rent has become hybridised through the intensity of technological intervention and made more complex by profits in transgenic agriculture managed by capital. Take, for instance, the case of transgenic productivity. Seasonal labour is still needed at certain moments of the production cycle. However, under these conditions, the 'reserve army' of rural workers exceeds by far the employment required by latifundia using genetically modified seeds and other forms of capitalist agriculture. Unemployed workers do not always have the possibility of complementing their income by working seasonally in neighbouring plots; often they take flight to neighbouring countries to engage in the capitalistic production of crops, which then compete with and displace production in traditional communal or *ejido* lands, as is the case with Mexican peasants abandoning their *milpas* and working in the capitalistic production of transgenic maize. Unwillingly, they become 'organic proletarian agents' of the disruption of their own traditional livelihoods and of the risks involved in polluting their rich eco-cultural patrimony of genetic resources (Alvarez-Buylla and Piñeyro 2013). This is the complex determination of capital dispossession and the extermination of the peasantry in the present geopolitics of sustainable development, where resistance and the possible *rexistence*[1] of the peasantry must be analysed (Gonçalves 2002; Leff 2002).

In brief, the problem of peasant persistence and peasant poverty lies in the actual exploitation and strategic needs of capitalism and the resistance strategies of the peasantry and indigenous peoples. But the challenge of understanding the workings of these processes arises from the 'poverty of available theory' to account for the complex ontological conditions that explain the global domination of techno-economic rationality in the modern world, the rootedness of the peasantry and indigenous peoples to a territory, and the condition of humanity and of life on the planet Earth (Leff 2014).

Marx constructed the first structural theory of a social structure that explains the exploitation of labour and, as a consequence, of nature – in short, for the production of poverty and land degradation – once capitalism was constructed as a consequence of the history of metaphysics. The concreteness of this phenomenon lies in Marx's method of inquiry. Marx stated that 'the concrete is concrete as a synthesis of multiple determinations'. The rootedness of the peasantry and indigenous peoples to their lands and territories is the result not only of a synchronic but also of a diachronic determination that transcends the historical process of articulation and subsumption of the traditional modes of production to the increasingly dominant capitalist mode of production. Even a genetic structuralist approach

(Goldmann 1959) proves insufficient to grasp the attachment of people to their territories according to a more ontological, historical and anthropological perspective. Cultural resilience and rootedness in nature might prove to be ontologically deeper and more transcendent than the logic of peasants' persistence and survival subjected to the capitalistic squeeze of their conditions of existence. Conditions of exploitation and the erosion of life have to be envisioned within the entropic degradation produced by the economic process (Georgescu-Roegen 1971).[2] The sustainability of life calls for a broader theoretical perspective: a questioning not only of the persistence of the dominant and subsumed modes of production, but of the kind of knowledge involved in the emancipation of peasants, indigenous peoples and human beings, and for the persistence of life on the planet (Leff 2014).

Ecological economics and political ecology take a different theoretical and political stance from that of traditional Marxism and eco-Marxism regarding peasants' and indigenous peoples' poverty, its historical and structural causes, and their responses to their persistence and survival, but primarily with regard to the construction of a sustainable economic system, of their sustainable livelihoods and a sustainable future.

However, a fundamental question remains within the domain of knowledge to transcend the domineering structure of capitalism and to construct a sustainable world: can the theory of value account for this theoretical challenge? The main shortcoming of the theory of value is not that it fails to include the discontinuity of labour in seasonal production processes, such as those of agriculture. The basic problem is that *nature* is not valued and that nature does not determine value or surplus value. Marx himself stated:

The value of labour-power is determined, as in the case of every other commodity, by the labour-time necessary for the production, and consequently also the reproduction, of this specific article. In so far as it has value, it represents no more than a definitive *quantity of the average social labour objectified in it*. Labour-power exists only as a capacity of the living individual ... For his maintenance he requires a certain quantity of the means of subsistence. Therefore the labour-time necessary for the production of labour-power is the same as that necessary for the production of those means of subsistence ... However, labour-power becomes a reality only by being expressed; it is activated only through labour. But in the course of this activity, i.e. labour, a definite quantity of human muscle, nerve, brain, etc. is expended, and these things have to be replaced. Since more is expended, more must be received. If the owner of labour-power works today, tomorrow he must again be able to repeat the same process in the same conditions as regards health and strength. His means of subsistence must therefore be sufficient to maintain him in his normal state as a working individual ... the owner of labour-power is mortal. If then his appearance in the market is to be continuous, and the continuous transformation of money into capital assumes this, the seller of labour-power must perpetuate himself 'in the way that every living individual perpetuates himself, by procreation' ... The labour-power withdrawn from the market by wear and tear, and by death, must be continually replaced by, at the very least, an equal amount of fresh labour-power. Hence the sum of means of subsistence necessary for the production of labour-power must include the means necessary for the worker's replacements, i.e. his children, in order that this race of peculiar commodity-owners may perpetuate its presence on the market. (Marx 1976 [1867]: 274–5)

In Volume II of *Capital*, Marx adds:

Working time is always production time, i.e. time during which capital is confined to the production sphere. But it is not true, conversely, that the entire time for which capital exists in the production process is necessarily therefore working time ... What is at issue here are not interruptions in the labour process conditioned by the natural limits of labour-power itself ... What is involved is rather ... an interruption conditioned by the nature of the product and its production, *during which the object of labour is subjected to natural processes of shorter or longer duration* ... while the labour process is either completely or partially suspended ... Between seed-time and harvest, the labour process is almost completely interrupted ... In all these cases, additional labour is added only occasionally for a large part of the production time ... therefore, the production time of the capital advanced consists of two periods: *a period in which the capital exists in the labour process, and a second period in which its form of existence – that of an unfinished product – is handed over to the sway of natural processes, without being involved in the labour process.* (Marx 1978 [1885]: 316–17, emphasis added)

Moreover, in the *Grundrisse*, Marx reflected:

> The fixed capital here allegedly acts quite by itself, without human labour, like e.g. the seed entrusted to the earth's womb … The time required here for the product to reach maturity, the interruptions of work, here constitute conditions of production. Not-labour time constitutes a condition for labour time, in order to turn the latter really into production time. The question obviously belongs only with the equalisation of the rate of profit. Still, the ground must be cleared here. The slower return – this is the essential part – here arises not from circulation time, but rather from *the conditions themselves in which labour becomes productive*; it belongs with the *technological conditions of the production process* … *Value*, hence also surplus value, *is not = to the time which the production phase lasts, but rather to the labour time,* [both] *objectified and living, employed during this production phase. The living labour time alone … can create surplus value, because (it creates) surplus labour time.* (Marx 1973 [1857–58]: 668–9, emphasis added)

What these citations of Marx reveal goes well beyond the fact that non-seasonal time and non-working time, which constitute conditions for the production process and for the reproduction of agricultural labour power, are not valued properly in the theory of value. They also reveal – and this is my crucial point of debate – that the natural processes involved in the production of commodities, in the value of labour force in general and in the reproduction of peasants' labour force in particular, are not valued. The problem is crystal clear: nature contributes to production, but only socially necessary labour time – the labour time necessary for production, and consequently for the reproduction of the labour force – as determined by technological progress, contributes to value and to establishing the rate of surplus value. The problem does not lie only in the fact that labour time fails to coincide with production time, but mainly in the fact that neither nature's contribution to production nor the destructive effects of production on nature are valued. While the poor peasant survives through the articulation of modes of production – often in extreme conditions of poverty, as capital does not pay for dignified, just and egalitarian standards of living in the reproduction of the labour power it needs – nature does not get paid at all for its contribution to the overall productivity of capitalist agriculture – or to the global economy. Simply stated, *nature has been externalised by the economy*; nature contributes to production but does not determine value, not in the way that the concepts of value and surplus value theory are structured in the Marxist theory of value.[3]

To overcome this theoretical fault, eco-Marxism addressed the hidden *second contradiction of capital*, disclosing the fact that capitalism destroys the ecological conditions for the reproduction of capital as well as the ways in which it does this (O'Connor 1998). However, displaying and internalising this forgotten contradiction will not transcend constraints of Marxist theory to envision a sustainable world order. The environmental crisis calls for a deconstruction of economic rationality and a transition towards an environmental rationality (Leff 1993).

In the course of these theoretical developments, the peasantry has survived and persisted through complex socio-cultural-political strategies of resistance and *rexistence* beyond its adaptation to the conditions of capitalist agriculture. But for how long can we expect nature to hold onto the biosphere's life support systems, when its resilience mechanisms have been eroded by capitalism? How can peasants survive without a territory that supports their livelihood?

3. From eco-Marxism to political ecology and environmental rationality

From the standpoint of ecological economics and eco-Marxism, economics and Marxism have remained without an adequate theory of value (Altvater 1993: 6).[4] Environmental economics is the economics of the environmental externalities of the economic system: that is, of the natural processes that contribute to production but are not accounted for by the principles of value formation, but rather are the buried and ignored ecological costs of the economic process. Ecological economics is, to a large extent, the economics of energy flows throughout the economic process, the economics of the metabolism of matter and energy governed by the law of entropy. Following the proposal of Howard Odum, ecological economics has attempted to construct an energy value theory. From Podolinsky to Neurath, and through the school of ecological anthropology – from Leslie White to Richard Adams and Roy Rappaport – there have been numerous attempts to complement Marxist labour value theory with a theory of energy value (Martínez Alier 1987).

The idea of combining an energy theory of value with Marx's theory of labour value seems to have been an original contribution of Podolinsky, who intended to determine the minimum conditions for human survival by analysing energy flow efficiency (Martínez Alier 1995a: 72). However wide the impact of this principle in ecological economics – and in determining the rationality of cultural organisation through energy flows in agriculture within the field of ecological anthropology (Rappaport 1971) – these attempts to complete Marx's theory of value have failed. Although, in principle, it should be easier to reduce complex matter and energy flows to basic energy unit measures than it is to transform complex labour into the abstract, simple and direct labour power that defines value as socially necessary labour time, it is impossible to internalise a homogeneous ecological measure of matter, energy and time within this unit of value. As Albert Puntí (1988) showed, 'the same quantities of energy coming from different sources have different times of production' (quoted in Martínez Alier 1995a: 53). In brief, the approaches of ecological economics lack a quantitative unit of matter, energy and time that could fit into the structural dialectic of value to surplus value, and that would enable us to establish a rate of exploitation of nature as a surplus ecological value.

Consequently, the limitations of the theory of value to determine peasant poverty and the persistence of the peasantry are not solved by adding the non-worked days to account for the total value of the reproduction of the rural labour force, as the failure to consider the contribution of nature to value formation is not resolved. As I have tried to prove in previous writings, a quantitative theory of value is untenable once its conceptual strength has collapsed with technological progress – the indeterminacy of value by the average productivity of technologies or by the more productive technology, and ultimately by the displacement of direct labour by scientific and technological knowledge in the production process – as one is left with the impossibility of defining a unit of value (socially necessary labour time) to produce exchange value by any homogeneous unitary measure of matter energy or labour time value.[5] Therefore, explaining peasant poverty in terms of value theory would involve a re-elaboration of the theory of labour value and of capital, not just by adding seasonal labour but by taking into account the contribution of nature's processes to value and price formation, not only in the cycle of the simple reproduction of capital but in its extended reproduction – something that has been abandoned by eco-Marxism as an impossible task.

This does not rule out the fact that capitalist agriculture is subsidised by peasant labour through the 'simple reproduction squeeze', or the fact that the rural production is often undervalued in order to fuel industrial development. The scale of production and the forms of property and technological development play important roles in capitalist agriculture by determining the economic surplus that can be appropriated and reinvested for the extended reproduction of capital. Today, natural forces of production are hybridised through biotechnology to fuel capitalist agriculture. Thus, a 'post-Marxist' theory of differential rent can be envisioned as a process of ecological distribution[6] whose workings go beyond the fact that the more productive plots are established on the best preserved and the most resilient land. The intervention of technology in the structure, chemistry and metabolism of the biosphere and the geosphere complicates the possible transformation of the flows of energy – of entropic degradation and negentropic potential – into economic value. As land is fertilised with petrochemical products, whose prices do not account for their environmental costs, it is impossible to include the restoration costs of exhaustible resources in the economic calculations of capitalist production, or the effects of this in terms of ecological distribution and accumulation by dispossession (Harvey 2004).[7] Moreover, how would differential rent account for the 'conservation' strategies of the 'green economy' and 'sustainable development', where peasant labour is involved and marginally paid for the preservation of their biodiverse territories to compensate for the ecological damages of the global economy, but which, in terms of value theory, appears as non-productive labour?

Following the above, poverty is not a homogeneous state of being, nor can it be reduced to its capitalist determinations. The peasant's 'simple reproduction squeeze' and the exhaustion of nature operate via very diverse and complex mechanisms in order to keep the 'treadmill of production' (Gould et al. 2008) moving. In what follows, I include in the category of peasantry not only people working the land (the *campesinado*) as a social class, but also the indigenous peoples who inhabit rural areas. The distinction between them is not only an ethnic question, or one of their miscegenation with the peasantry, but a question of the degree to which they maintain (or do not maintain) their cultural identities and traditional practices, and their degree of integration into the capitalist system and the global economy.

Peasants' actual ways of survival and persistence and their forms of 'being in the world' are the result of history. Capitalism drove and accentuated the divide of rural peasantry from industrial proletarians and urban dwellers through the dualist construction of society that separated nature from culture. The CMP structured the dialectical, functional and systemic relation between rural and urban areas. No wonder we keep going back to the origins of capitalism and to Marx himself to understand what triggered this condition of peasantry in modernity and up to the present day.

However, if capitalism has not expelled peasants completely from rural areas and from agricultural production, can that be explained simply by Marx's theory of differential rent or by some kind of diffuse 'obstacles derived from some natural features of agricultural production' (Mann and Dickinson 1978)? Is value theory a conceptual tool for understanding peasant poverty? Or is the theory of value responsible for misvaluing the work of the peasantry?

In fact, by construing the theory of value as the source of the fundamental contradiction between capital and industrial labour, Marxism explained the structural condition that reduces the value of labour and increases surplus value. But it simply did not value the 'workings' of nature – the generativity of *physics*; ecological productivity and resilience – and of the peasantry who work together with nature to lower the value of the reproduction of the labour force of industrial workers and of peasants themselves. Despite the fact that the theory of value is the critical theory of capitalism, it is nevertheless inscribed in the techno-economic ontology of modernity – Heidegger's world of *Gestell*, of the disposition of all entities as objects and the calculative appropriation of the world

(Heidegger 1977).[8] Technological change, which determines the socially necessary labour time as the unit of value, does not operate outside the 'ontology of nature' to determine the value of subsistence commodities required to fulfil the basic needs of the proletariat or for the reproduction of the peasantry; therefore, it cannot account for the ecological conditions necessary for the extended reproduction of capital. In the theory of value and surplus value, the 'productive consumption of nature' has become the unvalued destructive (entropic) consumption of nature.

In the 'ecological perspective', the major problem is not only that of discontinuous labour time in agriculture and the value of agricultural labour power, but of the contribution of nature in establishing the value of the means of subsistence and of any commodity, in a way that would allow capitalism – and any other mode of production – to internalise the ecological conditions for its extended reproduction in space and time. This problem has no solution within the theory of value or within the structure of the capitalist mode of production. It calls for the deconstruction of economic rationality and the construction of *another productive rationality*. Beyond a shift in economic paradigms, it implies the deconstruction of economic rationality and the construction of an environmental rationality, a turn from the techno-economic ontology of modernity to the ontology of life (Leff 1995; 2004; 2014).

4. Peasants' persistence in a political ecology perspective: the struggle for life

The enigma of peasants' persistence not only contradicts the Leninist prognosis of the disappearance of peasants from the face of the earth (being either proletarianised in capitalist agriculture or absorbed by industry or tourism). As shown by Chayanov (1974), the family peasant unit does not seek to maximise profits or to obtain the average rate of profit. While capitalist agriculture profits from this condition of traditional petty commodity production, peasants have not merely persisted by becoming functional to capital; rather, over a longer time span, indigenous peoples or peasants have survived by resisting dispossession by colonisation and capitalistic domination. They have resisted through *cultural resilience*, through the deep cultural rooting of their ontological existence in their ethnic territories, and through their innovative adaptations, in the construction of new life territories, to displacement and the erosion of the ecological conditions of their habitats.

From the standpoint of environmentalism, the questions we pose are not only about the conservation of biodiversity for nature's sake or the persistence of the peasantry within the process of modernisation and continuous capital accumulation, but about the survival of the living planet and of human life. In this perspective, theory is concerned with more than just the disappearance of traditional cultures and life forms as a result of capitalist entropic use and its destructive consumption of nature. The inquiry into the environmental question focuses critical thinking on the sustainability of life on the planet. Here, the outstanding question arises from the ineluctable *entropic degradation of nature induced by the economic process*. Economic growth not only feeds on the non-valued conditions of life and on scarce natural resources but transforms all matter and energy consumed in the process of production (and consumption) into degraded energy, ultimately in the form of unrecyclable matter and irreversible heat. These are the workings of the economic process on nature, on the complex structure of the biosphere, and on the life support systems of the planet. This is the fatality of the economic process that induces the 'entropic death of the planet' (Georgescu-Roegen 1971; Leff 2004; 2014).

The persistence of the peasantry, their ways and means of survival and their emancipation strategies cannot be circumscribed by their condition within the prevailing domination of the capitalist system and its economic rationality. The becoming of their being is deployed in the resistance and the *rexistence* of their cultural being within the context of an environmental rationality and the construction of a sustainable world. This implies the possibility of constructing a sustainable economy. The reversal of the unsustainable mode of production and the transition to a sustainable one is not brought about by an adjustment of value accounting to equalise the economic distribution of the seasonal work of the 'persistent peasantry', nor by the restructuring of value theory or the ecological reform of economics to internalise negative environmental externalities. Environmental rationality challenges eco-Marxism, ecological economics and political ecology for the construction of an alternative mode of production: one that is based on the conservation and enhancement of ecological conditions and the productive forces of nature, and which is embedded in socio-cultural-ecological relations of production – in the web of life – and embodied in diverse cultural beings.[9]

In brief, a sustainable economic process cannot be achieved – as environmental economics intends to do – by internalising externalities, having first recoded those externalities – ecological breakdown, pollution, biodiversity, climate change, greenhouse gases, environmental goods and services – in economic terms: that is, having first capitalised nature and then imposing the commodification of nature. Nor can we ecologise the economic process by confining economic behaviour to the ecological conditions necessary for the reproduction of nature (Passet 1979) in order to attain a 'steady-state economics' (Daly 1991). Georgescu-Roegen's 'bio-economics' is a more radical critique of economic rationality after Marx, underlying and expressing the 'second contradiction' of capital, the ineluctable self-destruction of the ecological bases of capitalism through the way in which the economic process activates and magnifies the workings of the law of entropy (Georgescu-Roegen 1971). However, this 'bio-economics' remains a critique of the thermodynamic unsustainability of the prevalent economic rationality rather than an economics based on the thermodynamic principles and ecological conditions needed for sustainable production.

If capitalist-induced *entropic degradation* is what is driving the ecological destruction of life support systems and cultural resilience, then the future persistence of the peasantry will not depend on its functional utility for capitalism, but on envisioning and constructing a sustainable mode of production, one based in the *negentropic potentials of life*. That is, a mode of production based on 'managing' the ecological conditions of the biosphere and internalising the material and symbolic conditions of human existence. This involves envisioning a 'labour process' that is oriented towards enhancing and magnifying the principle of life: from the process of photosynthesis to the eco-technological productivity of the biosphere.[10]

A sustainable negentropic paradigm of production is built on the complex articulation of three orders of productivity: ecological, technological and cultural. Ecological productivity is based on the ecological potential of different ecosystems. Ecological measures show that the most productive ecosystems, those of the humid tropics, produce biomass at natural annual rates up to about 8 per cent. This ecological potential can be enhanced through scientific research, ecological technologies and sustainable management practices to define and guide the cultural and economic value of the techno-ecological output of different productive processes (Leff 1995: Chapter 5). Such ecological technologies and management practices include high-efficiency photosynthesis, the management of secondary succession – the regeneration, growth and evolution of natural ecosystems after slash-and-burn practices in traditional shifting agriculture – the selective regeneration of valuable species in ecological processes, associated multiple cropping, agro-ecology and agroforestry, and cultural innovation.

This alternative paradigm of production is articulated in a spatial and temporal frame of non-modern cultural imaginaries and ecological practices. A rich diversity of peoples and cultures and their different territorialities opens up a new theoretical perspective of historical time and space as the manifestation of an 'unequal accumulation of times' (Santos 1996). This new perspective abandons the linearity of the Eurocentric conception of time and incorporates a different spatial and temporal frame into the analysis of cultural and territorial relations. As Milton Santos argued, different temporalities cohabit in geographical space. The simultaneity of different temporalities is not considered by a hegemonic modern time that orders life and production in other cultures. This alternative conception of historical time has important political implications for social movements, such as the actuality of ancestry invoked by the Afro-Colombians of the Pacific and the '*buen vivir*' of Andean peoples, opening up the question of co-evolution of peoples/cultures and nature/territories. In the culture of original peoples, such as the Inca tradition that prevails among the Andean people today, ecological floors were articulated through principles of complementariness and reciprocity that commanded the organisation of geographical space (Murra 1975; Estermann 2006). Their processes of territorialising, which are based on their ecological conditions and cultural practices, clearly differ from the logic of space occupation and the territorial division of labour in the capitalist world. Thus, ultimately, what is at stake in political ecology are conflicts over territories; not only the clash of interested parties over the appropriation of land and natural resources, but the confrontation of alternative modes of production and patterns of space construction, of ways of territorialising and inhabiting the world, and of 'being sustainable in the world' (Leff 2012; 2014: Chapters 3, 6).

The privileged spaces in which to deploy a strategy of *negentropic production* are, obviously, the rural areas of the world that are inhabited by indigenous and peasant peoples.[11] This new paradigm of production can be contested in the academic world, but even if it could triumph in the intellectual arena, it would only be able to confront the established economic world order through social movements in the field of political ecology. The social agents of this historical transformation are not the industrial proletariat or urban citizens, but the inhabitants of rural territories: the peoples of the earth and the ecosystem dwellers. The agents for the construction of a *negentropic society* are the persistent peasants and indigenous peoples. This brings us to the following questions: where and how do these people stand on the Earth? What are their attachments to their territories? What are their imaginaries of sustainability? And what is their potential for becoming social actors in the construction of a sustainable world?

The peasant struggles of the twentieth century (Wolf 1972), from the Mexican agrarian revolution to the Via Campesina and MST (Movimento dos Trabalhadores Rurais Sem Terra) movements, with their distinctive categories of peasantry and revolutionary strategies, focused on their attachment to, their claim to and their appropriation of land as a basis for survival and to maintain their traditional cultural organisation. Today, environmental struggles claim not only a piece of land but a *territory*, a space to be restored and reconstructed from their 'deep' cultural roots – for example, 'profound' Mexico (Bonfil Batalla 1987) – as the habitat where they can deploy their *habitus*, their imaginaries and practices in order to preserve and envision their sustainable life worlds.[12]

The new socio-environmental indigenous and peasant movements for the re-appropriation of nature emerge in light of this post-Marxist and post-structuralist perspective. Emblematic examples are the struggles of the *seringueiros* in the Brazilian Amazon region, who, from their syndicalist claims to the land where they worked as proletarians of the rubber industry in the late nineteenth century, have established their *extractive reserves* as a strategy of sustainable production (Porto-Gonçalves 2001).[13] A new peasantry is arising from ecological ground that has been marginal though functionally linked to the capitalist system. The very regions that remained at the margins of the market and were occupied by traditional peoples are those that harbour the planet's greatest natural wealth in water and biodiversity. Thus, in the face of the colonising and exploitative character of the new geopolitics of globalisation and sustainable development, a series of critical and creative responses from different Latin American peoples are emerging in the conflictual field of political ecology.

The imaginaries that root ecosystem dwellers to their territories are manifest as strategies of resistance–*rexistence*; these are expressed in the political discourse of the Afro-Colombian movement called 'Process of Black Communities' (Proceso de Comunidades Negras), in the reinvention of their identities and in their strategies for the re-appropriation of their rich patrimony of biodiversity (Escobar 1999; 2008). We can trace this political existential ontology in the discursive strategies of present socio-environmental movements in Latin America. Thus, the Process of Black Communities on the Colombian Pacific coast claimed its rights to:

1. Reaffirmation of being (of being black) ... from the point of view of our cultural logics, of our particular worldviews, of our vision of life in all its expressions, social, economic and political ... 2. Territory (a space for being) ... and to live according to what we think and what we want as a form of life ... to a habitat where the black people develop their being in harmony with nature. 3. Autonomy (for the practice of being) ... in relation to dominant society and to other ethnic groups and political parties, from the standpoint of our cultural logic ... 4. To construct our own perspectives for the future ... from our cultural vision, our traditional productive practices ... and social organisation. (Escobar et al. 1998, cited in Escobar 1999: 180–1)

These principles are spreading in the claims of indigenous peoples for autonomy, territory and dignity. They are visible in the emergence of cultural and environmental rights in different cultural organisations and in resistance and emancipation movements, in defence of their cultural rights to a territory and productive practices in many Third World countries and in all latitudes of the Latin American region – from the Amazonian cultures to the neo-Zapatista movement in Mexico, from the Mapuche in the far south of the continent to the

Seris or Comcaac in the arid north of Mexico (Leff et al. 2002). One recent expression is that of the Tipnis movement in Bolivia in defence of their ecological patrimony and in opposition to the modernisation of their territories, in the environmentalism of peasant movements, and in their innovative processes for the construction of sustainability in rural areas (Barkin et al. 2009). These are the social points of anchorage of an emergent environmental rationality (Leff 2004).

Obviously, there is not just one true and valid strategy to construct sustainability. Nor can there be any triumphant optimism that indigenous resistance and peasant persistence will prevail and not be absorbed by modernity or swept away by the inertia of entropic degradation induced and fuelled by the world economic order. The question is not only one of analysing the efficacy of these resistance–*rexistence* movements from the standpoint of political ecology and environmental sociology. The most critical question emerges from an ontological inquiry into the inscription of the thermodynamic, ecological and symbolic conditions of life within the social imaginaries of the sustainability of traditional peoples (Leff 2014: Chapter 4), into the persistence of their attachments to their historical and territorial roots, such as those being expressed today by the imaginary of 'good living' ('*buen vivir*', '*suma qamaña*' or '*sumak kawsay*'). Thus, the persistence of the peasantry and of traditional peoples could be theorised beyond its functional interdependence with capitalist agriculture; peasants and indigenous peoples could be seen as supporters of another world order, one that is still possible, if we trust that peasants and humanity have not been engulfed by the progress of the entropic death of the planet, and if we can envision sociologically and enact politically a sustainable future.

Notes

1 *Rexistence* is a neologism coined by Carlos Walter Porto-Gonçalves and adopted by this author. It expresses the ontological, epistemological and political turn from movements that resist colonialism and the impacts of the global economy on the deterritorialisation of original, traditional or local cultures to those that reconstruct their livelihoods and world lives and are rooted in the reinvention of their identities, in their cultural modes of existence and their social imaginaries for the sustainability of life (Porto-Gonçalves and Leff 2015; Leff 2014; 2015).

2 A metaphor might be useful to understand the capitalistic draining of peasant territories. The introduction and institutionalisation of the CMP are analogous to planting eucalyptus in certain ecosystems where it grows quickly by absorbing water and nutrients

from the soil, drying the land, and sucking the blood and squeezing the lives of the people. Thus, capital is implanted and extends its roots deep into the conditions of sustainability of ecosystems and the subsistence of their peoples; capital pumps out all the energy necessary for its continuous growth and expansion, consuming and exhausting the conditions for the sustainability of life and the reproduction of peasants, of nature, and eventually of the capitalist system itself.

3 It is not value theory that exploits and externalises nature, but the ontological condition of capital, which then becomes the object of critical theory. Thus, Marx unveiled the will and the mechanisms of exploitation constituted and instituted in economic rationality, particularly in the CMP. However, Marxism does not deconstruct nor escape the metaphysical thought that constructs objectified reality from the point where critical reflection emerges and is inscribed. For more on this argument, see Marcuse (2005).

4
But in the course of economic development, the scarcity of goods in relation to human needs is compounded by the fact that they are no longer at wide enough disposal; *to scarcity comes to be joined shortage*. Paradoxically, it is the scarcity of resources which makes rational economic calculation both possible and necessary. But its very successes in growth and expansion have led to *shortage* in the vital quality of nature, which in turn undermines the principle of *scarcity* and thus economic rationality itself. (Alvater 1993: 6)

5 For a broader argument and justification, see Leff (2000).

6 Martínez Alier defines ecological distribution as:

the unequal distribution of ecological costs and its effects in the variety of ecological movements, including movements of resistance to neoliberal policies, compensation for ecological damage and environmental justice … [Ecological distribution designates] the social, spatial and temporal asymmetries or inequalities in the human use of environmental resources and services, commercial or not, and in the decrease of natural resources (including the loss of biodiversity) and pollution loads. (Martínez Alier 1995b)

7 An example of this is the low price of Mexican oil that fuels the artificially high productivity of capital-intensive monocultures in the US, including maize, which then competes with maize that is produced traditionally, on a smaller scale and using lower concentrations of agrochemicals. This produces unequal competition with Mexican peasants' production, and the peasants remain poor because of these complex capitalist determinations.

8 Critical thought remains inscribed within metaphysical calculative thinking. From that standpoint, it reveals the exploitative nature of the capitalist system, it views the proletariat as the objective subject of history, and it claims justice for the dispossessed peasantry, squeezed by the law of value and oppressed by the techno-economic rationality of modernity.

9 It is impossible for me to develop a detailed argument and give sufficient support to this theoretical proposal in this chapter. I therefore deal with it very succinctly and refer the reader to my previous texts.

10 Photosynthesis is the negentropic transformation of radiant solar energy into biomass, from which complex forms

of life have emerged (Schrödinger 1944). To maintain this evolving, complex organisation of life, entropy works in the metabolism of food chains and in all industrial metabolisms throughout the economic process. Notwithstanding this ineluctable entropic effect, negentropy can be conceived as the overall process that forms and maintains the life support systems of the planet. Thus, sustainability is constructed by a dialectic of negentropic and entropic processes.

11 It is interesting to note the coincidence and overlap of the preserved biodiverse regions of the world on the one hand, and the persistence in these territories of cultural diversity on the other (Boege 2009).

12 In words of Arturo Escobar: The territory is conceived as a multidimensional space, fundamental for the creation and recreation of the communities' ecological, economic and cultural practices ... We can say that in this articulation of cultural identities and appropriation of the territory underlies the political ecology of the social movement of the black communities. The demarcation of collective territories has led activists to develop a conception of territory that emphasises articulations between settlement patterns, space use and use-meaning practices of resources. (Escobar 1999: 260)

13 Chico Mendes (1944–88), leader of a peasants' socio-environmental movement that fought against hegemonic economic forms of exploitation of nature, proposed the strategy of extractive reserves as a new 'agrarian reform', anticipating and countering the approaches of 'sustainable development': Clean Development Mechanism (CDM) strategies, REDD (Reducing Emissions from Deforestation and Forest Degradation) programmes and genetic latifundia (Porto-Gonçalves 2002).

References

Altvater, E. (1993) *The Future of the Market*. London and New York NY: Verso.

Alvarez-Buylla, E. and A. Piñeyro (eds) (2013) *El maíz ante los transgénicos. Un análisis integral sobre el caso de México*. Mexico City: CEIICH-UNAM and UCCS.

Barkin, D., M. Fuentes and M. Rosas (2009) 'Tradición e innovación: aportaciones campesinas en la orientación de la innovación tecnológica para forjar sustentabilidad', *Trayectorias* 11 (29): 39–54.

Boege, E. (2009) El Patrimonio biocultural de los pueblos indígenas de México. Hacia la conservación in situ de la biodiversidad y agrodiversidad en los territorios indígenas. Mexico City: Instituto Nacional de Antropología e Historia and Comisión Nacional para el Desarrollo de los Pueblos Indígenas.

Bonfil Batalla, G. (1987) *México profundo*. Mexico City: Grijalbo.

Chayanov, A. (1974) *La organización de la unidad económica campesina*. Buenos Aires: Nueva Visión.

Daly, H. (1991) *Steady-state Economics*. Washington DC: Island Press.

Escobar, A. (1999) *El final del salvaje. Naturaleza, cultura y política en la antropología contemporánea*. Bogotá: CEREC/ICAN.

— (2008) *Territories of Difference. Place, movements, life, redes*. Durham NC and London: Duke University Press.

Escobar, A., L. Grueso and C. Rosero (1998) 'El proceso organizativo de las comunidades negras en el Pacífico Sur Colombiano' in S. Álvarez, E. Dagnino and A. Escobar (eds), *Cultures of Politics/Politics of Cultures: Revisioning Latin American social movements*. Boulder CO: Westview Press.

Estermann, J. (2006) *Filosofía Andina. Sabiduría indígena para un mundo nuevo*. La Paz, Bolivia: Segunda Edición and Instituto Superior Ecuménico Andino de Teología (ISEAT).

Fossaert, R. (1977) *La Société. Tome 2: Les structures économiques*. Paris: Seuil.

Georgescu-Roegen, N. (1971) *The Entropy Law and the Economic Process*. Boston MA: Harvard University Press.

Goldmann, L. (1959) *Recherches dialectiques*. Paris: Gallimard.

Gould, K. A., D. Pellow and A. Schnaiberg (2008) *The Treadmill of Production: Injustice and unsustainability in the global economy*. Boulder CO: Paradigm Publishers.

Harvey, D. (2004) 'The "new" imperialism: accumulation by dispossession', *Socialist Register* 40: 63–87. Available at http://socialistregister.com/index.php/srv/article/view/5811#.Ut2eEvszHIV.

Heidegger, M. (1977) *The Question Concerning Technology*. New York NY: Harper & Row.

Leff, E. (1993) 'Marxism and the environmental question: from critical theory of production to an environmental rationality for sustainable development', *Capitalism, Nature, Socialism* 4 (1): 44–66.

— (1994) *Ecología y capital: racionalidad ambiental, democracia participativa y desarrollo sustentable*. Mexico City, Siglo XXI Editores.

— (1995) *Green Production: Towards an environmental rationality*. New York NY: Guilford.

— (2000) 'The scientific-technologic revolution, the forces of nature and Marx's theory of value', *Capitalism, Nature, Socialism* 11 (4): 109–130. Originally published in 1980 as 'La teoría del valor en Marx frente a la revolución científico-tecnológica' in E. Leff (ed.), *Teoría del Valor*. Mexico City: Universidad Nacional Autónoma de México (UNAM). Revised edition published as 'La teoría objetiva del valor, la revolución científico-tecnológica y las fuerzas productivas de la naturaleza' in Leff (2004).

— (2002) 'La Geopolítica de la Biodiversidad y el Desarrollo Sustentable: economización del mundo, racionalidad ambiental y reapropiación social de la naturaleza' in A. E. Ceceña and E. Sader (eds), *La Guerra Infinita. Hegemonía y Terror Mundial*. Buenos Aires: CLACSO-ASDI, pp. 191–216.

— (2004) *Racionalidad ambiental: la reapropiación social de la naturaleza*. Mexico City: Siglo XXI Editores.

— (2012) 'Political ecology: A Latin American perspective'. Mimeograph.

— (2014) *La apuesta por la vida. Imaginarios sociales e imaginación sociológica en los territorios ambientales del Sur*. Mexico City: Siglo XXI Editores.

— (2015) 'Political ecology: A Latin American perspective', *Desenvolvimento e Meio Ambiente* 35. 'Dossier: Pensamento ambiental latino-americano: movimentos sociais e territórios de vida.'

Leff, E., A. Argueta, E. Boege and C. Gonçalves (2002) 'Más allá del desarrollo sostenible. La construcción de una racionalidad ambiental para la sustentabilidad. Una visión desde América Latina' in E. Leff, E. Ezcurra, I. Pisanty and P. Romero (eds), *La transición hacia el desarrollo sustentable. Perspectivas de América Latina y el Caribe*. Mexico City: PNUMA/INE-SEMARNAT/UAM, pp. 479–578.

Mann, S. A. and J. A. Dickinson (1978) 'Obstacles to the development of a capitalist agriculture', *Journal of Peasant Studies* 5 (4): 466–81.

Marcuse, H. (2005) *Heideggerian Marxism*. Edited by R. Wolin and J. Abromeit. Lincoln NE and London: University of Nebraska Press.

Martínez Alier, J. (1987) *Ecological Economics: Energy, environment and society*. Oxford: Basil Blackwell.

— (1995a) *De la economía ecológica al ecologismo popular*. Montevideo: Nordan Comunidad and ICARIA.

— (1995b) 'Political ecology, distributional conflicts and economic incommensurability', *New Left Review* I/211.

Marx, K. (1973 [1857–58]) *Grundrisse: Introduction to the critique of political economy*. Harmondsworth, UK: Penguin Books.

— (1976 [1867]) *Capital: A critique of political economy*. Volume I. Harmondsworth, UK: Penguin Books.

— (1978 [1885]) *Capital: A critique of political economy. Volume II*. Harmondsworth, UK: Penguin Books.

Murra, J. (1975) *Formaciones económicas y políticas del mundo andino*. Lima: Instituto de Estudios Peruanos (IEP).

O'Connor, J. (1998) *Natural Causes: Essays in ecological Marxism*. New York NY: Guilford.

Passet, R. (1979) *L'économique et le vivant*. Paris: Payot.

Porto-Gonçalves, C. (2001) *Geo-grafías. Movimientos sociales, nuevas territorialidades y sustentabilidad*. Mexico City: Siglo XXI Editores.

— (2002) 'Latifundios genéticos y existencia indígena', *Revista Chiapas* 14: 7–30.

Porto-Gonçalves, C. W. and E. Leff (2015) 'Political ecology in Latin America: the social reappropriation of nature, the reinvention of territories and the construction of an environmental rationality', *Desenvolvimento e Meio Ambiente* 35. 'Dossier: Pensamento ambiental latino-americano: movimentos sociais e territórios de vida.'

Puntí, A. (1988) 'Energy accounting: some new proposals', *Human Ecology* 16 (1): 79–86.

Rappaport, R. (1971) 'The flow of energy in an agricultural society', *Scientific American* 225 (3): 116–32.

Santos, M. (1996) *A natureza do espaço*. São Paulo: Hucitec.

Schrödinger, E. (1944) *What is Life?* Cambridge: Cambridge University Press.

Wolf, E. (1972) *Las luchas campesinas del siglo XX*. Mexico City: Siglo XXI Editores.

8 | SOUTH AMERICAN PEASANTS AND POOR FARMERS FACING GLOBAL ENVIRONMENTAL CHANGE: A DEVELOPMENT DILEMMA

Elma Montaña

Climate change scenarios for Latin America call our attention to significant changes in hydrological and climate patterns and processes. Of special concern is the greater frequency and intensity of extreme climate events, which threaten not only the quality of life of people, but also their livelihoods. Especially vulnerable are rural people, who are highly dependent on climate and water resources.

Although all agricultural producers are likely to be affected by these changes, research financed by CLACSO-CROP on the vulnerability of rural communities in the watershed basins of Argentina, Bolivia and Chile has shown that expected drought and diminishing river flows would particularly compromise the well-being of the smallest producers and peasants of these socio-ecological systems, who are already affected by other stressors, such as globalisation, restricted fiscal policies and long-established situations of poverty and inequity.

The three river basins studied are vulnerable to these expected environmental changes: the Mendoza River basin in central-western Argentina; the Pucara (Tiraque-Punata) River basin in Cochabamba, Bolivia; and the Elqui River basin in the Coquimbo region, Chile. These are dryland territories, and in the three cases drought is already a major limitation for agriculture. Climate change scenarios produced by the Intergovernmental Panel on Climate Change (IPCC) raise new concerns about drought periods, not only because of their increasing frequency but also because of their length and severity. Reduced snow accumulation in the Andes mountains and a shrinking of the region's glaciers also negatively affect the main source of river water. In addition to droughts and diminishing river flows, there is the expected increase of mean temperatures and the associated evapotranspiration (which has an impact on irrigation water demand), as well as heatwaves, frost, storms and hail.

This chapter presents the situation of peasants, smallholders and small farmers in these three river basins; they are not homogeneous in their characteristics, but they share a common subordinate position in these hydraulic societies. It explores the situation of poor peasants in light of climate change – especially drought – and examines the ways in which these situations project on the issue of poverty persistence. Then, it examines the effects of the responses to climate change on peasantry persistence and explores the possible outcomes of diverse adaptation options. Finally, it identifies an opportunity to link climate change adaptation to poverty reduction policies, although this could be achieved only by changing the development paradigm.

1. Agricultural production in three dryland river basins

The drylands under study correspond to three basins in the so-called 'South American Arid Diagonal', where not only climate factors but also water availability in particular represent serious constraints to agricultural productivity (Figure 8.1).

At 33 degrees south latitude, just like other rivers of the Andean system, the Mendoza River originates in the central Andes in Argentina. It flows through the piedmont to the eastern plains, where it reaches the Guanacache wetlands in the lower part of the basin. In the province of Mendoza, which has a mean annual rainfall of about 200 mm in the piedmont, agriculture is possible only through irrigation, so a regulating dam has been built just before the river reaches the piedmont. It is in the piedmont where the 'Northern Oasis' lies and where agricultural activities (grape growing and horticulture) are conducted.

Grape growing accounts for about half of the cultivated area of the Mendoza River basin, and is followed by horticulture (23 per cent) (CNA 2002). Agriculture in the basin is highly integrated with the industrial sector, since 99 per cent of grape production is destined for wine making. Twenty-three thousand irrigators in the basin account for 89 per cent of surface water use (DGI 2007). In the basin, however, only 45 per cent of farmers irrigate with surface water; 27 per cent irrigate with groundwater only (CNA 2002); and 28 per cent use both surface and groundwater.

The rest of the agricultural sector in the basin consists largely of extensive goat husbandry performed by *'puesteros'* or peasant families – most of them of indigenous origin – who are scattered on the non-

8.1 The three river basins studied

irrigated area downstream of the oasis. The study in the Mendoza River basin encompassed producers in both the oasis and the non-irrigated areas.

In Chile, on the other side of the Andes, between 29 and 30 degrees south latitude, the Elqui River basin extends from the mountains to the Pacific Ocean. Water drawn from the river makes agriculture possible in the valley all the way down to the Pacific coast. The river is regulated by two dams: one in the mountains and the other in the agricultural valley. As in Mendoza, climate and water conditions vary according to height above sea level, but the region is considered semi-arid. Again, here there are two contrasting scenarios: large non-irrigated areas and a small oasis, where agricultural production is concentrated.

In the Elqui River basin there are three main economic activities: agriculture (within the irrigated area), mining and tourism. The main crops are fruit trees (citrus, avocado, papaya and cherimoya), which account for 39 per cent of the irrigated area. A few small-scale producers and most medium- and large-scale producers target their production to national and international markets and operate in the global agribusiness sector. Vegetables, which rank second in cultivated area (29 per cent of the total surface), are grown in the lowlands of the basin, where water is also obtained from springs and infiltration near the city of La Serena, the main regional market. Pulse and root vegetables rank third in area cultivated (13 per cent) (Dattwyler Cancino 2008). In the upper reaches of the valley, vineyards producing table and wine grapes (mainly for the production of *pisco*, a type of brandy) are highly profitable for capitalised firms.

Mining is a traditional activity in the region. There is artisanal mining and industrial mining, the latter having a much greater impact. Mining is carried out in the mountains, far from irrigated areas, but competes with agriculture for water and manpower.

As in the Mendoza River basin in Argentina, there is almost no cattle raising in the Elqui River basin, although there is goat breeding by small-scale subsistence farmers (*crianceros*) in the non-irrigated areas of the basin, similar to the Mendocinean *puesteros*. These goat producers are almost the only subsistence producers in the basin, since agriculture – which is very competitive – has expelled most of the weaker farmers and smallholders. There remain some small-scale agricultural producers who are mostly engaged in horticulture. Many of these small-scale farmers, rural workers and especially the *crianceros* are the rural poor in the Elqui River basin. As in the Mendoza River basin case, irrigated and non-irrigated communities were studied.

Finally, the Pucara basin is located in the department of Cochabamba, in the geographical centre of Bolivia. The river rises in the highlands of the province of Tiraque, flows through altitudinal thresholds that range between 2,800 and 4,600 metres above sea level (MASL) and empties in the Valle de Punata. Water problems in the area are associated with a gradual depletion of water sources, contamination, groundwater overexploitation, overlapping irrigation systems and related conflicts, disputes between water use sectors, legal voids and contradictory regulatory policies.

Three rural communities were studied in the Pucara basin: the highlands of K'aspi Kancha (3,600–3,900 MASL), and two downstream areas located in the '*abanico de Punata*' (Punata fan) – Huaña Kahua in the upper part of the Municipio de Punata and Chirusi in the southern part, both some 2,700 MASL. In the upper part of the basin, K'aspi Kancha has a cool climate and receives 650 mm per year of rainfall. Some producers draw water from two rustic dams operated by the users' association, while others grow crops without irrigation. Further down, Huaña Kahua and Chirusi have a dry and mild climate. With about 300 mm of rainfall, these areas are semi-arid and highly dependent on irrigation. Water is drawn from the river, some reservoirs and a few wells. Water flows and tube wells in the same basin are used for domestic water supply and irrigation. Water scarcity is more acute in Chirusi, leading to water quality and quantity problems.

There is a relative homogeneity in the spectrum of producers in the basin, especially when compared with the cases of Argentina and Chile. In the three Pucara areas there are diversified smallholders growing the mix of crops that best fits their location. In the highlands of K'aspi Kancha, most agricultural production is oriented towards Andean root vegetables, mainly potato (Figure 8.2), and broad beans, both of them for self-consumption and sale. To a lesser extent, these crops are also grown together with cereals such as oats and barley – as feed for the producers' own cattle and for sale – and vegetables such as onions and green peas. Quinoa has only recently been introduced. Most households raise animals: oxen for ploughing (tractors are rare), some horses, pigs, poultry or other farm animals that are integrated into agricultural production and/or supplement the family diet. At a lower altitude, in Huaña Kahua, the main economic activities are agricultural production (fruit trees – mainly peach – corn and various vegetables) and artisanal activities (mostly the production of *chichi*, a fermented beverage made from maize and other cereals), complemented with jobs in construction and services.

In Chirusi – in the south of Municipio de Punata, and the third area under study – the main agricultural activities are corn production

8.2 Potato sowing in a communal plot in K'aspi Kancha Alta, Pucara River basin (*source*: Montaña, del Callejo and Encinas, fieldwork, October 2010)

(both for seed and self-consumption) and small-scale dairy farming associated with the growing of alfalfa as cattle fodder.

In the three river basins, a longstanding coexistence with water scarcity has bound the social structure to the deliberate management of water, and has shaped coupled nature–society systems that can be identified as 'hydraulic societies' (Worster 1985). Here, the social fabric is strongly associated with an intensive use of water resources within a framework of techno-economic order imposed for the purpose of mastering a difficult environment. While space becomes territory through water allocation, water appropriation and use give rise to and reproduce a scheme of social and political relations in which quotas of power are distributed. As long as the distribution of power is regulated and exercised through deliberate water distribution and management, water acquires the capacity to express – and shape – asymmetric relationships between hegemonic and subordinate actors. It is among the latter that the status of the peasants in these basins is determined, not only by unfavourable socio-economic conditions but also by concurrent environmental situations (including the lack of water), an example of the so-called double exposures (Leichenko and O'Brien 2008) that feed spirals of poverty. In this context, the expected effects of climate change will certainly affect the well-being and subsistence of these smallholders and peasants, and even the conditions for their persistence.

2. Being a peasant in a hydraulic society

A peasant is usually a small-scale producer who works a small plot of land based on family work. A number of features help to characterise peasant economy (Boltvinik, Chapter 1, Section 3, this volume): the peasant unit is an interdependent organic structure combining production and consumption functions basically to satisfy family needs and – ultimately – to secure its survival; its resource endowment is limited, so the peasant unit is subject to different restrictions concerning land – and, in the case of drylands, water as well – among other production factors; and production is marked by a mix of crops and activities and subject to constant decision making, which means it is flexible. But even if the use of the family labour force is probably the most distinctive characteristic of the peasant economy, identification is not so clear when part of the household income comes from sources other than work on a plot of land – whether those sources are agricultural or not. Similarly, the other characteristics mentioned above may be more or less clear in different cases, and typological boundaries become blurred in a range of situations that go from the pure peasant to the pure proletarian.

This is the case in the basins analysed. The universe of the producers studied ranges from traditional peasants to smallholders and small or poor farmers, depending on the equation that results from combining the characteristics listed above, which are defined in relation to the economic model of each country and the orientation of its economic, agricultural and social policies as well as the history of the territories.

In Mendoza, the most dynamic portion of the grape-growing and wine-making sector is made up of agribusiness firms, most of them export oriented and owned by foreign capital. Nevertheless, small farmers and smallholders are numerous, as more than half of the agricultural plots in the basin are 5 hectares or less (CNA 2002). This is explained by the history of the construction of oases in Mendoza, which took place between the end of the nineteenth century and the beginning of the twentieth century with the arrival of European immigrants. Thus, at one end of the spectrum, there are representatives of the 'new viticulture' that is part of global agribusiness and, at the other, there are small grape growers with traditional vineyards and peasants who are mostly engaged in horticulture. Among the latter, there are many families of Bolivian origin who resort to their social and family labour force and networks for successful agricultural production.

Beyond the oasis, in the lower reaches of the Mendoza River basin, the Lavalle desert has a scarce and scattered population, most of it descended from the indigenous Huarpes. Holding no legal water rights and with highly diminished river flows (most of the water is consumed upstream in the oasis), these groups barely subsist on extensive goat breeding in an arid xerophytic environment, trapped in spirals of desertification and poverty. They fit better within the more traditional definitions of peasantry, although occasionally they resort to temporary wage labour.

The agrarian social structure in the Elqui basin offers more contrasts. The capitalised sector has been practically monopolised by export companies using strict business logic. There are almost no smallholders integrated into the more dynamic agricultural circuits: as producers, they have already been expelled from this sector by the big players under the strict rules of competition, and they have been integrated as the labour force. They have not even been integrated into the exporters' productive chains. As one fruit exporter put it: 'They can't meet our quality standards and to teach them would be complicated and expensive. We prefer to do it ourselves.' Smallholdings have been bought out by *fundos* (large country estates) and irrigation water ownership has concentrated under a water market system. There remain only some small horticultural producers working for the local market and for their own consumption while complementing their income with temporary jobs, either in the agricultural sector or elsewhere (Figure 8.3). The poor of the oasis also comprise field hands who have temporary jobs, many of them in agriculture.

Beyond the Elqui irrigated oasis, and restricted by the scarce water coming down the creeks, there is a meagre population of small-scale goat breeders (*crianceros*) who fit into the most traditional peasant definition (Figure 8.4). In the desert areas, *crianceros* who own their plots of land coexist with others who pay *talaje*, a kind of rent, for summer grazing. The main product of these small goat breeders is artisanal cheeses sold on the informal market through

8.3 Smallholder of Gabriela Mistral, Elqui River basin (*source*: Elma Montaña, fieldwork, December 2010)

intermediaries, who purchase the produce on site. These families usually supplement their income with state subsidies, which are not enough to raise them out of poverty. Where mining operations upstream of their land have deprived them of water (a minimum flow coming from the mining site uphill is supplied through a hose), the *crianceros* receive benefits from the mining companies – almost as compensation. Practically waterless, only a few *crianceros* are able to maintain their small orchards, which were once tended by their parents and grandparents. This is an ageing population that needs external contributions to survive.

Finally, as mentioned earlier, the Pucara Basin producers are the most homogeneous as a group and the ones who best fit the most traditional peasant typology. They have a long farming tradition supplemented with activities other than agriculture, which, in most cases, are highly diversified with products for both domestic

8.4 *Crianceros* of Talcuna Creek, Elqui River basin (*source*: Elma Montaña, fieldwork, December 2010)

consumption and the market. In K'aspi Kancha, as well as in Huaña Kahua and Chirusi, households are usually led by middle-aged to elderly men and have an average of five members, as others have emigrated (although many of them still contribute to the support of the family). In these households, all members are responsible for different activities in a production scheme in which all products are interdependent. It is in Chirusi where activities are most diversified, probably because water scarcity forces the peasants to ensure family subsistence from off-farm jobs.

In the three areas of the Pucara basin, agricultural tasks are performed by both men and women. Women combine farm work with other productive activities done from the home, such as *chicha* and cheese making and weaving textiles for sale. Men usually have occupations – more or less temporary and, in some cases, even permanent – to complement household income; these can include working as hired drivers (sometimes using their own vehicle), bricklayers or machine drivers.

Salaried work is rare among the members of the peasant units of production. The concept of *ayni*, however, remains strong. *Ayni* is a system of reciprocity, mutual work or assistance between two or more families in sowing, harvesting, home building, and even in exchanging water turns. Community social organisation is strong and so are family bonds. The nuclear family, the extended family and family associations also play a role in the organisation of production. Family bonds and contributions to household support are maintained even by those who have emigrated: they take out loans in the event of an emergency, when required for land improvements and even for daily subsistence.

The broad spectrum of producers in the three basins – small farmers, smallholders and peasants – determines different social situations for facing and responding to climate change challenges.

3. The impact of global environmental change on peasants

As the three basins under study are located in drylands, river flow reduction is one of the impacts where climate change scenarios provide less uncertainty. If this reduction occurs, it is possible that irrigators at the tail end of the irrigation systems will receive less water than the amount to which they are entitled. Agribusiness firms and wealthier farmers seek to settle at the head of the distribution systems or canals to ensure that they get the right amount of water. As they are located in areas with better access to water, they are more likely to succeed in their agricultural activities and, in turn, to buy better (and more expensive) lands. Higher temperatures and evapotranspiration reinforce this pattern, concentrating wealthier producers in the upper and cooler areas with higher thermal amplitude, and relegating poor producers to the lower and warmer parts where they try hard to keep their farms viable. The hotter and drier lower Mendoza and Elqui River basins are in fact the most frequent locations for small farmers and peasants. Longer and more severe droughts associated with climate change will increase environmental risks, reinforce the current spatial segregation patterns ('water flows uphill towards money') and perpetuate poverty spirals.

Smallholders are also less likely to benefit from a far more common adaptive practice: access to groundwater. As they irrigate with surface water only, they are more vulnerable to river flow reductions than those who have alternative water sources. Water wells are far beyond the reach of peasants. But, in the Mendoza River basin, for instance, there are small-scale producers who were better off in the past and managed to build a well on their farms. But today, due to decreasing profits, these chronically impoverished farmers are unable to maintain the well, keep the pump in good condition, or bear the energy costs of pumping water. Their traditional low profit-yielding farms prevent them from bearing these costs. This is an example of the way in which exposure to water-related factors, aggravated by previous economic exposures, reinforces the circular patterns of poverty and vulnerability that are so common among peasants.

Almost all large producers in the Elqui basin have at least a well on their farm (and also a reservoir and efficient mechanised irrigation systems) to make up for water deficits. This is not the case for small-scale horticultural producers, who have no well and are compelled to sow smaller surfaces or not sow at all. The greater the economic power of a producer, the greater his possibilities of displaying adaptation resources, mainly technological. If this is a general rule for the three basins – and it holds especially true for the Mendoza and Elqui basins – in the case of the latter, and given the neoliberal macro-economic policy of Chile, all production factors, including climate and water, end up revealing the advantages and disadvantages of each producer in a scenario dominated by the rules of crude competition. The Chilean water market is another example of a common good turned into a commodity to the detriment of smallholders.

Chilean and Argentinian smallholders and peasants who face droughts have to settle for a passive adaptation: irrigate less and/ or irrigate the crops that are more profitable. In these cases, there are double exposures and a spiral of vulnerability and poverty: the worse they irrigate or the less they irrigate, the less they earn, the poorer they are, and the fewer their possibilities for efficient water use. In Bolivia, the difference lies in social organisation: trade unions and other irrigators' associations in the Pucara basin maintain their systems using the few material and financial resources available and a large amount of manpower. They do not depend so much on the state as on the users' organisations, but they try to make up for their lack of financial resources with personal and family work and with solidarity and mutual aid mechanisms that constitute a sort of safety net in times of crisis, including climate- and water-related extreme events.

Droughts are especially harsh for goat breeders in non-irrigated areas of the basins in Argentina and Chile. These peasants do not hold water rights and depend on surplus water flows that have not been claimed or used by others. The lack of permanent flows and of irrigation systems tends to make them more vulnerable when they face more severe droughts and greater climate variability, and aggravates their poverty. But it is also true that the role played by past and present (and certainly future) social and economic exposures is just as important as climate and water – or even more so. Even 'natural' factors that affect poverty have a social origin, such as river flows diminished by upstream consumption and global environmental change itself. In any case, 'natural' and social factors are combined, increasing the likelihood of these groups being poorer not only in terms of their material living conditions but also in terms of other factors that impoverish them: the need to migrate in their search for higher income, and difficulties in maintaining family bonds and the feeling of belonging to their home town. If goat breeders in the Mendoza and Elqui River basins are equally poor, the competitiveness of the Chilean regulation system puts the latter on the verge of extinction. In the case of Argentina, the state is more willing to meet some of their needs, even though it has not succeeded in helping the smallest producers work their way out of poverty.

The manner in which droughts are faced in each case is very much related to water governance. In Mendoza, irrigation water supply is proportional to the land area (regardless of crop type) and water is inherent to the land, so it cannot be used on other farms. This system prevents a more 'rational' use of water in the sense that the supply hardly meets the real demand. Some farmers will need more water and other farmers will have surplus water, and there is no way to change this within the law. The situation in Chile is quite the opposite: the Water Code and the water market stipulate that water can be used anywhere by those who bought shares. The share system favours water use efficiency since the irrigator can derive benefits from the sale of surplus water. Although the water market is – at a basin level – an incentive for efficient water use, as projects covering more hectares could be cultivated with the same water supply, an analysis at the actors' level shows that it is a very competitive system in which water is concentrated in the hands of the most powerful producers, which makes small-scale producers in the system more vulnerable. The water market is added to the land market and the labour market, combining asymmetrical powers that turn against the interests of small farmers and peasants. Again, the law of the strongest further impoverishes those who are already poor.

The competition laws of the Chilean model are best expressed in the clash between mining companies and goat breeders in the non-irrigated areas of the Elqui basin. While large-scale agricultural producers in the Elqui oasis fear the harm they face or that could be inflicted by mining activities in terms of water availability (not without a certain resignation, since they do not object to free competition), small-scale *crianceros* located downstream from mining exploitation lost their water a long time ago, and with it the possibility of breeding their goats, of attending to their small orchards, of raising their families there, and of avoiding emigration and the loss of territorial bonds. They changed their lifestyle, surrendered the relative control they had over their food, and, finally, lost their identity as *crianceros*, settling for the meagre security that mining companies provide them with. They depend on the mining company to buy the cheese they produce with the few goats they still raise. It is evident that the system will disappear when old tenant farmers die or when they get sick and are forced to relocate with their children to the valley or to the city of La Serena. This does not seem to be of great concern in a society in which efficiency is an undisputed value and survival of the fittest is 'naturally' accepted. In this paradigm, the *crianceros* do not embody the values of agricultural productivity, water use efficiency or a locational rationality because they are isolated and scattered in areas with no infrastructure or services. This explains why there is not greater concern over their ongoing disappearance. Inasmuch as poverty means deprivation of rights, these peasants have lost them to the point that they run the risk of disappearing. Here is where we find the poverty limit: extinction.

In Mendoza the situation is similar, although here the peasants of the desert (the *puesteros*) have lost out to the prestigious grape growers and wine makers. Centuries of increasing agricultural and urban water consumption in the oasis have reduced the flow in the lower Mendoza River basin, depleting the Guanacache wetlands and sealing the fate of the goat breeders, who were already affected by desertification and extreme poverty. In the case of Mendoza, however, the *puesteros* are included in the government agenda and receive state grants through different arrangements. Whereas in Chile similar grants are aimed solely at improving productive performance, in Argentina they also address basic needs, most of the time in response to extreme climate events. In both basins there are political devices that make use of ideological structures – such as the cult of 'water tamers' in Mendoza's oases (Montaña 2011) or the law of the survival of the fittest in Chile – to blur or ignore the rights of subordinate groups such as the Elqui *crianceros* or the *puesteros* of the Huarpe communities of Guanacache in Mendoza.

Poverty in goat-breeding communities poses a paradoxical dilemma. As income from goat breeding means that the population is living on the edge of subsistence, they are forced to resort to other means of earning a living, such as taking temporary jobs in the oasis or in urban sectors or receiving government grants made available through different sources. The rural households in the desert of north-eastern Mendoza are much more diversified in their income sources than the small grape growers in the oasis. In this sense, goat breeders would be less vulnerable to the negative impacts of climate and water factors. In the social sciences, it is usually believed that income diversification tends to make households less vulnerable to climate change and that it provides greater possibilities of adopting a broader spectrum of adaptive strategies. Although it is true that incomes in households in the desert are more diversified than those of producers engaged exclusively in agricultural activities, oasis dwellers closer to urban areas are afforded a wider range of possibilities without having to emigrate. Finally, beyond analytical considerations, the fact is that the poverty of goat breeders is so extreme that they do not have many choices for improvement or adaptation.

In Bolivia, the difference lies in the political and economic environments: policies are devised to revitalise indigenous cultures in harmony with nature. This creates a favourable setting for resolving conflicts, taking into consideration the interests of the commons. Conflictual situations in the Pucara basin are mitigated by a relative homogeneity of producers and of cultural typologies. Even so, conflicts exist and increase during droughts: there are traditional disputes between irrigators and producers with no access to water, and between irrigators themselves, as well as upstream and downstream conflicts between the communities in the territories where the headwaters are located and the producers downstream. In the Pucara basin, this last type of situation is the most notorious.

Greater water scarcity in the three basins leads to even more serious conflicts over water. The conflicts are solved – to a certain extent – according to the institutionality in force and also to the amount of power that each user exerts in the community. If conflicts are solved by strictly applying formal, institutional water arrangements and technical rationalities, 'rationality is context-dependent, the context often being power', according to Flyvbjerg (1998). Channelled by water conflicts, the exercise of power deprives the weakest actors of their rights and impoverishes them.

The three rivers in these basins have been regulated to make up for spring and autumn irrigation water deficits. As there are dams, earlier spring snowmelt associated with climate change does not exert a great impact on agriculture. In the Mendoza River basin, however, as regulation does not ensure ecological flows, a more intense and deliberate use upstream (by the social groups with the most power) noticeably reduces the possibilities of water reaching the tail end of the basin, where desert communities have settled. This is another case in which the adaptation of some increases the vulnerability of others. The subordinate position of the indigenous *puesteros* is where an important part of the vulnerability of these peasant communities lies.

In times of global environmental change, investments in dams and canals are now, more than ever before, considered an unquestionable mission of the society of Mendoza and a guarantee for development. Nevertheless, although agriculture is important in the regional economy, the development of irrigation systems mainly benefits landowners and excludes the poorer rural groups: salaried employees, farm hands and seasonal workers. In an inequitable labour market, a paradox could occur in which better conditions to face adverse climate and water impacts encouraged landowners to expand their activities and hire a larger number of rural workers. If not properly compensated, as is usually the case, these workers would join the ranks of the rural poor, even if they held full-time, formal jobs. If the goal is to make adaptive processes diminish processes of poverty, then adaptation with equity should be at the forefront.

There is a critical phenomenon common to all three basins: migration. In Argentina and Chile, where migration is mostly local or regional, goat breeders move to the agricultural oasis for the harvest and petty crop producers take temporary urban jobs to supplement the meagre incomes from their land. This trend, which has been sustained for decades, has been increasing as small-scale producers not only lose competitiveness, and, little by little, their niche becomes less relevant in the agricultural circuit, but also fail to cope with climate change challenges.

In the case of the Pucara basin, the presence of many landowners is a factor that favours their attachment to the territory. But there is also a long tradition of local migration (to towns such as Tiraque or Punata, or farther away to Cochabamba or Santa Cruz, or even to other countries), which applies to one family member or to the whole family, usually those that are newly formed. Many young people migrate temporarily to north-east Argentina and Mendoza, where they stay for several months to work in agriculture in order to send some funds to their families in Bolivia. There are also whole families who leave their home country to look for a place where they can settle down.

In almost all cases, migration is not a proactive alternative but a reaction to some deprivation. Whether for study or work or for other reasons, poverty underlies most migration. If poverty is perceived as a violation of human rights (OHCHR 1998; 2004), the loss or deprivation of family life, of the sense of belonging to a home town and of decisions concerning the course of one's life are also factors of poverty that turn these migrations into processes of poverty production.

Finally, the incidence of global environmental change under conditions of poverty is related to the political context of each country.

The population of the Pucara basin is poorer than the populations in the other two basins. Bolivia is considered the poorest country in South America, and its poverty patterns, which have developed throughout history, have increased within the globalised economy. Notwithstanding the deprivations to which many households in the Pucara basin are subjected, analysis shows that sometimes traditional lifestyles are interpreted as 'poverty'. Despite the fact that poverty undoubtedly exists, these peasant communities also show strong resilience and an enormous potential to adapt to global environmental change. This is not the case of households in Chile and Argentina, which are governed by rules devised by formal 'modern' institutions.

On the other hand, Chile is seen as a country where efficiency, order and seriousness within the framework of a 'modern' economy help pave the way to success. In Chile, the values of the market economy are undisputed and poverty reduction objectives are usually posed as adjustments or corrections to these market laws. From the standpoint of that neoliberal paradigm, in order to help the poor and improve their standard of life, they should be provided with capacity-building support and the means to become competitive and to earn their own place in the system.

In the three river basins, producers tend to diversify and integrate production chains that minimise biophysical and social risks. But while in Chile this is carried out according to neoliberal capitalist logic, in Bolivia it is part of a diversified life and production tradition that combines agricultural and cattle-raising activities, production for domestic consumption and for commercial purposes, mutual aid and reciprocity systems, and so on. The objective here is not merely revenue generation; it is also the equilibrium of the household or productive unit within the framework of family relations and relations with neighbours and with the reference community, all of which operate as a safety net in adverse situations.

But as capital advances and the world becomes globalised, it is more and more difficult to maintain this peasant profile. The combination of climate and hydrological impacts and social exposures directs productive transformations towards less diversified, market-oriented economic units, thus increasing vulnerability. As commercial activities grow and consumption becomes increasingly separated from production, food security and, above all, food sovereignty are threatened.

4. Water, poverty, food sovereignty and territorial rights of peasants

From a relational perspective, 'poor people are those who are subjected to deprivation of multiple material, symbolic and spiritual goods that are indispensable for the autonomous development of their essential and existential identity' (Vasilachis de Gialdino 2003). Poor people are affected by 'poverty production' processes that are inherent in the logic of capitalist accumulation (Álvarez Leguizamón 2005; Øyen 2002; 2004). Poverty can also be conceived as a violation of one or several parts of the human rights' spectrum (OHCHR

1998; 2004). From this viewpoint, 'the poor' encompasses not only those who have a low income or unsatisfied material needs, but also those who cannot exert their right to decent work or to work in their home town, to share daily family life without being forced to migrate, to be deeply rooted in the land, to 'live in culture', to be valued in the context of respect for diversity, and so on. When poverty is seen from this broader perspective, it is associated with territorial rights and with the appropriation and use of natural common goods.

Water scarcity, a critical issue in drylands, is linked with poverty. There are different types of scarcity and, just like poverty itself, most of them are socially constructed. Physical scarcity occurs when water availability is limited by nature. Economic, managerial, institutional and even political scarcity occurs when people are barred from accessing an available source of water because they are in a situation of political subordination (Molle and Mollinga 2003). Water scarcity tends to be interpreted as a 'naturally' generated physical situation, which disregards the social fabric in which this scarcity occurs.

How does water scarcity affect peasants' poverty? The links between water and poverty have been analysed from different viewpoints. A restricted concept of poverty that considers water as a fluid necessary to meet basic needs would be mainly concerned with how scarcity affects the water supply for domestic uses: drinking, food security, sanitation and health purposes. This would be the basic version of 'water security'.

A less simplistic view would go beyond domestic uses and focus on how water scarcity affects food production, especially in subsistence economies. A sufficient water supply (along with other forms of ecosystem services, such as soil) allows peasants to grow food for family consumption, bartering or selling. But this is not enough to overcome multifaceted and multidimensional impoverishment processes. In drylands especially, water availability for irrigation provides smallholders and peasants with the possibility of maintaining their food sovereignty[1] while developing resilience. In drylands, having a small plot with irrigation water to grow petty crops makes it possible to meet household subsistence needs and is also the first condition necessary for people to project their future life and their family's life in their place of origin. The possibility of working on their own land reduces the vulnerability of those who have to resort to salaried jobs or to move in search of gainful employment. In dryland rural communities, access to irrigation water is a necessary – though not sufficient – condition for people to maintain their traditional life-styles, to 'live in culture' and to 'live well'.[2] Depriving rural communities of these territorial rights would lead to their impoverishment, while ensuring the exercise of these rights would cast doubt on the hegemonic development model.

In times of climate change and drought intensification, it is necessary – now more than ever – to uncover the special situations and mechanisms of the water-poverty equation. The fact is that climate change will have a direct and an indirect impact through adaptation policies that are not always equitable and in which the adaptive strategies that benefit some could increase the vulnerability of others. On the other hand, this issue is important because it presents an opportunity to achieve synergic effects between climate change adaptation and poverty reduction. These issues are discussed further in the final section of this chapter.

5. Persistence of the peasantry or persistence of poverty?

Based on the evidence presented above, and with regard to the relationship between climate change impacts and poverty in a broader sense (for all social groups), the effect of extreme climate and water events is not new, but rather a pre-existing limitation that has an impact on itself and enhances other factors that interact in *poverty production processes* (Øyen 2002; 2004). Climate and water impacts on agricultural production are obviously a major concern, since agriculture is inherently bonded to nature. The specifics in the case of smallholders could probably lie in the fact that – as exemplified when referring to spirals of poverty – the negative impacts of climate change tend to be greatest on the smallest agents, contributing to an increase in the process of social differentiation (Ellis 1996: 51–2), and polarising capitalist relations of production in favour of agribusiness and capitalised firms. This is especially true since climate change scenarios often anticipate drastic and unpredictable extreme events that producers with limited room for manoeuvre would find difficult to manage. From this standpoint, peasants would be the most severely affected: the more vulnerable and disadvantaged the producer is in terms of games of power, the greater the impact of climate change. This perspective could be used to introduce climate change effects to support the traditional Marxist arguments that predict the disappearance of the peasantry due to the excessive pressure exerted by the capitalist economy.

However, climate change could also be a factor in the persistence of the peasantry. The intrinsic characteristics of the peasant mode of production are linked to its resilience, if we understand resilience as the tendency of a system to maintain its integrity when subject to disturbance (UNDP 2005) or its ability to recover from the effect of an extreme load that may have caused harm (UKCIP 2003). Particularly auspicious is the inherent flexibility of the peasant unit, which mixes crops that best suit the context and conditions (climate, hydrological and markets, among others) and are subject to constant reviews and decision making. This unit of production and consumption is capable of combining the available production factors in the best possible way to comply with whatever requirement is needed to meet family needs and – ultimately – to ensure its survival. These features grant the peasant mode of production a capacity for resilience. This is not too different from what Ellis says in relation to the peasant's ability to persist, recognising his capacity to withstand the pressure of capitalist production and reproduce himself almost indefinitely (Ellis 1996: 51–2).

It is in Bolivia where producers most clearly match the peasant profile and show the greatest resilience to climate change and the challenges of globalisation, as the Pucara peasant communities have acquired, strengthened and incorporated agro-meteorological practices (the combination of different crops and crop varieties, adjustment of planting schedules and staggered plantings, management of different ecological layers, cultivation work such as preparation for sowing, crop combination, etc.) over centuries of experience. Theirs is an ingrained adaptive learning capacity.

Unstable climate and water resources tend to increase agricultural risks and discourage some farms from growing certain crops in specific locations; even if they always have the possibility to move or to produce other crops, peasants are left with more economic space, at least for growing crops with a generalised demand in the local and national markets (beans, rice and corn, for example). Confronted with adverse agricultural conditions, peasants are less demanding than capitalist units since they do not seek profits but just need to fulfil their reproduction needs, and – if necessary – they could self-exploit and increase the amount of work invested in production.

Again, expected changes in climate and water could be interpreted as favouring the persistence of the peasantry.

In practice, these assumptions are developed in a complex manner. Let us analyse the case of Chile. The increasing competitiveness of dynamic markets compels agricultural producers to engage in permanent innovation, developing a capacity to adapt to economic and climatic stressors. Export companies and capitalised farmers tend to use all the resources that money can buy in order to cope with droughts: they move to areas with more water, buy more water shares than they actually need in regular conditions, drill wells, reduce water consumption by means of mechanised irrigation systems, build reservoirs on their farms, select crop varieties that are more resistant to water stress, and so on.

Like more fertile lands, those that are better situated to confront the threats of extreme climate and hydrological events will undoubtedly give rise to differential land rents that will be appropriated by the owners. The spatial distribution of this new differential rent may coincide with the existing one or modify it by increasing the value of locations that were less prized. In the cases studied here, and in connection with droughts, more intense water shortages render the areas in the upper irrigated oases and closer to water sources more attractive and strengthen already established socio-spatial segregation patterns.

On the other hand – and going back for a moment to Lenin's (1971 [1899]) explanation of the disappearance of the peasantry because of social differentiation – the strict Chilean neoliberal economic model and economic policies favouring competition have put a lot of strain on small producers and smallholders, expelling them from the agricultural circuit. This has been further exacerbated by the impact of mining and tourism – the industries where the proletarian seasonal labour force goes, leading to a scarcity in the supply of cheap labour for the agricultural sector. Fruit exporters in the Elqui basin state that the lack of manpower is the most serious problem they face and that the search for technological innovations mainly seeks to reduce the demand for labour. They still have access to labour, but they want better conditions and blame the Chilean state for not providing the infrastructure and general living conditions required by the inhabitants of the oasis for them to remain rooted in the rural areas and not be forced to migrate to the city of La Serena.

The above endorses the fact that capitalism in agriculture is only viable when it coexists with the peasant economy (Boltvinik, Chapter I, Section I, this volume) and reveals the existence of an economic space conducive to the persistence of the peasantry.

This example also points to the seasonality of agriculture and to the fact that the social cost of seasonality is absorbed by the peasants, who are constantly searching for an additional income and are condemned to live in poverty. This Chilean example in particular shows that seasonality is not exclusive to agricultural work. There is also a demand for seasonal wage labour in other sectors of the economy, both rural (mining and tourism) and urban (tourism and the service sector, among others). It is not only capitalist agriculture that depends on the proletariat to get cheap labour; other capitalist economic activities do so as well.

Temporary manpower is required by different sectors, but not all peasants can meet the demands for these positions or are willing to transform their lifestyle or migrate. This is the case for the *crianceros* of the non-irrigated areas, some because of old age and others because they refuse to undergo drastic changes. Many of them are considered 'non-viable' by Chilean economic and social policies, and, since they are no longer functional to the capitalist economy, they turn from being exploited to being excluded.

It is interesting to note that post-Fordist capitalist restructuring is transforming production, especially in urban settings (manufacturing and services), into a more flexible model in which processes are shorter and subject to constant changes and adjustments to meet the needs of dynamic markets. Information and communications technology (ICT) helps keep command posts in command centres and not necessarily in production centres, qualified jobs tend to disappear and unskilled labour tends to rise, perpetuating the demand for wage labour in 'flexible' forms, many of them temporary.

The Mendoza River basin provides a good example of this. The agricultural oasis surrounds the metropolitan area of Mendoza and contains smaller urban centres. The territorial configuration is such that it provides rural dwellers with easy access to urban and peri-urban areas. Thus, a peasant can live on his plot, devote part of his time to agricultural activities, and supplement his income with salaried work in the city, sometimes a temporary job. These urban job opportunities add to the seasonal demand for jobs in agriculture, multiplying the conditions for a mass of workers who need to sell their labour power in order to persist and grow. From this statement, it could be assumed that what will surely persist is the proletariat, but not necessarily in the peasant form. Some of the existing peasants will certainly continue selling their labour power and occupying the subordinate space that is functional to capitalist agricultural production. Others, however, will mutate – totally or partially – into an urban proletariat. The situation is different in the Pucara basin, where peasants face less pressure from the capitalist economy and can turn to other cultural, social and economic means to avoid supplementing their income with wage labour (although they still migrate). But in the cases studied in Chile and Argentina, peasantry – at least in the interpretation that emphasises that their main income comes from their plot of land – has no guarantee of persistence. Poverty certainly does.

6. Pro-peasant adaptation to climate change

The discussion on the issue of peasant persistence has shown that climate change reinforces pre-existing factors but it also creates some new features or variations. Another approach for discussing peasant persistence in the light of climate change is to examine the effects of responses to climate change on the persistence of the peasantry, and to explore the possible outcomes of diverse adaptation options.

Generally speaking, there are two main options for addressing climate change challenges: mitigation and adaptation. Mitigation means implementing policies to reduce greenhouse gas emissions and enhance carbon sinks (IPCC 2007), and is a substantive way to address climate change that could produce results in the longer term. The other way is to adapt, taking initiatives and measures to reduce the vulnerability of natural and human systems to actual or expected climate change effects (ibid.).

Adaptation is a very important topic of discussion in the field of science, policy making and management, and there are many ways to address it. McGray et al. (2007: 17–23) identify two roughly distinct perspectives in approaching adaptation: one focuses on creating response mechanisms to specific impacts associated with climate change, and the other on reducing vulnerability to climate change through building capacities that can help deal with a range of impacts (Figure 8.5). This typology will be useful for exploring the impact that adaptive actions could have on peasants in the three river basins.

In the three cases analysed, the adaptive measures that focus almost exclusively on improving the situation vis-à-vis specific climate and water impacts (see '4. Confronting climate change' in Figure 8.5) do not seem adequate. The construction of hydraulic infrastructure or investments in modern irrigation technologies might contribute to improving the situation of peasants, but they would address only the 'natural' or material portion of poverty situations, as defined by the interaction between natural or material factors and other factors pertaining to the social or symbolic sphere. Social causes of water scarcity would, in this case, be overlooked.

Adaptive strategies that make it possible to manage the risks associated with global environmental change ('3: Managing climate risk' in Figure 8.5) seem to be more appropriate to break spirals of poverty. Such strategies could include introducing information on hydrological variables into decision making in order to reduce their negative effects on production and means of life; creating monitoring and early warning systems or improving the existing ones so that they can fulfil these tasks; systematising this information and having agricultural producers incorporate it into their decisions on crop selection and agricultural practices; and implementing insurance mechanisms in times of drought.

However, in basins where social power is very asymmetric and where peasants are also wage workers employed by large producers, the risk posed by the two intervention strategies mentioned above is that their positive effects may be appropriated by capitalised producers. This is because the rural labour market and the social regulation system in general operate as barriers preventing these benefits from reaching the poorest sectors. We would be disregarding a set of market and policy mechanisms that operate as poverty production processes.

A more adequate way of facing the situation would be to develop response capacities to different stressors (natural and social) by setting up or strengthening systems (social and natural) in order to solve problems or overcome negative situations, especially among the poorest groups of the population ('2. Building response capacity'

1 Addressing Drivers of Vulnerability	2 Building Response Capacity	3 Managing Climate Risk	4 Confronting Climate Change
UGANDA: Providing women with crossbred goats and instruction in graze-free feeding *(Karamoja Agropastoral Development Programme)*	**BRAZIL:** Participatory reforestation in Rio de Janeiro's hillside favelas to combat flood-induced landslides *(City of Rio de Janeiro)*	**TANZANIA:** Monitoring salinization of drinking water and drilling new wells to replace those that are no longer usable (**South**South/North)	**INDONESIA:** Managing coral reefs in response to widespread coral bleaching *(WWF)*
BANGLADESH: Diversification of livelihood strategies in areas vulnerable to flooding (**South** South/North)	**MONGOLIA:** Reinstating pastoral networks to foster appropriate rangeland management practices in arid regions *(National University of Mongolia)*	**MALI:** Teaching farmers to collect climate data and integrate it into their planting decisions *(Government of Mali/Swiss Agency for Development and Cooperation)*	**NEPAL:** Reducing the risk of glacial lake outburst floods from Tsho Rolpa Lake *(Government of Nepal)*
CUBA: Vaccination program to eradicate diseases in low-income areas *(Cuban Ministry of Health)*	**TANZANIA:** Reviving traditional enclosures to encourage vegetation regeneration and reduce land degradation *(Ministry of Natural Resources and Tourism, Tanzania)*	**BANGLADESH:** Using nationally standardized risk assessment procedures to develop a community adaptation plan of action *(Local government)*	

8.5 A continuum of adaptation activities: from development to climate change (*source:* McGray et al. (2007: 18)) in Figure 8.5). Examples of this would include facilitating access to information and to technical assistance; developing planning systems to change agricultural practices (which must be fully participatory if poverty is to be overcome effectively); creating or strengthening community systems to face extreme climate, water and market situations collectively; reinforcing the links between government and scientific systems and productive agents; and improving or completing the regulatory framework.

In all of these options, there is the risk not only that powerful actors may seize these initiatives but that the adaptive actions of some of them may increase the vulnerability of others. Thus, any adaptive strategy to address global environmental change should also address the objectives of poverty reduction, while taking due consideration of its effects in terms of equity. If we recognise that capitalised agriculture has a symbiotic relationship with the peasantry, and we assume that poverty production processes are relational phenomena that involve not only the poor but also the same system that benefits some to the detriment of others, then interventions to reduce inequalities are processes that will alleviate the poverty of the weakest – the peasants.

There is no doubt that the best adaptation efforts seem to focus on reducing vulnerability in its broader sense, including sensitivities associated with natural and social exposures, and developing capacities and providing the necessary resources to strengthen resilience ('1. Addressing drivers of vulnerability' in Figure 8.5). These are actions that address development objectives, but not those prescribed by the orthodox model. From a critical perspective, development should include the 'right to not develop', the 'right to difference' and the objectives of 'good living' in all of their dimensions, including economic independence, social equity, personal safety, health and education, access to equal opportunities, freedom of personal and community choices, and other territorial rights. This is the kind of adaptation that may favour the persistence of the peasantry and – especially relevant – may alleviate their poverty.

Following this line of action, adaptive practices could contribute to the persistence of the peasantry in various ways:

• Some may be channelled through existing economic mechanisms: for instance, granting subsidies for drilling and maintaining wells and to meet the energy costs of pumping. In Argentina, many of the wells that small producers are still using were drilled thanks to subsidies given by the welfare state in the 1970s, and energy costs are currently being subsidised. In Bolivia, many community wells – and other irrigation infrastructure – have been paid for with international cooperation funds and state subsidies. On the other hand, even if subsidising climate change adaption could be more acceptable than subsidising the peasantry, the Chilean example resists such a concept. However, adaption initiatives oriented towards building resilience go beyond adapting to drought, hail or cold, and subsidies can be applied to a broad range of purposes: to provide better production conditions, to improve quality of life, to develop a variety of personal, familial or community skills, or even to make rural settings more attractive.

- While also appealing to relatively common economic practices, some measures could enhance climate change resilience by addressing double exposures, as well as by contributing to peasant persistence: cluster forming, vertical integration with capitalised firms, horizontal integration in cooperatives, and so on.

- Assuming that wage income will increase its share in the total income of peasants, operating on the labour market to mitigate asymmetries and ensure better working conditions constitutes a good option for addressing drivers of vulnerability in the cases of Argentina and Chile, where wage workers are numerous.

- Land market regulation and better planning of urban sprawl over agricultural land could relieve the pressure on small suburban properties, mitigating the double exposures borne by smallholders who are located near urban centres.

- Processes of change in favour of peasants could be driven by consumption. The preferences of consumers who believe that 'small is beautiful' or of those seeking fair trade or organic products could benefit the position of small farmers and peasants in the agri-food system.

- Beyond market mechanisms, and taking Bolivia as an example, adaptive actions may be based on social organisation: mutual aid, reciprocity and solidarity could be encouraged. Resilience could also be built into the field of values. A strategy could be elaborated that emphasises and promotes an awareness of peasants' contribution to biodiversity, to the conservation of heritage landscapes and to the preservation of cultural diversity (Montaña and Diaz 2012). The fact that the human rights of peasants are violated could also be highlighted, promoting a political space that is more favourable to their persistence.

The initiatives listed above can all be framed within the concept of addressing vulnerability drivers, and could – eventually – be more easily accepted and implemented under the umbrella of climate change adaptation. But, in truth, most of them are similar to the alternatives that have already been proposed to provide better production and living conditions in order to favour peasants' persistence. We have already failed in implementing them. What could make a difference now?

Values in the symbolic field constitute an arena in which vulnerability and poverty could be fought; moreover, these are the types of value that make it feasible to adopt the strategies listed above. Adaptation, conceived as a process for building resilience for peasants, poor and vulnerable people, requires a change in the development paradigm towards a new ethics of conservation, one that promotes a multicultural paradigm that values small-scale production and lifestyles and understands their connections with nature. We have known this for some time. But what is new is that, while the political and economic spaces defending the right of farmers tend to shrink, the idea of climate change adaptation oriented towards the most vulnerable seems to be consolidating. It is an opportunity that we must seize.

Notes

1 This is the right of all people to healthy, culturally appropriate food produced through ecologically sound and sustainable methods, and their right to define their own food and agriculture systems.

2 *Suma qamaña* in the Aymara language, *sumak kawsay* in Quechua and *buen vivir* in Spanish all refer to a concept that relates to 'living in harmony and balance, in harmony with the cycles of the Mother Earth, of the cosmos, of life and of history, and in balance with all forms of existence' (Huanacuni Mamani 2010: 37). *Good living* involves the right to think and to choose and to have autonomy to decide (Espinoza 2010: 3). This concept has been adopted both by the new Political Constitution of the Plurinational State of Bolivia (2009) and by the Political Constitution of Ecuador (2008).

References

Álvarez Leguizamón, S. (2005) *Trabajo y producción de la pobreza en Latinoamérica y el Caribe: Estructuras, discursos y actores.* Buenos Aires: CLACSO.

Boltvinik, J. (2011) 'Poverty and persistence of the peasantry'. Background paper for the International Workshop on Peasant's Poverty and Persistence, CROP and El Colegio de México, Mexico City, 13–15 March 2012, Chapter 1, this volume.

CNA (2002) *Censo Nacional Agropecuario.* Buenos Aires and Mendoza: Instituto Nacional de Estadística y Censos (INDEC) and Dirección de Estadísticas e Investigaciones Económicas (DEIE).

Dattwyler Cancino, E. (2008) *Minería, agricultura y recursos hídricos en la cuenca del río Elqui: aspectos económicos, sociales y ambientales.* Memoria para optar al trato de Ingeniero Civil Ambiental, Facultad de Ingeniería, Universidad de La Serena. La Serena: Universidad de La Serena.

DGI (2007) *Diagnóstico Preliminar sobre la Gestión de los Recursos Hídricos de la Provincia de Mendoza. Oferta Hídrica.* Mendoza: Departamento General de Irrigación (DGI). Available at www.dgi.gov.ar.

Ellis, F. (1996) *Peasant Economics: Farm households and agrarian development.* Cambridge: Cambridge University Press.

Espinoza, R. (2010) 'Perú: el buen vivir, alternativa indígena a la crisis global de la civilización occidental'. Available at www.servindi. org/actualidad/opinion/22327.

Flyvbjerg, B. (1998) *Rationality and Power: Democracy in practice.* Chicago IL: University of Chicago Press.

Huanacuni Mamani, F. (2010) 'Reflexiones del buen vivir: artículos, notas y comentarios del buen vivir en el Ecuador y en el mundo', 31 March. Available at https:// reflexionesdelbuenvivir.wordpress. com/2015/03/31/fernando-huanacuni-mamani/.

IPCC (2007) *Fourth Assessment Report: Climate change 2007.* Geneva: Intergovernmental Panel on Climate Change (IPCC). Available at www. ipcc.ch/report/ar4/.

Leichenko, R. and K. O'Brien (2008) *Double Exposure: Global environmental change in an era of globalisation.* New York NY: Oxford University Press.

Lenin, V. (1971 [1899]) *El desarrollo del capitalismo en Rusia.* Mexico City: Ed. de Cultura Popular.

McGray, H., A. Hammill, R. Bradley, with E. L. Schipper and J. E. Parry (2007) *Weathering the Storm: Options for framing adaptation and development.* Washington DC: World Resources Institute.

Molle, F. and P. Mollinga (2003) 'Water poverty indicators: conceptual problems and policy issues', *Water Policy* 5: 529–44.

Montaña, E. (2011) 'The "water-tamers" and the construction of the hydraulic society in Mendoza, Argentina'. Paper presented at the XIV World Water Congress, Porto de Galinhas, Pernambuco, 25–29 September.

Montaña, E. and H. P. Diaz (2012) 'Global environmental change, culture and development: rethinking the ethics of conservation', *International Journal of Climate Change: Impacts and Responses* 3 (3): 31–40.

OHCHR (1998) *Derechos humanos y pobreza extrema.* Resolution 25. Geneva: Office of the United

Nations High Commissioner for Human Rights (OHCHR).

— (2004) *Los derechos humanos y la reducción de la pobreza; un marco conceptual.* Geneva: Office of the United Nations High Commissioner for Human Rights (OHCHR).

Øyen, E. (2002) 'Poverty production: a different approach to poverty understanding' in N. Genov (ed.), *Advances in Sociological Knowledge Over Half a Century.* Paris: International Social Science Council (ISSC).

— (2004) 'Knowledge about poverty production as a key word to poverty reduction'. Paper presented at the NFU Conference, Bergen, 30 November.

UKCIP (2003) *Climate Adaptation: Risk, uncertainty and decision-making.* Oxford: UK Climate Impacts Programme (UKCIP). Available at www.ukcip.org.uk/wp-content/PDFs/UKCIP-Risk-framework.pdf.

UNDP (2005) 'Compendium on methods and tools to evaluate impacts of, and vulnerability and adaptation to, climate change'. UNDP Adaptation Policy Framework. United Nations Framework Convention on Climate Change. Available at http://unfccc.int/adaptation/nairobi_work_programme/knowledge_resources_and_publications/items/5501.php.

Vasilachis de Gialdino, I. (2003) *Pobres, pobreza, identidad y representaciones sociales.* Barcelona: Gedisa.

Worster, D. (1985) *Rivers of Empire: Water, aridity and growth of the American West.* New York NY: Pantheon Books.

9 | FINANCIALISATION OF THE FOOD SECTOR AND PEASANTS' PERSISTENCE

Kostas Vergopoulos

Since the breakout of the subprime financial crisis in the United States (September 2008), the paradoxes of the world economy have kept building to the point where they have become a huge and hardly decipherable puzzle. Hopes for a rapid stabilisation notwithstanding, international volatility seems to be rebounding, mainly from its epicentre in the industrialised and developed countries, out to the rest of the world. Should the remaining regions of the world engage in the process of economic downturn, they will do so to the extent that they suffer the consequences of the degradation of the former and that they were overconfident about their own exclusively export-led economic growth models. When the Western economies' engines break down, this must necessarily imply, as an inevitable consequence, a slowdown for other parts of the world that are dependent on them. Much has been said about some supposed new 'dynamics' coming from emerging economies. Today, we discover that the so-called emerging dynamics were in fact based in Western consumerism, fuelled by credit from emerging nations. And now we have exhausted consumerism from one side and export-led growth from the other.

Industrial outsourcing to emerging countries has generated surpluses there, with consequent trade deficits in Western nations. The heavily indebted Western countries are those whose productive bases have been most heavily impacted by relocations, while the creditor nations are those that have benefited from such relocations – especially in their export-led economic sectors. Too many international imbalances, too many structural deficits and accumulated international surpluses, and too much funding that led to gigantic amounts of accumulated debt have gravely shaken international confidence and stability. Meanwhile, the current severe lack of confidence is an expression of some much deeper structural distortions on both sides of the world system.

The greatest paradox today lies in the fact that those responsible for the 2008 crisis are now back in business and trying to overcome the crisis by implementing the same policies that fostered and precipitated it some years ago. Once again, as the French politician Talleyrand said about the Bourbons following the monarchy's restoration in France after 1815, today's financiers and speculators 'neither learned nor forgot anything'[1] (Dyssord 2001 [1942]). Today, the world system is about to sink back into a funding crisis, even worse than that of 2008, inasmuch as its leaders are repeating their previous conduct and using the same practices as before. Only this time, they are proceeding more purposefully, with less visibility and certainly without the mitigating circumstance of *not knowing what is going to happen.* Currently, the lack of visibility is so striking that not only are more and more people resigned to the inevitability of the capitalist crisis, but they are also discovering some benefits from it, especially in terms of so-called economic consolidation through the extension of liberal reforms that enhance 'flexibility' and 'free and perfect' competition, in order, supposedly, to ensure conditions of economic 'viability'.

Since 2008, those responsible for the financial speculative bubble have been desperately trying to mitigate its consequences, substituting new alternative speculative bubbles in its place, such as the financialisation of commodities and food prices. In recent years, a food financial bubble has emerged and grown, in the hope that it could work as a buffer against the violent consequences of the bursting of the other financial and housing bubbles. The value of commodities and food products appears to be a safe haven when other virtual financial values are breaking down. The only people who do not admit the existence of such a 'food bubble', as *The Washington Post* candidly notes, are precisely those who benefit most from it: that is, the Wall Street financial food market traders. There should also be a mention here of the institutional regulators of the Commodity Futures Trading Commission (CFTC), a public authority, who insist that they lack statistical evidence on financial investors' impact on the determination and volatility of food prices. As frequently happens, everyone knows what is going on, except the beneficiaries of the current state of affairs and, obviously, those who are supposed to supervise them!

1. The food tsunami

During the World Economic Forum's annual meeting in Davos in January 2012, most participants were astonished by the fact that 'major changes were taking place so swiftly'. However, often in history, immense changes have taken place in a rather rapid and irrepressible way. Economic history has shown repeatedly that in the middle of a crisis, a number of major events occur in rapid succession. The key event during the past three or four years has been a quick acceleration of food prices combined with decreasing production and the breakdown of productivity in the world food economy. Once again, these troublesome developments have been correctly attributed to the financialisation of food economies. Most of the Davos Forum participants agreed that 'financial positions in the food area have become increasingly relevant components in both individual and institutional international speculators' portfolios' (Curwin 2012).

Also noteworthy is the increasing dysfunctionality of agriculture. Even in the United States of America, the Department of Agriculture acknowledges the current food economy impasse. Here, the uncontrollable increase in food prices is now reaching unprecedented levels and there has been a steep decline in agricultural productivity by acre of cultivated area, as well as a decrease in US cereal stocks, even falling below the 1996 figures. The upcoming world struggle for food security will necessarily be linked to new international conflicts. Even the Arab Spring might be interpreted by historians of the future as reflecting new international competition among 'ever-increasing populations having to share ever-decreasing food supplies' (ibid.). In turn, the worldwide struggle for water and against the threat of pervasive desertification represents an overwhelming limiting factor for many agricultural and food projects in many nations, including the developed countries. The scenario envisioned by the nineteenth-century British economist David Ricardo (1772–1823) now seems to be evident: the intensification of agricultural production as a consequence of a dramatic increase in demand for foodstuffs. Currently, this situation coexists not only with the financialisation of food and agrarian products, but also with a deterioration in productive conditions. As a result, not only is there declining agricultural productivity by cultivated area, but also an increase in food prices and a structural inflation of agrarian production costs. While, in the short term, increased prices are basically due to speculation in financial food futures, they also derive from the structural penetration of capitalism in agrarian production, which is proving to be a deeply destabilising factor within the overall capitalist system. If foodstuffs are capitalist products, their prices are the sum not only of the labour income necessary for their production but also of profit revenue for respective capitalist entrepreneurs and rent revenue for landowners. In other words, in the face of inflation of foodstuff prices, all types of income in non-food sectors should decrease proportionally. The overall global valorisation of capital is severely impacted by structural increases in foodstuff prices and related revenues. And all this occurs even though the income of direct producers keeps shrinking – and does so even more today than it did in the past.

In Davos, the unlikely issue arose of finding out 'whether globalisation was in the process of undermining its own initiators, to wit, the developed countries – in other words, the United States, the European Union and Japan' (De Schutter 2012). With the outsourcing of productive activities to emerging countries, the developed nations were ultimately forced to retreat to the financial sphere, with the concurrent pathology of inevitably bursting bubbles. Similarly, in Davos, Olivier De Schutter – a United Nations Special Rapporteur on the Right to Food – drew attention to the fact that the world food situation was showing 'seeds of dystopia', entailing the risk of 'rolling back the globalisation process' (ibid.). In other words, the failure of globalisation, which seems to be happening – namely through excessive financialisation – implies a risk of de-globalisation and de-financialisation: that is, the risk of fragmentation is falling back onto economies' own domestic frameworks. This 'regression' appears to be the agenda of the day.

As speculative funds race towards agri-food values, the very initiators of the globalisation process are currently experiencing the destabilising effects resulting from the financialisation of the agrarian and food sectors. Those who moved forward most swiftly in terms of globalisation, and, therefore, of financialisation, are now the first to suffer its consequences. The American economist Kenneth Rogoff, a Harvard scholar, readily compares the current dysfunctions and turmoil in the agri-food chain to some sort of 'coronary crisis in capitalism' (Rogoff 2012). This capitalist circuit heart attack might be of a financial nature or due to the food economy: both are just as likely to volatilise and destabilise capital's profitability and, consequently, its valorisation system.

Persistent imbalances in international trade have created huge monetary surpluses; these are not directed towards enhancing the stability of the world system, but rather are put to uses that result in more destabilisation of the world economy, such as financial and food speculation. The food economy financialisation, which in the beginning could have been perceived as a buffer for the financial crisis, eventually turned out to be far more destabilising than the initial financial shock it was intended to mitigate. With excessive and outrageous deregulation, new types of investors and new investment vehicles have been established in this stage of the international economic scenario, within a framework of financial profusion and beyond any control. Thus, it turns out that agri-food financialisation is actually creating more problems for capitalism than it is solving.

2. The bubble and the contemporary food crisis

As has been reported by Frederick Kaufman (2011), the tools for agri-food financialisation were indeed set up well in advance, namely by the ominous Goldman Sachs financial group during President Bill Clinton's two successive terms. First of all, the financial group had already introduced its financial innovation into the agri-food area – its agri-food financial derivative product the Goldman Sachs Commodity Index (GSCI) – during the 1990s. This composite index included the prices of twenty-four primary commodities: precious metals, energy products, coffee, cattle, maize, pork, soya products and wheat. Later, by 1999, the CFTC, giving in to pressure from Goldman Sachs, opened the financial instruments to external 'business operators' and futures contracts; their reported profits were $13 billion in 2003 and today they are in the hundreds of billions of dollars. As reported by the author of the investigation, the entrance of traders and international banks into the foodstuff domain is tantamount to the invasion of the food arena by 'true carnivores' (ibid.). The outcomes of such a mutation are not only instability and volatility in food prices, but also a rapid growth in starving populations in the world (estimated at 250 million people in 2012) and people living under insecure food conditions (who, in 2012, represented more than 1 billion individuals worldwide). Moreover, hunger and food insecurity, as traditional symptoms of underdevelopment, are now assuming unprecedented dimensions not only in developing countries but also within developed Western nations. In its estimation of the food situation worldwide, the United Nations Food and Agriculture Organization (FAO) did not hesitate to describe the world situation in 2011 as a 'true agri-food tsunami' (FAO 2011).

This agri-food tsunami now prevalent in the world food situation is attributed to both the financialisation of agri-food values and the penetration of the capitalist mode of production into the sphere of agrarian production. Both processes, instead of serving as a stabilisation buffer for the worldwide financial chaos, are in fact extending and aggravating it. They create more instability and social tensions within the world economy, and particularly in the conditions of agri-food supply and its prices. If, as suspected, speculation on food commodities is merely the apparent tip of the iceberg, structural mutations created by the extension of capitalism into the agri-food sphere are really the root of the problem. Disturbing as speculation is, the hidden truth is even more alarming – not only for the millions of hungry people but also for the speculators and capitalist investors themselves.

3. Peasantry's poverty and persistence

For the past three decades, the world food economy has been experiencing globalisation coupled with financialisation, and undergoing destabilising consequences not only to food supply and security but also to the conditions for the overall reproduction of capital's valorisation system. Instability and growing pressures on the foodstuff markets are closely associated with instability and equally increasing pressures on the financial markets. In fact, the permanent and constant element through all these mutations is the farming world, constantly subjected to mere subsistence conditions.

Julio Boltvinik, from El Colegio de México, raises two crucial questions (see Chapter 1). Why don't peasants disappear, given the forecasts of their eventual extinction by innumerable agrarian analysts from the nineteenth century onwards? And why do peasants still live in conditions of poverty, despite constant increases in the prices of their products? These two questions entail two other vital questions. Why is it that food security policies and the return to original forms of family agri-food production are now being encouraged within both national and regional economies? And to what extent is the notion of food security compatible with those of globalisation and financialisation?

For a number of years already, the World Bank and its previous American president Robert B. Zoellick, as well as the FAO, with its directors-general Jacques Diouf and José Graziano da Silva, have emphatically encouraged and financed through every possible means a worldwide implementation of 'food security' programmes based on the consolidation of family farming forms of agrarian production. These measures were intended not only to counteract the extreme emergency in the world food situation but also to overcome the impasse of the past three decades – 1980–2010 – which were marked by globalisation and financialisation tendencies that exhausted agrarian supply in the local markets. The current mutations have to overcome the unproductive deadlock wrought by the preceding phase (FAO 2009; Fresco and Rabbinge 2011).

4. Family farming

The immediate answer to these questions refers directly to the benefits of family farming, as opposed to the impact of the capitalist mode of production in the agrarian area. Just as shown almost a century ago by Russian economist Alexander Chayanov (1888–1937), a specialist in agrarian economy, the family mode of production permits the maximisation of the agrarian product or foodstuff, while minimising prices and production costs (Chayanov 1966 [1930]). Its competitive edge lies in the family's excessive workload provided for free. Capitalist forms of production, on the other hand, are always too volatile, over-dependent as they are on the market's own volatility and vicissitudes. Furthermore, they inflate agricultural prices through additional structural expenses, as they have to pay not only the wages of agrarian workers and profits for entrepreneurs, but also rent revenues for landowners in order to ensure access to productive lands. Capitalist forms of production intrinsically entail not only fluctuations, instability and volatility in the supply of foodstuffs but also structurally increasing food prices, in order to pay for the components of those prices. Conversely, the family mode of production does not need to finance profit or land rent, but utilises only family labour. And this labour is based on remuneration criteria much lower than those of urban wage systems.

In addition, peasant family members' labour is supplied in amounts far beyond those that could be established by contract or considered necessary. Under family production conditions, peasant families' excess labour is maximised without any special compensation, which would be particularly high under the conditions of the capitalist mode of production. If the salaried person works for a boss under the conditions of an employment contract, the peasant and his/her family offer their labour unconditionally, inasmuch as they are working on their own account. Although owners of their land, and despite being entrepreneurs within the family enterprise, peasants mobilise the entire family's potential labour power while earning the equivalent of a labourer's wage, and quite often receiving a much lower income than that.

Within this theoretical context, the peasant family's poverty is a prerequisite for their survival, social incorporation and persistence as a form of production. The poorer peasants are, the more 'competitive' they become relative to other forms of agri-food production. Economic and financial capitalist cycles are both volatile and recurrent while peasant forms persist, although the benefits and costs of the two forms of production are evaluated differently depending on economic momentum and current circumstances. During the phase of prosperity, one tends to encourage overall capitalism: that is, the capitalist rush and extension into areas not yet formally capitalised – agriculture indeed, but also healthcare, education, pensions and retirement, public and social welfare enterprises. 'Less government and more freedom' (for freedom read privatisation) is the slogan of triumphant integrative capitalism. 'Rescue by the government, social services and non-capitalist modes of production' is the slogan of beleaguered capitalism looking for stability.

During the ascending phase of the economic cycle, capital always seeks to extend into and hopefully incorporate all of those areas that were previously beyond its reach. So, in the ascending phase, capitalism remains extensive and inclusive. However, the complete incorporation of non-capitalist areas implies inevitably the exhaustion of sources necessary for its own profitability. In contrast, when the capitalist system enters the declining phase of the cycle, old truisms begin to emerge that we had forgotten and stopped worrying about: social safety nets to cushion the blows dealt by integrative capitalism. Triumphant capitalism during the 1950s and 1960s, after World

War II, absorbed 'new areas' such as aspects of the reproduction of the labour force and leisure time consumption for workers through the standardisation of production and through mass consumption. This led to a severe decline in profit rates for the overall system, as at the end of the 1960s the extension of capitalism into new areas had nearly exhausted the quantity of non-market goods that could be transformed into market goods.

With the new wave of so-called globalisation, after the 1980s, the problem of the extinction of sources of profitability rebounded. The financialisation of the agri-food economy since the 1990s, and later the rush of capital to agri-food financial values after the 2008 crisis, exacerbated the original problem of the scarcity of non-market areas and goods. Nowadays, the real problem for the capitalist system is no longer how to incorporate more non-capitalist areas; rather, it is the opposite: how to reduce capitalist spheres of production and foster non-capitalist forms to avoid paying profits and land rents at the overall systemic level.

In the history of economic thought, Adam Smith made the 'mistake' of equating the price of labour with its production and reproduction costs. It is a mistake because if wage workers' 'labour power' as a commodity were to be paid its true capitalist value, then capitalism would be simply impossible, as Marx showed when reviewing the approaches of the founding fathers of classical political economy (Marx 1968 [written 1862–63; first published 1905–10]). If all commodities were sold and purchased at their cost of production, no room would be left for profit at the global macro-economic level, unless, as ironically stated by Rosa Luxemburg – pushing the reasoning into reductio ad absurdum – this would imply that capitalists were stealing from each other (Luxemburg 1951 [1913]). In order for capitalist profit to be structurally possible at a macro-economic level, at least one commodity must be sold and purchased at a lower price. Under the capitalist mode of production, labour necessarily has to be paid for at a lower price relative to its presumed cost of production and also relative to its theoretically presumed price.

In other words, for the profitability of the capitalist system – and for the profitability of capital – at least one commodity should be produced by means of a non-capitalist mode of production, so as to avoid paying profit or land rent revenues.

This particular commodity, which in fact is not a commodity like the others, is labour power, or the labourer's ability to work. Capitalists buy this 'commodity', although at strictly cost price: that is, not including in the price paid for it (the worker's wage) the respective margin either of profit or of land rent or even of workers' wage costs. If the supply of this special commodity, whose price includes the feeding and reproduction costs of the working-class family, were to be supplied by the capitalist mode of production, its price – the worker's wage – should cover both the entrepreneurial profit and the land rent income, which would wreak havoc on the profitability of the capitalist system. Family agriculture's guardian angel makes sure that this particular 'commodity' is sold on the market at a price precluding any profit or any income whatsoever for the landowner, which necessarily could put a strain on the price of all other capitalist commodities. Under the capitalist mode of production, the supply of this 'special' commodity called labour power must be ensured through a non-capitalist (i.e. family) process in order to keep its price substantially, structurally and permanently low.

Consequently, peasant poverty, far from being a simple conundrum, is in fact nothing more than the hidden, necessary and complementary face of the contemporary capitalist moon. Indeed, it is merely a necessary condition for the general profitability of the capitalist system. Marx pointed out many times that capitalism is not only the production of commodities, but also – and basically – the permanent and endless transformation of non-market goods into market goods, with the benefits accrued to capital through the appropriation of the production of previously non-market goods. The air we breathe, noted Friedrich Engels, is free, although capitalism appropriates it, turning it into particular profit. If we had to pay taxes for breathing, if we were to pay a profitable fee to someone supplying the air to us, it would be all the more difficult for capital to maintain its profitability in capitalist production sectors.

Not every capitalist extension into new areas necessarily implies new additional overall profits, improving the conditions of general profitability. It often implies a capture of profits or a transfer of profits created in other sectors and, consequently, a diminishing rate of profit for the overall capitalist system. Extension into new areas and innovation could prove beneficial to the overall profitability only under one very strict condition: that increasing productivity is coupled with diminishing costs of production and the lowering of final prices. However, if extension and inclusion imply a lowering of productivity coupled with ascending costs of production and final prices, profitability could not be enhanced and would certainly deteriorate.

Capitalist and non-capitalist forms of production complement each other, and the former could not absorb the latter without running the risk of creating a deadlock. Overall, all-inclusive capitalism remains nothing but an illusion, which, furthermore, often turns out to be a cause of instability and regression for the global system of capital.

Today, a return to family-based forms of agri-food production is considered more and more seriously as a remedy for the 'overall capitalist' impasse that the previous historical phase – that of globalisation and financialisation – pushed us into. Now, there appears an urgent need for de-globalisation and de-financialisation in the production and distribution of foodstuffs, in order to stabilise the whole economic system and especially its global profitability for the formally capitalist sectors. This explains why peasants' poverty is not just a vestige of the past but a condition for the new incorporation of peasants into the contemporary economy. Peasants' poverty, instead of being a handicap, represents the competitive advantage of this type of production and a way out of the current impasse.

By the same token, we can understand not only why peasants remain poor, but also why they certainly will not disappear and why the capitalist mode of production in the agri-food sector is now tending to restore the land to its traditional residents and workers. As for the third question, it should be noted that food security seems to prevail today as a central policy issue more than ever before; this is due to the food disasters that took place during the previous phase, that of overall financial capitalism and the ruthless financialisation of the agri-food sectors. The financial rush to these sectors not only deeply disrupted the profitability conditions of capital in general, but also resulted in new food tensions in both developing and developed countries.

The current new shift towards peasant family farming is the result of the need to maximise agricultural production while minimising its costs and prices. However, given the actual conditions of food distribution systems, the initial problems of supply instability and the volatility in the prices of foodstuffs are quite likely to persist. This is due not only to the financialisation of agri-food supply, but also to the pre-eminence of commercial channels in the transformation and distribution of agri-food products and primary commodities. Such a danger can be avoided only if the transformation and distribution of foodstuffs are entrusted to peasants' associations as a complement to their home finances, and this needs to occur with the political, moral and economic support of the authorities. If, however, the expansion of capitalism into non-capitalist spheres turns out to be a source of instability for the system, it should not lead us to the conclusion that a return (to the conditions of subjugation) of non-capitalist forms of production should be without problems for the system's perennial functioning. If contemporary capitalism benefits from the family organisation of agri-food production, it does not mean that the latter also benefits from the former. The relation between the two worlds – capitalist and peasant – might well turn out to be as deeply opposite and antagonistic, but also as deeply functional, as it has been in the past. In economic history, both versions of this contradictory relation have often been witnessed. In any case, if a major part of foodstuff production is now in the process of being entrusted to family units, this will not be the first time in economic history that we have witnessed an economic and social switch in production techniques – even if this switch goes in the opposite direction to what some still consider as permanently and endlessly 'progressive'. Many times in history, 'backwardness' and even 'retrocession' in some areas have been the condition needed for the 'advance' of others. Certainly, capitalism remains a 'total' system, but this does not imply that all areas of this system are and remain, at any given moment, of the same productive nature.

Note

1 This quote is attributed to Talleyrand (1815) in his biography.

References

Chayanov, A. (1966 [1930]) *The Theory of Peasant Economy*. Homewood IL: Richard D. Irwin, Inc. Also re-published in 1986 by Manchester University Press with a new prologue by Teodor Shanin.

Curwin, T. (2012) 'Thinking about food at Davos'. CNBC, 22 January. Available at www.cnbc.com/id/45855922 (accessed 26 June 2015).

De Schutter, O. (2012) 'Taking back globalization', *Project Syndicate*, 24 January. Available at www.project-syndicate.org/commentary/taking-back-globalization (accessed 26 June 2015).

Dyssord, J. (2001 [1942]) *Les belles amies de Talleyrand*. Paris: Nouvelles Éditions Latines.

FAO (2009) *World Summit on World Food Security*. Rome: Food and Agriculture Organization of the United Nations (FAO).

— (2011) *The State of Food Insecurity in the World: How does international price volatility affect domestic economies and food security?* Rome: Food and Agriculture Organization of the United Nations (FAO). Available at www.fao.org/docrep/014/i2330e/i2330e.pdf (accessed 26 June 2015).

Fresco, L. and R. Rabbinge (2011) *Keeping World Security on the Agenda: Implications for the United Nations and the CGIAR*. Washington DC: World Bank and Consultative Group on International Agricultural Research (CGIAR). Available at www.worldbank.org/html/cgiar/publications/issues/issues11.pdf (accessed 26 June 2015).

Kaufman, F. (2011) 'How Goldman Sachs created the food crisis', *Foreign Policy Review*, 27 April. Available at http://foreignpolicy.com/2011/04/27/how-goldman-sachs-created-the-food-crisis/ (accessed 26 June 2015).

Luxemburg, R. (1951 [1913]) *The Accumulation of Capital*. London: Routledge and Kegan Paul.

Marx, K. (1968 [written 1862–63; first published by K. Kautsky in 1905–10 in three volumes]) *Theories of Surplus Value*. London: Lawrence & Wishart.

Rogoff, K. (2012) 'Coronary capitalism', *Project Syndicate*, 1 February. Available at www.project-syndicate.org/commentary/coronary-capitalism (accessed 26 June 2015).

POLICY, SELF-RELIANCE AND PEASANT POVERTY

10 | THE RISE AND FALL OF THE AGRARIAN WELFARE STATE: PEASANTS, GLOBALISATION, AND THE PRIVATISATION OF DEVELOPMENT

Farshad A. Araghi

This chapter explores the rise and demise of the post-war global agrarian welfare state. Following an exploration of the role of agrarian welfare systems in managing labour and food supplies in the rise of capitalism, the chapter traces the origins of the modern agrarian welfare state to global peasant movements, and rural–urban nationalist political alliances that foisted nation state-based divisions of labour into the global developmentalist projects sponsored by the United States following World War II. It then analyses the unravelling of the 'development compromise' and its substitution by the 'neoliberal consensus', whose core components were: 1) the reorganisation of the world division of labour as a way of displacing diverse 'home markets' with a 'world market' organised around a truly global division of labour; 2) the creation of a massive and actually or potentially mobile migratory global army of labour; and 3) the operationalisation of the law of value as a basis for global wage determination, and as a result, as I will argue, an endemic 'crisis of under-reproduction' of labour and nature. The chapter links the latter with what it conceptualises as the 'privatisation of development' that has at its centre not the abandonment of the agrarian welfare state but its privatisation to the advantage of agri-food corporations. The movement for food sovereignty and counter-enclosure movements in general are symptomatic of poor people's quest for a global de-commodification of food.

1. Colonialism as an agrarian welfare regime

I conceptualise colonialism as an agrarian welfare system for European capitalism. The reconfiguration of the global division of labour under the British hegemony around the needs of the now dominant regime of industrial capitalism in the nineteenth century led to a reorganisation of land use on a global scale. Reorganising world trade in accordance with the law of value (Araghi 2003), Great Britain and its European competitors embarked on a massive global land grab in the their scramble for colonies.

The colonial land grabs enforced various racialised and gendered regimes of forced labour as a way of constructing export-dependent monocultures that subsidised the reproductive needs of European labour and capital (McMichael 2012). The year 1834 marks the passage of the Poor Law Amendment Act and the beginning of a systematic attempt by the English liberal industrial bourgeoisie to dismantle the traditional and rudimentary welfare system[1] that had developed piecemeal from the sixteenth century. The agrarian welfare regime of capital originated in this period, in that the agrarian programme of emerging industrial capital sought to construct a value-based global division of labour, a project that expressed the coming of age of industrial capital in the nineteenth century. The Great Irish Famine of 1845 to 1849 is particularly illustrative of the relational character of the emerging global food regime of capital: one in which forced under-consumption, witnessed in the stark form of starvation and death, followed by evictions, dispossessions, rural depopulation, depeasantisation and massive global migration, became the corollary of a growing English taste among the ruling class for beef consumption. As Rifkin (1992: 57) notes:

> the Irish food crisis only served to help the British ... Between 1846 and 1874 the number of cattle exported from Ireland to England more than doubled, from 202,000 to 555,800 head. By 1880 Ireland had been virtually transformed into a giant cattle pasture to accommodate the English palate.

India repeated the same experience; by the late nineteenth century it had become a major exporter of rice and wheat and, during the famine of 1881, it exported much of its surplus to England:

> Londoners were in effect eating India's bread. 'It seems an anomaly,' wrote a troubled observer, 'that, with her famines on hand, India is able to supply food for other parts of the world' ... Grain merchants, in fact, preferred to export a record 6.4

million cwt. of wheat to Europe in 1877–78 rather than relieve
starvation in India. (Davis 2001: 26–32)

In the settler colonies, the continued extermination of indigenous
populations and the seizure of extremely productive lands, along
with continuing plantation slavery (Tomich 1990; 2004) and
unpaid family labour, provided the consumption needs of urban
industrial capital, its workers, and urban consumers. In this way, an
increasingly globally organised system of forced under-consumption
lowered food costs, which in turn lowered the value of labour power
and enhanced the rate of surplus value. Peace and profit were, as a
result, maintained in Europe.

The agrarian welfare policy of the colonial period was thus
depeasantisation, proletarianisation and urbanisation at home, and
peasantisation, ruralisation and the super-exploitation of coerced
labour in the colonies. This was done by reorganising trade with the
colonies in accordance with the initial formation and solidification of
global value relations (Araghi 2003). Trade in luxuries, which had
characterised the first part of the long colonial period, thus gave way
to trade in agricultural commodities, which eradicated the need for
wage supports and non-market subsistence alternatives in the North,
and, in so doing, subsidised the reproductive needs of European
labour and capital (Mintz 1985). A global division of labour led,
as a direct consequence, to the emergence of a global food regime
(Friedmann and McMichael 1989) based on the international
integration of peasant and coerced labour and formally free urban
wage labour. However, the emergence of socialist movements at
home and global peasant and anti-colonialist movements in the
colonies on the one hand, and the rise of European nationalisms and
global warfare on the other, marked the political end of this from the
late nineteenth to the early twentieth centuries.

2. Developmentalism and the transformation of the agrarian welfare state

Two victories in two world historical revolutions during the
twentieth century – the Russian Revolution of 1917 and the
Vietnamese Revolution of 1975 – mark the beginning and the end
of what I term long national developmentalism. The first revolution,
along with the emergence of a powerful wave of peasant, nationalist

and anti-colonialist movements on the one hand, and inter-capitalist rivalry, militarism, war and the rise of an unmanageable fascist alternative on the other, forced a global reformist retreat on classical liberalism. The economic content of the retreat came from Keynesianism, in the form of an abandonment of *laissez faire* for a mixed economy model; the social and political content of this model adapted three innovations drawn from the Russian Revolution: the bureaucratic welfare state; the recognition of postcolonial peoples' nationalist and developmentalist aspirations and the acknowledgement of postcolonial peasantries as a political force; and the resulting necessity – if reluctantly and following a tortured path – of adopting an agrarian reform platform to accommodate the demands of revolutionary and/or nationalist peasantries. That this reformism, which at the same time formed the foundation of US hegemony in the three decades or so following World War II, was a practical retreat from colonial globalism can be seen in the dominant discourse of state officials, politicians and economists.

The origins of national developmentalism can be traced back to Wilsonian reformism, which was itself in part a response to socialist and fascist alternatives that were offered to the deepening crisis of colonial liberal globalism, a crisis that was demonstrated by imperial rivalry, nationalism, protectionism, the scramble for colonies, rebellions in those colonies, World War I, and the developing alliance between the socialist and the anti-colonialist movements. Thus, during the height of World War I, and indeed prior to the October Revolution, Woodrow Wilson sent his adviser and confidant Edward House to Europe to advocate a negotiated peace and a new post-war order. As House put it to the British:

> my plan is that if England, the United States, Germany and France will come to an understanding concerning investment by their citizens in underdeveloped countries, much good and profit will come to their citizens as well as to the countries needing development. (cited in Levin 1968: 24)

The October Revolution changed the course of events for the rest of the world. World historically, the emergence of the Soviet Union as the first major national developmental state facilitated the later rise of the welfare state in the West and later still the era of national developmental states in the Third World after the conclusion of World War II, when fascism was dead and colonialism was dying. Indeed, by participating in the war against fascism, colonial peoples had learned how to defeat colonialism itself. There followed a powerful wave of national liberation movements, leading to the final break-up of the old colonial blocs.

For the emerging postcolonial states, the economic content of political independence quickly came to be defined as inward-oriented, nationally based industrial growth, or what I call national developmentalism. However, in the Cold War context there were soon two distinguishable kinds of national developmentalism: socialist or state-led national developmentalism; and Western-oriented, market-led national developmentalism. Regarding the latter, while the New Dealers in the United States had a clear programme for the reconstruction of Europe and Japan in the aftermath of World War II, they were ambivalent about the place of postcolonial nationalisms in the emerging international order. In particular, unlike European colonialists in the era of colonial liberal globalism, US policy makers had yet to learn what to do with peasant societies in the expanding international economy.

Quite the reverse was true for the Soviet Union, which, based on its own revolutionary heritage, had a ready-made formula stipulating 'the correct attitude towards anticolonial nationalist movements' (Araghi 2009: 124). This formula was to link the national and colonial question with the peasant question by carrying anti-colonial and nationalist struggle into the countryside and actively supporting the demands of an insurgent peasantry. Indeed, it was clearly the success of this formula and the rapid expansion of state and socialist nationalisms that put the Third World and its development on the agenda of the United States. The urge to respond on the part of the United States came from the fact that the expansion of state and socialist nationalisms would have restricted the political and commercial space of the global free trade and free enterprise regime, the implementation of which was being sponsored by the United States. Ultranationalists – that is, state or socialist nationalists – had either to be contained by military force or to be incorporated by more peaceful, commercial and political, means.

Incorporation, however, meant that the United States had to compromise its internationalism with Third World nationalism; this

meant acknowledging the demands of Third World urban bourgeoisies and insurgent peasantries. The main components of this
compromise were embodied in the market-led national developmentalism promoted by the United States: import-substituting industrialisation policies and US-sponsored land reform programmes. The
first element was to promote a managed nationalism that recognised
the yearnings of the urban populations of the postcolonial nations for
modernity and national industrialisation; the second was to placate
their peasantries. As to the latter, after decades of peasant unrest
and mobilisation for socialist and nationalist revolutions in Asia and
Latin America, the United States developed its first programmatic
solution to the peasant question in the 1950s and 1960s.

That solution was land reform, American style. The development
of the American discourse on land reform is an interesting case of
what I have called 'discourse formation in world historical context'.
This discourse had four elements:

1. It emphatically expressed itself in individualistic and explicitly
   anti-communist terms.
2. In addition to these terms, in contained insistent ideological
   references to America's own past experience with family farming,
   as embodied in the free land movement and the 1862 Homestead
   Laws as its model.
3. However, it in fact borrowed its *raisons d'être* and content from
   Leninist agrarian programmes.
4. But, at the same time, it radically altered the political goal of those
   programmes.

The United States was able to borrow this Leninist formula because
national developmentalism, with the regime of colonial liberalism in
retreat, was, in relative terms, a regime of accommodation, in the
Gramscian sense of the concept (Gramsci 1971; Sassoon 1982). Land
reformism, as the emerging agrarian programme of the United States
in the Third World, was thus designed to placate postcolonial peasant
movements by accommodating their land hunger within a market-
led framework. As such, it turned the Leninist agrarian strategy on
its head: if the Leninist agrarian programme was intended to build
broad-based political alliances by linking the peasant question to the
national question, the purpose of US agrarian policy was precisely

the reverse – to demobilise Third World peasant movements and, more particularly, to unlink them from urban nationalist and/or socialist movements.

That this was the political impulse behind US Third World agrarian programmes can be seen from the discourse on land reform articulated by US policy makers in the 1950s and 1960s. Thus, as Dean Acheson (1951: 660) warned in 1951:

> [for] millions of people in the world, there is no more urgent problem than the impoverishment resulting from primitive methods of cultivation of the land under antiquated systems of landownership. Soviet propagandists have dangled promises of great change to those impoverished and hungry people, and to many, in such a state, it may have seemed that any change must be an improvement.

That same year a US representative to the Economic and Social Council of the United Nations said that 'land reform is important not only because of its potential effect on incentives to production. It has a far larger significance. It can mean the difference between explosive tensions and stability' (Lubin 1951: 468). This was reinforced by views such as those of Lester Mallory, the Deputy Assistant Secretary for Inter-American Affairs, who stressed that 'land reforms ... will arm its millions of subsistence farmers, tenants, and squatters against the blandishments of communism by giving them pride of possession and the kind of incentive that every human being has a right to have' (Mallory 1960: 821). Indeed, the importance of land reform as an American global political imperative was captured earlier in Acheson's (1952: 202) comment before the Food and Agriculture Organization (FAO) of the United Nations: '[T]he subject of land reform ... is a matter which we in the Department of State have believed is absolutely foremost in our whole international relations.'

The Cuban Revolution spurred the assimilation of agrarian reformism into the discourse of 'development compromise'. As Carl Rowan, the Deputy Assistant Secretary for Public Affairs, affirmed in 1962: 'It would have been nice if the United States and the Latin American leaders had found before now the coincidence of events and vision to which we have now come. *Unfortunately, however, the*

example of Cuba was needed first' (Rowan 1962: 379, emphasis added).
Lester Mallory illustrates my point. As he noted in 1960:

> This issue of 'land reform' or 'agrarian reform,' about which
> we have heard so much … is unquestionably one of the
> most burning issues in the world today and is at the heart
> of revolutionary movements in the Orient, the Middle East,
> and Latin America. The Communists' championship of
> the 'land reform' movement has tended to give the term a
> vaguely communistic connotation. This circumstance has been
> exploited by the enemies of the movement, particularly the great
> landholders abroad who have for centuries resisted any reduction
> in their privileged status and are deaf to all arguments that
> they stand to lose everything, soon, if they do not cooperate in
> promoting orderly reform. Too many of them ignore
> the proverb: 'For want of a nail a Kingdom was lost.' (Mallory
> 1960: 816)

Referring to the experience of Mexico, Edwin Martin, the Assistant
Secretary for Inter-American Affairs, observed:

> When the Mexican revolution began in 1910, land holdings in
> Mexico had become highly concentrated. An essentially feudal
> land system gave the Mexican farmer little stake in the political
> or economic life of the country. The aspirations of the people for
> land were not satisfied by peaceful evolutionary methods, and
> frustration gave way to revolution. The problem was not unlike
> that in several of the Latin American countries today and one
> which they must correct with constructive programmes if they
> are to avoid the costly experience of Mexico. (Martin 1963: 960)

Another US official added: 'We can look at Mexico today and
thank the Lord its revolution occurred and matured before Sino
Soviet imperialism had become militant and powerful' (Mallory
1960: 820).

Thus, by 1960, a year after the Cuban Revolution and the land
redistribution that followed, land reform had become such an
integrated component of US development discourse that John F.
Kennedy (1961) could argue that:

the leaders of Latin America, the industrialists and landowners are, I am sure, ready to admit past mistakes and accept new responsibilities. For unless all of us are willing to contribute our resources to national development, unless all of us are prepared not merely to accept, but initiate, basic land and tax reforms, unless all of us take the lead in improving the welfare of our people, then that leadership will be taken away from us and the heritage of centuries of Western civilization will be consumed in a few months of violence.

There were, then, two questions regarding US-led agrarian reformism as it spread in the 1960s: first, why land reform? As just argued, the answer came from the Leninist tradition, but with an American anti-communist twist. The second question was: land reform how? The answer to this came from persistent ideological references to US history. Ideologically, the creation of family-sized farms – as opposed to collectivisation – was seen as a way of creating a stable and highly conservative social base on which to construct US agrarian policy. Thus, Dean Acheson, in offering the United States Draft Resolution on Land Reform submitted to the United Nations Economic and Social Council, had noted that:

> the peasants of Eastern Europe, like the peasants of Russia, have learned that Soviet 'collectivisation,' or land reform imposed from the top, brings worse oppression than before … we have regarded our family-sized farms … being of fundamental importance to the prosperity and stability of the entire nation. Our democracy has its roots in a sound land policy. (Acheson 1951: 660)

As a result, the US concept of agrarian reform, according to the US Delegate to the FAO Conference on World Land Tenure Problems, was:

> based on the thought that men everywhere cherish that which is their own, and that there are few human instincts stronger than the desire of men and women to possess a little spot of earth which they can call their own. Farm and home ownership in any nation makes for stability of government. (Hope 1951: 999)

This was only in part because, as Oliver Freeman, the US Secretary of Agriculture, later noted, 'efficiency and progress is stimulated by individual ownership and personal incentive' (Freeman 1964: 387). It was more fundamentally tied to the relationship between land ownership and the character of political regimes emphasised by both Acheson and Hope: as Charles Brennan, another US Secretary of Agriculture, put it: '[The] American pattern of family farming has long been accepted as one of the basic strengths of our democracy … The love of freedom is deeply rooted in the family farm … This love of freedom is the real backbone of democracy' (Brennan 1951: I–V).

Leaving rhetorical references to freedom, democracy, efficiency and family farming to one side, the ideological and political impulse behind US Third World agrarian programmes can easily be inferred from the land reforms that the American military government implemented immediately following World War II in Japan, and thereafter in South Korea and Taiwan. These reforms were a direct response to powerful peasant movements and communist-inspired tenant unions, and were explicitly designed to undercut the political and ideological orientation of these movements. Cumulatively, the reforms reduced tenancy in Japan from 49 per cent in 1945 to 9 per cent in 1950, with peasant land ownership increasing from 31 per cent to 70 per cent during the same period (Ogura 1968: 17). In Taiwan, between 1948 and 1959, tenancy decreased from 36 per cent to 14 per cent while peasant ownership increased from 33 per cent to 59 per cent (Chen 1961: 312). In South Korea, peasant ownership increased from 14 per cent in 1945 to 70 per cent in 1965 while tenancy reduced from 49 per cent to 7 per cent (Morrow and Sherper 1970: 38–41).

In a similar fashion, land reforms were carried out in Germany and Italy, with the same objective: to prevent the growth of communist tendencies. Southern Italy in particular was the scene of demonstrations, strikes and land occupation in the early post-war period (Tarrow 1967). Thus, in Sicily, Calabria and Lazio between 1944 and 1949, peasant cooperatives with a total membership of a quarter of a million took over more than 165,000 hectares of land, displacing the former owners of that land (Ginsborg 1984: 94).

While the consequences of the many land distribution programmes in the Third World that were implemented under national developmentalism differed according to local geographies, ecologies, the kind of crops cultivated, prior political histories, existing land tenure systems, strength of the landholding classes, geopolitics and the local balance of forces, they had far-reaching impacts for the future of Third World peasantries. In general, land reforms of this era successfully transformed extant landlord–peasant relations that were based on various historical forms of direct domination and led to a proliferation of near-subsistence family-sized farm units, some of which were capable of accumulation. Thus, as Llambi (1989) and Katzmann (1978) have shown, in some regions – such as northern Ecuador, the Argentine Pampas, southern Brazil, western Venezuela and northern India – the reforms, when combined with privileged access to credit and marketing (Edelman 1980) or labour markets (Lehmann 1982), led to the emergence of capital-accumulating family farms producing overwhelmingly for the market and worked by owners with some hired labour.

However, this occurred in only a minority of cases. The majority of near-subsistence family-sized farm units were petty commodity producers and depended heavily for their production and subsistence needs on state subsidies. Indeed, even where land was available, the reforms in general left most of the productive land in the possession of large owners. In Latin America, for example, the number of family farms with an average of about 2 hectares increased by 92 per cent between 1950 and 1980. However, in 1980, 20 per cent of large commercial holders continued to occupy 80 per cent of the land area, while about 80 per cent of petty landowners occupied a mere 20 per cent of the cultivated area (de Janvry et al. 1989).

In sum, the political and ideological character of land reforms during the national developmentalist era led to the creation of masses of potentially mobile peasantries. Ironically, a global agrarian programme that, in Stolypin's fashion, had sought to create a class of peasant proprietors as a stable social base for the postcolonial states *ipso facto* created the conditions for a process of depeasantisation on a world scale. In this connection, two important dynamics should be noted. First, state credit and subsidies promoted the expansion of monetised and commodity relations into the countryside and increasingly exposed the emerging small farms to market forces. Second, while formally nation state-based divisions of labour and national home markets were promoted as a way of accommodating the demands of the postcolonial bourgeoisies in the Third World, the emerging world market and global division of labour substantively undercut and derailed home market formation and nation-based divisions of labour.

The politics of world market formation in this period are brilliantly captured by Harriet Friedmann's (1982) historical analysis of the post-war international food order between 1945 and 1972. Sponsored by the United States to dispose of its mounting grain surpluses as food aid or concessional sales, the post-war food order depressed world prices of grain and encouraged Third World food imports and indeed food import dependency. As Oliver Freeman, the aforementioned US Secretary of Agriculture, put it in 1964:

> American agriculture is proportionally more concerned with expanding exports than is American industry. Production from one acre out of every four harvested in 1963 was exported. Our agricultural exports have been increasing rapidly in recent years. In the 1963–64 fiscal year US agricultural exports reached a new record high level of $6.1 billion – $1 billion larger than the previous year. All of this increase was in commercial sales for dollars. In the year just ended our exports were 35 percent larger than in 1959. (Freeman 1964: 384–5)

Between 1950 and 1970, the US share of world exports had increased by 90 per cent for soya beans, 50 per cent for maize and 35 per cent for wheat (Tubiana 1989: 25). As American diets were adopted on a world scale, local food production declined in Latin America, Asia, the Middle East and Africa, and, by the early 1970s, Asia and Latin America, formerly surplus-producing regions, became dependent on food imports. In the Third World as a whole, the ratio of food imports to food exports increased from 50 per cent in the period between 1955 and 1960 to 80 per cent in 1980 (Manfredi 1978: 16). In other words, the reorganisation of world agriculture to the advantage of American farmers contradicted the political rhetoric that stressed balanced national development and expanding petty capitalist ownership in the Third World countryside.

The global food order in the post-war period should be seen not only as a response to farm politics in the United States (Friedmann 1982) but also as a way of containing socialist nationalisms of the time (Cleaver 1977; Wallerstein 1981; Dowie 2001; Ross 1998). Thus, the public financing of US agricultural exports as food aid was motivated by the ongoing politics of the reformist accommodation of the period rather than by the narrow economics of mercantilist capital accumulation. Indeed, even though in practice the Green Revolution led to increased technological and input dependency, and even though in practice food aid led to depeasantisation and food dependency in the Third World, both programmes were ideologically reformist components of national developmentalism.

Increased food import dependence spatially reconfigured populations in the Third World. Thus, between 1960 and 1980 in all regions of the South, both the rural population as a percentage of the total population and the agricultural labour force as a percentage of the total labour force declined significantly (World Bank 1984; UN 1980; ECLAC 1988). As independence became synonymous with modernisation, and the latter was equated to urban industrialisation, postcolonial national developmentalist states welcomed the availability of cheap food in the form of food aid or credit-financed concessional food sales such as US Public Law 480, with attendant low interest rates and long repayment periods. The resulting poverty among the new small landowners, who were now free from bondage, combined with the postcolonial state's urban bias in terms of state resource allocations (Lipton 1974), led to a substantial draining of rural population growth through out-migration. Thus, the number of Third World rural migrants increased by 230 per cent between 1950 and 1975 compared with the previous twenty-five years (World Bank 1984; UN 1980; ECLAC 1988).

Hence, Third World peasantries were being located in national markets and at the same time as they were being exposed, through cheap food imports, to world market competition with capitalised and heavily subsidised farms in the North. Nation-based peasantisation and global depeasantisation thus expressed the contradictions of national developmentalism and the post-war national developmentalist compromise.

To relate this to the debate between the advocates of the permanence versus the disappearance of the peasantry, it is apparent from a close examination of the national developmentalist period that peasantisation and depeasantisation are neither unilinear nor mutually exclusive national processes. Both the metaphysical 'peasants for ever' theses and the teleological or functional theses on the 'destiny' or function of the peasantries within capitalism thus miss Marx's methodological caveat that 'the concrete is concrete because it is the concentration of many determinations, hence unity of the diverse' (Marx 1973: 100; cf. Araghi and McMichael 2002; 2006). As a world historically concrete account of peasantries under national developmentalism, analysed as a historical regime of political capitalism, this analysis offers an alternative conclusion: that peasant dispossession in the form of nation-based rural class differentiation in this period occurred at a sluggish rate and in the end was subordinated to peasant dispossession via urban displacement.

Therefore, if we redefine the nation state-based demographic concepts of push and pull migration factors (Harris and Todaro 1970) from a global perspective as global push factors – derived from the post-war food order, food aid and dumping – and global pull factors – from the postcolonial equation of national independence with industrialisation and urbanisation – it was the historical mix of both that explains what I call relative depeasantisation, which was a defining character of global dispossession under national developmentalism. The relative depeasantisation witnessed in the period between the 1950s and the 1970s was a reflection of simultaneous peasantisation and depeasantisation processes and the relative protection of national agricultures through subsidies, price supports and state financing of agricultural inputs, which slowed down the rate at which millions of newly created small peasant landowners were exposed to global push factors. Hence, if we define the rate of de-ruralisation[2] as the contribution of rural out-migration to rural population decline, it appears that all developing countries for which data are available experienced accelerating declines in their rural populations due to net rural out-migration (UN 1980). In Latin America and in the Middle East, this decline was by more than 50 per cent (ibid.). While *relative depeasantisation* was indeed a defining character of global dispossession under national developmentalism between the 1950s and the 1970s, as we will see in the next section, it can be distinguished from the absolute depeasantisation that defines the historical character of global dispossession in the late twentieth century and beyond under postcolonial neoliberal globalism.

3. Globalisation and the privatisation of the agrarian welfare state

By the early 1970s, a major systemic crisis had been created by the contradictions of national developmentalism, and in particular demands for more independence and control over national resources by the South under the aegis of structuralism, and the contradictions of a Keynesian accommodation of northern working classes through full employment policies that, as a result, generated significant wage inflation, combined with global competitive pressures, a profit squeeze, stagflation, and the North's inability to either suppress or accommodate the South (Armstrong et al. 1991). Neither Keynesianism at home nor national developmentalism abroad seemed compatible with the requirements of capital accumulation, and hence capital withdrew from both reformist social compacts. The *retreat from development* was a component of a systemic counteroffensive that emerged in the 1970s and 1980s and sought to reverse the protection of society from the market (cf. Polanyi 2001). As this project evolved, it came to include the following features:

- withdrawal from the post-war Keynesian social compact with labour in the North through flexibilisation, casualisation, deproletarianisation and the spatial mobility of capital (Araghi 2009; 2010a);
- withdrawal from the agrarian welfare state, with a resulting deepening of depeasantisation;
- dismantling of nation state-based agricultural versus industrial divisions of labour that had come to symbolise independence and nationhood for postcolonial states as the socio-economic content of national developmentalism (Araghi 2000);
- reconstruction of global value relations (Araghi 2003) that had been undercut during the period of national developmentalism to accommodate the project of home market construction;
- dismantling of the post-war aid-based food order as a component of the agrarian welfare state (Araghi 2007);
- reconstruction of a global food regime modelled on the colonial liberal food regime of the late nineteenth century where the British workshop of the world is replaced by consumption hubs in the North; and

- socialisation of finance as a means of subsidising aggregate demand and the deployment of a global debt regime as a means of restructuring the world's division of labour (Araghi 2010b).

From an instrumental point of view, the last component – the creation of the debt regime – was central to the counteroffensive strategy of reshaping the world's many home markets to fit the needs of an emergent world market. Without it, the only alternative was a strategy of militarisation and a reversion to the colonial liberal globalism of the late nineteenth century. That this was unthinkable in the post-Vietnam era was a point well understood by Robert McNamara, who, as the Secretary of Defense between 1961 and 1968, was responsible for the massive, but in the end ineffective, use of military violence during Vietnam's war for national unification. Thus, McNamara's strategy during his long World Bank presidency between 1968 and 1981 was dubbed by Bank staff as 'pushing money out the door' (George and Sabelli 1994); during his presidency the Bank's lending increased thirteen-fold, from $953 million in 1968 to $12.4 billion in 1981, and, in a sense, debt became the continuation of war by other means. Commercial banks followed suit as their petrodollar lending to the South increased by 4,400 per cent between 1972 and 1981 (ibid.). It was thus in this era that policy lending under the rubric of rural development and poverty reduction paved the way for the rise of an agro-industrial export model.

The bestowal of the Nobel Prize in Economic Sciences on Friedrich Hayek in 1974 and on Milton Friedman in 1976 presaged the coming of the neoliberal age, and with it postcolonial neoliberal globalism. With détente, the communist 'threat' was relaxed for the moment in order to deal with more serious threats of internal wage inflation and the external unruliness of postcolonial nationalisms. There then followed major realignments in established political parties, and, in particular in the United Kingdom and the United States, the creation of new institutions such as the Trilateral Commission, the World Economic Forum and the G7, and the activation of existing interstate institutions such as the World Bank and the International Monetary Fund (IMF) in the service of a programmatic withdrawal from national developmentalism, Keynesianism and public welfare institutions.

As part of this process of realignment, the political use of food as a coercive way of dealing with the Third World was developed by senior figures in the Nixon administration. Of course, food aid had always had a broadly defined political dimension, as demonstrated by the Egyptian experience under Nasser in 1966 (Dethier and Funk 1978) and the US withholding food aid from Bangladesh at the height of the 1974 famine until the newly born state abandoned plans to try Pakistani war criminals (Sharma 2002). From 1973 onwards, however, food in the service of national developmentalism clearly gave way to commercial and subsidised exports as a mechanism for dismantling nation state-based divisions of labour in the Third World. In this light, it is not surprising that as early as 1974 commercial food exports by the US had increased to $20 billion, while food aid shipments had declined to $1 billion (Rosenfeld 1974: 21; Hopkins 1984). Moreover, between 1973 and 1986, the European Community matched the commercial, export-oriented and nationally protectionist policies of the US; thus, a food regime that managed the disposal of food surpluses in a manner that was divorced from price regulation gave way to the need for markets for commercial agrarian dumping. As a direct consequence, between 1980 and 1987, the rate of increase in agricultural production in the United States and Europe taken together exceeded the rate of increase in domestic consumer demand by 100 per cent (Watkins 1991; Srinivasan 1989: 40). The contradictions of this 'structural overproduction' (Watkins 1991), due in no small measure to the use of export subsidies, was, at least in part, the impetus behind the transformation of the General Agreement on Tariffs and Trade (GATT) into the World Trade Organization (WTO), as we will see.

The 'new' free market economics, or what we may call the second *laissez faire*, while fiercely anti-institutionalist in rhetoric, in fact actively developed its own interventionist institutions. Thus, by the late 1980s, the latter were enforcing a comprehensive set of anti-reformist economic policies that came to be known as the Washington Consensus, and which included the following elements: the privatisation of the state and state functions, and hence the privatisation of the public sphere; the privatisation of welfare and law and a vast expansion of the legal dominion of property rights, tax reform and upward income redistribution; the deregulation of labour markets and deproletarianisation policies; trade and market liberalisation; and currency devaluations. Hence, while national developmentalism was characterised by mixed economies and the formal subsumption of labour to capital, both colonial liberal globalism and postcolonial neoliberal globalism were characterised by attempts to construct a global division of labour based on the real subsumption of labour to capital.

The privatisation of the agrarian welfare state to the advantage of northern transnational agribusinesses and capitalist farms forms the context in which the relative depeasantisation and displacement of the post-war period gave way to absolute depeasantisation and displacement under postcolonial neoliberal globalism. It was in this period that the 'invisible hand' of the debt regime – standing at $2.5 trillion at the beginning of the 1980s – functioned as the 'visible foot' of the global enclosures of our times. The policy lending of the McNamara era evolved into debt-enforced structural adjustment in the global agrarian sector, leading to:

- the deregulation of land markets and the reversal of land reform policies originating in the national developmentalist era;
- drastic cuts in farm subsidies and price supports and the disengagement of both postcolonial states and the World Bank from irrigation support;
- the expanded use of agrarian biotechnologies and the expanded commodification of seeds and seed reproduction;
- a marked, and growing, dependence on chemical, biological and hydrocarbon farm inputs; and
- the promotion of agro-exports at the expense of food crops through an expansion of livestock agro-exports, expanded cash crop production for export as animal feed, and the export of niche luxury foods, fresh fruits, vegetables and ornamental flowers for the global centres of overconsumption.

The power relations that guided the subsumption of formerly protected home markets by the world market created a world division of labour marked by unmediated exchange relations. These types of exchange relations brought together formally equal but substantively unequal participants, thereby forcing millions of petty producers in the South to compete with heavily subsidised agro-industrial food transnational corporations (TNCs) in the

North (McMichael 2008). The inability to compete led in turn to massive peasant dispossessions by displacement. Thus, the global enclosures of postcolonial neoliberal globalism, which are similar to the enclosures of colonial liberal globalism, have led to the creation of a massive reserve army of migratory labour.

I distinguish between two forms of this reserve army: the actual and the potential reserve armies of migratory labour. This distinction is based on the theoretical difference between ownership of the means of production and ownership of the means of subsistence. The distinction is relevant to historical conditions under which peasant differentiation through capital accumulation in national countryside are subordinated to processes of global urban capital accumulation and corporate agro-food capital accumulation. More specifically, the sluggish rate of peasant differentiation in national countryside has led to the creation of masses of semi-dispossessed peasantries; that is, those who have lost their non-market access to their means of subsistence but still hold formal and/or legal ownership to some of their means of production. While corporate capital and its chain of subcontractors appropriate their surplus labour via the provision of credit, seeds and other inputs, and market access, it leaves the labour process and partial ownership of the means of production in the hands of the direct producers. As I develop the argument elsewhere (Araghi 2003), this is a form of production of absolute surplus value by commodity-producing labour power. Hence, while the loss of ownership of the means of production is simultaneously the loss of non-market access to the means of subsistence, the reverse is not always the case within the historical context under consideration. Partially dispossessed peasantries of the South today are part of the potentially or partially mobile reserve army of migratory labour. The latter comprises a major proportion of the world slum population, which is currently estimated at 1 billion (UN 2003), and a concrete analysis of their conditions, needs and demands is crucial for understanding the emerging mass movements of resistance among the peasantries of the South.

The agrarian programme of capital in the era of postcolonial neoliberal globalism has thus intensified depeasantisation via displacement across the global space. In other words, if simultaneous peasantisation and depeasantisation were the distinguishing

characteristics of the agrarian programme of national developmentalism, simultaneous depeasantisation and deproletarianisation are the
defining features of the agrarian programme of postcolonial neoliberal globalism. However, in order to understand the profound consequences of postcolonial neoliberal globalism's agrarian programme
for the world's peasantries in the present period, it is necessary to
consider the transformation of the food regime of the post-war era
into what I will call the 'enclosure food regime' (cf. McMichael 2005;
Friedmann 2005; Pechlaner and Otero 2010).

I use the concept of an enclosure food regime to emphasise the
exclusionist and violent character of the agrarian programme of
postcolonial neoliberal globalism. This programme has the double
aim of:

1. finally dismantling postcolonial nation-based divisions of labour
   that were at the core of national developmentalism; and
2. reorganising world production and exchange relations on the basis
   of global value relations.

The enclosure food regime of our times is a historical form of
the food regime of capital, the emergence of which marks a radical
departure from the reformist-based food order of the era of national
developmentalism. Theoretically, the construction of truly global
value relations requires the construction of a global division of
labour at the expense of home markets, national divisions of labour
and national food security. In this sense, the post-war food regime
represented a political retreat from colonial liberal globalism's project
of constructing value relations on a global basis. The enclosure food
regime, as the agrarian programme of a re-energised reglobalising
capital, represents a reversal of the suspension of global value
relations, with drastic consequences for the large number of agrarian
direct producers who become redundant on a daily basis, and who
are thrown out of collapsing national divisions of labour into the
vortex of globalisation as masses of surplus labour in motion.

Thus, the specific character of the enclosure food regime is the
enclosure of the spaces of existence of the world's peasantries. As
a spatial regime of dispossession, it devours national agricultures,
land and means of subsistence, and frees labour power for global
consumption. Key to this project was the transformation of the

GATT into the WTO and the latter's enforcement of the Agreement on Agriculture that had been negotiated by the former. It is not in a figurative sense that I characterise the Agreement on Agriculture as the agrarian programme of capital in the era of postcolonial neoliberal globalism: Daniel Amstutz, a former chief executive officer of the futures trading and commodities division at Cargill, the world's largest global grain trading company, was the US Chief Negotiator for Agriculture and led the negotiations in the Uruguay Round, thus playing a critical role in drafting the Agreement on Agriculture (Ritchie 1993). Following completion of the negotiations, he returned to Cargill, and later was charged with drafting food and agricultural policies for the Iraqi Constitution (Choudry 2006: 3).

At its core, the Agreement on Agriculture was an agreement between the United States and Europe to resolve their overproduction crisis by expanding the space of commercial dumping in the South. This required:

1. an international legal framework for the purpose of eradicating the legacies of national developmentalism, most particularly nation-based divisions of labour; and
2. a discursive system that delegitimised agrarian nationalism and, in its place, rationalised the commodification of food security.

However, there is a central contradiction here. As noted presciently by Kevin Watkins (1991: 40) in his early critique of the GATT Uruguay Round, doing away with formal and informal export subsidies in the US and the European Union has not been on the agenda; the 2007 US Farm Bill makes this quite clear. The invisible hand is not going to supplant the visible foot; it cannot, as it would be tantamount to a major transfer of payments and differential advantage from the North to the South. In addition, it would result in a massive reduction in the size of the mobile surplus labour population, which, as undocumented and under-reproduced labour power, serves as the basis for metropolitan agricultures. Thus, in the United States and Europe, agro-food TNCs are the primary recipients of depeasantised Southern migrant labour, who are now increasingly living in enclosed forced – and indeed slave – labour camps in the heartlands of metropolitan agriculture (Brass 1999).[3]

Indeed, what a *New York Times* editorial in 2003 called 'hypocrisy' and 'the one way street of globalization' are in fact systemic aspects of the agrarian programme of capital under the enclosure food regime. Subsidies to agriculture by the Organisation for Economic Co-operation and Development (OECD) member states increased by 65 per cent between 1995 and 2005, and the total amount of subsidies (what the OECD calls producer support estimates, or PSEs) in the US, the EU and Japan came to a total of $192 billion in 2014, of which $106 billion were expended in the twenty-eight EU countries, $44 billion in Japan and $41 billion in the US.[4] Moreover, these subsidies are notable in that they are so inequitably distributed: the top 10 per cent of recipients receive more than 70 per cent of all farm subsidies, with allocations going to agro-food TNCs (Environmental Working Group's Farm Subsidy Database). This can be contrasted with the situation facing the marginalised surplus labour population: according to Green and Griffith (2002), 3 billion of the world's poor earn less than the subsidies received by the average dairy cow in the European Union, which amounts to $2.20 per day.

Accounts of agricultural subsidies often focus attention on the direct corporate recipients and the costs to taxpayers. However, it is important to note that, from a value theory viewpoint, the subsidisation of agro-food capital functions to:

1. overproduce food commodities and drive down the price of domestic food and wage costs, thereby benefiting not only the direct corporate agro-food recipients of subsidies but also all fractions of capital;
2. subsidise overconsumption in the North;
3. depress the price of food commodities in the world market to the advantage of urban consumers and all fractions of non-agrarian capital in the South;
4. rapidly and massively displace agrarian petty commodity producers;
5. forcibly deflate wages through coerced under-consumption, the under-reproduction of labour, and deproletarianisation strategies; and
6. vastly expand a globally mobile population of agricultural refugees.

Thus, from a value theory viewpoint, the subsidisation of agro-food capital is wholly consistent with the solidification of a global food regime of capital that deepens value relations on a world scale.

4. Conclusion

'Agrarian development in reverse' has been a core component of neoliberal globalisation. With respect to land rights, this period has witnessed a vast expansion of corporate land rights at the expense of small and partial landholder remnants of the developmentalist era on the one hand and the rise of powerful 'counter-enclosure' movements on the other. Specifically, with the privatisation of agrarian welfare states that operated to the advantage of transnational agribusiness and capitalist farms, the relative abrogation of public land rights and the displacement of the post-war era have been followed by aggressive global enclosures and a massive contraction of land rights for the world's agrarian populations, as well as absolute depeasantisation on a world scale (Araghi 2009; 2010a). Especially since the financial crisis of 2007 (Araghi 2008; 2010b), a 'food bubble' has been forming that is partly substituting the collapsed 'housing bubble'. Currently, a global land grab, unprecedented since colonial times, is underway as speculative investors – who now regard 'food as gold' (Henriques 2008) – are acquiring millions of hectares of land through purchases in the global South, often involving the eviction of local producers and forced expropriations under the rubric of confronting the global food and energy crises (McMichael 2010; 2011). According to the latest Oxfam study:

> In developing countries, as many as 227 million hectares of land
> – *an area the size of Western Europe* – has been sold or leased since
> 2001, mostly to international investors. The bulk of these land
> acquisitions has taken place over the past two years, according
> to on-going research by the Land Matrix Partnership. (Oxfam
> 2011, emphasis added)

According to a former World Bank official, the number of dispossessed and displaced peasants in India who will 'migrate from rural to urban India by the year 2015 is expected to be equal to twice the combined population of UK, France, and Germany' (Sharma 2007). The Indian state is using the Land Acquisition Act of 1894 to acquire land for 500 planned special economic zones: 125,000 hectares of agricultural land are being enclosed in the first stage of these clearances, with about the same amount to be acquired in the second stage. Here, then, de-ruralisation means the state-sponsored substitution of rural space with enclosed economic zones. The scale and pace of change in farmer bankruptcies and peasant dispossession led to a 52 per cent increase in the rate of farmer suicide in four major states between 1997 and 2005, compared with a 23 per cent increase among the non-farmers. Sainath (2007) thus notes that these states 'might be termed ... Special Elimination Zone[s] for farmers this past decade'.

In Mexico, the privatisation of development and its historical welfare state took the form of privatisation of the *ejido* following the signing of the North American Free Trade Agreement[5] (Barros Nock 2000; Akram-Lodhi 2007: 1446). According to an analysis by Oxfam (2003), the threefold increase in US maize exports since the early 1990s has led to a 70 per cent fall in the price of domestically produced maize. Particularly affected are 3 million peasant maize producers. Nearly 50 per cent of the Mexican rural population, and fully 70 per cent of those living in the maize-producing states of Chiapas, Oaxaca and Guerrero, now live in extreme poverty. As a result, many leave their villages to urban centres, or, of course, to the US – every year at least 300,000 displaced Mexicans migrate to the United States.

I use these examples not to show a uniform experience or the destiny of the millions of poor people and semi-migrants who have emerged as a result of the privatisation of development and its welfare state. In fact, the era of 'de-globalisation' (1917–73) has important lessons for our times: it showed that global social movements in fact imposed severe limitations on unbounded capital accumulation and successfully forced into retreat the agrarian programme of colonial liberal globalism for six decades. Neoliberal globalism is a *de*socialising project, and this is its Achilles heel.

Notes

1 For an interesting historical account of the rise of the welfare state in connection with social movements, labour unions and political reformism, see Hicks (1999).

2 Thus, as data indicate (UN 2004), the percentage change in the world urban population was about two times higher than the percentage change in the total world population. Between

1950 and 2003, the urban population in the less developed regions grew by a staggering 593 per cent. Similarly, while the growth rate of the urban population in more developed regions was 28.6 per cent between 1975 and 2003, the corresponding figure in the less developed regions was 65 per cent during the same period. Since urbanisation is always followed by lower rates of natural population growth, these data indicate a *shift in the structure of population* from rural to urban (i.e. de-ruralisation as a result of both rural to urban migration and the transformation of rural settlements into urban places). Accordingly, between 1975 and 2000, the rate of urbanisation was 4.3 times faster in less developed regions compared with more developed regions. Despite a reduction in birth rates in most areas, especially in urban areas, the less developed regions have experienced high rates of urban population growth as a result of rural to urban population transfers. In other words, the urban areas of the less developed world have increasingly absorbed most of the growth in total world population as well as most of the population growth in urban areas worldwide.

Thus, between 1995 and 2000, the urban areas of the less developed regions were absorbing 92 per cent of the annual increment of the world urban population (ibid.). Similarly, between 2000 and 2005, 76 per cent of the total population increase in the world was due to growth in the urban population in less developed regions. The trend towards global de-ruralisation can be seen in the 15 per cent *decline* in the rural population of the less developed regions between 1975 and 2003.

3
[M]odern day slavery around the world is ongoing and systematic,

including within the United States. In Florida, significant numbers of workers are in slavery and/or forced labour at any given moment within the agriculture industry. Indeed, in the last decade there have been six successful federal government criminal prosecutions in Florida for forced labour and slavery resulting in up to 15 year prison terms and the freeing [of] over 1000 workers ... Forced labour and slavery are driven by the economic and legal context in which farm workers find themselves. These violations are enabled by 1) discriminatory and inadequate labour laws; 2) failure to ensure basic economic and social rights; and 3) economic structures enabling slavery through concentrated buying power, which has driven down wages and fuelled inhumane working conditions ... Farm workers are among the poorest labourers in the United States economy ... Undocumented workers earn less than half [that of farm workers with legal status]. (NESRI 2005; see also Maxwell 2002; the International Labour Organization (ILO) also published on this subject in 2001)

A 2007 report by the ILO specifically explores the linkages between globalisation, migration, labour market deregulation and forced labour. In the last decade there were at least 2.45 million persons in forced labour, and their numbers have been increasing (ILO 2007).

4 See *OECD.STAT* at http://stats. oecd.org/viewhtml.aspx?QueryId=66824 &vh=0000&vf=0&l&il=&lang=en.

5 For a critical analysis of empirical studies with differing (and inadequate) definitions of poverty, which nonetheless all confirm the rise of poverty in Latin America in the 1980s, see Boltvinik (1996).

References

Acheson, D. (1951) 'Conference on world land tenure problems', *Department of State Bulletin* 25: 660–4.

— (1952) 'Statement by Secretary Acheson before FAO meeting at Rome', *Department of State Bulletin* 26: 200–2.

Akram-Lodhi, H. (2007) 'Land, markets and neoliberal enclosure: an agrarian political economy', *Third World Quarterly* 28: 1437–56.

Araghi, F. (2000) 'The great global enclosure of our times: peasants and the agrarian question at the end of the twentieth century' in F. Magdoff, H. Buttel and J. B. Foster (eds), *Hungry for Profit: The agribusiness threat to farmers, food, and the environment*. New York NY: Monthly Review Press.

— (2003) 'Food regimes and the production of value: some methodological issues', *Journal of Peasant Studies* 30: 41–70.

— (2007) 'Food regimes in longue durée'. Paper presented at the Joint Annual Meetings of the Agriculture, Food and Human Values Society and the Association for the Study of Food and Society, University of Victoria, Victoria, British Columbia, 30 May – 3 June.

— (2008) 'Political economy of the financial crisis: a world-historical perspective', *Economic & Political Weekly* 43 (45): 30–2.

— (2009) 'The invisible hand and the visible foot: peasants, dispossession and globalisation' in A. H. Akram-Lodhi and C. Kay (eds), *Peasants and Globalisation: Political economy, rural transformation and the agrarian question*. New York NY: Routledge.

— (2010a) 'Accumulation by displacement: global enclosures, food crisis, the ecological contradictions of capitalism', *Review: A Journal of the Fernand Braudel Center* 34 (1): 113–46.

— (2010b) 'The end of "cheap ecology" and the crisis of "long Keynesianism"', *Economic & Political Weekly* 44 (4): 39–41.

Araghi, F. and P. McMichael (2002) 'Contextualizing (post)modernity: a world-historical perspective'. Unpublished manuscript.

— (2006) 'Trayendo lo histórico mundial de regreso: crítica del retroceso postmoderno en los estudios agrarios', *Revista ALASRU* [Asociación Latinoamericana de Sociología Rural] 3: 2–38.

Armstrong, P., A. Glyn and J. Harrison (1991) *Capitalism since 1945*. Oxford: Basil Blackwell.

Barros Nock, M. (2000) 'The Mexican peasantry and the *ejido* in the neo-liberal period' in D. F. Bryceson, C. Kay and J. E. Mooij (eds), *Disappearing Peasantries? Rural labour in Africa, Asia and Latin America*. London: Intermediate Technology Publications.

Boltvinik, J. (1996) 'Poverty in Latin America: a critical analysis of three studies', *International Social Science Journal* 48: 245–60.

Brass, T. (1999) *Towards a Comparative Political Economy of Unfree Labour: Case studies and debates*. London and Portland OR: Frank Cass Publishers.

Brennan, C. F. (1951) 'Preserving the family farm', *Family Farm Policy Review*, 11 June.

Chen, C. (1961) *Land Reform in Taiwan*. Taipei: China Publishing Company.

Choudry, A. (2006) 'Bilateral free trade and investment agreements and the US corporate biotech agenda' in *Special Release: A publication of Pesticide Action Network Asia Pacific*

(PANAP) and People's Coalition on Food Sovereignty (PCFS). Penang, Malaysia: Pesticide Action Network Asia and the Pacific. Available at www.foodsov.org.

Cleaver, H. (1977) 'Food, famine and the international crisis', *Zerowork* 2: 1–47.

Davis, M. (2001) *Late Victorian Holocausts: El Niño famines and the making of the Third World.* London: Verso.

de Janvry, A., E. Sadoulet and L. W. Young (1989) 'Land and labour in Latin American agriculture form the 1950s', *Journal of Peasant Studies* 16: 369–424.

Dethier, J. J. and K. Funk (1978) 'The language of food: PL 480 in Egypt', *Middle East Report* 145: 22–8.

Dowie, M. (2001) *American Foundations: An investigative history.* Cambridge MA: MIT Press.

ECLAC (1988) *Statistical Yearbook for Latin America.* New York NY: United Nations Economic Commission for Latin America and the Caribbean (ECLAC).

Edelman, M. (1980) 'Agricultural modernisation in smallholding areas of Mexico: a case study in the Sierra Norte de Puebla', *Latin American Perspectives* 27: 29–49.

Freeman, O. L. (1964) 'Improving the effectiveness of U.S. assistance to international rural development', *Department of State Bulletin* (14 September): 376–88.

Friedmann, H. (1982) 'The political economy of food: the rise and fall of the postwar international food order', *American Journal of Sociology* 88 (Supplement): S248–S286.

— (2005) 'From colonialism to green capitalism: social movements and emergence of food regimes' in F. H. Buttel and P. McMichael (eds), *New Directions in the Sociology of Global Development: Research in Rural Sociology and Development.* Volume 11. Oxford: Elsevier.

Friedmann, H. and P. McMichael (1989) 'Agriculture and the state system: the rise and fall of national agriculture, 1870 to the present', *Sociologia Ruralis* 29: 93–117.

George, S. and F. Sabelli (1994) *Faith and Credit: The World Bank's secular empire.* Boulder CO: Westview Press.

Ginsborg, P. (1984) 'The Communist Party and the agrarian question in southern Italy, 1943–48', *History Workshop Journal* 17 (1): 81–101.

Gramsci, A. (1971) *Selections from the Prison Notebooks of Antonio Gramsci.* Edited by Q. Hoare and G. Nowell-Smith. London: Lawrence & Wishart.

Green, D. and M. Griffith (2002) *Dumping on the Poor: The Common Agricultural Policy, the WTO and international development.* London: CAFOD. Available at www.iatp.org/files/Dumping_on_the_Poor_The_Common_Agricultural_Po.htm.

Harris, J. and M. Todaro (1970) 'Migration, unemployment & development: a two-sector analysis', *American Economic Review* 60: 126–42.

Henriques, D. (2008) 'Food is gold, so billions invested in farming', *New York Times,* 5 June.

Hicks, A. M. (1999) *Social Democracy and Welfare Capitalism: A century of income security politics.* Ithaca NY: Cornell University Press.

Hope, C. R. (1951) 'The U.S. concept of agrarian reform as a foundation for world peace', *Department of State Bulletin* 25: 988–1000.

Hopkins, R. (1984) 'The evolution of food aid', *Food Policy* 9: 345–63.

ILO (2007) *Eradication of forced labour.* Geneva: International Labour Office (ILO).

Katzmann, M. T. (1978) 'Colonisation as an approach to regional development: Northern Parana, Brazil', *Economic Development and Cultural Change* 26 (4): 709–24.

Kennedy, J. F. (1961) 'Address at a dinner at the San Carlos Palace in Bogota', *The American Presidency Project*. Available at www.presidency.ucsb.edu/ws/index.php?pid=8495.

Lehmann, D. (1982) 'Peasantisation and proletarianisation in Brazil and Mexico' in S. Jones et al. (eds), *Rural Poverty and Agrarian Reform*. New Delhi: Allied Publishers.

Levin, N. G. (1968) *Woodrow Wilson and World Politics: America's response to war and revolution*. New York NY: Oxford University Press.

Lipton, M. (1974) *Why Poor People Stay Poor: A study of urban bias in world development*. London: Temple Smith.

Llambi, L. (1989) 'Emergence of capitalised family farms in Latin America', *Comparative Studies in Society and History* 31: 745–74.

Lubin, I. (1951) 'Land reform problem challenges free world', *Department of State Bulletin* 25: 467–74.

Mallory, L. D. (1960) 'The land problem in the Americas', *Department of State Bulletin* (November 28): 815–22.

Manfredi, E. M. (1978) *World Economic Conditions in Relation to Agricultural Trade*. Washington DC: US Department of Agriculture.

Martin, E. M. (1963) 'The economic revolution in Mexico', *Department of State Bulletin* (23 December): 959–63.

Marx, K. (1973) *Grundrisse: Foundations of the critique of political economy*. New York NY: Vintage Books.

Maxwell, B. (2002) 'Slavery alive in Florida agriculture industry', *St. Petersburg Times*, 3 July.

McMichael, P. (2005) 'Global development and the corporate food regime' in F. H. Buttel and P. McMichael (eds), *New Directions in the Sociology of Global Development: Research in rural sociology and development*. Volume 11. Oxford: Elsevier.

— (2008) *Development and Social Change: A global perspective*. Thousand Oaks CA: Pine Forge Press.

— (2010) 'Agrofuels in the food regime', *Journal of Peasant Studies* 37 (4): 609–29.

— (2011) 'The food regime in the land grab: articulating "global ecology" and political economy'. Paper presented at the International Conference on Global Land Grabbing, University of Sussex, Brighton, 6–8 April.

— (2012) *Development and Social Change: A global perspective*. Thousand Oaks CA: Pine Forge Press.

Mintz, S. W. (1985) *Sweetness and Power: The place of sugar in modern history*. New York NY: Viking.

Morrow, R. B. and K. H. Sherper (1970) 'Land reform in South Korea', *US Department of State Spring Review of Land Reform* 3: 1–67.

NESRI (2005) 'Modern day slavery in U.S. agriculture: legal failure and corporate complicity'. New York NY: National Economic and Social Rights Initiative (NESRI). Available at www.nesri.org/resources/modern-day-slavery-in-us-agriculture-legal-failure-and-corporate-complicity.

Ogura, T. (1968) 'The economic impact of postwar land reform in Japan', *FAO Land Reform, Land Settlement and Cooperatives* 2: 14–43.

Oxfam (2003) *Dumping Without Borders: How US agricultural policies are destroying the livelihoods of Mexican corn farmers*. Oxfam Briefing Paper 50. Washington DC: Oxfam International. Available at http://policy-practice.oxfam.org.uk/publications/dumping-without-borders-how-us-agricultural-policies-are-destroying-the-livelih-114471.

— (2011) 'Land and power: the growing scandal surrounding the new wave of investments in land'. Oxfam Briefing Paper 151. Oxford: Oxfam GB for Oxfam International. Available at www.oxfam.org/en/research/land-and-power.

Pechlaner, G. and G. Otero (2010) 'The neoliberal food regime: neoregulation and the new division of labour in North America', *Rural Sociology* 75: 179–208.

Polanyi, K. (2001) *The Great Transformation: The political and economic origins of our time*. Boston MA: Beacon Press.

Rifkin, J. (1992) *Beyond Beef: The rise and fall of the cattle culture*. New York NY: Dutton.

Ritchie, M. (1993) 'Breaking the deadlock: the United States and agriculture policy in the Uruguay Round'. Institute for Agriculture and Trade Policy, 17 April. Available at www.iatp.org/files/Breaking_the_Deadlock_Agriculture_and_Environm.htm.

Rosenfeld, S. S. (1974) 'The politics of food', *Foreign Policy* 14: 17–29.

Ross, E. B. (1998) *The Malthus Factor: Population, poverty, and politics in capitalist development*. London: Zed Books.

Rowan, C. T. (1962) 'New directions in foreign policy', *Department of State Bulletin* (5 March): 378–81.

Sainath, P. (2007) 'Nearly 1.5 lakh farm suicides from 1997 to 2005', *The Hindu*, 12 November. Available at www.thehindu.com/todays-paper/nearly-15-lakh-farm-suicides-from-1997-to-2005/article1946744.ece.

Sassoon, A. S. (1982) *Approaches to Gramsci*. London: Writers and Readers Publishing Cooperative.

Sharma, D. (2002) 'Famine as commerce', *India Together*, August. Available at www.indiatogether.org/agriculture/opinions/dsharma/faminecommerce.htm.

— (2007) 'Displacing farmers: India will have 400 million agricultural refugees', Share the World's Resources, 22 June. Available at www.globalresearch.ca/displacing-farmers-india-will-have-400-million-agricultural-refugees/6127.

Srinivasan, T. N. (1989) 'Food aid: A cause of development failure or an instrument for success?', *World Bank Economic Review* 38: 39–65.

Tarrow, S. (1967) *Peasant Communism in Southern Italy*. New Haven CT: Yale University Press.

Tomich, D. W. (1990) *Slavery in the Circuit of Sugar: Martinique and the world economy,1830–1848*. Baltimore MD: Johns Hopkins University Press.

— (2004) *Through the Prism of Slavery: Labour, capital, and world economy*. Lanham MD: Rowman & Littlefield.

Tubiana, L. (1989) 'World trade in agricultural products: from global regulation to market fragmentation' in D. Goodman and M. Redclift (eds), *The International Farm Crisis*. London: Macmillan.

UN (1980) 'Pattern of urban and rural growth'. Population Studies no. 68. New York NY: United Nations (UN).

— (2003) *The Challenge of Slums: Global report on human settlements 2003*. New York NY: Earthscan Publications.

— (2004) *World Urbanisation Prospects: The 2003 revision*. New York NY: United Nations (UN).

Wallerstein, M. B. (1981) 'Food for war – food for peace: United States food aid in a global context', *American Political Science Review* 75: 787–8.

Watkins, K. (1991) 'Agriculture and food security in the GATT Uruguay round', *Review of African Political Economy* 18: 38–50.

World Bank (1984) *World Development Report*. Washington DC: World Bank.

11 | OVERCOMING RURAL POVERTY FROM THE BOTTOM UP

David Barkin and Blanca Lemus

The possibility of overcoming poverty seems like a chimera in today's societies. The definitions of poverty are conditioned by the political contexts in which we operate, or, in some cases, by the proposals of new strategies that we would like to use in order to (re-)build the world. In this short essay we focus on the latter: those proposals that can guide us in moving forward to overcome the growing socio-political, economic and environmental obstacles that prevent us from understanding the possibility that poverty can be eradicated only by promoting a strategy that would free people, as members of communities, to implement their responses to forging their own solutions to the challenge.

Poverty is presently defined in terms of access to basic human needs which, in turn, is directly related to individuals' ability to obtain employment which, in turn, is tied to their capabilities, in a society dependent on private accumulation to create these opportunities – both in the labour force and in the realm of human development. Because of this, the possibilities of successfully confronting these challenges are inherently limited by the difficulty of creating social solidarity in the community and by the state's inability to supplement the inadequate mechanisms offered by the private sector. Even worse, in the name of generating employment opportunities, society has implemented important modifications in the received social contract that compromise basic guarantees of a decent wage or minimally acceptable working conditions, which were enshrined in the original formulation of Article 123 of the Mexican Constitution.[1] This situation is further aggravated by society's insertion into the 'international division of labour', which places workers everywhere in direct competition with each other, wherever they are, regardless of the political or social conditions to which they are subjected. In this process, we are also finding a dramatic 'race to the bottom' with regard to environmental standards, as corporations are (implicitly) permitted to disregard environmental standards in the name of competitiveness, even as these same actors shrilly proclaim their commitment to programmes of social and environmental responsibility. We consider it important to focus here on the underlying factors that people might refer to in their efforts to avoid the problem of poverty.

To begin with, it is useful to present an alternative proposal for measuring well-being, perhaps the most important factor relating to poverty, in contrast to the measures of gross domestic product (GDP) or its components. We refer to the proposal by King Jigme Singye Wangchuck of the Kingdom of Bhutan, made in 1972, to implement an alternative system to assess a country's richness according to an index of 'gross domestic happiness' (GDH). This concept proposes to measure the richness of nations by evaluating the real well-being of their citizens – their happiness – measuring smiles instead of money or material possessions, as does GDP. The initial idea was to ensure that 'prosperity is shared by the whole of society and well-balanced concerning cultural traditions conservation, environmental protection with a government that responds to the needs of those being governed' (Revkin 2005).[2]

Although personal income in Bhutan is one of the lowest in the world, life expectancy increased around twenty years from 1984 to 1998, from forty-three to sixty-six years; the literacy rate jumped from 10 per cent in 1982 to 60 per cent today; and the infant mortality rate fell from 163 deaths per 1,000 inhabitants to 43.[3] This change in approach to development has been reinforced by the country's strong commitment to environmental conservation. Bhutan's legislation defines 70 per cent of the country as 'green areas', including 60 per cent as forests. Even though this small country faces a very high unemployment rate, the perception of its inhabitants concerning their quality of life as 'good' has been significant enough for the indicator GDH to be considered seriously in many other countries.

In the World Values Survey, a project in process since 1981, Ronald Inglehart, a political scientist at the University of Michigan, found that Latin American countries, for example, recorded much more subjective 'happiness' than their economic levels would suggest.[4] In the same manner, a multinational team organised by the Inter-American Development Bank published an extensive report evaluating the process, using its own methodology, and concluded that the data regarding individual perceptions and values in a variety of countries of the region reveal huge discrepancies with statistics concerning living conditions or the opinions of government agencies. Certainly, there is a large gap between income and people's levels of satisfaction; these differences are not limited to monetary questions, because they include, in accordance with the studies, questions about the nature of the sources of employment and the quality of urban life, among others (Lora 2009). In fact, '[t]he evidence suggests that once people have their basic material needs adequately met, the correlation between income and happiness quickly begins to fade' (Alexander 2012: 2). We can add, quoting Albert Einstein, 'not everything that can be counted counts; and not everything that counts can be counted'. This is because measuring happiness includes subjective aspects, not material ones, such as the influence of social relations, autonomy and self-determination, among other factors.

This is not the place to review the endless discussions about poverty indicators or their meaning. In many other circles, scholars are trying to understand what makes people happy and the determinants of a good quality of life. The academic community seems incapable of defining these terms, because of our inability to incorporate concepts of uncertainty. It is clear, however, that there is a growing realisation that current definitions dominant in the social sciences do not contribute to an appropriate understanding of the issue.[5]

In this situation, then, a new understanding of poverty is more urgent than ever. An essential question is: what elements are necessary for an individual or a society to escape from poverty? It seems clear that an answer would include some of the GDH's index components, such as education and medical services. This would require a change in emphasis of social policy from simply delivering the services to ensuring that they adequately prepare people for a productive life in their communities. In Cuba, striking results were achieved in these sectors without particularly stellar results in economic growth (Pollitt 2009; Backer and Molina 2010). It is now clear, however, that our efforts to advance towards a better quality of life cannot be limited to these instruments of social policy. In spite of improvements in education and medical care, it is evident that throughout the world we are suffering a deterioration in our quality of life, resulting from the weakening or destruction of social and solidarity networks (with a direct increase in personal and social violence) and the accelerated destruction of the ecosystems on which we depend. The inability to guarantee a basic package of social services and economic assistance, accompanied by a shocking deterioration of environmental quality, has an extreme effect on the quality of life in virtually all countries. This is a multi-factorial theme and, for this reason, questioning the essential meaning of progress requires a multidisciplinary vision and a revaluation of some of the fundamental elements that we normally associate with 'traditional' society.

Generally speaking, when problems such as well-being or poverty are being discussed, we must refer to the development policies that create the social dynamics that prevent improvements in the quality of life. These policies are promoting a transformation that distances us from their stated objectives. It is evident that the principles of economic advance offered by economists do not offer appropriate solutions. This is clear once we examine the process of development; Gilbert Rist describes this process with an enlightening definition of development in his classic work:

> *'Development' consists of a set of practices, sometimes appearing to conflict with one another, which require – for the reproduction of society – the general transformation and destruction of the natural environment and of social relations. Its aim is to increase the production of commodities (goods and services) geared, by way of exchange, to effective demand.* (Rist 2008: 13; italics in original)

It is not necessary to analyse this definition in greater detail – as Rist did in his classic analysis of the concept – to realise how inappropriate the present development policies to promote a better quality of life are. Rist offers an interesting explanation, starting by pointing out that, although cooperation and international help are necessary and often valuable, they 'have little impact, compared with the many measures imposed by the implacable logic of the economic system' (ibid.: xi). Without pretending to reproduce his argument, it is enough to highlight three suppositions in development practice that impede society's advance: social evolutionism, individualism and economicism (ibid.: 9).

In the rest of this chapter, we propose to introduce reflections relating to two paradigms offering alternatives to 'development' and then examine practices beyond official solutions. These alternatives are emerging philosophical and analytical approaches that can stimulate the intellectual work that must accompany the search for new ways of understanding. We begin with an analysis based on academic literature, but then continue with reflections emanating from the social movements motivating and triggering scholarly work and the resolute resistance of official institutions, which continue intransigently in not exploring the possibilities of alternative models. These two important alternatives are *degrowth* and *'good living'*, as it is called by the Andean groups where the term originated (in Quechua and Aymara). Two areas of academic work are related to these paradigms: ecological economics (and its close relative, political ecology) and social and solidarity economics.[6] An extensive literature has been accumulating around these two ideas in a process that threatens them, as many new contributors are trying to expand their scope in an effort to bring them closer to the methodologies and content of mainstream analysis.

1. Degrowth

The 'new' field of 'degrowth' emerged from the critical diagnosis of the current situation: an international elite and a 'global middle class' are causing havoc to the environment through conspicuous consumption and the excessive appropriation of human and natural resources. Their consumption patterns lead to further environmental and social damage when imitated by the rest of society in a vicious circle of status-seeking through the accumulation of material possessions.[7]

In the international meeting where this statement emerged, its adherents offered a critique that extended to transnational corporations, financial institutions and governments, insisting on the profound structural causes of the crisis. Similarly, they indicated that the measures to confront crises by promoting economic growth will only deepen social inequalities and accelerate environmental degradation, creating a social disaster and generating economic and environmental debts for future generations, especially for those who live in poverty.

Those attending the conference declared that the main challenge today is how to conduct the inevitable transition (as they see it) to economic degrowth, which has beneficial effects for the environment through a process that will be implemented in an equitable manner at national and global levels. The proposals offered by participants following this school of thought embraced all the dimensions of productive and social activity. The adherents to this line of analysis are optimistic with regard to the possibility of implementing changes in lifestyles and community organisation to reduce the ecological footprint of different social groups, and thereby liberate social resources to attack the root causes of poverty. In their critique of the current model there is a clear tendency to protect and strengthen individuals' rights and to reduce the scale of social and productive activity, emphasising the local over the global. At this Second International Conference on Economic Degrowth, however, there was a persistent effort to focus on the design of reforms that could be discussed and implemented within the current organisational framework of the affluent societies from which most of the participants came; the few efforts to examine the possibility of implementing these changes in the current system of capitalist organisation came to naught.

Although this school of thought places its intellectual roots in the field of ecological economics, it does not propose mechanisms to challenge the fundamental contradictions arising from the current organisation of society and its economy. On the basis of their ambiguous pledge to reduce the scale of production and consumption by the wealthy in the 'advanced' countries, their proposals are committed to the possibility of a soft transition to a 'de-scaling' and towards a 'stationary state' economy. This 'degrowth' school proposes the option of reorganising 'affluent' societies in order to release resources that would create political and productive spaces; this would allow them to redeploy their energy to their own social fulfilment and guarantee appropriate living standards for their people. Many of these proposals are technological, offering new physical and productive solutions that ignore institutional and corporate structures that would prevent these changes, while also completely ignoring their dependency on the countries of the global South for an even more austere lifestyle in the affluent countries.[8]

2. Good living or *sumak kawsay*

The concept of 'good living' is a translation or adaptation of an expression in Quechua, the language of the descendants of many

Incan peoples in Ecuador, Peru and Bolivia. It is defined in the preface of the new Ecuadorian Constitution as 'a new form of public coexistence, in diversity and harmony with nature, to achieve the good way of living, the "*sumak kawsay*"'. Elevated to a constitutional principle,[9] *sumak kawsay* recognises the 'rights of nature' and a new complex citizenry 'that accepts social as well as environmental commitments. This new citizenry is plural, because it depends on its multiple histories and environments, and accepts criteria of ecological justice that go far beyond the traditional dominant vision of justice' (Gudynas 2009).

As expressed by Alberto Acosta, one of its important protagonists on the Ecuadorian scene:

> The basic value of an economy, in a Good Living regime, is solidarity. A different economy is being forged, a social and solidarity economy, different from economies characterised by supposedly free competition, that encourages economic cannibalism among human beings and feeds financial speculation. In accordance with this constitutional definition, they hope to build relations of production, exchange and cooperation that promote efficiency and quality, founded on solidarity. We talk about systematic productivity and competitiveness, based on collective advances rather than individuals who are arbitrarily added together as is often the practice at present. (Acosta 2010: 9)

In contrast to current policies designed to address the problem of the existence of growing segments of society that require charity or official transfer payments for their survival, this approach towards a social and solidarity economy offers a stark contrast with the proletarian organisation of community life. This approach far exceeds the reforms proposed by many participants in the debates, which were based on economistic visions that do not consider abandoning individual or corporate accumulation in order to improve collective well-being. *Sumak kawsay* requires a reorganisation of social life and economic production, transforming the essential function of the market and shaping it so that it can serve society rather than determine social relations, as it does at present.[10]

Sumak kawsay is a concatenation of economic, social and political equalities, which support a different organisation of society and its relationship with nature. These equalities, expressed in our political language, would include equality and freedom, social justice (productive and distributive) as well as environmental justice; it is evident that dramatic actions are required to reverse the currently existing inequalities (Acosta 2010). If this principle were applied, it would constitute a solid base for reorienting the productive apparatus and political and cultural relations, reversing inequalities that violate rights and prevent the possibility of an effective democracy. Progress, in this sense, would be defined in terms of a social and productive organisation that generates equality directly and that produces social justice through direct democracy.

These are just two examples of a broad search for alternative ways of understanding people's relationships to their environments and proposals for shaping their communities, as well as for conducting research and implementing proposals for change. What is particularly notable about the virtual flood of these proposals is the legitimacy they have gained in international academic institutions and the intransigence of many existing institutions and the dominant paradigms in the principal disciplines to seriously consider the need to rethink the way in which social science analysis is conducted. The titles themselves are revealing with regard to the proposals being offered: *An Epistemology of the South: The reinvention of knowledge and social emancipation* (Santos 2009); *Decolonising Methodologies* (Smith 2012); *Sharing Power* (Borrini-Feyerabend et al. 2007).

3. Operationalisation

The principles examined in this text are an integral part of a long tradition: declarations from and action by social movements reacting to the dramatic changes that are imposed on the social and economic system and are designed to reorganise society for the benefit of elites. They take us back to the dawn of the French Revolution in the Paris Commune, to Richard Owens' commune and to the intentional communities of Protestant and Jewish sects, as well as to the workers' struggles of the nineteenth century. Most of them were suppressed in one way or another, with tragic massacres committed by forces at the service of a particular model of economic organisation, which repeatedly tries to condemn a growing segment of the world's population to diverse forms of poverty.

Today, individuals who are looking for another model of progress realise that Schumacher's *Small is Beautiful* (1973) still has a lot to teach us. We are also obliged to consider the fact that Marshall Sahlins' affirmation might now be truer than ever: hunter-gatherers offer a model of a really affluent society:

> The world's most primitive people have few possessions,
> but they are not poor. Poverty is not a certain small amount
> of goods, nor is it just a relation between means and ends;
> above all, it is a relation between people. Poverty is a social
> status. As such it is the invention of civilisation. It has grown
> with civilisation, at once as an invidious distinction between
> classes and more importantly as a tributary relation that
> can render agrarian peasants more susceptible to natural
> catastrophes than any winter camp of Alaskan Eskimo.
> (Sahlins 1972)

Might we not ask, as some scholars and critics do: did medieval peasants work less than today's industrial working class?

These reflections pose many questions. Today it is relatively easy to document the fruitless dynamic of anti-poverty programmes such as the international Millennium Development Goals effort and their national correlates, including the widely praised '*Oportunidades*' programme of the Mexican government, or the destructive effects of society's current organisation. We can turn to measurements of life expectancy, educational levels, morbidity and mortality rates by age, social or gender groups. Similarly, we can include diverse indicators of social, economic and geographic inequality, and indices of access to social and cultural infrastructure. We can add diverse efforts that document the lack of correlation between increases in production and improvements in human well-being. In turn, the deterioration in working conditions and the restriction of freedom of association in unions and their effectiveness to protect internationally agreed working rights are now widely recognised. The degradation of health and safety conditions in the workplace and the erosion of the social welfare system, particularly for people of advanced age, are also intensifying in the present stage of globalisation.

However, most of these problems – and our improved capacity to measure them – avoid the fundamental criticism of alternative visions. In other words, a description of society's current organisation and its productive apparatus, with all the symptoms enumerated above, does not consider the way in which the process contributes to the enrichment of a few at the expense of the majority and of our ecosystems. After all, while this concentrated (and dynamically growing) control persists, the possibility of alleviating the deepening poverty and exclusion of significant segments of society will be minimal (or nil).

But efforts to achieve true social and environmental progress and a fuller appreciation of the ways in which society's current organisation systematically generates the conditions that deepen the roots of poverty also need to take note of society's dependence on the extraction of natural resources, both renewable and non-renewable. It would be necessary to reduce this dependency, as well as the system that integrates people into the labour market in 'dead-end' employment. It would also be important to develop mechanisms to identify the need for ecosystem rehabilitation and the possibilities of effectively protecting vulnerable areas and species in danger of extinction, incorporating processes to integrate local populations in these tasks, and taking advantage of their knowledge and own organisations, with appropriate recognition that would allow them to live with dignity. Not all these tasks are readily quantified, in spite of our recognition of the importance of revaluing the significance of these environments relative to material production. In the rest of this chapter, we will focus on the promises offered by an alternative vision of society derived from the organisation and practices of myriad communities throughout the Americas who have explicitly chosen to reject their wholesale integration into the global market system.

To escape from the poverty that oppresses most peasants, many rural groups propose their own forms of collective organisation to administer the social and natural resources that the communities control. These organisations do not emerge spontaneously; rather, they are the product of concerted and long-term processes of social control and cooperation as well as a collective commitment to the sustainable management of their resources. To do this, the communities must also ensure an appropriate and diversified productive structure that allows members to satisfy their basic needs as well as to produce goods that can be used for exchange with other communities in the region and elsewhere to procure the items they need to assure their well-being. Although there are many examples of these alternative organisations of rural society and production, most social science thinking and analysis focuses on the impoverishing effects of international economic integration on the masses of peasants and rural labourers who have been thrust into poverty by the structural conditions of rain-fed subsistence agriculture. There are at least two different explanations of this process: 1) the proposal offered in the background paper for the CROP conference, based on seasonal variations in economic opportunities and labour demand (Boltvinik, Chapter 1): and 2) the semi-proletarianisation of the peasantry. The latter is the version favoured by traditional analysts and dominant in the United Nations' Food and Agriculture Organization (FAO), and is anchored in orthodox economic models that explain their poverty through the structural features of the labour markets in which they can find employment opportunities, albeit in disadvantageous conditions.

The analysis presented here summarises an alternative approach to escape from these limitations of systemic poverty, based on the proposals of diverse indigenous and peasant groups for their own organisation of the rural production process as part of their diagnosis of the functioning of the market economy. Their collective commitments to an alternative framework for production and social integration, grounded in the basic principles that shape their social and political organisation, offer a realistic but challenging strategy for local progress. These principles, widely agreed upon in broad-based consultations among the communities, are: autonomy, solidarity, self-sufficiency, productive diversification, and the sustainable management of regional resources (Barkin 2000; 2005). Their emphasis on local (regional) economies, the use of traditional and agro-ecological approaches in production and the integrated management of ecosystems are the basis for their guarantee of a minimum standard of living for all their members and for a corresponding responsibility to participate, thus eliminating the phenomenon of unemployment. An integral part of this approach is the explicit rejection of the notion that people in rural communities conceive of themselves exclusively as farmers, or even as resource managers; rather, in these societies, it is more revealing to understand their decisions as the result of a *complex* allocation of their time among numerous activities of individual and collective benefit.

4. Communality

There are a number of fundamental conceptual principles underlying the organisation of the societies involved in constructing a structure that is capable of moving towards the 'good living' (*buen vivir*) as discussed in the Latin American literature (Huanacuni 2010). These principles facilitate the societies' efforts to eliminate the concept of poverty from their social reality, with a concomitant commitment to productively incorporate all their members into socially useful occupations. In the case of Mexico, the principles have been codified by a number of 'organic intellectuals' who have been actively involved in innovative approaches as part of the process of consolidating social capacities in their communities, a self-conscious process of organisation contributing to a strengthening of tradition (Díaz 2007; Martínez Luna 2010).[11] They have suggested the category 'communality' to encompass these principles, which include: 1) direct or participative democracy; 2) the organisation of community work; 3) community possession and control of land; 4) and a common cosmology, which includes the notion of the Earth as mother (Pachamama) and respect for community leadership. This development reflects an epistemological contribution that incorporates the appropriation of nature in a way that is dramatically different from that conceived by the dominant institutions of the Western project of 'civilisation' and embedded in most development programmes.

Communality, in this sense, is not simply the aggregation of individual interests into a collective whole, as suggested by the historical notion of 'social contract' (in Hobbes, Locke and Kant), which should lead to a 'just society'. It is not:

> An agreement in which each person adheres to the contract to safeguard his own individual interest; if the contract, the political association, does not safeguard them, the individual has the right to break the contract, because (s)he agreed to the arrangement in terms of an egotistical interest, and thus if it does not respond in these terms, the individual may refuse to continue abiding by the contract. (Villoro 2003: 48–9)

In contrast, in the context of a peasant association adhering to the principles discussed above, a social contract means the following:

> Since I accept the contract, on the understanding that I am committed to the well-being of the group as a whole, even if it might advance against my own particular interests, I will continue to respect the terms of the contract.

> Democracy is, in this sense, a political association which, at the same time, is an ethical agreement, because it is the way in which a public group can guarantee the freedom of everyone in the group, while also remaining a guarantor of autonomy. (ibid.: 49)

Communality, then, is a complex composite concept, one that embodies the totality of the collective commitment to individual welfare in the context of an individual commitment to collective well-being. It is an implicit arrangement to go beyond the limits of material considerations and to accept a different responsibility to the community and to its ecosystem, an obligation grounded in tradition, and in cosmology, to respect the community within its environment.

Although it emerged from the very specific conditions of the struggles in the highlands of Oaxaca to reclaim forest resources,[12] the doctrine of communality is increasingly recognised as relevant for understanding the many local fights for self-governance, for autonomy in the management of social organisation, and for the right to decide on the best uses of resources controlled by the people involved in these struggles.[13] As such, the doctrine is a direct challenge to inherited notions of the sovereignty of the nation state, of the unquestioned right and ability of national governments to decree the disposition of the nation's resources without reference to the considerations of the local peoples, as in the case of Mexico, where subsoil rights are constitutionally conferred on the state.

Without going into more detail, we wish simply to point out that the Oaxacan version of this conceptual approach is by no means exceptional. Similar approaches are evident in the current efforts among the Andean peoples to codify and operationalise the heritage of the *sumak kawsay* (*buen vivir*), the explanations of the Zapatistas of their own developments ('*mandar obedeciendo*'), the struggles of the Huichol people, or Wixárika[14] (in their sacred site, Wirikuta), and the myriad other manifestations of peoples throughout the Americas defending their customs, their territories, their societies, and indeed their very existence.

5. Implementing alternative societies

This book proposes to explain the persistence of poverty among the peasantry. We are examining this phenomenon in the context of the search for alternative explanations – how and why do our societies perpetuate this situation? And why do the societies continue to persist in their stubborn ties to the land, to their traditional structures for production and reproduction? Because of this, many of our colleagues are convinced that these societies are condemned to disappear, to sink into a miasma of sub-proletarian wretchedness.[15] They view the peasantry as an antiquated social form, with the fate of its peoples sealed in misery. The explanations for this tragic situation may be those of unequal exchange, or more creative ones such as the seasonality of agricultural production, offered in Julio Boltvinik's background paper in this volume.

The approach suggested in this chapter is quite different. What appears as poverty in many rural societies is the result of deliberate choices made by their members to shape or reshape their communities on the basis of different principles, focusing on satisfying their own basic needs and assuring an ever more effective ability to govern themselves and negotiate their autonomy, in the face of intensifying efforts to integrate them into global markets and the logic of rationalities based on individual benefit and monetary valuations of social relations and natural resources.[16]

The evidence for this peculiar situation is provided by the concerted efforts made by societies throughout the Americas to forge solutions on their own, or in alliance with other communities, or in collaboration with outside agents. Throughout the world there are numerous social movements defending their territory and proposing alternatives that lead to a better quality of life, although not necessarily more consumption. What is striking is the volume of literature documenting these efforts; this relates to both those who are 'bringing up to date' the long-held traditions of many groups who tenaciously defend their ideological and cultural heritages (Toledo and Barrera Bassols 2008) as well as those who are searching out new paths, controlled by themselves (see, for example, Baronnet et al. 2011; Zermeño 2010).

The process is not limited to ethnic communities. It is interesting to note the significance for many peasant communities of the consolidation of one of the largest peasant organisations in the world, Vía Campesina. This group integrates local small-scale farmer organisations from around the world, with a view to promoting local capacities for self-sufficiency based on technologies that combine the benefits of organic cultivation, where appropriate, with the intensive use of the producer's own equipment and knowledge to increase production. This approach, known as agro-ecology, is widely acknowledged to be appropriate for overcoming many of the considerable obstacles that impede the successful expansion of small-scale farming in the Third World (Altieri and Toledo 2011; Holt-Giménez 2010). Evaluations of the implementation of these strategies reflect the benefits not just of the productive gains from a production system reoriented to local needs and distribution systems, but of their contribution to strengthening local communities and environmental balance (Rosset and Martínez Torres 2012).

There is no space here to delve into the details of these innovative strategies, many of which do not offer material solutions to poverty when measured by ownership or access to a certain package of commodities. Instead, they address a much more thoroughgoing reconceptualisation of the possibilities for a different meaning of the concept of 'quality of life', and therefore of the social and material significance of poverty. In this different context, then, it might be that much of the poverty to which most of the literature is addressed has its origins in the individualism and alienation of the masses whose behaviour is embedded in the Western model of modernity, a model of concentrated accumulation based on a system of deliberate dispossession of the majority by a small elite. The collectivism implicit in the proposals offered by communities that are implementing their own areas of conservation[17] is accompanied by the social concomitant of solidarity, which pervades the processes inherent in these alternative strategies. The realisation of the importance of people becoming involved in identifying and protecting their territories is an integral part of a complex dynamic that examines the significance of the place-based nature of cultures and their survival. As a result, peoples around the world are being accompanied in their efforts to protect these areas by a global alliance of such communities and organisations that seek to promote these efforts; the Indigenous Peoples' and Community Conserved Territories and Areas forum (www.iccaconsortium.org) is promoting and documenting the practice in dozens of countries and in hundreds of initiatives in which people are able to improve measurably their living conditions as part of processes that enable them to govern themselves more effectively while also contributing to ecosystem protection and rehabilitation (Borrini-Feyerabend 2010; Ibarra et al. 2011).

In this context, then, we reiterate the underlying principles of this construction – distilled from the practice of many recent experiences – that help avoid the 'syndrome' of poverty: autonomy and communality; solidarity; self-sufficiency; productive and commercial diversification; and sustainable management of regional resources (Barkin 2009). In many of these circles, the collective commitment to ensure that there are no individuals without access to their socially defined basic needs implies a corresponding obligation of every single person to contribute to the strengthening of the community's productive capacity, to improve its infrastructures (physical, social and environmental), and to enrich its cultural and scientific capabilities. Poverty, in this light, is an individual scourge – created by the dynamics of a society based on individualism and its isolation – that is structurally anchored in the very fabric of society. To escape from this dynamic, the collective subject that is emerging in the process offers a meaningful path to overcoming the persistence of poverty in our times.

Notes

1 As originally written, this guarantee was considered a groundbreaking guarantee for unions and workers' rights (Compa 2012).

2 We are grateful to Gabriel Torres González of CIESAS-Occidente (Centro de Investigaciones y Estudios Superiores en Antropología Social) for our discussions of this topic and his contributions. He is in the process of conducting a study of this phenomenon in Mexico.

3 For recent developments on this approach, see Bhutan's Gross National Happiness Commission (www.gnhc. gov.bt/).

4 See 'Human beliefs and values: a cross-cultural sourcebook based on the 1999–2002 Values Surveys', a study conducted at the Survey Research Center of the University of Michigan.

5 In fact, concern over the divergence between well-being and

standard measures of progress is such that, in the UK, a Royal Commission was charged with providing guidance for public policy to reduce the gap (Scott 2012). There is also the burgeoning field of 'economics of happiness' that is responding to this concern, albeit principally within the confines of orthodox economics (cf. Figart and Marangos 2011; Carabelli and Cedrini 2011).

6 Some consider 'degrowth' to be a response to the disenchantment with the colonisation of 'ecological economics' by many analysts of a neoclassical (orthodox) tendency, who 'escaped' from 'environmental economics' due to its inability to incorporate issues of biological diversity and social justice into its analysis; frequently, these analysts make this transition or academic migration without transforming their methodologies or even their paradigms (Barkin et al. 2012). In contrast, political ecology – more firmly rooted in Marxist political economy – suffers less criticism. Similarly, 'social and solidarity economics' is suffering from a confusion generated by competing or incompatible social and political objectives; the notions of solidarity and equality that motivated cooperative and union movements of the past are being compromised by present-day social policies of the state, by community organisations at the service of corporations, and by religious charities (Barkin and Lemus 2011). Recently, other academic and political groups have intensified their attempts to influence the evolution of these alternative approaches by accepting the participation of transnational companies that claim their own right to take part, since their 'social and environmental responsibility' investments make them worthy of strictly controlled (by

them) rewards as 'socially responsible companies' (as they are called in Mexico) (cf. Utting and Clapp 2008).

7 See the 'Declaration of Barcelona 2010', which was produced at the Second Conference on Economic Degrowth for Ecological Sustainability and Social Equity, convened in Barcelona in March 2010. For more information on this paradigm, see www.degrowth.eu, among other sources.

8 Two additional conferences were held after this chapter was completed, in Venice in September 2012 and in Leipzig in September 2014. What is striking about the keynote addresses and the available papers from these events is their continued and unbridled optimism about the possibility of slowing or even stopping economic growth without generating insurmountable problems for the viability of the capitalist system or the governance institutions that support it (see www.venezia2012.it and www.degrowth.de/en/leipzig-2014/archive/).

9 The Bolivian counterpart, 'good living' (from the Aymara language *suma qamaña*), is in the preface of its new Magna Carta. One of the most prolific writers on the subject is Fernando Huanacuni Mamani, whose works are widely available on the internet (see Huanacuni 2010). See also Tortosa (2011).

10 This point is central in Karl Polanyi's (2001) works, where the need to '(re-)embed' the market in society is emphasised in place of the current organisation of the economy that allows it to dominate social relations. An extensive discussion on the 'good living' topic is presented in the magazine *América Latina en Movimiento*, published in Ecuador and available online at www.alainet.org; numbers 452–4 of 2010 and 462 of 2011 are highly recommended.

11 This characteristic was central to the thinking of Eric Wolf, an

anthropologist who was very influential in Mexico and who emphasised that one of the keys to the success of traditional societies is the leadership's ability to selectively innovate, carefully identifying what elements can be discarded or modified while staunchly defending others that are judged to be critical for the continuity of the community (Wolf 1982).

12 For two detailed studies that offer a historical review of these struggles in Mexico, see Klooster (2000) and Mathews (2003).

13 Evidence of this recognition is shown by the inclusion of panels for examining the concepts examined here (*buen vivir* and communality) in the meetings of the International Congress of Americanists in Vienna in August 2012 and in the II (Mexican) Congress of Anthropology and Ethnology in Morelia in September 2012.

14 Smith's (2012) insightful analysis of the development of similar processes among peoples in Oceania and Southeast Asia serves to reinforce the argument that there are myriad examples worldwide of peoples with unique ethnic origins in national states asserting the significance of their own proposals for constructing alternatives to global development programmes. For detailed examples of case studies of these processes, see collections such as that assembled by Apffel-Marglin et al. (2010) and others cited below in this chapter.

15 This is an important line of analysis repeatedly emphasised in the meetings of the Mexican Association of Rural Studies (cf. Cartón de Grammont and Martínez Valle 2009) as well as among other groups of students of rural problems (see, for example, Pérez Correa 2007).

16 The significance of the rejection of a monetary valuation of social and natural phenomena is enormous; for example, the widespread acceptance of apparently value-free concepts such as 'social capital' and 'natural capital', which offers a justification for placing prices and values on elements outside the market by asserting the need to assign them 'relevance', also facilitates their transformation into a new category of quasi-'commodities' that contributes to other mechanisms for personal and collective alienation. Fine (2010) offers an introduction to this problem.

17 A recent development in this regard is the recognition of the importance and prevalence of 'Indigenous Peoples' and Community Conserved Territories and Areas'. This has become sufficiently significant to encourage a number of organisations to create a global ICCA forum (cf. www.iccaconsortium.org).

References

Acosta, A. (2010) 'Sólo imaginando otros mundos, se cambiará éste: Reflexiones sobre el Buen Vivir', *Sustentabilidad(es)* 2.

Alexander, S. (2012) 'The optimal material threshold: toward an economics of sufficiency', *Real World Economics Review* 61: 2–21.

Altieri, M. A. and V. M. Toledo (2011) 'The agroecological revolution in Latin America: rescuing nature, ensuring food sovereignty and empowering peasants', *Journal of Peasant Studies* 38 (3): 587–612.

Apffel-Marglin, F., S. Kumar and A. Mishra (eds) (2010) *Interrogating Development from the Margins*. New Delhi: Oxford University Press.

Backer, L. C. and A. Molina (2010) 'Cuba and the construction of alternative global trade systems: ALBA and free trade in the Americas', *University of Pennsylvania Journal of International Economic Law* 31 (3): 679–752.

Barkin, D. (2000) 'Overcoming the neoliberal paradigm: sustainable popular development', *Journal of Developing Societies* XVI (1): 163–80.

— (2005) 'Reconsiderando las alternativas sociales en México rural: Estrategias campesinas e indígenas', *Polis* 5 (15): 7.

— (2009) 'Principles for constructing alternative socio-economic organisations: lessons learned from working outside institutional structures', *Review of Radical Political Economics* 41 (3): 372–9.

Barkin, D. and B. Lemus (2011) 'La Economía Ecológica y Solidaria: Una propuesta frente a nuestra crisis', *Sustentabilidad(es)* 5.

Barkin, D., M. E. Fuente Carrasco and D. Tagle Zamora (2012) 'La Significación de una Economía Ecológica Radical', *Revista Iberoamericana de Economía Ecológica* 19: 1–14. Available at www.redibec.org/IVO/REV19_01.pdf.

Baronnet, B., M. Mora Bayo and R. Stahler-Sholk (2011) *Luchas muy otras: Zapatismo y autonomía en las comunidades indígenas de Chiapas.* Mexico City: UAM-X-Ciesas-UNACH.

Boltvinik, J. (2011) 'Poverty and persistence of the peasantry'. Background paper for the International Workshop on Peasant Poverty and Persistence, CROP and El Colegio de México, Mexico City, 13–15 March 2012, Chapter 1, this volume.

Borrini-Feyerabend, G. (2010) *Bio-cultural Diversity Conserved by Indigenous Peoples & Local Communities: Examples & analysis.* Tehran: Indigenous Peoples' and Community Conserved Territories and Areas (ICCA) Consortium and Centre for Sustainable Development (CENESTA).

Borrini-Feyerabend, G., M. Pimbert, M. Taghi Farvar, M. Taghi, A. Kothari and Y. Renard (2007) *Sharing Power: A global guide to collaborative management of natural resources.* Gland, Switzerland: International Union for Conservation of Nature (IUCN).

Carabelli, A. M. and M. A. Cedrini (2011) 'The economic problem of happiness: Keynes on happiness and economics', *Forum for Social Economics* 40 (3): 335–59.

Cartón de Grammont, H. and L. Martínez Valle (eds) (2009) *La pluriactividad en el campo.* Quito: Flacso-Ecuador.

Compa, L. (2012) *Justice for All: The struggle for worker rights in Mexico.* Washington DC: American Center for International Labor Solidarity. Available at http://digitalcommons.ilr.cornell.edu/reports/34.

Díaz, F. (2007) 'Comunidad y comunalidad' in S. Robles and R. Cardoso (eds), *Floriberto Díaz. Comunalidad, energía viva del pensamiento.* Mexico City: Universidad Nacional Autónoma de México (UNAM), pp. 34–50.

Figart, D. M. and J. Marangos (eds) (2011) *Living Standards and Social Well-being.* London: Routledge.

Fine, B. (2010) *Theories of Social Capital: Researchers behaving badly.* London: Pluto.

Gudynas, E. (2009) 'La ecología política del giro biocéntrico en la nueva Constitución de Ecuador', *Revista de Estudios Sociales* 32: 34–47.

Holt-Giménez, E. (2010) 'Linking farmers' movements for advocacy and practice', *Journal of Peasant Studies* 37 (1): 203–36.

Huanacuni, F. (2010) *Vivir bien/Buen vivir: Filosofía, políticas, estrategias y experiencias regionales.* La Paz: Convenio Andrés Bello and Instituto Internacional de Integración. Available at www.reflectiongroup. org/stuff/vivir-bien.

Ibarra, J. T., A. Barreau, C. Del Campo, C. I. Camacho, G. J. Martin and S. McCandless (2011) 'When formal and market-based conservation mechanisms disrupt food sovereignty: impacts of community conservation and payments for environmental services on an indigenous community of Oaxaca, Mexico', *International Forestry Review* 13 (3): 318–37.

Klooster, D. (2000) 'Institutional choice, community, and struggle: a case study of forest co-management in Mexico', *World Development* 28: 1.

Lora, E. (ed.) (2009) *Beyond Facts: Understanding quality of life.* Cambridge MA: Harvard University Press for the Inter-American Development Bank and David Rockefeller Center for Latin American Studies, Harvard University. Available at http://idbdocs. iadb.org/wsdocs/getdocument. aspx?docnum=1775002.

Martínez Luna, J. (2010) *Eso que llaman comunalidad.* Oaxaca: Consejo Nacional para la Cultura y las Artes, Centro de Apoyo al Movimiento Popular Oaxaqueño, A. C., Fundación Harp Helu, Secretaría de Cultura de Oaxaca, Mexico.

Mathews, A. S. (2003) 'Suppressing fire and memory: environmental degradation and political restoration in the Sierra Juárez of Oaxaca, 1887–2001', *Environmental History* 8 (1): 75–108.

Pérez Correa, E. (2007) *La Enseñanza de Desarrollo Rural: Enfoques y perspectivas.* Bogotá: Pontificia Universidad Javeriana.

Polanyi, K. (2001) *The Great Transformation: The political and economic origins of our time.* Boston MA: Beacon Press.

Pollitt, B. (2009) 'From sugar to services: an overview of the Cuban economy', *International Journal of Cuban Studies* 2 (1): 91–104. Available at http://mrzine.monthlyreview. org/2010/pollitt061010.html.

Revkin, A. C. (2005) 'Happy little kingdom', *New York Times*, 4 October.

Rist, G. (2008) *The History of Development: From Western origins to global faith.* Third edition. London: Zed Books.

Rosset, P. M. and M. E. Martínez Torres (2012) 'Rural social movements and agroecology: context, theory, and process', *Ecology and Society* 17 (3): 17. Available at www.ecologyandsociety. org/vol17/iss3/art17/.

Sahlins, M. (1972) *Stone Age Economics.* Oxford: Blackwell. Quote taken from www.eco-action.org/dt/affluent. html.

Santos, B. de S. (2009) *Una epistemología del Sur. La reinvención del conocimiento y la emancipación social.* Mexico City: CLACSO-Siglo XXI.

Schumacher, E. F. (1973) *Small is Beautiful: Economics as if people mattered.* New York NY: Harper & Row.

Scott, K. (2012) *Measuring Well-being: Towards sustainability?* London: Routledge.

Smith, L. T. (2012) *Decolonising Methodologies: Research and indigenous peoples.* Second edition. London: Zed Books.

Toledo, V. M. and N. Barrera Bassols (2008) *La memoria biocultural: La importancia ecológica de las sabidurías tradicionales*. Barcelona: Icaria.

Tortosa, J. M. (2011) 'Sobre los movimientos alternativos en la actual coyuntura', *Polis: Revista de la Universidad Bolivariana* 30.

Utting, P. and J. Clapp (2008) *Corporate Accountability and Sustainable Development*. New Delhi: Oxford University Press.

Villoro, L. (2003) *De la libertad a la comunidad*. Mexico City: Fondo de Cultura Económica por el Instituto Tecnológico y de Estudios Superiores de Monterrey.

Wolf, E. (1982) *Europe and the People Without History*. Berkeley CA: University of California Press.

Zermeño, S. (2010) Reconstruir a México en el Siglo XXI: Estrategias para mejorar la calidad de vida y enfrentar la destrucción del medio ambiente. Mexico City: Océano.

THIRD PART: CLOSING THE BOOK

12 | DIALOGUES AND DEBATES ON PEASANT POVERTY AND PERSISTENCE: AROUND THE BACKGROUND PAPER AND BEYOND

Julio Boltvinik

This chapter starts with the dialogue on the background paper (Chapter 1) that has taken place in this book. This task is carried out in the first two sections of this chapter: in section 1, clarifications, precisions and backups to the paper are analysed, while in section 2, my replies to criticisms are presented. Section 3 provides an enriched version of the distinctive features of agriculture and how it contrasts with industry, which were presented in Chapter 1 and systematised by Bernstein in Chapter 5, and section 4 lists some of the pending issues that could not be covered in depth because of length constraints. Section 5 closes the chapter and the book, outlining two typologies of replies to the central theoretical questions addressed in this volume.

1. Commentaries and criticisms to the background paper: clarifications, precisions and backups

As originally intended, the background paper received numerous commentaries and criticisms in some of the seminar papers (summarised in Table 12.1 at the end of the chapter), although the dialogue with Bartra started in 2008 and the one with Arizmendi two months before the seminar. In this section, I present clarifications, precisions and backups on the background paper, and I include my replies in section 2. These exclude the dialogue with Bartra, which has been covered in two chapters of the book (Chapters 1 and 2).

Table 12.1 enumerates twenty-five observations numbered sequentially and grouped by author. In this and the following section, I identify them by their number in Table 12.1.

I start with a caveat.

A caveat on the different meanings of the word 'agriculture' in English and Spanish. The word *agriculture*, despite deriving in both English and Spanish from the same Latin word, has different meanings. The *Collins English Dictionary* defines agriculture as 'the science or occupation of cultivating land *and rearing* crops and *livestock*'. The definition in *Webster's New World Dictionary* is practically the same. The *Diccionario de la Lengua Española* of the Real Spanish Academy defines *agricultura* as: '1. Tillage or cultivation of the land; 2. Art of cultivation of the land.' And María Moliner's *Diccionario de Uso del Español* gives practically the same definition. Thus, *in English, agriculture includes livestock raising, but not in Spanish*. These different meanings of the word agriculture in the two main mother languages of the contributors to this book have represented a serious communication problem. Translations become deceiving: when you translate this word from Spanish to English you broaden its meaning, whereas in translating from English to Spanish you narrow it. An exact Spanish translation of the English 'agriculture' would be *agricultura y ganadería*.

Clarifications I: On the genesis and the theoretical bases of my theory. I shall first explain how I came up with my 'theory' on peasant poverty and persistence, and what are its theoretical bases. Then I will clarify some points about what I do and do not say. As stated in the background paper (Chapter 1, section 1), my theoretical position started from a theory on peasant poverty only (Boltvinik 1991; 2007). These two initial texts quoted Chayanov (mainly on the slave mode of production) and Brewster (1970 [1950]) on family farms, but did not rely at all on Marx or Marxists. This initial position reflected my training in agricultural economics and rural development at the School of Development Studies at the University of East Anglia (1972–73)[1] and the fact that I was working with the United Nations Development Programme (UNDP) on its Regional Project to Overcome Poverty in Latin America (1988–91). It was later, in the initial rounds of my (almost) permanent (and friendly) debate with Armando Bartra, that I discovered that my theory on peasant poverty also constituted a theory on the persistence of the peasantry, and that I perceived the necessary symbiosis between capitalist agriculture and the peasantry, as can be seen in a later text (Boltvinik 2009). Still, Marx, Kautsky and Lenin were not present in my arguments.

It was in preparing the background paper (2010–11) that I became involved in these authors' views on the peasantry.

So, despite the perception of some authors of this book, *my theory on peasant poverty and persistence is not based on Marx*. I consider myself a non-dogmatic, non-orthodox Marxist. But my Marxist background and my agricultural economics and rural development backgrounds remained separate until recently. It might be said that, having already outlined my theory on the peasantry from outside Marxism, I was able to read Marx from a perspective that allowed me to be aware of the fact that he neglects the discontinuous production processes in agriculture in his theory of value, despite his great clarity, in Volume II of *Capital*, on the differences between working time and production time in agriculture. The sequence of chapters in the background paper reflects genetically how I read Marx (and Kautsky and Lenin) with respect to agriculture. I found that both in Volume I of *Capital* and in the reproduction schemes of Volume II there were no references to discontinuities, and on that basis I formulated my critique of Marx's theory of value. In conducting this analysis, and also in reading Lenin and Kautsky, I brought together my Marxist and my agricultural economics backgrounds.

I find it understandable that the discontinuities of the labour process in agriculture are not included in Marx's schemes of simple and amplified reproduction, as the schemes are built from a capital-centric perspective and these discontinuities *apparently* do not pose a problem for the reproduction of total social capital. The same can be said of mainstream current macro-economics, where these discontinuities are also absent. It is only for people-centric perspectives, focused on human life (which are also very much present in Marx's gigantic and revolutionary *Werke*), that the discontinuities pose a problem, and this *appears to be* only a human problem. To paraphrase Leff's statement on nature (Chapter 7), the *reproduction of human life has been externalised* from macro-economic models, Marxist and non-Marxist.

In some of the chapters in the book, there are some misinterpretations of what I say in the background paper, and so it is necessary to clarify what I say and what I do not say.

Clarifications II: Things I never say

- I never say that absorbing the costs of seasonality *is the only cause* of peasant poverty. Although in some non-nuanced expressions (for example in section 1 of the background paper) I say that 'peasant poverty is determined by the seasonality of agriculture', the correct statement, reflecting my real intention, would have been that 'peasant poverty is determined *mainly* by the seasonality of agriculture'. In section 13 of the paper (somewhat late), I give a numerical hypothetical example through which I show that 'even if we eliminate (through assumptions) the *other poverty factors of peasant producers*' (low productivity and the undervaluation of labour power), they would 'continue to be poor in a market where price levels are determined by the operating logic of capitalist firms'. My acknowledgement of these other factors expresses the fact that seasonality, for me, has never been the only factor of peasant poverty. Some authors underestimate or forget the importance of prices in the determination of family farmers' or peasants' income – not those who emphasise unequal exchange, but certainly those who emphasise the factors behind the low volume of peasant production: small plots, low-quality land, archaic technology, and so on. But explaining poverty as a consequence of these type of factors implies circular reasoning, for one could easily make the contrary argument: that they lack capital and have small plots because they are poor. This has been argued convincingly by Galbraith (1979: Chapter 1). The equation for the income of a family farm (assuming only one crop, which is totally sold, and no hiring of wage labour), is $Y = QP$, where Y is income, Q is the quantity of product, and P is the net price, once market-bought input costs per unit of product are deducted. This makes it clear that peasants can be poor as a consequence of low production levels (Q) and/or low price levels (P). Although both low P and low Q can be causes of peasant poverty, arguments relating to low prices are not involved in circular reasoning, unlike arguments about low quantities.

• I did not state that *capitalism is impossible in agriculture* or that industry cannot deal with living organisms, as Welty, Mann, Dickinson and Blumenfeld (WMDB) (no. 5 in Table 12.1) imply when they state that both the fact that capitalism has successfully penetrated many branches of agricultural production and the fact that some industries rely on micro-organisms in their processes 'undermine essentialist arguments about agriculture'. What I do say is that capitalist agriculture, to the extent that it requires seasonal labour power, is dependent on the existence of a poor population willing, and capable, to work seasonally for low wages, and thus that pure capitalism in agriculture (not combined with peasant or poor family farms) is impossible. As long as such a supply of labour is available (whether it comes from nearby peasant units or from far away), capitalist agriculture can thrive. There is indeed an omission in the background paper in that it does not mention exceptions such as the fact that some industries do deal with micro-organisms, but this omission does not undermine the consequences: labour processes are still (almost always) *continuous in industry* and *discontinuous in agriculture*. I also omitted to say that agricultural discontinuities are greater in some plant species or varieties than in others (see 'Precisions on seasonality' below).

• Nor do I say (or think) that capitalist accumulation is a function of the congruence between production time and working time, as WMDB state that I do (no. 9). As Bernstein (Chapter 5) points out, the background paper's focus is 'on the reproduction of rural households ... it broadens often capital-centric arguments about the uneven development of capitalism'. Explaining capitalist accumulation is completely alien to the theory of peasant poverty and persistence postulated in the background paper.

Clarifications III: Things I do say

• I *do* say that capitalist agriculture is dependent on seasonal labour power provided by poor peasants. So Bernstein (no. 20) is right, *empirically speaking*, when he says that there *might be* other sources, besides peasants, of seasonal labour. Students and teachers can be – and sometimes are – hired during their off-school months; the non-active population (housewives, for example) or the unemployed can also be hired. But this is contingent and anomalous. If you are going to plant fruit trees, you have to be sure that you will have (for many years to come) a sufficient supply of able, efficient and cheap seasonal labour. Migrant labour coming from poor countries to work in agriculture in the rich countries mainly consists of members of poor peasant families. So *conceptually Bernstein is not right*: in a society with full employment, where all who are willing to work are working, only those employed in discontinuous processes of production (such as agriculture or teaching/learning) are available to be hired in some seasons. The rest of the working population is occupied throughout the year. This is why poor peasants and capitalist agriculture have to live in symbiosis.

Precisions on seasonality

• Seasonality is not only a consequence of the differences between production time and working time, which is what is assumed both by the Mann–Dickinson thesis and by Contreras (1977). Take corn (or maize), the most important crop in both the US and Mexico. Relying on information on sowing and harvesting dates from the US Department of Agriculture (www.nass.usda.gov/) for Iowa, the state with the largest acreage of maize in the US, I have calculated the length of production time and working time using two procedures: 1) taking the *most frequent* dates for *starting* sowing and the most frequent dates for *ending* harvesting; and 2) taking the period from the *first to sow* until the *last to harvest* for Iowa as a whole. In the first case, the production period would be 183 days (2 May to 31 October); in the second, it would be 210 days (22 April to 17 November). The same two options can be used for calculating working time, taking only the peak labour demand tasks (planting and harvesting) that require seasonal labourers to be hired. Using the most common dates, the number of working days is 40 (15 for planting and 25 for harvesting); using dates for Iowa as a whole, working days are 103 (43 for sowing and 60 for harvesting). In both cases, working days are part of the production period. The rest of the year is non-production time and therefore also non-working time: that is, it is non-agricultural time (NAT). This is the complement of the agricultural production time or agricultural time (AT), and therefore NAT + AT = 365. The two NAT values are therefore 365−183 = 182 days (1 November to 1 May) and 365−210 = 157 days (18 November to 21 April). The exact calculation is not important here. What I want to convey is that *there are not two but three 'agricultural' periods in a year*: 1) working time (40 or 103 days); 2) the production period without working time, which, in the words of Marx, is the period when 'the unfinished product is handed over to the sway of natural processes' (143 or 107 days, so the total production time is 183 or 210 days); and 3) NAT or non-production time (the winter or dry season, which equates to 182 or 155 days). Of the 365 days of the year, as we see now, the working days (counting only the two periods of peak labour requirements) account for between just over 10 per cent to 28 per cent, and the longest non-working period is winter or dry season, or the period from the end of harvesting to the beginning of sowing (182 or 155 days). The latter is greater than the difference between production time and working time (210–103 = 107 or 183–40 = 143). These three periods are different in the case of winter wheat, which is sown before the winter and harvested the following autumn; in this case, the production period is very long, almost one year, and NAT is almost zero. Nevertheless, winter time is still a non-working period. So, going back to WMDB, accumulation can never be a function of the congruence between production time and working time, as agricultural time also involves such 'essentialist' facts of life as the winter or the dry season.

- Some authors (for example, Mann and Dickinson 1978) make a false identity between biological (or chemical processes), which take time, and *plant growth*, which also takes time but *is also attached to a specific period of the year* (e.g. spring for planting; autumn for harvesting) when the specific climatic conditions (temperature, rain, etc.) that it requires are present. The gestation periods of cows, pigs and rabbits (around 280, 115 and 31 days respectively) take time but they can become pregnant at various seasons, as heat periods are not tied to seasons. So, in cattle raising, you can have pregnant cows, and deliveries, all year round. Cows produce milk throughout the year. Livestock production is not seasonal. This is even more applicable to chemical or bacterial reactions, for example in brewing. When some authors say that the achievement of factory-like production in hog and chicken rearing reflects the possibility of attaining the same in plant cultivation, they are neglecting the seasonal and climatic determination of this last activity. Hothouses introduce a degree of man-made climatic control, but at a very high cost and they require irrigation.

- I did not state it explicitly, as I assumed it was evident, that seasonality manifests itself in diverse rhythms in different *plants*. Grains are, generally, an annual crop. In some weather conditions, two cycles per year are possible if irrigation facilities are available, as in north-western Mexico. Some vegetables have shorter periods of growth than grains (lettuces and peas, for instance), so they can be harvested twice a year even in colder weather like that of Iowa, but even in these cases the winter (November–March) is NAT. Other vegetables (such as onions, tomatoes and potatoes) can only be harvested annually (information from Iowa State University, Extension and Outreach, web page). Fruits, some of which are perennial plants, have a variable harvest period but this is also mostly annual. Seasonality *seems to be present in all agricultural products (in the Spanish sense of the term, i.e. plant rearing)*. WMDB state: 'Yet, to say that the production of many agricultural commodities reflects the confluence of these natural features is not the same as saying that all agricultural commodities are subject to the same logic'; while this remains valid for *agriculture* in the English sense, it is not valid for the Spanish sense.

Backups I: Unexpected findings in Lenin's and Danielson's thinking. The generalised interpretation of Lenin's position is that *capitalism would take over direct production in agriculture*, in a similar way as it did in handicrafts, displacing the peasantry, which would then vanish as peasants would differentiate into capitalists and proletarians. But reading Lenin closely leads one to nuance this sharply defined position. In *The Development of Capitalism in Russia* (1964 [1899]: 175–90), Lenin arrives at ten conclusions; the first six are as follows (the page references are those for each conclusion; I am excerpting Lenin's text rather than reproducing it verbatim):

1. *The contemporary Russian peasantry are immersed in a commodity economy* and thus subject to all its inherent contradictions. The peasantry is completely subordinated to the market (ibid.: 175).
2. These contradictions show that the system of economic relations in the 'community' village does not constitute a special economic form ('people's production', etc.) but is an ordinary petty-bourgeois one. *The Russian community peasantry are not antagonists of capitalism, but, on the contrary, are its deepest and most durable foundation* (ibid.: 175–6).
3. The sum total of all the economic contradictions constitutes what we call the *differentiation of the peasantry*, which peasants themselves characterise by the term '*depeasantising*'. The old peasantry is not

only 'differentiating', it is being completely dissolved – it is ceasing to exist (ibid.: 176–9).

4. *The differentiation of the peasantry creates two new types of rural inhabitants*: the first is the rural bourgeoisie or the well-to-do peasantry. The size of their farms requires *the formation of a body of farm labourers and day labourers* (ibid.: 179–80).

5. *The second new type is the rural proletariat, the class of allotment-holding wage workers.* This covers the poor peasants, including the completely landless; *however, the most typical representative of the Russian rural proletariat is the allotment-holding farm labourer, day labourer, unskilled labourer, building worker or other allotment-holding worker.* Insignificant farming on a patch of land, the inability to exist without the sale of labour power, an extremely low standard of living – these are the distinguishing features of this type. Our literature frequently contains *too stereotyped an understanding of the theoretical proposition that capitalism requires the free, landless worker.* This proposition is quite correct in that it indicates the main trend, but *capitalism penetrates into agriculture particularly slowly and in extremely varied forms. The allocation of land to the rural worker is very often in the interests of rural employers themselves, and that is why the allotment-holding rural worker is a type to be found in all capitalist countries.* In *assigning the indigent peasants to the rural proletariat,* we are saying nothing new, only the Narodnik economists persist in speaking of the peasantry in general as being something anti-capitalist (ibid.: 180–1).

6. The intermediary link between these post-reform types of 'peasantry' is the *middle peasantry, which covers his maintenance in perhaps only the best years*, and his position is extremely precarious. *In most cases, the middle peasant cannot make ends meet without* resorting to loans, to be repaid through labour service, and without *the sale of his labour power.* Every crop failure flings masses of middle peasants into the ranks of the proletariat (ibid.: 183–4).

What Lenin calls the 'rural proletariat' (allotment-holding worker[2]) is what most authors in this book call peasants. Thus, his thesis on the proletarianisation of the peasantry is built through an *act of labelling*. Lenin was aware of the symbiosis between agricultural capital and 'allotment-holding workers' but did not link it explicitly to seasonality. His implicit explanation of the dominance of allotment-holding workers (instead of landless workers) in agriculture, that capitalism penetrates slowly in agriculture, involves circular reasoning. Paradoxically, to explain why the allotment-holding rural worker is present in all capitalist countries, he resorts to the interests of the rural employers. This is linked to the tendency, noted by Djurfeldt (1982: 141), for the big *latifundistas* to divide parts of their land into parcels where they settle their workers. Djurfeldt adds that this is complemented by legislative action, which he illustrates with the British Small Holding Act of 1892, the Danish *husmandsbevaegelse* and the Swedish *egnahem-srörelse*. Then he adds that 'it is a way of decreasing the cost of labour in a capitalistic enterprise, which in more recent times also has been the specific aim of land reforms in many Latin American countries' (for a longer quote, see Chapter 1, section 6).

Lenin (1964 [1899]: Section X, Chapter IV) was confronted with the Narodnik theory of the 'freeing of winter time'. He describes 'the essence' of this theory of N. F. Danielson (who he refers to as 'N.-on' or 'Nicolai-on') as follows:

> Under the capitalist system *agriculture becomes a separate industry*, unconnected with the others. *However, it is not carried on the whole year but only for five or six months*. Therefore, the capitalisation of agriculture leads to 'the freeing of winter time', *to the 'limitation of the working time of the agricultural class to part of the working year'*, which is the *'fundamental cause of the deterioration of the economic conditions of the agricultural classes'*. (ibid.: 323, emphasis added)

Lenin attacks this theory: 'Here you have the whole of this *celebrated* theory, which bases the most sweeping historical and philosophical conclusions solely *on the great truth that in agriculture jobs are distributed over the year very unevenly!*' Lenin's critique reminds the reader of Bernstein's critique of my theory (Chapter 5), which is also based on that *great truth*:

> To take this one feature, to reduce it to absurdity by means of *abstract* assumptions, to *discard all the other specific features of the complex process which transforms patriarchal agriculture into capitalist agriculture* – such are the simple methods used in this latest attempt to restore the romantic theories about pre-capitalist 'people's production'. (Lenin 1964 [1899]: 319, emphasis added)

Lenin qualifies Danielson's theory as an 'inordinately narrow' and 'abstract postulate'. In order to show this, 'he indicates five aspects of the actual process that are either entirely lost sight of, or are underrated by our Narodniks'. My ability to judge the cogency of Lenin's argument is limited as I have had no access to the works of Danielson, which, apparently, are not available in English, Spanish or French. Hussain and Tribe (1983) cite a German-language edition of Danielson's book *Russian Economy after the Peasant Emancipation* (written under the pseudonym Nicolai-on). I highlight aspects three to five of Lenin's critique which relate directly to my theory:

'Thirdly, capitalism presupposes the complete separation of agricultural from industrial *enterprises*,' says Lenin, rephrasing the Narodnik thesis. And replies: 'But whence does it follow that this separation does not permit the combination of agricultural and industrial *wage-labour*? We find such a combination in developed capitalist societies everywhere'. He adds that unskilled workers 'pass from one occupation to another, now drawn into jobs at some large enterprise, and now thrown into the ranks of the workless'. Lenin quotes *Capital*, Volume I, where Marx uses the expression 'nomad labour', and Volume II, where he says that 'such large-scale undertakings as railways' withdraw labour power that 'can come only from certain branches of the economy, for example, agriculture' (Lenin 1964 [1899]: 324–6).

'Fourthly, if we take the present-day rural employers, *it cannot, of course, be denied that sometimes they experience difficulty in providing their farms with workers*,' says Lenin, adding: 'But *it must not be forgotten that they have a means of tying the workers to their farms, namely, by allotting them patches of land*. The allotment-holding labourer is a type common to all capitalist countries. One of the chief errors of the Narodniks is that they ignore the formation of a similar type in Russia' (ibid.: 326). 'Fifthly, it is quite wrong to discuss the *freeing of the farmer's winter time* independently of the general question of capitalist surplus-population' (ibid.: 326, emphasis added).

* * *

Lenin tries to subsume the specific idleness of agricultural labour in winter in the general problem of the industrial reserve army, and attributes this approach to Marx. But Lenin argues inadvertently against himself when he quotes Marx underlining the seasonality of agricultural activities: 'There are always too many agricultural labourers for the ordinary, and always too few for the exceptional or temporary needs of the cultivation of the soil' (Marx 1976 [1867]). Lenin comments: 'So that, notwithstanding the permanent "relative surplus population", the countryside seems to be inadequately populated.' So, instead of subsuming the seasonal unemployment of agriculture as part of the surplus population, Lenin makes it clear, non-voluntarily, that it is an *independent characteristic*. Lenin refers to Chapter 13 of Volume II of *Capital*, where Marx discusses the difference between 'working time' and 'production time'. He notes that, in Russia, compared with other European countries, *this difference is a particularly big one*, and quotes Marx again, in this case backing up Danielson's thesis, again inadvertently (I add, in brackets, a sentence that precedes the two quoted by Lenin):

> [We see here how the distinction between production period and working period, with the latter forming only a part of the former, *constitutes the natural basis for the unification of agriculture with rural subsidiary industries* ...]. In so far *as capitalist production later manages to complete the separation between manufacture and agriculture, the rural worker becomes ever more dependent on merely accidental subsidiary employments and his condition thereby worsens. As far as capital is concerned ... all these differences in the turnover balance out. Not so for the worker.* (Marx 1978 [1885]: 319; 1957 [1885]: 241; different translations)

Lenin comments (agreeing with Danielson, who is backed up by Marx):

> So then, the only conclusion that follows from *the specific features of agriculture* ... is that *the position of the agricultural worker must be even worse than that of the industrial worker. This is still a very long way from Mr. N's theory that the freeing of winter time is the fundamental reason for the deterioration of the conditions of the 'agricultural classes'. If the working period in our agriculture equalled 12 months ... the entire difference would be that the conditions of the agricultural worker would come somewhat closer to those of the industrial worker.* (Lenin 1964 [1899]: 327)

Going back to Danielson, 'the conversion of agriculture *in a separate industry*' must be based on the text just quoted from Volume II of *Capital* (he had an ongoing relation with Marx and Engels, and translated the three volumes of *Capital* into Russian). Additional evidence for this is that the paragraph from which the last quote from *Capital*, Volume II is taken by Lenin refers to Russia! The phrases quoted by Lenin and the one I added are at the end of a long paragraph in which Marx had previously stated:

> Thus the more unfavourable the climate, the more the agricultural working period, and hence the outlay of capital and labour, is compressed into a short interval, as for example in Russia. 'In some of the northern districts, field labour is only possible during from 130 to 150 days in the course of the year, and it may be imagined what a loss Russia would sustain, if out of the 65 million of her European population, 50 million remain unoccupied during six or eight months of winter, when all agricultural labour is at a standstill.' ... particular cottage industries have grown up everywhere in the villages. 'There are villages, for instance, in Russia in which all the peasants have been for generations either weavers, tanners, shoemakers, locksmiths, cutlers, etc.' ... These cottage industries, incidentally, are already being pressed, more and more into the service of capitalist production. (Marx 1978 [1885]: 318–19; the text previously quoted appears after this)

Kautsky (1988 [1899]: 181–2) gives the following succinct account of the forced specialisation of peasants in agriculture, which coincides in general terms with the Marx–Danielson view:

> Originally peasants were both farmers and industrialists. The development of urban industry eventually forced them to devote themselves exclusively to agriculture. Nevertheless, the peasant family retained a number of manual skills. Wherever agriculture begins to fail as the sole source of income these can be resurrected, but not as handicrafts working directly for the customer. The isolated peasant cannot compete with the urban handicrafts, which have access both to larger markets and all the other advantages of the town. As commodity-production, rural industry can only

develop as production for a capitalist, a merchant or a putter-out, who establishes the link with distant markets inaccessible to the peasant.

The theory of the freeing of winter time can be seen as an obvious (but very little known) precedent of my theory. The Narodnik theory refers to one of the non-working periods defined above (in the section 'Precisions on seasonality'): the winter or the NAT. Winter unemployment is explained by Danielson as a result of the development of capitalist industry, which converts peasants into *specialised producers* within the social division of labour. In a preceding stage, which Lenin calls patriarchal peasantry, peasants were occupied in the winter in various crafts (as the preceding quote of *Capital* makes clear). Some of these crafts were ruined first by capitalist-promoted cottage industries, and later by manufacturing and rural industry (the period to which Marx refers as *unification of agriculture with rural subsidiary industries*). But at some point, as Marx says, capitalism manages *to complete the separation between manufacturing and agriculture*. At this point, local crafts had been completely (or mostly) displaced by industrial products, now relocated mostly to towns. Marx maintained that, with this 'complete separation of agriculture and manufacture', the '*rural worker becomes ever more dependent on merely accidental subsidiary employments and his condition thereby worsens*', and, as stated by Lenin, our Narodnik theorists expressed this as the '*limitation of the working time of the agricultural class to part of the working year*, which is the *fundamental cause of the deterioration of the economic conditions of the agricultural classes*'. What they are saying, together with Marx, is that the growing social division of labour, or branch specialisation – which was highly praised, correctly, by Adam Smith as one of the forces of the wealth of nations – finds an exception in agriculture. *People involved in agriculture, given the discontinuity of agricultural work, are damaged by the growing division of labour.* In a given state of technological development, the limitation of the working time of the *vast majority of humanity* means that the wealth they are able to create (which is a function of working time) is severely diminished, and this has to be reflected in the economic conditions of this population. The quotations from Marx and Lenin show that they both agree on this, although Lenin expresses the opposite by saying 'this is still a very long way from Mr. N's theory'.

As a general conclusion as to how Lenin's text strengthens my theory, I can make the following two points. Firstly, if one looks more closely into Lenin's peasant differentiation analysis, it confirms the symbiosis between capitalist agriculture and poor peasants, rather than the disappearance of peasants; the latter (whom Lenin labels proletarians) provide cheap seasonal labour to the former. Lenin provides no argument on why this symbiosis should be unstable or why it should tend to be displaced by pure capitalist relations: that is, relations between capital and landless labourers. Secondly, Danielson's theory of the 'freeing of winter time', based on Marx, is reluctantly and partially accepted by Lenin 'as worsening the position' of the agricultural worker. Lenin's description also shows that *the peasant's access to land is (sometimes) carried out voluntarily by rich farmers to guarantee their provision of labour power.* This undermines positions such as Leff's – that the poverty of peasants is explained as a consequence of dispossession of their land. History shows that dispossession and re-possession are frequently sequential.

Backups II: Kautsky's views on why capitalism needs the peasantry. As shown in Chapter 1, section 6, Kautsky (1988 [1899]) implicitly argues, for demographic reasons, that the peasantry is an integral part of the capitalist mode of production in agriculture and that he *expects a symbiotic relationship between peasantry and capitalism to last a long time.* Also, he quotes Marx, arguing that, as long as bourgeois relations subsist, 'agriculture necessarily proceeds in an incessant cycle of concentration and fragmentation of the land'.

Akram-Lodhi and Kay (2009) state that 'the establishment of agrarian capital began, according to Kautsky and Lenin, with the deepening use of non-rurally produced simple manufactures in rural society', as 'urban manufactures were cheaper than rural' ones; this coincides with what was said in the previous subsection. This increased the need for money and, as a consequence, according to Kautsky, led to 'the commoditization of agricultural production' (ibid.: 8). And this, in turn, led to competition and social differentiation.

But Akram-Lodhi and Kay add that Lenin and Kautsky 'did not propose that rural transformation was subject to "path-dependence", i.e. self-reinforcing tendencies':

Kautsky, in particular, but also Lenin, argued that the process of agrarian change could take multiple forms ... Agro-industrial capital ... might in particular circumstances *prefer to sustain a non-capitalist rural economy because of the unique characteristics of agricultural production. These characteristics include seasonal and biological aspects*, as well as the capacity of family based agricultural production to depress real wages by working longer and harder ... In such circumstances, according to Kautsky, *agro-industrial capital would restrict itself to food processing, farm inputs and rural financial systems, using science, technology and money to subsume petty commodity production to the demands of agro-industrial capital* ... For Kautsky there was no tendency for the size distribution of farms to change over time, as might be inferred if capitalist agriculture overwhelmed peasant farming. (ibid.: 10–11, emphasis added)

The depeasantisation thesis – assumed by many to be *the* thesis sustained by both Lenin and Kautsky – is completely transformed into a thesis on the persistence of the peasantry, at least for Kautsky, thus confirming the position adopted in the background paper.

Hamza Alavi and Teodor Shanin (1988), in their introduction to the English edition of *The Agrarian Question*, highlight some points that characterise it. Below, I summarise, and discuss, three that are closely related to the topics of this chapter.

The demographic role of the peasantry

Alavi and Shanin note that Kautsky's arguments are often misread. This could be partly due to the fact that Kautsky started his book with certain preconceptions that he modifies 'quite radically ... in the light of his findings as the analysis progresses'. Initially, he presumed that ... capital would eliminate petty commodity production; the peasantry would be dissolved ... But rural censuses in Germany did not show a progressive concentration of land in fewer hands. So, as 'Kautsky proceeds with his analysis ... he defines with increasing clarity the significant structural differences between the conditions of peasant production and petty commodity production in manufacturing' (ibid.: xiii). By Chapter 7, Kautsky finds himself 'explaining why such a tendency does not prevail; why the peasantry may even persist within the general framework of capitalism'. Alavi and Shanin add that, in the section 'Shortage of labour power' –

from which I quoted extensively in Chapter 1, section 6 – we *'find him pointing out the functional role of small farms as "production sites" for labour-power needed by the capitalist large farms and industry'*. They quote Kautsky: 'The growth in the number of large farms curtails the supply of rural labour power while, at the same time, increasing the demand for it ... This in itself is sufficient to ensure that despite its technical superiority, the large farms can never completely prevail' (ibid.: xiii–xiv).

Alavi and Shanin contrast Kautsky's view with that of Lenin, which they characterise as the classical notion of the inevitable transformation of rural Russia through polarisation, and conclude that Kautsky's perception is significantly different from Lenin's (ibid.: xiv). As can be seen, my interpretation of Lenin's views differs from that of Alavi and Shanin.

The question arises on the relations between two functions of the peasantry, both of which are assumed to explain its persistence: the production of labour power, attributed by Kautsky; and the provision of cheap seasonal wage labour, attributed in Chapter 1 by me. In Kautsky's view, it is the integration of the production unit and the household unit that explains the peasant's capacity to procreate, whereas he argues that both domestic servants and free wage workers do not have this capacity *as they lack an autonomous household unit.* This is obvious for domestic servants; however, in the case of free wage workers there is a missing argument, namely that they cannot form a household as they are *nomadic workers.*

In contrast, Kautsky (1988 [1899]: 163, emphasis added) says that small farms supply labour power for themselves and also produce a surplus. In explaining this function, Kautsky notes that their 'bit of cultivation of their own land *does not take up all of their time and they hire themselves out as day labourers on larger farms,* or they provide a surplus of workers via their children, for whom there is no room on the family farm' (ibid.). In my theory, all active members of a family might be able to alternate work on their own land with wage work on other farms, which corresponds with Kautsky's phrase highlighted in italics. The difference is that Kautsky does not emphasise seasonality as the explaining factor. Nevertheless, his demographic theory and my seasonal theory complement each other. His theory explains why capitalist farms, which do not reproduce labour, *need peasant households to procreate.* My theory explains that capitalist farms, which have to hire labour power mostly in peak seasons, *need a reliable, seasonal, cheap supply of labour.*

Overexploitation of peasant labour power
'The lower-than-average price of labour-power that is realised in agriculture reinforces its functional significance for capitalism.' Although for Kautsky large-scale agriculture is more effective than peasant farming, peasants survive because they are ready to accept 'underconsumption' and 'excessive labour', underselling permanent wage workers.

Technological progress and historicity of the peasants
Despite his position on peasants' persistence and their functionality for capitalism, Kautsky insisted 'on the historical nature of the peasantry'. The element that made these two positions compatible is, according to Alavi and Shanin, Kautsky's idea that the 'end of the peasantry would come about as a result of technological progress rather than from the impact of capitalism' (Alavi and Shanin 1988: xvi). Kautsky is completely right. Seasonality makes capital dependent on a cheap seasonal supply of labour, but, as Goodman, Sorj and Wilkinson have argued, complete mechanisation releases this dependence:

> New plant breeding techniques have permitted the complete mechanisation of cultivation in major crop sectors. [They then provide two examples.] Today with the precision planting of monogerm seeds ... the production of sugar beets in the US is completely mechanised. *The growers have become independent of migrant labour* [p. 35, quoting Rasmussen]. Tomato picking in California, until 1964 had been a manual operation performed by Mexican workers ... Successful industrial appropriation of this task was achieved by ... a harvesting machine and a new variety of tomato plant with fruit that would ripen at about the same time and be able to withstand machine handling. (Goodman et al. 1987: 34–5)

Alavi and Shanin appraise Kautsky's main achievements. The example that is most clearly related to the debates in this book is that Kautsky:

traced the regularities and stages through which peasant firms were transformed under the impact of capital: the *agriculturalization of the peasant, i.e. the increase of farming activity as against the self-supporting crafts*; the commercialisation and monetisation of their economic activities; and the *increasing engagement in extra-farm wage labour*. (Alavi and Shanin 1988: xxxi)

Luis Cabrera and agricultural capitalism's needs for peasants. According to Schejtman and the United Nations Economic Commission for Latin America (Schejtman 1982: 27), 'Luis Cabrera was perhaps the most influential of the agrarian intellectuals of the first stage of the Mexican revolution'. Arnaldo Córdova describes Cabrera's position: 'it was necessary to "reconstruct the *ejidos*, making sure that these are *inalienable*"' (quoted in ibid.: 28). The purpose of this reconstruction was that the *ejidos* would become part of an agrarian structure in which fully exploited agricultural medium and large enterprises would coexist with *ejidos*. These would be constituted using land appropriated from the big latifundia, which *would allow day labourers* to have more income so that they would not become Zapatistas and take up rifles (ibid.: 28, quoting Luisa Paré). In 1912, in his position as a deputy to the Federal Congress, Cabrera presented a project for a law that would reconstitute the *ejidos*. The speech he gave on that day is reproduced in Silva-Herzog (1964: 200–8). I translate some excerpts that are highly pertinent to the debates in this book (specific page numbers are given in brackets):

> Before protecting the small rural property, it is necessary to solve another agrarian problem ... This consists in liberating the people from the economic and political pressures exerted by the *haciendas*, within the limits of which the proletarian villagers are kept as prisoners. For this, it is necessary to think of reconstituting the *ejidos*,[3] making sure that they are inalienable, taking the land required from the large surrounding big properties. (p. 200) ... What you are going to hear is the bare but moving observation of the facts. The *hacienda* ... has two types of servants or workers: the *annual peon* and the *task peon*. The annual peon is the *acasillado* peon who lives in the *hacienda* together with his family. The task peon is the one who renders

his services occasionally, for the sowing or harvesting period. The annual peon has the most insignificant wage that a *human beast* can have ... lower than what is required for his subsistence, even lower than the amount required for the subsistence of a mule. Why does this wage exist? (p. 202) ... For the following reasons: the *hacienda* ... calculates it can pay an average of 120 pesos for the four months in which it needs the labour of the peon; this means that it would have to pay 30 pesos per month or one peso per day. But if it received the peon and let him go again, *it would have the difficulties associated with the search for arms.* He needs to seek the permanence of that peon in the *hacienda*, so he dilutes the wage for four months over the whole year, paying a daily amount of 0.31 pesos per day, or the same 120 pesos per year. [If the merely repressive means of retaining the peon fails,] he uses other economic means to attract him. I am going to enumerate them. The price at which the peons of the *hacienda* have the right to acquire maize [is below the market price]. This ... represents a small increase in the peon's wage ... barely sufficient for him not to starve to death (p. 203) ... He also receives as a complement to his wage the *casilla*, a half, third or eighth part of the *casilla* that is his dwelling ... Next, there is the credit he has in the *tienda de raya* [the *hacienda* store]. (p. 204) [Here he receives] as credit every day what he needs to eat, which is deducted from his weekly wage ... and he gets loans in Holy Week, on All Saints Day and at Christmas Eve ... These loans are made without any intention of them being repaid by the peon. What, then, is the purpose of these loans if the peon cannot repay them and the owner of the *hacienda* has no intention of collecting them? It doesn't matter; he will collect the debt in the blood of the peon's children and grandchildren ... The three annual loans are not, apparently, an increase in the peon's wages, but that is what they really are. (p. 205) ... Lastly, another way of increasing wages is given to a select group of peons ... a small piece of land, around a quarter of a hectare, which the peon has the right to cultivate ... [I]t is therefore the most interesting one for our purposes. *As long as it is not possible to create a system of smallholders' agricultural exploitation that replaces the big exploitations and latifundia, the agrarian problem should be solved through the exploitation of* ejidos *as a way of complementing wages.* (p. 206, emphasis added)

In this astonishing text, Cabrera shows an extreme solution, not foreseen in my seasonal theory: wages are paid only for the days worked (as my theory says) but the workers are retained in the hacienda by spreading these wages throughout the year and indebting the peons until they become *peones acasillados* (a sort of prisoner). This retention is performed to guarantee that, in the following peak periods, the hacienda will have labour to do the work. In Cabrera's speech it becomes clear who pays the social cost of seasonality and the recruiting difficulties involved for wage-paying entrepreneurs. It is like a reductio ad absurdum performed in real life, not in thought. It shows the extremes to which capitalist enterprises would have to go to solve the recruitment problems of seasonal agriculture if there were no poor landholding peasants around to voluntarily provide seasonal labour. Cabrera's speech is also enlightening because he sees only two possible futures: 1) the agrarian reform he proposes, which is equivalent to the practice mentioned by Lenin of giving small parcels of land to the peasants so that they can complement their seasonal wages; and 2) production based totally in smallholdings. *Cabrera does not conceive the possibility of a completely capitalist system operating in agriculture, as he knew it would be impossible.* His speech is a very strong reinforcement of the theory of peasant poverty and persistence presented in Chapter 1.

2. Reply to commentaries and criticisms

Welty, Mann, Dickinson and Blumenfeld. I will not repeat those points already covered in the previous section; instead, I will start with commentaries numbered 4 to 6 in Table 12.1, all of which relate to the alleged 'essentialist' (a term used derogatorily) view of agriculture in the background paper. Goodman, Sorj and Wilkinson would receive the same criticism from WMDB:

> The key to understanding the *uniqueness of agriculture* ... lies neither in its social structure nor in its factor endowment. Rather *agriculture confronts capitalism with a natural production process.* Unlike sectors of handicraft activity, agriculture could not be directly transformed into a branch of industrial production. There was no industrial alternative to the biological transformation of solar energy into food. (Goodman et al. 1987: 1)

TABLE 12.1 Contributors' criticisms of and disagreements with the background paper's account of peasant poverty and persistence

Author(s) and chapter	Disagreements and criticisms in relation to the background paper (BP)
Bartra (Chapter 2)	1. Seasonality is not the most important explanation of peasant persistence. Peasants' function as a buffer of differential ground rents is more important. 2. More than subsidies, diversification is the solution to peasants' poverty. 3. Peasant *exploitation* is polymorphous, absorbing the costs of seasonality; wage work, unequal market exchange and absorption of ground rent are other forms.
Welty, Mann, Dickinson and Blumenfeld (Chapter 3)	4. Take issue with the BP's *ontology* of industry and agriculture and its '*essentialist*' view of agriculture'. 5. Think that the BP maintains that *capitalism is impossible* in agriculture and that industry *cannot deal* with living micro-organisms, so that any example in either case would be a proof against the theory. 6. Question the distinction between organic and inorganic features of production, i.e. 'essentialist, ontological distinctions' between agriculture and industry, as a basis to account for differences in their development. 7. The BP is said to blur the distinction between the use value of labour power and its exchange value. 8. It passes over the fact that, in capitalism, the maintenance and reproduction of labour power are almost entirely privatised. 9. The BP regards 'capitalist accumulation as a function of the congruence between production time and labour time per se'. 10. Disagree with its proposal to subsidise peasant agriculture in the global South.
Arizmendi (Chapter 4)	11. Introduces the distinction between critical and normative theory as the correct framework with which to evaluate Marx's theory of value with respect to its neglect of discontinuities. 12. Criticises the BP's step to try to formulate a general theory of value as being unnecessary.
Bernstein (Chapter 5)	13. Finds the highly abstract nature of its theory problematic, that abstractions 'are not grounded in theory as history' and that the theory (and its assumptions) are not tested empirically. 14. Does not answer questions such as: Why are some farmers or peasants not poor? Does all capitalist farming depend on seasonal cheap labour? 15. Lacks a move to periodise and explore the development of agriculture in capitalist society. 16. Instead of the two-sector (capitalist and peasant farming) model of the BP (with barely any reference to the wider capitalist economy), proposes the notion of fragmented classes of labour.

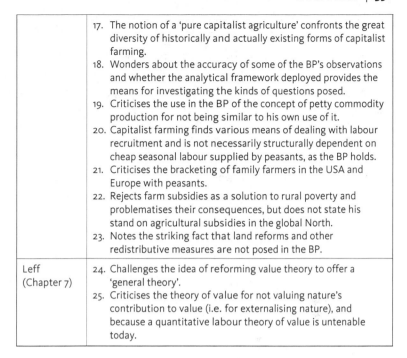

	17. The notion of a 'pure capitalist agriculture' confronts the great diversity of historically and actually existing forms of capitalist farming. 18. Wonders about the accuracy of some of the BP's observations and whether the analytical framework deployed provides the means for investigating the kinds of questions posed. 19. Criticises the use in the BP of the concept of petty commodity production for not being similar to his own use of it. 20. Capitalist farming finds various means of dealing with labour recruitment and is not necessarily structurally dependent on cheap seasonal labour supplied by peasants, as the BP holds. 21. Criticises the bracketing of family farmers in the USA and Europe with peasants. 22. Rejects farm subsidies as a solution to rural poverty and problematises their consequences, but does not state his stand on agricultural subsidies in the global North. 23. Notes the striking fact that land reforms and other redistributive measures are not posed in the BP.
Leff (Chapter 7)	24. Challenges the idea of reforming value theory to offer a 'general theory'. 25. Criticises the theory of value for not valuing nature's contribution to value (i.e. for externalising nature), and because a quantitative labour theory of value is untenable today.

In this transformation (*photosynthesis*) lies the miracle of life as we mostly know it. This is indeed *a very essential fact*. I do not regard *essentialism* as something negative, as WMDB do, and I will defend it. But first I will clarify whether my position is essentialist and how far it is, in this respect, from the Mann–Dickinson thesis (MDT).

WMDB qualify the description of distinctive features of industry and agriculture in Chapter 1 as an 'ontology' of industry and agriculture, and add that it is based on an 'essentialist view of agriculture' taken from John Brewster. 'Ontology' is a branch of philosophy that deals with *being in itself*; it studies the more general characteristics of reality (Bunge 2001: 155). Apparently, WMDB object to all essentialist approaches, although the MDT accepts the 'non-identity of production time and labour time' (Mann and Dickinson 1978: 477) and its corollary of seasonal labour *as facts of agriculture*. 'In the literature on family farming, the employment of seasonal wage labour is acknowledged, but its importance is generally underplayed,' they say, and add: 'However as *labour time* may be almost entirely suspended between, say, sowing and harvesting, *seasonal wage labour becomes extremely important in the determination of the value of the agricultural commodities produced*' (ibid.). However, they want to distance themselves from essentialist and determinist approaches. In Chapter 3, WMDB do this by criticising my position, which they regard as essentialist. But in the MDT *it becomes clear how important the natural (and essential) features of agriculture* (as well as the contrast with industry) *are in their theoretical position*. Mann and Dickinson (ibid.: 478) express caveats ('the theoretical approach which we have sketched out here must only be used in conjunction with a social and historical analysis') that communicate how they want their theoretical position to be construed or used, rather than what it really is:

> The argument that *it is the natural characteristics of the production process which ultimately inhibit capitalist development must not be misinterpreted as natural determinism.* Indeed, *the relationship to objective, natural processes is much closer in agriculture than in industry*; but an explanation based on nature *alone* does not explain why some spheres of agriculture become capitalistic relatively rapidly while other spheres are characterised by non-capitalistic forms. In a general sense, *the inability to control natural factors affects all forms of agricultural production* ... An appeal to nature alone is an ahistorical argument.

This paragraph shows a pendular movement from non-willing naturalism to the rejection of its essentialist or deterministic consequences. This is present in the first sentence and repeated in the second. Finally, the last two sentences quoted, taken together, repeat the pendular movement.

This shows that the only difference between the MDT and my theory with regard to their natural (essential) features is that I do not reject their consequences and do not express caveats as to their use.

Describing features of a human activity (agriculture) and contrasting them with those of industry, as Chapter 1 does – or as Bernstein does when he draws a table of these comparisons – are descriptive activities. This would constitute an *ontology* if these characteristics were seen as the more general features of agriculture and industry. Neither I nor the MDT identifies what each one does as ontology. If one is called ontology, then both should be. But the specific critique by WMDB is that my ontology is said to rest on 'an essentialist view of agriculture drawn from the writings of John Brewster'. This is inexact: the distinctive features of agriculture are part of the prevailing conventional wisdom of people working in agriculture (not only academics, but also managers, consultants, and so on), as the following text illustrates:

> From a management perspective, *agriculture is quite distinctive.* This distinctiveness primarily relates to the *time-dependent biological nature of agricultural production … Industrial production, being independent of the natural environment, is mechanical.* In contrast, the *biological nature of agricultural production* causes it to be strongly influenced by the natural environment. In consequence, *agriculture has its own innate rhythms and significant elements of agricultural production are not under the farmer's control.*[4]

I conclude that enumerating some distinctive features of agriculture is not necessarily an essentialist activity. Many relativists would agree that those features do, in fact, distinguish agriculture from industry. The feature of agriculture on which I base my theory of peasant poverty and persistence is seasonality, which, as we have seen, is also strongly emphasised by the MDT. But as I do not regard essentialism as a negative quality, I do not write caveats as Mann and Dickinson and WMDB do. WMDB define essentialism as follows:

> An essentialist argument generally claims that there are natural or inherent traits that characterise a particular group or category and *that these irreducible traits constitute its very being,* but this type of essentialism has been called into question by a number of critics of *modernist thought.* (Chapter 3, section 2)

They quote Diana Fuss's book *Essentially Speaking: Feminism, nature, and difference* (1989) as an example of this critique. It refers not to essentialism in agriculture but to essentialism in human beings.

When referring to human beings, essentialism is expressed through the concepts of human essence and human nature. I wrote a long discussion based on Erich Fromm and Ramón Xirau (1968), György Márkus (1978) and Martha Nussbaum (1992), and pointed out that there are other important authors who have defended essentialism and universalism. Just to mention three of them: from the philosophical field, Thomas Hurka in his *Perfectionism* (1993); from the social sciences, Len Doyal and Ian Gough in *A Theory of Human Need* (1991); and, from the natural sciences, Steven Pinker's *The Blank Slate: The modern denial of human nature* (2002). For reasons of space, nevertheless, I had to delete the discussion mentioned, which showed that there are many distinguished scholars today who strongly defend essentialist approaches and illustrated the force and consistency of their arguments.

Replies to criticisms, as has been seen, take up a lot of space. The replies to other criticisms by WMDB not addressed in the main text are presented in Table 12.2. I do the same with some of Bernstein's criticisms: some will be replied to at length, and others in a compact form in Table 12.2.

Bernstein's commentaries (numbers 13 to 23). Bernstein's criticisms are combined with praise and are very helpful. I do not agree with some of his points, but they provide good grounds for reflection. The first one (13) says that he 'finds the highly abstract nature' of the theory expounded in Chapter 1 'problematic', as 'abstractions are not grounded in theory as history', and that the theory and its assumptions 'are not tested empirically'. This commentary is linked to numbers 15 ('lacks a move to periodise and explore the development of agriculture in capitalist society') and 17 ('the notion of a pure capitalist agriculture confronts the great diversity of historically and actually existing forms of capitalist farming'). Commentary number 20 (on sources of seasonal labour for agricultural capitalism) has already been dealt with in the previous section. Since some of his commentaries refer to what Chapter 1 does *not* contain, Bernstein clarifies that 'the point is not to suggest that one paper can cover everything' but rather to 'enquire whether the analytical framework provides the means for investigating the kinds of questions noted'.

My first answer to this group of commentaries is that *theories are necessarily abstract*. For instance, both the Marxist theory of value and the neoclassical theory of prices are highly abstract. But Bernstein's main critique is that my abstractions are not grounded in 'theory as history'. The expression 'theory as history' comes from the title of J. Banaji's book; in the foreword to it, Marcel van der Linden (2010: xi) explains the meaning of this expression:

> If we are to understand historical processes truly and in depth, then we ought to do full justice to the empirical record. But that is not all. We also have to reveal the abstract determinations which are hidden 'behind' the concrete, and which 'lead towards a reproduction of the concrete by way of thought' [quotes Marx's *Grundrisse*]. If we disregard this necessary dialectic of the abstract and the concrete, one of two kinds of errors is likely to result. Either we remain entrapped in a descriptive narrative of a mass of empirical details failing to reach the abstract determinations that identify and convincingly *explain* the real nature of a historical process in its totality. Or, we superimpose 'forced abstractions' on history, which are not grounded in a thorough analysis of its concrete specificities, and which, therefore, are to a large degree arbitrary and superficial, or even purely subjective preferences.

This text demolishes the position assumed by WMDB (Chapter 3, section 2) when they say (opposing my theory in Chapter 1 in a binary fashion) that 'we hold that historically specific and commodity-specific analysis are always preferable to an explanatory framework based on an essentialist ontology'. I agree fully with the view of Bernstein, Banaji and van der Linden, and would be very happy to be able to engage in an effort to ground *fully* my theory in history. Let me just clarify that it is not completely detached from history, as can be seen in many arguments of a historical concrete nature to which I refer in Chapter 1 and in this chapter (using examples from Mexico, Russia, Germany and USA, mainly from the nineteenth and twentieth centuries), as can be seen in the perception of these facts by Marx, Kautsky, Lenin, Cabrera and many contemporary authors. What is lacking is a systematic historical appraisal of my theory and a contrast with complementary or rival theories.

The notion of a pure capitalist agriculture (number 17) refers to an agriculture in which all production takes place in capitalist enterprises that hire seasonal labour in the peak seasons and a smaller number of permanent workers. This is not an empirical or historical category but an ideal type category. If it does not exist (and I think it does not), this is evidence in favour of my theory, which maintains that such a pure capitalist agriculture is impossible.

On commentary number 21, which refers to the bracketing of family farmers with peasants, Alavi and Shanin (1988) state that 'the possible Marxist designation of the difference between peasants ... and the highly capital-intensive family farmers', which came from Kautsky's vision, has 'escaped theoretical specification, becoming a blind spot'. However, they add that a 'conceptual step forward within a Marxist frame of reference' has been suggested by Danilov:

> In Danilov's view the distinction based on the respective relations of production which delimits family labour from wage-labour under capitalism, must be supplemented by a further distinction based on *qualitative differences in the forces of production deployed*. Peasant production is family agriculture where natural forces of production, land and labour predominate. Farmers ... represent family farms in which the man-made forces of production, mostly industrial in origin, come to play a decisive role. The particularity of family farming as a form of organisation of production does not disappear thereby, but the characteristics of its two different types can be distinguished more clearly. (ibid.: xxxv)

Alavi and Shanin say that modern agricultural technologies have altered the criterion of the optimal size of the labour team, lowering it for some branches of contemporary agriculture. A family farm is not necessarily at any advantage over a large enterprise but nor is it debarred from utilising new technology. They add that, given some conditions:

> it is often more effective and stable than a parallel large enterprise based on wage labour. Subsumed under capitalism as the dominant mode of production, it can secure higher or safer profits for agribusiness while at the same time providing an improved livelihood for its own members – an equation which facilitates the continuation of family farms as a social form, at least for a time. (ibid.: xxxiv–xxxv)

Orlando Figes (1987: 123–4) adds: 'Danilov moves away from assuming the exclusivity of market relations and/or relations of production in determining the rural social form and emphasises instead the changing nature of production forces as an objective system distinguishing peasants from farmers.'

Strikingly, the authors just cited agree with Brewster on one central point, quoted extensively in section 4 of the background paper: in 1950, Brewster pointed out the competitiveness of family farms, both before and after mechanisation. Two other interesting points in these quotations are the role of the development of productive forces in a field of thought obsessed with social relations of production, and the idea that the fully mechanised family farm of rich countries *is subsumed under the capitalist mode of production.*

Arizmendi's and Leff's commentaries on the theory of value. I will broach here the commentaries (numbers 11 and 12 in Table 12.1) by Arizmendi, and the two commentaries (24 and 25) by Leff. All of them refer to the validity of Marx's theory of value and the possible reforms of it. Arizmendi introduces the distinction (absent in Chapter 1) between critical and normative theory as the correct framework within which to evaluate Marx's theory of value with respect to its neglect of the consequences for workers of the discontinuities of the labour process in agriculture (11). He therefore disagrees with my attempt in Chapter 1 to formulate a general theory of value as an unnecessary step (12). He says (in Chapter 4, section 3) that the genuine problem I pose is not solved 'by questioning the Critical Theory of Value'. His position is that: 'The premise that the value of labour power must invariably be equivalent to the satisfaction of needs, thus guaranteeing the process of social reproduction of the worker ... disregards the unavoidable violence contained and unleashed by the commodification of human labour power.'

In Chapter 1, section 11, I showed that by introducing the seasonality of agriculture in Marx's Simple Reproduction Scheme (SRS), *the conditions of equilibrium that Marx uses to demonstrate the possibility of reproduction of capital are not sufficient to reproduce the agricultural labour force.* I argued that the SRS needs an additional equation that establishes the payment of wages to the agricultural labour force for 365 days a year; but, in doing this, a discrepancy arises, as goods produced incorporate as value only the work done in, say, 100 days a year, not in 365, so the SRS equations would be unbalanced. I solved this discrepancy by arguing that the rural wage worker who works for 100 days a year, for example, but consumes (together with his or her family) a livelihood over 365 days, *not only objectivises in his work value for the 100 days of living labour, but also (like machines or working animals) transfers to the value of goods produced the value of his means of subsistence during the 265 days not worked.* Arizmendi replied (in an unpublished text not included in his chapter) that the consumption of value of the labour force, 'when not configured as a commodity is destruction of value'.

I normatively reject this phrase for the reasons given. I conclude that, if the agricultural wage worker reaches the harvest carrying the accumulated value of the means of subsistence consumed between the end of the sowing period and the beginning of harvest (*objectified past labour*), he or she will transfer this value together with the new value that his or her new *living labour* generates when working on the harvest. This rebalances the equation and we would have an SRS valid for both continuous and discontinuous processes. This I called a *general theory of value*. Arizmendi replied, in a text not included in his chapter, that the postulate of equality of the value of the labour force and the peasant's wage has both a critical and a normative sense. Regarding the former, he says:

> *Critical for its negation*, as the *specificity of peasant wage labour consists in the fact that such equality is not met.* As *peasant wage labour is discontinuous* labour, it receives as payment *a form of time-wage: seasonal time-wage.* Time-wage implies that the worker is paid only for the hours effectively worked; in *seasonal time-wage*, he/she is not paid for the working year, but only for the season when she/he works. The conclusion is: *the law of peasant labour wage is the violation of the law of value in the relation between capital and labour.*

Arizmendi generalises to *seasonal time wages* what Marx said in Chapter 20 ('Time-wages') of Volume I of *Capital*:

> If the hour's wage is fixed in such a way that the capitalist does not bind himself to pay a day's or a week's wage, *but only to pay wages for the hours during which he chooses to employ the worker* [... the] capitalist can now wring from the worker a certain

quantity of surplus labour *without allowing him the labour-time necessary for his own subsistence.* (Marx 1976 [1867]: 686)

An important insight I derived from my discussion with Ariz-mendi is that *this form of exploitation, in which the worker's life apparently does not matter, is only possible in practice because agriculture is only partially capitalist.* Previous theoretical reflection (sections 10–12 of Chapter 1) highlighted that 'pure capitalism in agriculture is impossible unless workers were paid for the entire year even though their labour power were only used for part of it, with the additional cost being transferred to consumers'. Arizmendi's statement that '*the law of peasant labour wage is the violation of the law of value in the relation between capital and labour*' is made possible by the presence of peasants with access to land that can provide, through direct production, at least some of their 'self-preservation'. Otherwise, people would die and the population growth required by capitalist accumulation would be destroyed. Empirical observation that confirms that the law of value is not met in peasant wage work takes place in a context where the form of peasant production is present. *Any theory of capitalism has to include, therefore, its necessary coexistence and articulation with the peasantry (or poor family farm).* As a positive theory, Marx's theory of value fails in this respect, and this failure is related to Marx's ambiguous stand with respect to the persistence of the peasantry.

Arizmendi expresses the *normative sense* he perceives in my assumption of equality between the value of labour and the wage paid to the agricultural wage worker as follows:

Normative, because its assertion makes sense as a guide in the fight to defend the historical–moral dimension of the peasant's labour-force reproduction ... it is vital to open our eyes *to the invention of forms of decommodification of labour power.* The struggle for a *rural moral economy* should go beyond the decommodification of labour.

I agree with Arizmendi on this and have therefore advocated a 'basic income' (or universal citizen income or UCI) which eliminates (totally or partially) the forced commodification of labour power. But respect for the law of value (in its normative sense and thus payment of wages for 365 days to all people working) would, by itself, totally eliminate the poverty of around 2 billion people in the world. I have previously said:

> The works of E. P. Thompson (1991) and Scott (1976) ... reflect the inescapable fact that *human life cannot be left to the market.* No society has done this. Labour power is not an ordinary commodity, whose value and employment rate can be decided by market forces. The moral element comes in inevitably. Rising the price of bread can balance the supply and demand of bread, but does not solve the hunger of the people. Any self-respecting economic science, *any political economy must also be a moral economy.* (Boltvinik 2010: 190)

Leff says that he will 'challenge [Boltvinik's] proposal to reform value theory to incorporate the full cost of peasants' labour force reproduction' and 'offer a "general theory of value"' (number 24 in Table 12.1). But instead of providing specific arguments on my proposed reform, he moves to what he considers a more general problem. So he subsumes the problem that I am addressing within the problem he wants to address. He argues (number 25) that 'the natural processes involved in the production of commodities' are not valued in Marx's theory of value; that 'neither nature's contribution to production nor the destructive effects of production on nature are valued'. He does not mention that, in non-Marxist economics, this neglect is also present.

According to Foster, Clark and York (2010: 61 ff.), many green thinkers share the idea that Marx 'attributes no intrinsic value to natural resources'. Given the importance of what is at stake here, I will describe the story of the Lauderdale Paradox, as narrated by Foster et al., in order to clarify Marx's standpoint. Foster et al. (ibid.: 53) say that 'self-styled sustainable development economists claim that there is no contradiction between the unlimited accumulation of capital and the preservation of the earth', which would be achieved by bringing market efficiency to bear on nature and its reproduction. Behind this, say Foster et al., is a distorted accounting deeply rooted in the workings of the system, which sees wealth entirely in terms of value generated through exchange. *In such a system only commodities for sale on the market really count.* External nature – water, air, living species – is seen as a 'free good'. In the usual calculus of the capitalist system, both the contributions of nature to wealth and the destruction of natural conditions are largely invisible. The fatal flaw of received economics can be traced back to its conceptual foundations. They argue that neoclassical economics meant the abandonment of:

> the distinction between wealth and value (use value and exchange value). With this was lost the possibility of a broader ecological and social conception of wealth. These blinders of orthodox economics ... were challenged by ... critics such as James Maitland (Earl of Lauderdale), Karl Marx ... Today, in a time of unlimited environmental destruction, such heterodox views are having a comeback. (ibid.: 54)

In analysing their ideas, Foster et al. achieve some very deep insights into the complex dialectic of wealth value or use-value value. 'The ecological contradictions of the prevailing economic ideology are best explained in terms of ... the "Lauderdale Paradox"', formulated in 1804:

> Lauderdale argued that there was an inverse correlation between public wealth and private riches, such that an increase in the latter often served to diminish the former. Public wealth, he wrote, 'may be accurately defined – *to consist of all that man desires, as useful or delightful to him.*' Such goods have use value and thus constitute wealth. But private riches, as opposed to wealth, required something additional ... consisting of '*all that man desires as useful or delightful to him; which exists in a degree of scarcity.*' (ibid.: 55)

As Foster et al. explain, Lauderdale holds that if exchange values were attached to goods that are necessary for life and were previously abundant, such as air, water and food, but are now of increasing scarcity, this would enhance individual private riches, and indeed the riches of the country (conceived as the sum of individual riches), but at the expense of the common wealth. They add that if one could monopolise water that had previously been freely available by placing a fee on wells, the measured riches of the nation would be increased at the expense of the growing thirst of the population.

Foster et al. add that wealth, as opposed to mere riches, was associated in classical political economy with what John Locke called the 'intrinsic value' and classical economists called 'use value'. While material use values had always existed and were the basis of human existence, commodities produced for sale embody something else: exchange value. Commodities have a twofold aspect: use value and exchange value. 'The Lauderdale Paradox was nothing but an expression of this twofold aspect of wealth/value.'

Foster et al. (ibid.: 56 ff.) say that Marx adhered to the Lauderdale Paradox and went beyond it:

> Indeed, Marx built his entire critique of political economy in large part around the contradiction between use value and exchange value ... Under capitalism ... nature was rapaciously mined for the sake of exchange value ... This was closely related to Marx's attempt to look at the capitalist economy simultaneously in terms of its economic-value relations and its material transformations of nature. Thus Marx was the first major economist to incorporate the new notions of energy and entropy ... into his analysis of production. (ibid.: 59)

The first sentence of this quote expresses a view that coincides greatly with that of Bolívar Echeverría (2010:12), who said that the central contradiction in *Capital* is the one between value (exchange value) and use value.

Foster et al. point out that, when analysing capitalist agriculture, Marx often refers to sustainability as a requirement for any future society – the need to protect the earth for successive generations. *A condition of sustainability, Marx insisted, is the recognition that no one owns the earth, which must be preserved for future generations*:

> From the standpoint of a higher socio-economic formation, the private property of particular individuals in the earth will appear just as absurd as the private property of one man in other men. Even ... all simultaneously existing societies taken together, are not the owners of the earth. They are simply its possessors, its beneficiaries, and must have to bequeath it in improved state to succeeding generations, as *boni patres familias*. (Marx 1981 [1894]: 911)

The strong presence of nature in Marx's thought is evident. However, green thinkers, such as Leff in this book (Chapter 7), frequently point out that the labour theory of value put Marx in direct opposition to the type of ecologically informed value analysis that is needed today. As a reaction to these claims, Foster et al. adopt an interesting position:

> Here it is important to understand that certain conceptual categories that Marx uses in his *critique of political economy*, such as nature as a 'free gift' and the labour theory of value itself, were inventions of classical-liberal political economy that were integrated into Marx's *critique* – insofar as they exhibited the real tendencies and contradictions of the system. Marx employed these concepts in an argument aimed at transcending bourgeois society and its limited social categories. The idea that nature was a 'free good' for exploitation ... [was] advanced by the physiocrats [and the classics] – well before Marx [... and] was perpetuated in mainstream economic theory long after Marx. Although accepting it as a reality of bourgeois political economy, Marx was acutely aware of the social and ecological contradictions embedded in such a view. (ibid.: 61–2)

Foster et al.'s vision is that Marx faced a strong tension between *what is* and *what ought to be*. For that purpose, it was paramount to maintain explicit the contradiction between use value and (exchange) value. For Foster et al., *Marx developed both a positive and a critical theory* describing how capitalism works and what it is, but also showing its contradictions from the perspective of a post-capitalist society: that is, from the perspective of *what should be*. Therefore, Foster et al. add that, 'as treating nature as "free good" was intrinsic to the operation of the capitalist economy, it continued to be included as a basic proposition underlying neoclassical economic theory'. This proposition is even explicitly held in mainstream environmental economics. They conclude:

> Misconceptions pointing to the anti-ecological nature of the labour theory of value arise due to conflation of the categories of *value* and *wealth* – since in today's received economics, these are treated synonymously ... In the capitalist logic there was no question that

nature was worthless (a free gift). The problem, rather, was how to jettison the concept of wealth, as distinct from value, from the core framework of economics, since it provided the basis of a critical – and what we now call ecological – outlook. (ibid.: 63)

Marx resisted the elimination of the wealth–value distinction. For Marx, those who saw labour as the only source of wealth attributed to it a supernatural creative power, as Foster et al. point out. Both in *Critique of the Gotha Program* (2010 [1891]: 341) and Volume I of *Capital* (1976 [1867]: 133–4, emphasis added) the old Marx defined his position:

> Labour *is not the source* of all wealth. Nature is just as much the source of use-values (and surely these are what make up material wealth!) as labour.
>
> Use-values ... the physical bodies of commodities, are combinations of two elements, the material provided by nature, and labour. If we subtract the total amount of useful labour of different kinds which is contained in the coat, the linen, etc., a material substratum is always left. This substratum is furnished by nature without human intervention ... *[L]abour is therefore not the only source of material wealth, i.e. of the use-values it produces.* As William Petty says, *labour is the father of material wealth, the earth is the mother.*

Capitalism's failure to incorporate nature into its value accounting and its tendency to confuse value with wealth were *fundamental contradictions of the regime of capital itself*, argue Foster et al. Those who fault Marx for not ascribing value to nature, they say – quoting Paul Burkett (2014) – should redirect their criticisms to capitalism itself.

Although the debate is obviously unfinished and incomplete, I feel that my theory on the poverty and persistence of the peasantry, having been exposed to the critical views of many experts from Mexico and other countries, has survived the storm. This – together with the backups analysed in this chapter that buttress my theory – means to me that it deserves (and needs) to be elaborated further and improved (taking into consideration the critiques received).

TABLE 12.2 Replies to some comments and criticisms not addressed in the text

Authors and numbers	Replies
WMDB 7, 8, 10	On **7** ('the BP blurs the distinction between the use value of labour and its value of exchange'). This is based on the alleged fact that I treat the exchange value of labour power (wage) as a value that directly corresponds with time worked. My short reply is: capitalism blurs the distinction through time wages (Chapter 20, Volume I, *Capital*); normatively, I say in the BP that wages should be independent of the number of days (hours) worked. On **8**, the BP is criticised (in other words) for not accepting at face value the 'freedom of the worker to starve'. My reply is (as stated above) that the works of E. P. Thompson and J. C. Scott reflect the inescapable fact that *human life cannot be left to the market. No society has done this.* Any self-respecting *political economy must also be a moral economy.* On **10**, they disagree with my proposal to subsidise peasant agriculture in the global South. Their argument is that this idea is not ripe because it goes against the dominant neoliberal credo. A similar argument is made by Bernstein (see below). I reply that, in this case, agricultural subsidies would have to be eliminated in the global North, which they do not propose, and that the intellectual attitude of equating *ought to be* with *is* helps explain why neoliberalism is dominant. Some countries in South America have implemented many non-ripe ideas successfully. As part of their commentaries against ontology and essentialism (see **4** to **6** in Table 12.1), WMDB refer to Lukács to criticise me for 'translating the concretely historical into supra-historical essences' and for adopting binary thought that serves the purposes of quietism. My reply is that, in the quoted phrase, Lukács was criticising two contradistinctions made by Tönnies in aspects that are quite distant from nature (community–society, civilisation–culture), whereas the distinction agriculture–industry is permeated by the presence of natural features, to the extent that man is unable to transform 'solar energy into food' – it depends on photosynthesis, a natural process that is non-modifiable by humans. Stating *this fact* cannot be seen as translating 'the concretely historical into supra-historical *essences*', as there is no concrete historical feature but rather a constant natural one. The same applies to the imputation of quietism to my thought: am I being accused of not fighting our dependence on photosynthesis?

TABLE 12.2 Continued

Authors and numbers	Replies
Bernstein 18, 19, 22	On **18**, where Bernstein expresses his doubt about the accuracy of the BP's 'observations about current realities, in the (mostly) timeless world of his abstractions, for example, concerning the "numerical importance of peasants in Latin America"'. He is right: every assertion has to be backed up with evidence, but then one requires not a paper but a book. The evidence on Mexico is discussed in Chapter 6 of this book by Damián and Pacheco.
	On **19**, Bernstein criticises my use of the concept of petty commodity producers 'as a descriptive synonym for peasants or family farmers rather than as a theoretically defined category'. My reply is that I use it exactly as Marx uses it, whereas his use of the term (seeing peasants as both wage workers and capitalist) implies imputing capitalist categories to non-capitalist forms of production.
	On **22**, Bernstein rejects my position of subsidising peasants in the South if it implies a redistributive policy from rich to poor, which it does, as this is ruled out by dominant neoliberal ideology. My reply would be the same as the one given to WMDB above. But Bernstein looks at the possible consequences within my model and points out, rightly, that if subsidies eliminate the main cause of peasant poverty, capitalist agriculture would not have the cheap supply of seasonal labour and would disappear. My reply is that this might indeed occur in the long run and would be very good for humanity.

3. The distinctive features of agriculture: a detailed version

In Chapter 5, Bernstein synthesised in a table the distinctive features of agriculture and industry as described in Chapter 1. As a result of my debates with Armando Bartra, I perceived the contrast between the character of machinery, the main means of production in industry, which are man-made, and soil, water and climate (nature), the main means of production in agriculture, which are not man-made. Machinery can be increased (and modified) at will, whereas nature can be modified and increased only within limits. Additionally, I perceived the importance of contrasting the typical flows of production in agriculture and industry. Starting from Bernstein's table, adding these two features and a column of consequences in agriculture, and making other slight changes, I have come up with an updated and completed version of the contrasts and consequences of conditions of production in agriculture and industry as presented in Table 12.3. I have included in the first two rows the traits of the

TABLE 12.3 Conditions of production in agriculture and industry: contrasts and consequences

Aspect	Industry	Agriculture	Consequences for agriculture
1. Character of the object of work and contents of production.	Almost always inert material. *Production* consists in modifying and/or assembling these objects.	Biological (seeds, plants). *Cultivation* consists in provoking, stimulating and taking care of the biological growth of the plant.	Uncertainty: the biological growth process can be interrupted or modified, by causes beyond human control.
2. Character of the main means of production.	Machinery produced by human beings.	Land (soil), water and climate – natural.	Absence in agriculture of a trend to equalise labour productivity among producing units, which gives way to *differential land rent*.
3. Work process 1.	Continuous.	Discontinuous (seasonal).	Seasonal work: the main determinant of peasant poverty and persistence.
4. Work process 2.	Activities are simultaneous (highly developed technical division of labour).	Activities are sequential (little technical division of labour).	Low presence and importance of economies of scale, in contrast to industry.
5. Location of the labour process.	Flexible: materials are moved to where machines and workers are.	Fixed by location of cultivated land: workers and machines are moved to the land.	Diseconomies in very large units.
6. Character of work product.	Almost always inert. It can be stored during long periods.	Frequently perishable. It has to get to consumers promptly or its character is modified.	Excess production can be more disastrous: prices can fall abruptly.
7. Flow of production.	Continuous in most branches of industry.	Products are obtained only at harvest time, usually once a year.	Financial requirements (of circulating capital) are strong as expenditures are dispersed over the production period, but income is concentrated in a few weeks.

object of work and of the main means of production in industry and agriculture. These two rows highlight that both the object of work and the main means of production are natural in agriculture. I illustrate that agriculture (in the Spanish sense of the term) consists in provoking, stimulating and taking care of the biological growth of plants; *that it is,* as Malita (1971: 302) has described it, *cultivation, not production,* and thus in sharp contrast to most industrial activities. This is reflected in the third row – the discontinuity of the labour process in agriculture – because, as Marx said in *Capital,* after planting, the labour process is interrupted almost completely and the unfinished product is left to the influence of natural processes. The second row refers to the characteristic of agriculture that explains both the rise of agricultural land rent and, according to Bartra, the persistence of the peasantry: the non-human-produced character of land, water and climate. The third row highlights the seasonal character of agriculture, which, in my view, is the main explanation for both the persistence of peasantry and its poverty. The last four rows add features of agriculture that contrast with industry; they explain the minor role of economies of scale in agriculture (row 4) and therefore that agriculture is less prone to the concentration of production (rows 4 and 5). Row 6 explains the urgent character of harvesting, especially in the case of highly perishable products (vegetables and fruits), in addition to its seasonality and the tremendous impact on prices of excess production. Row 7 illustrates that, while the flow of products is continuous in most industries, in agriculture products are obtained only at harvest time; this occurs mostly once a year, and is usually concentrated in a few weeks. Financial requirements (of circulating capital) are strong, as expenditures are dispersed over the production period but income is concentrated in a few weeks.

4. Pending issues for discussion

The text of the previous sections outgrew their expected length, and so I had to eliminate most of the contents (which I had partially written) of this section, which deals with issues (and authors) not discussed in the book, and had to change its title and outlook. The main elements to be included in it were as follows:

a I had written a long account of what I had labelled 'An alternative theory of capitalist agricultural development', developed by Goodman, Sorj and Wilkinson (1987). This theory is centred on the processes of *appropriationism* and *substitutionism* adopted by capital to control agriculture, which I regard as quite relevant to understanding the relationship between peasant units and capital and thus throwing light on the central issues of this book. The following excerpts from the introduction synthesise how they construe those concepts and give an idea of their importance:

The key to understanding the *uniqueness of agriculture* ... lies neither in its social structure nor in its factor endowment. Rather *agriculture confronts capitalism with a natural production process.* Unlike sectors of handicraft activity, agriculture could not be directly transformed into a branch of industrial production. *There was no industrial alternative to the biological transformation of solar energy into food.* The industrialization of agriculture therefore took a decisively different path ... determined by the *structural constraints* of the agricultural production process, represented by *nature as the biological conversion of energy, as biological time in plant growth and animal gestation, and as space in land-based rural activities.* Unable to remove these constraints directly ... industrial *capitals* have responded by adapting to the specificities of nature in agricultural production ... [D]iscrete elements of the production process have been taken over by industry – broadcast sowing by the seed drill, the horse by the tractor, manure by synthetic chemicals ... *This discontinuous but persistent undermining of discrete elements of the agricultural production process, their transformation into industrial activities, and their incorporation into agriculture as inputs we designate as appropriationism.* The products of agriculture likewise presented unique problems for industrial production. Their destiny as food impeded simple replacement by industrial products. Nevertheless, *the emergence of the food industry, we would argue, represents a similarly discontinuous but permanent process to achieve the industrial production of food which we denominate substitutionism ... the agricultural product,* after being reduced to an industrial input, *increasingly suffers replacement by non-agricultural components. Appropriationism is constituted*

> *by the action of industrial capitals to reduce the importance of*
> *nature in rural production, and specifically as a force beyond their*
> *direction and control.* This was achieved initially by relaxing the
> constraint of land as space via mechanization, and subsequently
> by the continuing struggle *to transform the secrets of biological*
> *production into scientific knowledge and industrial property* ...
> The logic of *substitutionism* has led to the creation of sectors
> of accumulation in the downstream stages of food and fibre
> manufacture ... [T]he tendential outcome of substitutionism
> is to eliminate the rural product, and thus the *rural* base
> of agriculture ... [T]he advent in the 1970s of modern
> biotechnologies, particularly genetic engineering ... mark a
> generalised advance in the industrial manipulation of nature,
> and have triggered a technological revolution in plant and
> livestock breeding, agrichemicals and food manufacture. (ibid.:
> 1–5, emphasis added)

It is worth highlighting that the authors start with the premise of the *uniqueness of agriculture* and regard it as *lying in a natural production process: the biological transformation of solar energy into food.* Although the starting point of the background paper is similar in stressing the natural and biological character of plant growth, the perspectives from which this essential feature is seen are different. Goodman et al. emphasise industrial capital's *lack of control* as it cannot replace the biological growth of the plant by an industrial process ('*as a force beyond their direction and control*'). They identify *biological time in plant growth and animal gestation* and *space in land-based rural activities* as constraints derived from its uniqueness. Chapter 1 emphasises the *discontinuous requirements of labour power* and its social consequences in capitalism. Although this acute consciousness of the natural character of plant growth is shared in this book by many authors, its social consequences are not as widely grasped.

b The general account of rural poverty that is present in some development studies centred on the crucial role of security in peasant societies and on adaptation to their realities. John Kenneth Galbraith's book *The Nature of Mass Poverty* (1979), in which he develops the concepts of *equilibrium of poverty* and *accommodation*[5] as the forces explaining rural poverty in the Third World, was to be discussed with other related works, such as Albert Hirschman (1958) and Raúl Prebisch (1963).

c I was to explore the demographic factor, including the relation between population and arable land, that was brought into the analysis by Galbraith and is also present in Chayanov. On the one hand, the position adopted by Gordon Childe in *Man Makes Himself* (1936) was to be made explicit: human beings, as a species, as *Homo sapiens*, have to be regarded as successful as they have survived for many millennia and have multiplied their numbers. This perspective leads to a paradox: Chinese and Indian societies would be regarded, in terms of their numbers, as the most successful human societies, although they are considered among the less successful in terms of their GDP per capita and the percentage living in poverty. As WMDB say in Chapter 3, three types of production processes have to be considered: the production of the means of subsistence, of the means of production and of labour power. India and China (peasant societies since antiquity) should be considered as very efficient producers of labour power.

d I had planned to examine James C. Scott's (1976) concepts of *subsistence ethics* and the *moral economy* of the peasantry.

e I would also have discussed George M. Foster's (1967) concept of the 'image of the limited good', a specific 'cognitive orientation' connected with other authors' ideas and with the category of 'ethos' used by Luis Arizmendi in this book, following Bolívar Echeverría.

f The concept of a 'culture of poverty', as developed by Oscar Lewis (1959) and criticised by, among others, Charles Valentine (1968), was to be included.

g I intended to explore the concept of the social character of the peasantry, which was developed and applied empirically by Fromm and Maccoby (1970) in a Mexican village.

The preceding five lines of thought (c to g) are closely interlinked and were to be developed in the same subsection. They would also be related to Jean-Paul Sartre's concept of '*exis*', which he enunciated thus:

Scarcity is a fundamental relation of our History … If a state of equilibrium is established within a given mode of production, and

preserved from one generation to the next, it is preserved as *exis*
– that is to say, both as a physiological and social determination of
human organisms and as a practical project of keeping institutions
and physical development at the same level. This corresponds
ideologically to a decision about human 'nature'. Man is a stunted
misshapen being hardened by suffering, and he lives in order to
work from dawn till dusk with these (primitive) technical means,
on a thankless threatening earth. (Sartre 2004: 125–6)

The concept of scarcity is central to any systemic understanding
of the world. While the Marxist project of the (future) society of
organised producers is based on overcoming scarcity and on replacing
the realm of necessity with the realm of freedom, the current
environmental crisis has put a serious question mark on this vision.
In the final analysis, the critical scarcity is that of food. If capitalist
agriculture is unsustainable, how are we going to supply food for 7.25
billion people, a number that is increasing by 42 million every year?
Is it possible to develop a sustainable agriculture that can provide
food for such an enormous volume of people?

h The unsustainable nature of capitalist agriculture and its
environmental crisis are rooted in the scission of cities and
countryside and thus in the interruption in the cycling of soil
nutrients, what Marx called the *ecological rift*. More specifically,
the position of Marx in ecological thinking was to be reviewed.
For these purposes, the following books were to be reviewed: Foster
et al. (2010), Magdoff et al. (2000), Foster (2000; 2002; 2009);
Burkett (2014); O'Connor (1998); Altvater (1993); Leff (2014);
González de Molina and Toledo (2014); and Klein (2014).
i A comparative analysis of the present book and similar books that
collect papers on the peasantry (classic and recent) was to be conducted in order to specify the contributions of this volume and its
distinctive character.

5. Different replies to the two central theoretical questions of this book: a sketch

The two central questions posed in the background paper
(Chapter 1), and to which the call for the seminar suggested that all
participants give their answers, were as follows:

1. What are the reasons for peasant poverty? In other words, why are most peasants poor?
2. Why has the peasantry as a distinct form of production been able to persist in the twenty-first century in the face of global capitalist development?

A third question also was posed:

3. Are the replies to the two previous questions related and, if so, in what way?

The purpose of this section is to assess how generalised are the replies to the two central questions in the book, and to build two *typologies of reply*. I consider replies both by the authors of chapters themselves and by other authors that are discussed in the book.

The following topics are not included as they are not strictly theoretical replies to the two questions: the account given on definitions of poverty and the peasantry, and the historical view of ideas on Question 2 (Introduction); Arizmendi's discussion on the various modes of subsumption of the peasantry to capital (Chapter 4); Damián and Pacheco's empirical findings on rural poverty, seasonality and persistence (Chapter 6); Montaña's case studies in three countries on the impact of water scarcity on peasants according to the degree of water commodification in each (Chapter 8); and Araghi's historical analysis of food regimes that promote peasantisation and/or depeasantisation (Chapter 10). Authors' proposals to reduce poverty and/or support the peasant economy are also not included.

Replies to the peasant poverty question (Question 1). I have identified the following replies to Question 1. I indicate in brackets whether the reply is associated with peasants' low levels of production, Q, or with the price levels, P, at which they sell and/or buy.

Chapter 1 or the background paper (Boltvinik)
1.1. 'Conventional answers': severe limitations of resources and technology and low labour productivity [Q].
1.2. Exploitation, including self-exploitation (Chayanov and Bartra) and labour-power undervaluation (Boltvinik) [P].

1.3. Seasonal theory: peasants absorb the cost of agricultural seasonality [P] (Boltvinik; see also replies to Questions 2 and 3).

Chapter 2 (Bartra)

2.1. Self-exploitation and polymorphous exploitation, including absorbing the cost of seasonality, buying dear and selling cheap, and labour-power undervaluation [P] (linked to replies to Question 2).

Chapter 3 (Welty, Mann, Dickinson and Blumenfeld)

3.1. In the highly commoditised, capitalist-dominated global economy, peasants are impoverished because of their low labour productivity. Social differentiation renders poor peasants either landless or forced to find additional forms of income to survive [Q].

3.2. Unpaid domestic labour, which keeps at a low level the value of commodity labour power [P].

Chapter 4 (Arizmendi)

4.1. Domination (subsumption) by capitalism, which absorbs and penetrates the peasant economy, placing it at its service [P].

Chapter 5 (Bernstein)

5.1. Social differentiation of the peasantry – which results from their character as petty commodity producers who internalise and combine the class locations of both capital and labour – leads to their doom.

5.2. 'Simple reproduction squeeze' caused by exploitation [P].

Chapter 7 (Leff)

7.1. Colonialism and capitalism resulted in an impoverishing process that entailed pillaging peasants' resources, degradation of the productivity of their ecosystems, dispossession of their territories, and the colonisation of their knowledge. In short, a historical process of entropic degradation of their environment and livelihood [Q].

Chapter 9 (Vergopoulos)

9.1. Peasants maximise production and minimise prices. If capitalism were to produce every commodity, profits would be impossible; at least one commodity, labour power, has to be produced non-capitalistically, to avoid paying profit and land rent revenues.

So peasant poverty is, for him, a necessary condition for the general profitability of capitalism [P] (see also replies to Question 2).

Chapter 11 *(Barkin and Lemus)*

11.1. Poverty originates in the individualism and alienation of the masses and the market is the main obstacle to escaping poverty.

Chapter 12 *(Boltvinik)*

12.1. Presents, through Lenin's words, Danielson's theory on Question 1 of the 'freeing of winter time', which is caused by the ruination of peasant handicrafts, which in turn is caused by the development of capitalist manufacturing or industry; this shows a strong coincidence with a text from Volume II of *Capital*.

12.2. Argues that Kautsky's position coincides with Danielson's, whose theory is a significant (but very little known) precedent to Boltvinik's theory.

12.3. Other issues listed and related to the central questions include Galbraith's theory of the *equilibrium of poverty* and *accommodation* as the forces explaining rural mass poverty.

12.4. The *demographic factor* in Questions 1 and 2, complementing Kautsky, as explored by Galbraith and Gordon Childe.

Replies to the peasant persistence question (Question 2)

Chapter 1 or the background paper *(Boltvinik)*

1.4. Classical Marxist position attributed to Lenin: disappearance of peasants (Ellis).

1.5. Exploitation breaks differentiation (simple reproduction squeeze: all surplus is extracted), contributing to persistence (Bernstein).

1.6. Seasonal theory (Boltvinik): symbiosis of agricultural capitalism and the peasantry, expressed by peasant seasonal wage labour in capitalist agriculture (see also 1.3 in the replies to Question 1 above).

1.7. The self-exploitation theory and the non-accumulation motives of peasants explain Question 2 (Chayanov).

1.8. Obstacles to capitalist development in agriculture explain Question 2 (Mann and Dickinson; Contreras).

1.9. Peasant households have to persist as they produce the labour power capitalist units require (Kautsky's demographic theory).

1.10. Peasants are functional for capitalism and thus persist, as they do not pursue profits, they can function at lower prices and thereby reduce differential rent, which is detrimental for non-agricultural capital (Bartra).

Chapter 2 (Bartra)
2.2. Serving as a buffer for differential rent, peasants are functional to capitalism (see 1.10 above).

Chapter 3 (Welty, Mann, Dickinson and Blumenfeld)
3.3. Question 2 is explained by the Mann–Dickinson thesis and its focus on natural and socio-historical obstacles to capitalist development in agriculture. Given these or similar obstacles, in agriculture and elsewhere, capitalism promotes, or is able to work with, many peculiar non-capitalist forms of production, whenever this enhances profits and/or diminishes risks.

Chapter 5 (Bernstein)
5.3. Question 2 is a non-question as poor and marginal peasants should not be considered peasants or farmers at all, but workers.

Chapter 7 (Leff)
7.2. Question 2 has to be understood on the basis of peasants' attachments to land and territory.

Chapter 9 (Vergopoulos)
Same as 9.1 above.

Chapter 12 (Boltvinik)
12.9. Kautsky's demographic theory with regard to Question 2 and my theory are complementary: Kautsky explains why capitalist farms, which do not reproduce labour, need peasant households to 'produce' labour power, while my theory maintains that capitalist farms need peasants to provide a reliable seasonal, cheap supply of labour.

* * *

Observing the broad list of replies to both questions, and taking into account the numerous topics not covered in these lists, one concludes that most chapters include a reply (or replies) to both questions, and/or present empirical evidence on them, or look at them historically – both the history of food regimes and the history of ideas. Thus the central questions have a strong and generalised presence in the book and the reader receives, in addition, a rich panorama beyond the specific replies (or theories) advocated by the contributors to the book.

I move now to building one typology for the replies to Question 1 and one for the replies to Question 2. In the case of Question 1, I have already classified replies according to whether the cause identified involves low levels of production (Q) or low prices of products and the labour force, and/or high prices for inputs (P). Tables 12.4 and 12.5 present the typologies of the replies to the two questions derived from the previous listing. They are not, obviously, the only possible typologies.

In Table 12.4, five types of reply to Question 1 are derived from the previous list by combining two or more specific replies in each type. Only the first type is classified as attributing low levels of production (Q) as the cause of poverty. It could be worded as follows: 'Peasants are poor because they produce very little.' As stated by Galbraith (1979: 1–22), these types of theory involve circular reasoning, as it could also be said that peasants have small plots and use traditional technologies because they are poor. In the case of dispossession, the question this theory cannot answer is why they are not dispossessed of all their land. The second type of reply involves the prices at which peasants buy and sell (P). Self-exploitation, exploitation or domination (subsumption) by capital, despite their differences, are all associated with peasants receiving low prices for their product and buying their inputs at high prices (P) through unequal exchange that might – or might not – involve contract farming (see row 2 in Table 12.4). This domination (subsumption) has other consequences, including dispossessing peasants of their capacity to decide, that are not captured in the table. This could be worded as: 'Peasants are poor because they are exploited, self-exploited, or dominated by (subsumed to) capital.' My theory that peasants are poor because they absorb the costs of seasonality (row 3) impinges on both the prices (P) at which they sell their product and the wages received for their seasonal work (W); both of these reflect only the time effectively worked, which, given seasonality, is only a fraction of the year. This has been classified in the same category as

Danielson's theory (backed up by Marx and Kautsky) of the 'freeing of winter time', which relates to the reduction in the time during which labour power can be deployed. So both theories are complementary: peasants cannot work in the winter, nor in the non-working time of the production period, and the prices and wages they receive do not compensate these losses. This might be worded as: 'Peasants absorb both winter and pre-harvest seasonality costs.' The fourth type of reply to Question 1 involves wages (W). The poverty of peasants results from the fact that they produce labour power non-capitalistically, lowering wages. This might be worded as: 'Peasants are poor because they subsidise capital by selling their labour power cheaply.' Lastly, the fifth type of reply identifies 'cultural explanations' (individualism, alienation and accommodation) for peasant poverty and the idea of the equilibrium of poverty, which attests that 'an increase in income could set in motion the forces that would eliminate the increase and restore the previous level of deprivation. Improvement would devour itself' (Galbraith 1979: 45).

Table 12.5 presents the typology of replies to Question 2. Type 1 denies the persistence of the peasantry: both Lenin and Bernstein consider poor landholding peasants as proletarians, not peasants. The five remaining types accept peasant persistence and their mottos could be written as 'peasants persist because': 'the production and seasonal-supply functions of their labour power are indispensable for agricultural capitalism' (Kautsky; Boltvinik, Chapter 1; Vergopoulos, Chapter 9; see row 2); 'by not requiring profits, nor rent, but only subsistence income, they become very competitive' (Chayanov; Bartra, Chapters 1 and 2; see row 3); 'capitalism cannot overcome the obstacles present in agriculture for its development' (Mann and Dickinson; Contreras; WMDB, Chapters 1 and 3; see row 4); 'peasants function as buffers for differential rents, which damage non-agricultural capital' (Bartra, Chapters 1 and 2; see row 5); and 'peasants' attachment to land is very strong' (see row 6). Two of the types (rows 2 and 5) refer to the peasant economy's functionality for capitalism, although for Bartra it is functional for non-agricultural capitalism, and in Kautsky's, Boltvinik's and Vergopoulos's replies it is functional for agricultural capitalism. The remaining three types refer to peasants' competitiveness (see row 3; Chayanov; Bartra), given their own attributes as simple commodity producers; to natural obstacles to capitalist development that would then be unable to displace the peasantry (row 4); and lastly

TABLE 12.4 Typology of replies to the peasant poverty question (Question 1)

Type of theory (reply)	Chapter and author of the reply	Impinges on Q, P, W, LP and/or O	Sustained or discussed	Comment and/or critique
1. Limitation of resources or technology; low productivity; dispossession or degradation.	1. Authors not identified 1. Boltvinik 3. WMDB 7. Leff	Q Q Q Q	D S S S	'Conventional' (circular reasoning)
2. Self-exploitation, exploitation or domination (subsumption); Functional for capitalism.	1. Chayanov 2. Bartra 5. Bernstein 4. Arizmendi 9. Vergopoulos	P P P P P	D D S S S	Includes unequal exchange, contract farming, etc.
3. Peasants absorb seasonality costs; working time reduced; 'freeing of winter time'	1. Boltvinik 12. Marx, Danielson and Kautsky	P, W LP	S D	Symbiosis of peasants and agricultural capital
4. (Re-)production of labour power is non-capitalist; done with unpaid domestic work.	3. WMDB 9. Vergopoulos	W W	S S	LP produced in non-capitalist way
5. Individualism and alienation; equilibrium of poverty and accommodation.	11. Barkin and Lemus 12. Galbraith	O O	S D	'Cultural explanations'

Key: Q = quantity produced; P = price; W = low and/or seasonal wages; LP = labour power deployed; O = other; S = sustained; D = discussed.

TABLE 12.5 Typology of replies to the peasant persistence question (Question 2)

Type of theory (reply)	Chapter and author of the reply	Sustained or discussed	Comment, clarification and/or critique
1. Non-persistence (doom).	1. Lenin (attributed to) 5. Bernstein, following Lenin	D S	Poor peasants *are* workers, not peasants. Labelling act by Lenin and Bernstein.
2. Symbiosis of capital and peasants (seasonal supply and production of LP).	1. Boltvinik 1. Kautsky 9. Vergopoulos	S D S	They are complementary.
3. Self-exploitation and non-accumulation motives.	1. Chayanov 2. Bartra	D S	It would predict persistence of artisans also.
4. Obstacles to capitalist development in agriculture.	1. Mann and Dickinson; Contreras 3. WMDB	D D	Omits equalisation of profit rates; thus obstacles identified are not real. WMDB do not reply to this critique.
5. Peasants function as buffers for differential rents.	2. Bartra	S	By being able to function with low income or prices.
6. Peasants' attachment to land.	7. Leff	S	Not convincing.

Key: LP = labour power deployed; S = sustained; D = discussed.

to a subjective property of peasants – their attachment to land. The second and fifth reply types are relational explanations: the role played by peasants within capitalism explains their persistence, and therefore peasants are not a mere remnant of previous modes of production, but rather they persist because they play a positive, new role within capitalism. The other three explanations can be conceived as 'resistance of the peasantry', either because their will to resist is very strong, or they have competitive advantages or the competitor (capitalist agriculture) has disadvantages.

The last column of Table 12.5 shows my criticisms of three of the reply types. The competitive advantage argued in row 3 would explain the persistence of all simple commodity producers (artisans), which has not happened. The Mann–Dickinson and Contreras theses, which are also supported by WMDB, identify false obstacles to capitalist development in agriculture, as they disregard the equalisation of the rate of profit analysed by Marx in Volume III of *Capital*. WMDB (Chapter 3) do not counter-argue against this critique. Lastly, explaining peasant persistence by the peasant's attachment to land forgets the great gap in economic, political and military power between the peasantry and capital. It also forgets that capital has not only dispossessed peasants, but in many periods and places it has allotted plots of land to them.

Notes

1 When I came back to Mexico I prepared and published three articles centred on peasant economies and technological innovations (Boltvinik 1975; 1976; 1979).

2 The Spanish translation of *The Development of Capitalism in Russia* (Lenin 1950 [1899]) uses the expression 'with *nadiel* land' instead of 'allotment-holding'. The translator explains (p. 51) that *nadiel* refers to the land given to peasants in usufruct (it could not be sold) after the abolition of serfdom in 1861; this land was communal property and was redistributed periodically among peasants for their cultivation. '*Nadiel*' in Russia and '*ejidos*' in Mexico had strong similarities.

3 See the footnote in Chapter 6,

section 1, by Damián and Pacheco, which explains what the *ejidos* are.

4 See 'The distinctive features of agriculture', New Zealand Digital Library, University of Waikato, Agricultural Information Modules Collection. Available at www.nzdl.org/ (accessed 23 August 2015).

5 In brief, *the equilibrium of poverty* argues that 'an increase in income could set in motion the forces that would eliminate the increase and restore the previous level of deprivation. Improvement would devour itself' (Galbraith 1979: 45). By *accommodation*, Galbraith refers to the fact that '[p]eople who have lived for centuries in poverty in the relative isolation of the rural village have come to terms with this existence' (ibid.: 62).

References

Akram-Lohdi, A. H. and C. Kay (2009) 'The agrarian question: peasants and rural change' in A. H. Akram-Lohdi and C. Kay (eds), *Peasants and Globalization: Political economy, rural transformation and the agrarian question*. London: Routledge, pp. 3–34.

Alavi, H. and T. Shanin (1988) 'Introduction to the English edition: peasantry and capitalism' in K. Kautsky, *The Agrarian Question*. Two volumes. London: Zwan Publications, pp. xi–xxxix.

Altvater, E. (1993) *The Future of the Market: An essay on the regulation of money and nature after the collapse of 'actually existing socialism'*. London: Verso.

Boltvinik, J. (1975) 'Economía Campesina e Investigación Agrícola', *Comercio Exterior* 25 (5): 525–32.

— (1976) 'Estrategia de Desarrollo Rural, Economía Campesina e Innovación Tecnológica en México', *Comercio Exterior* 26 (7): 813–26.

— (1979) 'Economía Campesina y Tecnología Agrícola'. Documentos para el Desarrollo Agroindustrial no. 3. Mexico City: Secretaría de Agricultura y Recursos Hidráulicos. Reprinted in 1982 in *Revista Chapingo* VII (35 & 36): 12–20.

— (1991) 'Presentación' in *Economía popular. Una vía para el desarrollo sin pobreza en América Latina*. Bogotá, Colombia: United Nations Development Programme, Regional Project to Overcome Poverty, RLA/86/004, pp. vii–lv.

— (2007) 'Hacia una teoría de la pobreza campesina', *Papeles de Población*, New Epoch, 13 (54): 23–38.

— (2009) 'Esbozo de una teoría de la pobreza y la sobrevivencia del campesinado. Polémica con Armando Bartra', *Mundo Siglo XXI* V (18): 27–41.

— (2010) 'Ingreso ciudadano universal y economía moral. Una propuesta para México' in E. Valencia (ed.), *Perspectivas del Universalismo en México*. Guadalajara: Universidad de Guadalajara.

Brewster, J. M. (1970 [1950]) 'The machine process in agriculture and industry' in K. A. Fox and D. G. Johnson (eds), *Readings in the Economics of Agriculture*. London: George Allen & Unwin, pp. 3–13. Originally published in 1950 in *Journal of Farm Economics* XXXII (1): 69–81.

Bunge, M. (2001) *Diccionario de Filosofía*. Mexico City: Siglo XXI Editores. Spanish edition of *Dictionary of Philosophy*. Amherst NY: Prometheus Books, 1999.

Burkett, P. (2014) *Marx and Nature: A red and green perspective*. Chicago IL: Haymarket Books.

Childe, V. G. (1936) *Man Makes Himself*. London: NCLC Publishing Society.

Contreras, A. (1977) 'Límites de la producción capitalista en la agricultura', *Revista Mexicana de Sociología* 39 (3): 885–9.

Djurfeldt, G. (1982) 'Classical discussions of capital and peasantry: a critique' in J. Harriss (ed.), *Rural Development: Theories of peasant economy and agrarian change*. London: Routledge, pp. 139–59.

Doyal, L. and I. Gough (1991) *A Theory of Human Need*. London: Macmillan.

Echeverría, B. (2010) 'Crítica a la posibilidad de una Teoría Crítica de György Márkus', *Mundo Siglo XXI* 21: 9–12.

Figes, O. (1987) 'V. P. Danilov on the analytical distinction between peasants and farmers' in T. Shanin (ed.), *Peasants and Peasant Societies*. <edition>Second edition</edition>. Oxford: Basil Blackwell, pp. 121–4.

Foster, G. M. (1967) 'Peasant society and the image of the limited good' in J. M. Potter, M. N. Díaz and G. M. Foster, *Peasant Society: A reader*. Boston MA: Little, Brown and Company.

Foster, J. B. (2000) *Marx's Ecology: Materialism and nature*. New York NY: Monthly Review Press.

— (2002) *Ecology Against Capitalism*. New York NY: Monthly Review Press.

— (2009) *The Ecological Revolution: Making peace with the planet*. New York NY: Monthly Review Press.

Foster, J. B., B. Clark and R. York (2010) *The Ecological Rift: Capitalism's war on the earth*. New York NY: Monthly Review Press.

Fromm, E. and M. Maccoby (1970) *Social Character in a Mexican Village*. Englewood Cliffs NJ: Prentice Hall.

Fromm, E. and R. Xirau (1968) 'Introduction' in E. Fromm and R. Xirau (eds), *The Nature of Man*. New York NY: Macmillan.

Galbraith, J. K. (1979) *The Nature of Mass Poverty*. Cambridge MA: Harvard University Press.

González de Molina, M. and V. M. Toledo (2014) *The Social Metabolism: A socio-ecological theory of historical change*. New York NY: Springer.

Goodman, D., B. Sorj and J. Wilkinson (1987) *From Farming to Biotechnology*. Oxford: Basil Blackwell.

Hirschman, A. O. (1958) *The Strategy of Economic Development*. New Haven CT: Yale University Press.

Hurka, T. (1993) *Perfectionism*. Oxford: Oxford University Press.

Hussain, A. and K. Tribe (1983) *Marxism and the Agrarian Question*. London: Macmillan.

Kautsky, K. (1988 [1899]) *The Agrarian Question*. Two volumes. London: Zwan Publications.

Klein, N. (2014) *This Changes Everything: Capitalism vs the climate*. New York NY: Simon and Schuster.

Leff, E. (2014) *La Apuesta por la Vida. Imaginación Sociológica e Imaginarios Sociales en los Territorios Ambientales del Sur*. Mexico City: Siglo XXI Editores.

Lenin, V. I. (1950 [1889]) *El desarrollo del capitalismo en Rusia*. Moscow: Ediciones en Lenguas extranjeras.

— (1964 [1899]) *The Development of Capitalism in Russia*. Moscow: Progress Publishers.

Lewis, O. (1959) *Five Families: Mexican case studies in the culture of poverty*. New York NY: Basic Books.

Magdoff, F., J. Bellamy Foster and F. H. Buttel (2000) *Hungry for Profit: The agribusiness threat to farmers, food and the environment*. New York NY: Monthly Review Press.

Malita, M. (1971) 'Agriculture in the year 2000', *Sociologia Ruralis* XI (3): 301–4.

Mann, S. A. and J. Dickinson (1978) 'Obstacles to the development of a capitalist agriculture', *Journal of Peasant Studies* 5 (4): 466–81.

Márkus, G. (1978) *Marxism and Anthropology: The concept of human essence in the philosophy of Marx*. Assen, The Netherlands: Van Gorcum. Spanish edition: *Marxismo y Antropología*. Mexico City: Grijalbo, 1985.

Marx, K. (1957 [1885]) *Capital: Volume II*. Moscow: Foreign Language Publishing House.

— (1976 [1867]) *Capital: A critique of political economy*. Volume I. Harmondsworth, UK: Penguin Books.

— (1978 [1885]) *Capital: A critique of political economy*. Volume II. Harmondsworth, UK: Penguin Books.

— (1981 [1894]) *Capital: A critique of political economy*. Volume III. Harmondsworth, UK: Penguin Books.

— (2010 [1891]) 'Critique of the Gotha Programme' in K. Marx, *Political Writings. Volume 3: The First International and after*. London: Verso, pp. 339–59.

Nussbaum, M. (1992) 'Human functioning and social justice. In defence of Aristotelian essentialism', *Political Theory* /source> 20 (2): 202–46.

O'Connor, J. (1998) *Natural Causes: Essays in ecological Marxism*. New York NY: The Guilford Press.

Pinker, S. (2002) *The Blank Slate: The modern denial of human nature*. New York NY: Penguin Books.

Prebisch, R. (1963) *Towards a Dynamic Development Policy for Latin America*. New York NY: United Nations.

Sartre, J.-P. (2004) *Critique of Dialectical Reason*. London: Verso.

Schejtman, A. (1982) *Economía campesina y agricultura empresarial. Tipología de productores del agro mexicano*. Mexico City: Siglo XXI Editores.

Scott, J. (1976) *The Moral Economy of the Peasant: Rebellion and subsistence in Southeast Asia*. New Haven CT: Yale University Press.

Silva Herzog, J. (1964) *El agrarismo mexicano y la reforma agraria. Exposición y crítica*. Mexico City: Fondo de Cultura Económica.

Thompson, E. P. (1991) *Customs in Common*. London: Penguin Books. See especially 'Chapter IV. The moral economy of the English crowd in the eighteenth century' and 'Chapter V. The moral economy reviewed'.

Valentine, C. (1968) *Culture and Poverty: Critique and counter-proposals*. Chicago IL: University of Chicago Press.

van der Linden, M. (2010) 'Foreword' in J. Banaji, *Theory as History: Essays on modes of production and exploitation*. Chicago IL: Haymarket Books, pp. xi–xv.

FOREWORD AUTHOR, EDITORS AND CONTRIBUTORS

Foreword author and editors

Lord Meghnad Desai is a Labour Party politician and has been a member of the House of Lords of the UK Parliament since 1991. He has been a member of the academic staff at the London School of Economics and Political Science (LSE) since 1965, and since 2003 has been Emeritus Professor. He founded and directed (1992–2003) the Centre for Global Governance at LSE. He has published extensively on a wide variety of topics: economics, econometrics, Marxian economics, politics, history and fiction. Among his recent books are *Marx's Revenge: The resurgence of capitalism and the death of statist socialism* (2002) and *Hubris: Why economists failed to predict the recession and how to avoid the next one* (2015).

Julio Boltvinik has spent over three decades studying and fighting poverty. He is a professor and researcher at the Centre for Sociological Studies, El Colegio de México, and has been a visiting professor in the UK and Mexico, as well as holding government positions, working for the United Nations Development Programme and being member of the Scientific Committee of CROP. As well as one hundred and fifty articles and book chapters, he has published books including *Social Progress Index: A proposal* (with A. Sen and M. Desai, 1991), *Poverty and Social Stratification in Mexico* (1994), *Poverty and Income Distribution in Mexico* (co-authored with E. Hernández-Laos, 1999), *Poverty in Mexico and the World* (co-edited with A. Damián, 2004), *Broadening Our Look: A new approach to poverty and human flourishing* (forthcoming) and *To Understand the Current Capitalist Crisis* (2010). He also writes the weekly column 'Moral economy' in the Mexican newspaper *La Jornada*, for which he received the Citizen National Journalism Award in 2001.

Susan A. Mann was Professor of Sociology and former Director of Women's and Gender Studies at the University of New Orleans in Louisiana. She also served as a former Chair of the Race, Class and

Gender Section of the American Sociological Association. Her books include *Reading Feminist Theory: From modernity to postmodernity* (2015), *Doing Feminist Theory: From modernity to postmodernity* (2012) and *Agrarian capitalism in theory and practice* (1990).

Contributors

Farshad Araghi works in the areas of global sociology, social theory, sociology of agriculture and human displacement, and world-historical analysis. He was a visiting professor at Cornell University and has won several teaching awards. For the past decade, he has been a co-editor of the *International Journal of Sociology of Agriculture and Food*. As well as articles, he has published chapters in books including *Peasants and Globalisation: Political economy, rural transformation and the agrarian question* (edited by A. H. and C. K. Akram-Lodhi, 2009) and *Hungry for Profit: The agribusiness threat to farmers, food and the environment* (edited by F. Magdoff, F. H. Buttel and J. B. Foster, 2001).

Luis Arizmendi is Director of the international journal *Mundo Siglo XXI*, an economist and sociologist. He has translated authors such as I. Wallerstein, N. Chomsky and E. Altvater, among others, and has given hundreds of lectures at various universities and research centres in Mexico, as well as participating in international conferences. He has been Professor of Political Economy for the past two and a half decades at the National Autonomous University of Mexico (UNAM). He is co-author of the book *Walter Benjamin: Iconoclastic kaleidoscope of modernity* (forthcoming), has edited many books, including *Horizons of the Turn of the Century* (2011), *Global Crisis and Civilization's Crossroads* (2014) and *Bolívar Echeverría: Transcendence and impact in Latin America* (2014), and has published many articles and chapters in books.

David Barkin is Distinguished Professor at the Autonomous Metropolitan University in Mexico City and a member of the Mexican Academy of Sciences. He has collaborated with communities in many parts of Latin America to implement projects promoting sustainable resource management based on local capacities for self-government and ecosystem management, as well as consolidating their ability to increase their production of basic necessities while generating new sources of income and employment. His publications include reflections on epistemology and paradigm shifts in social sciences and the contributions of non-Western societies to produce alternative models for social and political organisation that are more conducive to planetary balance.

Armando Bartra teaches in the Faculties of Philosophy and Economics at the National Autonomous University of Mexico (UNAM) and is a researcher and professor in the Graduate Division in Rural Development of the Autonomous Metropolitan University. He is the Director of the Institute for Rural Development 'Maya' (an NGO) and edits the supplement *La Jornada del Campo* in the daily newspaper *La Jornada*. He has published over twenty books and about a hundred papers in journals and collected volumes. His most recent books are *The New Heirs of Zapata: Peasants in motion* (2012), *Hunger. Carnival. Two perspectives of the crisis of modernity* (2013) and *The Barbarian Mexico: Plantations and hunting areas during the dictatorship of Porfirio Díaz* (2014).

Henry Bernstein is Emeritus Professor of Development Studies at the School of Oriental and African Studies, University of London, and Adjunct Professor at the College of Humanities and Development, China Agricultural University, Beijing. He was editor, with Terence J. Byres, of the *Journal of Peasant Studies* (1985–2000) and founding editor, again with Byres, of the *Journal of Agrarian Change*, of which he became Emeritus Editor in 2008. His 'little book on a big idea', *Class Dynamics of Agrarian Change* (2010), has been translated into Chinese, Japanese, Portuguese, Spanish and Turkish, with Bahasa and French forthcoming.

Emily R. Blumenfeld is a writing facilitator in the area of the transformative and therapeutic uses of language. She has published both literary and scholarly writing, and her writing and work centre on themes of social justice, women's equality, and the well-being of mothers and children.

Araceli Damián is a professor and researcher at the Centre of Demographic, Urban and Environmental Studies at El Colegio de México, where she teaches courses on social policy and poverty, and has been a visiting researcher at the Universities of Bristol and Manchester. Her research topics focus on the multidimensional nature of poverty and how to measure it (basic needs, income and time poverty). She has published extensively on various topics related to poverty, including in the Mexican daily newspaper *El Financiero* (2003–13) and in books such as *Adjustment, Poverty and Labour Market in Mexico* (2000), *Poverty in Mexico and in the World: Realities and challenges* (co-edited with J. Boltvinik, 2004), and *Time: The missing variable in the study of poverty and well-being* (2014).

James Dickinson teaches in the Sociology Department at Rider University in Lawrenceville, New Jersey. He edited (with Bob Russell) *Family, Economy and State: The social reproduction process under capitalism* (1986). His current work explores the built environment of older industrial cities and the visual culture of the street.

Enrique Leff is a Mexican environmental sociologist, a researcher at the Institute for Social Research and a professor at the Faculty of Political and Social Sciences, both at the National Autonomous University of Mexico (UNAM). He works in the fields of sociology, epistemology and environmental philosophy; political ecology and ecological economics; and environmental education and training. He was coordinator of the United Nations Environmental Programme's Environmental Training Network for Latin America and the Caribbean (1986–2008) and of the UNEP Office in Mexico (2007–08), and edited UNEP's 'Latin American Environmental Thought' series. His most recent book, of the many he has published, is *Betting for Life: Sociological imagination and social imaginaries in the environmental territories of the South* (2014).

Blanca Lemus is a medical doctor with a doctorate in work environment and community health from the University of Massachusetts. She retired from the University of Michoacán (Mexico) and collaborates with David Barkin on issues relating to the social and solidarity economy as well as with communities forging alternative models for creating a balance between society and nature, assuring greater control over their territories and their members' well-being.

Elma Montaña is Assistant Director for the Science Programmes of the InterAmerican Institute for Global Change Research (IAI). She was previously a researcher at the Human, Social and Environmental

Sciences Institute (INCIHUSA) at the National Scientific and Technological Research Council of Argentina and Professor of Urban and Rural Sociology at the School of Political Sciences of the National University of Cuyo, Mendoza, Argentina. At INCIHUSA, she led a research team working on territory construction, water management and the social dimensions of global environmental change in drylands, themes that she has also developed in development programmes and projects in rural areas and in urban and regional planning. She has published *Scenarios of Climate Change and Rural Poverty: A territorial perspective* (2012).

Edith Pacheco is a professor and researcher at the Centre for Demographic, Urban and Environmental Studies of El Colegio de México, with an interest in labour markets, gender and agricultural work. Her most recent publication (co-authored with B. García) is 'The economic interests in Mexican families: the role of wives in the last 20 years' in *Mexicans: A balance of demographic change* (2014).

Kostas Vergopoulos is Professor of Economics at the University of Paris VIII. His fields of specialisation are agrarian economics, international and European economy and development economics. He has taught widely in Latin America and the USA and has been an international consultant to organisations such as ASEM (Asia-Europe Meeting), UNESCO and the United Nations Development Programme. His publications include *Capitalism and the New Peasant Question* (with a contribution by Samir Amin, 1974) and, more recently, *The Big Rift: The deconstruction of the world system* (2008), *After the End: The disaster economy and the day after* (2011) and *Greece–Europe: An inappropriate relation?* (2012).

Gordon Welty is Professor Emeritus at Wright State University in Ohio and Associate Professor of Sociology at Mercy College, New York. He is the author of book chapters and articles including 'A critique of the theory of the praetorian state' (in G. Caforio (ed.), *The Sociology of the Military*, 1998), 'Contribución a la crítica de Chayanov: la Teoría de la Unidad Laboral Familiar' (*Mundo Siglo XXI* 28 (VIII), 2012) and 'La Regulación de los Negocios Empresariales en EU' (*Mundo Siglo XXI* 31 (IX), 2013).

INDEX

Note: Page numbers followed by figure or table number in parentheses refer to that figure or table. An n following a page number denotes an endnote.

The term 'peasant(s)' appears over 1,000 times across the book; therefore, it was impossible to index it without it being an arbitrary selection. Nevertheless, it is indexed when it is paired with other words such as 'poverty' and 'rich'. The associated terms 'peasantry' and 'peasantisation' are also indexed.

dysfunctionality for capital of, 302; emergence of, as an object of policy, 177; 75–6; employment in, declining, (Table 5.3), 218–19; essentialist views of, 119–20; global valorisation of, 32; industrialisation of, 109 (as unsustainable, 23); markers of, in the broad sense of the term, 175–6; natural character of main means of production used in, 38; new sociology of, 10; penetration of capitalism into *see* capitalism: penetration of, into agricultural production; as an object of policy and politics, 177; relationship with industry, 174–8; uniqueness of, 409–10; women's employment in, 127 *see also* farming *and* production time, different from working time

agro-ecology, 359
agro-export model of colonialism, 109
agro exports, promotion of, 34
agro-food capitalism, 175, 335; profitability of, 142; subsidisation of, 337
agroforestry, 261
agrofuels, production of, 100, 111
Akram-Lohdi, A. H., 383–4
Alabama, checking immigrant status in, 131
Alavi, Hamza, 19, 384–7, 396
Alliance for Progress, 102, 104
allotment-holding farm labourers, 377–9, 421n2
alternative societies, implementation of, 358–60
Amstutz, Daniel, 335
ancestry, actuality of, 261
Anderson, James, 99
Andes, reduced snow accumulation in, 269
anti-colonial 9, 319
anti-communism, 320, 321, 323, 330
anti-imperialist movements, 11
anti-Vietnam War, movement, 11
appropriationism, 409–10
Araghi, Farshad, 33–5, 413
Argentina, 30–1; watershed communities in, 269–98

Aristide, Jean-Bertrand, 137
Arizmendi, Luis, 22, 24–6, 38, 369, 390, 397–406, 411, 413, 414
ASERCA programme (Mexico), 213
Asian Development Bank, xix
'Asiatic Mode of Production', xx
austerity, 115
autonomy, 355, 360; as a claim of indigenous people, 263; in social organisation, 357
ayni, concept of, 278–9

background paper, xx, 1–2, 20–6, 37, 88n1, 119, 247, 355, 358, 369–73, 384, 389, 397, 410, 412–3, 415
Banaji, J., 195n10, 395
Banco Nacional de Crédito Ejidal, 207
Bangladesh, food aid withheld from, 331
Barkin, David, 35–7, 415
Bartra, Armando, xxviii, 21–2, 23, 25, 38, 46, 62–8, 151, 153–5, 194n4, 369, 370, 390, 406, 413, 416, 418; *El capital en su laberinto*, 109, 111, 114; *El hombre de hierro*, 93
Bartra, Roger, 151, 152
basic income, 399
basic needs, *see* needs
beans, and fixing of nitrogen, 67, 116n2; as occupier of labour-force, in Mexico, 230; as part of milpa, 94; bean-maize combination, 67; general demand in Bolivia, 289, import dependence in Mexico, 101; intensive work in sowing of, 231
Beauvoir, Simone de, 126
Bernstein, Henry, 26–7, 58, 88n3, 373, 378, 390, 392, 394–7, 405, 406, 414, 416, 418
Bhutan, 346
bio-economics, 260
biodiversity, 260; 265n6; conservation of, 30, 259; peasants' contribution to, 296; resources of, 263
biofuel *see* agrofuels
biomass, production of, 260–1
biotechnology, 256; revolution in, 62–3
Black Death, xxiii
blackness, reaffirmation of, 263